Still Reading Romance

Still Reading Romance

Identity and Engagement with Popular Romance Fiction

Edited by Josefine Smith and
Kathleen W. Taylor Kollman

ROWMAN & LITTLEFIELD
Lanham • Boulder • New York • London

Rowman & Littlefield
Bloomsbury Publishing Inc, 1385 Broadway, New York, NY 10018, USA
Bloomsbury Publishing Plc, 50 Bedford Square, London, WC1B 3DP, UK
Bloomsbury Publishing Ireland, 29 Earlsfort Terrace, Dublin 2, D02 AY28, Ireland
www.rowman.com

Copyright © 2025 by The Rowman & Littlefield Publishing Group, Inc.

All rights reserved. No part of this publication may be: i) reproduced or transmitted in any form, electronic or mechanical, including photocopying, recording or by means of any information storage or retrieval system without prior permission in writing from the publishers; or ii) used or reproduced in any way for the training, development or operation of artificial intelligence (AI) technologies, including generative AI technologies. The rights holders expressly reserve this publication from the text and data mining exception as per Article 4(3) of the Digital Single Market Directive (EU) 2019/790.

British Library Cataloguing in Publication Information available

Library of Congress Cataloging-in-Publication Data

Names: Smith, Josefine, 1986- editor. | Taylor Kollman, Kathleen W., 1975- editor.
Title: Still reading romance: identity and engagement with popular romance fiction / edited by Josefine Smith and Kathleen W. Taylor Kollman.
Description: Lanham: Rowman & Littlefield, 2025. | Includes bibliographical references and index. | Summary: "This book questions the cultural capital of traditional archetypes, explores the experience of romance readers, and examines how romance and cultural studies researchers create quantitative, qualitative, and mixed methods research"— Provided by publisher.
Identifiers: LCCN 2024050974 (print) | LCCN 2024050975 (ebook) |
 ISBN 9781538182291 (cloth) | ISBN 9781538182307 (ebook)
Subjects: LCSH: Romance fiction—History and criticism. | Women—Books and reading. | Feminism and literature. | LCGFT: Literary criticism.
Classification: LCC PN3448.L67 S75 2025 (print) | LCC PN3448.L67 (ebook) |
 DDC 809.3/85—dc23/eng/20241220
LC record available at https://lccn.loc.gov/2024050974
LC ebook record available at https://lccn.loc.gov/2024050975

For product safety related questions contact productsafety@bloomsbury.com.

∞™ The paper used in this publication meets the minimum requirements of American National Standard for Information Sciences—Permanence of Paper for Printed Library Materials, ANSI/NISO Z39.48-1992.

Contents

Acknowledgments ix

Introduction: Development of the Project 1

SECTION 1: VISITING ROMANCELANDIA: POPULAR ROMANCE FICTION AS A COMMUNITY 11

1 Re-Reading Romance: Exploring Practitioner, Reader, and Industry Perceptions of the Genre 15
 Jacqueline Burgess and Gaja Kolodziej

2 From Private to Public: #Bookstagram as a Safe Space for Romance Readers 31
 Ayşegül Rigato

3 Romance Readers' Perceptions of New Adult Fiction 45
 Josefine Smith

4 Which Women Want What?: The Shifting Demographics and Perspectives of Romance Readers 59
 Natalie Duvall and Matt Duvall

5 Social Media, Critical Analysis, and Feminist Action: Popular YA's Role in Disseminating Theory Online 71
 Jessica Caravaggio

SECTION 2: A REAL MEET CUTE: ROMANCE READING AS SOCIAL PRACTICES   89

6   Beyond the Bodice Ripper: Why Erotic Romance is Feminist Literature   93
Joann Stout

7   Reading Historical Romance / Reading Romance Historically   111
Lise Shapiro Sanders

8   Romance Reading as a Social Activity   129
Anna Michelson

9   Escaping the Negativity of "Escapism": Rethinking Romance Reader Notions of Why They Read   143
Andrea Barra

10   Love, Romance, Sex, and Happily Ever After: A Feminist Exploration of Women who Read Romance Novels   165
Jessica M. W. Kratzer

SECTION 3: UNDER THE COVERS: TEXT ANALYSIS   191

11   Coming of Age and Coming Out: The Intersection of New Adult and Queer Romance   195
Kathleen W. Taylor Kollman

12   Getting Love Out of the Margins: Race, Disability, Sexuality, and the Idea of a Happy After for Marginalized People   209
Trinidad Linares

13   Retellings and Re-readings—Romance, Representation, and Reimaginations in *Self-Made Boys*: A Great Gatsby Remix *(2022)*   235
Christina M. Babu

14   Mr. Darcy as the Perfect Book Boyfriend, or the Impact of BookTok on Male Characters in Romance Books   249
Louise Schulmann-Darsy

15   Reading Romance and Erotic Literacy   271
Sara Partin and Josefine Smith

Conclusion   293

Bibliography	321
Appendix A: Demographic Results	349
Appendix B: Survey	355
Appendix C: Tables for Chapter 8	373
Appendix D: Participant Reading List for Chapter 10	377
Appendix E: Tables and Figures for Chapter 14	383
Appendix F: Contributor Book Recommendations	387
Index	393
About the Editors' Statements	407
About the Contributors	409

Acknowledgments

The editors would like to thank all the contributors and our contacts at Bloomsbury, including Charles Harmon and Lauren Moynihan. We would also like to thank Sarah McGinley and Pamela Lang for additional peer review support.

Josefine would also like to thank Corinne Bertram, Psychology Professor at Shippensburg University, for a multitude of conversations about revising surveys, the Shippensburg University IRB for continued support with this project, and Nicole Hill, Dean of the College of Education and Human Services, for illuminating exploratory methodology. I would also like to thank Erika Schmitt for reading and asking questions about the project and the constant support of kindred spirits. Finally, I would like to thank my family (my husband Eric and my children) for reminding me to take a breath and without whom all of this would be pointless.

Kathleen would also like to thank Kristen Rudisill for an engaging course in popular romance fiction and her mentorship; Jolie Sheffer, for first introducing me to Janice Radway's work; Heidi Ruby Miller, who showed me that science fiction romance is an engaging and delightful subgenre; Carrie Gessner, Rachel Porter, and Robin Hershkowitz for talking romance novels with me; the romance communities at both Seton Hill University and Bowling Green State University; and of course to my husband Tom, for keeping romance in my real life.

Above all, we are grateful to Janice Radway and the romance community for the authors, fans, and scholars who have directly and indirectly inspired this work.

Introduction
Development of the Project

This project has followed a winding path. In 2019, Josefine Smith wanted to explore some of the questions originally posed by Janice Radway. Through her research, Radway hoped to provide a different, more empirical approach to understanding reader engagement with popular texts and if that engagement subverts or reinforces patriarchal structures. As a romance reader herself, Smith found the positioning of romance readers as ignorant victims duped by a commodifying system extremely problematic. In devaluing popular romance fiction as a simple static object in the patriarchal structure, this perspective creates a bias for researchers positioning the genre within a feminist framework. While Smith was not interested in exploring feminist or sexist nature of romance fiction, Janice Radway's reflections about collecting data to illustrate the reading process as being a useful supplement to rhetorical analysis of those texts and qualitative reader-response research were interesting.[1] Smith was particularly intrigued by the survey Radway developed.

Smith developed a research plan to disseminate a revised version of the survey to attempt to compare the findings to that of Radway's and to explore a specific subgenre, New Adult fiction. Smith first disseminated the survey in the winter of 2019–2020. Instead of finding a specific romance book group as Radway did, the survey was disseminated to various social media romance groups. In order to get a larger participant pool and data set, Smith posted the survey to 5 Facebook groups during the winter of 2019. Then a series of events delayed the project. Smith had a baby, and the pandemic swept the world. Between work and family, the research project got derailed. Then in 2022, Smith put out a call for collaborators on the discussion forum at the Popular Culture Association's annual conference. While connecting with interested colleagues, Smith met Kathleen Kollman, and both researchers were excited about the idea behind an interdisciplinary project exploring the social and cultural dynamics of romance reading. This collection is tethered to Janice Radway's *Reading the Romance*, in that the survey was developed from her original survey and has similar interest in the feminist and cultural relationship with romance reading as a process.

RESEARCH ABOUT READING ROMANCE

Janice Radway was born in 1949 and received degrees from Michigan State and SUNY Stony Brook. Her 1977 Ph.D. dissertation was on the confluence of popular and literary fiction.

Reading the Romance was an attempt to marry her interests in literary and cultural studies and take a much more anthropological approach in her methodology, rather than the textual analysis most favorable to literary studies at the time. Since the original edition of *Reading the Romance* came out in 1984, Radway has taught at three different universities, served as a department chair, been the editor of *American Quarterly*, and served as president of the American Studies Association. As of this writing, she is a Professor Emerita at Northwestern, focusing on communication, American studies, and gender studies. In addition to her most famous book, she has edited collections of American studies essays, written on the phenomenon of book clubs, the early history of book publishing in the U.S., and fan zines, particularly in relation to girlhood.

Thus, Radway's scholarly output has broadly been about American books and publishing, through the lens of feminist theory, but romance novels unto themselves are but one set of data she has examined rather than her primary concern. Conversely, for many scholars and aca-fans working with romance novels, it is "romancelandia" itself that is the focus, examined with a multiplicity of methods and theories.

The present study is based on Radway's questionnaire that formed the basis of her book. Radway began her study several years earlier, with a shorter article version of her findings published in a 1983 issue of the journal *Feminist Studies*. As will be discussed at length throughout our contributors' chapters in the present volume, Radway conducted both qualitative and quantitative analysis of the reading habits of a set of women who routinely bought, read, and discussed romance novels, aided by the book recommendations of Dorothy Evans (a.k.a. "Dot"), a bookstore employee in the pseudonymous Midwestern town of Smithton. Dot's regular clientele greatly trusted her taste in books, and Radway interviewed Dot in addition to her customers.

The 1983 article version of Radway's work does not include the deeper examination of sets of romance novels, nor does it spend much time on the qualitative data from readers other than Dot. By the time of the article's publication, Radway was already at work on the full book-length version, so there is much overlap. However, it is clear in the article that Radway had not yet fully formed a lot of her ultimate conclusions, as the article ends on a note of being quite confident in the novels' tendency to reinforce hegemonic patriarchy, even though the readers were in some ways subverting that by even taking personal time to read at all.[2] The full book, however, presents a more nuanced take on these questions, once Radway goes deeper into her data set.

Reading the Romance, then, is an example of mixed methods in cultural studies research: qualitative and quantitative interviews and survey data combined with a macro-level variation of textual analysis, peppered throughout with grounding in feminist theory and gender studies, American and cultural studies, literary studies, ethnography, and audience reception theory, among other areas. This is largely why so many later scholars first encounter the book not in courses on romance fiction or popular fiction but in theory and research methods.

As we see in Radway's updated introduction to the 1991 edition of the book, she did have some mixed feelings about the end result of *Reading the Romance* after its initial publication, writing toward the end of the introduction that, in the intervening years, she had determined what was needed in further research on the subject "is a recognition that romance writers and readers are themselves struggling with gender definitions and sexual politics *on their own terms* [emphasis in original] and that what they may need most from those of us struggling in other arenas is our support rather than our criticism or direction."[3] Indeed, it is our hope that this present volume may offer a bit more of that, while remaining respectful of Radway's groundbreaking contributions to popular romance studies.

During the 1980s and 1990s, feminist academics like Radway became interested in popular romance research and set a foundation for contemporary popular romance fiction research.[4] Earlier scholars like Tania Modleski explored the narrative meaning of popular romance texts.[5] Radway's research provided an ethnographic and reader-response perspective. At its foundation, popular romance fiction is an interdisciplinary field, with scholars from a spectrum within the social sciences and humanities interested in romance readers and the meaning imbued in the genre.[6] As other scholars have reflected on *Reading the Romance* in other venues—articles, conference roundtables, and subsequent books—romance fiction makes researchers reflect on readers as victims or critical consumers and popular culture as a subjugator or subverter. Either way, it shapes its readers and our society at large.

Contemporary scholars doing romance research have responded to changes in methodology trends and shifts in audience population, as well as dramatic differences in novel content over time. Kollman, for example, found a dramatic increase in feminist themes when looking at a sample of paranormal romance novels of several subgenres from the early 2000s to late 2010s,[7] and Maleah Fekete noted dramatic changes in content from 1980 to 2016.[8] Eric Selinger observed in 2014 that "Radway's work has also been controversial, and its reception within the field of popular romance studies has sometimes been marked by 'harsh and even unforgiving critiques,'"[9] even as participants in a retrospective roundtable on her work found much to celebrate. This same roundtable also found much in Radway's work to inspire the next generation of scholars to update the study, calling for new research to reflect progress made by third- and fourth-wave feminism. Some scholars have dived into the idea of ethnography of the romance world with both feet, such as Catherine M. Roach, who documented her journey as a fledgling romance novelist while critically examining the genre and its readers in her 2016 book *Happily Ever After: The Romance Story in Popular Culture*.[10] In most cases, however, research on romance communities and texts since Radway have leaned into the idea of the "aca-fan," an academic who is also a fan of the material they are examining. While Smith and Kollman would not argue that one *must* be a fan to engage with a particular cultural phenomenon (and in fact being a very engaged fan can often hinder one's research by burning the scholar out on something they used to love or leave one open to criticism of lack of objectivity), a certain detachment from the community or text being examined is also not ideal, as a measure of insider interest, affinity, respect, and knowledge can help bridge the gap between in- and out-community understanding. The biggest area needing updating in taking Radway's survey from the twentieth to twenty-first centuries is an acknowledgment of the move away from patriarchal standards in contemporary romance novels as well as their writers and audiences.

PROJECT GOALS

The ultimate purpose of the present volume, then, is to allow a multiplicity of voices to examine and explore the romance community and texts from a variety of standpoints, thereby providing readers with the best of all possible worlds: authors, aca-fans, cultural studies scholars, publishers, those with varying degrees of involvement with the romance genre, and a wide swath of career phases and disciplinary affiliations. We felt that keeping the data to merely one or two researchers would not capitalize on the potential of disciplinary and positional diversity. Despite using the same data set, then, we all come at it in different ways. Furthermore, we have noted, too, the gaps in the survey, even as updated as it is, and several of us in this volume speak to those lacks and gaps, arguing for even more diversity of perspectives to be represented through future projects. These questions should not remain even as static as we have left them, but should be taken up again by other projects to explore even more granular aspects of readership and authorship and identity. We hope, too, that it does not take another forty years to do so, as the technological and social landscape is changing ever faster, creating communities of greater specialized interests within broader romancelandia.

The premise of updating the survey and distributing it more widely was largely in an effort to see how romance readers' habits and opinions differed from Radway's initial interviews (held between 1980 and 1981) and readers in the early 2020s, as the scope, topics, and popularity of romance novels—not to mention feminism, social movements, and massive technological advancements—have changed quite a lot in the intervening forty years between our two books' publications.

In addition to her interviews and surveys, Radway also did analyze sections of novels, but does so on a much more collective scale, taking the novels themselves as data points, and sometimes quoting passages that offer trends of themes or tropes without mentioning the name of the novel or author except in footnotes. Part of the reason for this is Radway's methodological concerns being more squarely on the readers themselves than the texts, but this is another area where we wanted to deviate by allowing our contributors (including ourselves) to use both our data as well as example texts much more fully. Furthermore, Radway herself in undertaking this study was not a romance novel fan or regular reader, and certainly not also a romance author.

This does not mean that *Reading the Romance* takes a dim view of readers, fans, and authors, but it does result in a distanced approach to her subject. Her distance as a scholar is something she discusses in the 1991 introduction added to later editions of the book, writing that an ethnography undertaken by scholars who are not members of the group comprising a study's participants results in the work being "an interpretation" of "my own construction of my informants' construction of what they were up to in reading romances," and that such studies "can never be pure mirror images of some objective reality."[11] She also states that if she were to redo the study, she would integrate more textual analysis.[12]

Again, our present work deviates in many ways from Radway's original approaches not only in updating the questions but in allowing contributors to put their own spin and emphasis on the data, speaking from many identity standpoints such as author, fan, reader, scholar, and with a wide variety of experiences and subtypes of romance novels to use as examples. We also did not conduct long-form interviews with anyone other than a select group of experts in our conclusion (as well as each other), rather than doing focus groups with readers or speaking with booksellers. The experience of reading and purchasing and engaging with romance fiction now often takes place exclusively on the internet: in Facebook groups, on Reddit, Twitter/X,

Threads, Instagram, TikTok, and other social media platforms, and e-book readers and online bookstores have made in-person, human bookseller recommendations much less likely to occur.

SURVEY: METHODOLOGY AND DEMOGRAPHICS

This survey was developed based on Radway's 1984 final survey. The original survey included 53 questions regarding reading behaviors of the participants, romance norms and tropes, and general popular culture engagement.[13] The survey used to collect this data set comprised the original questions, not including informed consent (Appendix B). The overall structure of the survey attempted to align with Radway's original spirit. Indeed, items were kept in their original form, with revisions only implemented to represent a contemporary shift and more diverse populations. Smith hoped to maintain questions originally developed by Janice Radway, with some minor revisions. She expanded the question of sex from Male or Female to be more inclusive and added non-Judeo-Christian traditions to the question capturing religious beliefs.

Because initially Smith was interested in exploring the genre broadly and then delving into the subgenre of New Adult fiction, she created a section of questions related to that subgenre that mirrored the questions about the romance genre as a whole.

The survey was distributed in two cycles, in 2019 and 2023. In 2019, the first version of the survey was distributed online through various social media by the primary researcher, Josefine Smith, with a total of 130 responses.[14] In 2021, a revised version of the survey was distributed by Josefine Smith and Kathleen Kollman, with additional questions about race/ethnicity, country of residence, and relationship status, and a total of 178 additional responses were received.[15] These forums for distribution fostered a convenience sampling recruitment model, as they were all groups we were members of in either personal or professional capacities. Two major revisions happened during distribution that stemmed from the differences in the sampling procedure. As Radway only sampled participants from a small New England town and all of her participants were white, she did not have any racial or nationality questions in her final survey. This quickly became apparent as an issue in the first survey cycle, as social media groups are not constricted by geography or racial groupings. Following a revision to the IRB application, Smith included a racial identity question and a nationality-focused question for the second survey cycle.

In developing this project, there are limitations that must be articulated. First, the gap between distribution cycles, particularly in light of the impact of the pandemic on the participants, could be seen as challenging as a confounding variable. The late addition of race and geographic location questions also impacts the type of analysis that can be performed.

Additionally, the threshold for what we determined to be useful data was rather low (completion of at least 25%), primarily because the survey was quite long, and it front-loaded research-specific questions, meaning that analysis could still be useful for exploratory analysis. This does result in a significant percentage of blanks, which have been removed for the review of results.

DEMOGRAPHIC RESULTS

The results from the original set of demographic survey items describe age, race, gender, religion, relationship status, education, children, and socioeconomic status. Eighty-five percent of participants were in young and middle adulthood (Appendix A, Fig 1). A majority (36.6%) were between the ages of 35 and 44 years, while about 20% were either in the age-group just above or below that middle range (28.2% were 24–34 years old and 20.8% were 45–54 years old). The majority of respondents who answered the question identified as female or woman (62.1%), and 2.5% identify along the gender spectrum: Agender, Gender Queer, Gender Fluid, and Trans Man, with a further .6 identifying as male (Appendix A, Fig 2). A majority of the respondents are notreligious: 41 identified Agnostic (20.8%), 43 respondents identified as Atheist (21.3%), and 4.5% selected N/A. The next most selected were "Christian but nondenominational" (39 respondents, about 19%) and Catholic (22 respondents, 10%). Interestingly, 21 respondents selected other, and other responses could be grouped within lapsed religious affiliation, more universal Christian identities, or pagan religions (Appendix A, Fig. 4). Most respondents were coupled (over 60%), with 106 married and 24 in a relationship. About 70 respondents were single at the time of the survey. 90 respondents reported having children. The vast majority had some form of higher education degree (91 respondents had a master's, 55 had a bachelor's degree, and 25 had a doctorate), and 31 had graduated from high school or had a GED (Appendix A, Fig 6). Almost half had a household income of over $100,000 (38 respondents had a household income of $100,000–$149,999, and 47 had a household income over $150,000) (Fig 8).

Data related to race and geographic location are a subset of the larger section, so there is a large amount of missing data (Appendix A, Fig. 9 & 10). A majority of respondents were white (114 respondents) and from North or Central America (109 respondents). Thus, the demographics indicate our respondents were primarily white women from North or Central America, middle class, and highly educated. It would be interesting to see how a more diverse demographic group would experience reading romance.

CONCLUSION

This collection considers romance reading as a cultural process from multiple vantage points. It is a mixed-methods, interdisciplinary volume that holds *Reading the Romance* as its connecting thread. Contributors herein consider *Reading the Romance* as a theoretical framework, as a survey design framework, or as a broader methodological framework. This collection is organized into three parts: popular romance genre as a collective, romance reading as a social practice, and culture-text interactions.

NOTES

1. Radway, Janice A. *Reading the Romance: Women, Patriarchy, and Popular Literature*. Chapel Hill: University of North Carolina Press, 1991, 7–11.
2. Radway, Janice A. "Women Read the Romance: The Interaction of Text and Context." *Feminist Studies* 9, no. 1 (1983).
3. Radway, Janice A. *Reading the Romance: Women, Patriarchy, and Popular Literature*. Chapel Hill: University of North Carolina Press, 1991, 18.
4. Eric Selinger and Frantz, 2014. "Introduction." *New Approaches to Popular Romance Fiction: Critical Essays*. Frantz, Sarah SG, and Eric Murphy Selinger, eds. McFarland, 2014.
5. Modleski, Tania. *Loving with a Vengeance: Mass-Produced Fantasies for Women*. New York: Methuen, 1984.
6. Valerie Walkerdine 1998; Light, Alison. "'Returning to Manderley'—Romance Fiction, Female Sexuality and Class." *Feminist Review* 16, no. 1 (1984): 7–25.; Hubbard, Rita C. "Relationship Styles in Popular Romance Novels, 1950 to 1983." *Communication Quarterly* 33, no. 2 (1985): 113–25.
7. Kollman, Kathleen W. Taylor. "Contemporary Paranormal Romance: Theories and Development of the Genre's Feminism (Or Lack Thereof)." *Researching the Romance Conference, 2018, Bowling Green, Ohio*, ScholarWorks@BGSU, 2018.
8. Fekete, Maleah. "Confluent Love and the Evolution of Ideal Intimacy: Romance Reading in 1980 and 2016." *Journal of Popular Romance Studies* 11 (2022): 1–30.
9. Selinger, Eric. "Reading the Romance: A Thirtieth Anniversary Roundtable, Editor's Introduction." *Journal of Popular Romance Studies* 4., no. 2, 2014, 1–2.
10. Roach, Catherine M. *Happily Ever After: The Romance Story in Popular Culture*. Indiana University Press, 2016.
11. Radway, *Reading the Romance*, 5.

12. Radway, *Reading the Romance*, 5–6.
13. Radway, *Reading the Romance*, 231–40.
14. The groups were: New Adult Book Club (https://www.facebook.com/NewAdultBookClub/), Colleen Hoover's CoHorts (https://www.facebook.com/groups/colleenhooverscohorts), The Wicked Wallflowers Coven (https://www.facebook.com/groups/wckdwallflowersgroup), *Heaving Bosoms: A Romance Novel Podcast* (https://www.facebook.com/HeavingBosomsPodcast/), and Kristen Callihan's Lounge (https://www.facebook.com/groups/CallihanVIPLounge). All groups are comprised of members of the romance community, including author fan pages and groups for romance fans in general.
15. On the subsequent distribution of the survey in 2021, we utilized Twitter/X, romance forums on Reddit, Facebook groups for Seton Hill University's Writing Popular Fiction MFA students and alumni (as romance comprises a huge amount of that program's student and faculty populations), romance Facebook groups distinct from the first cycle, our personal Instagram accounts, and our personal Facebook accounts. We also asked as part of our call for participants that respondents share and repost our call and link to the survey, thus ensuring snowball sampling.

Section 1

VISITING ROMANCELANDIA

POPULAR ROMANCE FICTION AS A COMMUNITY

In her work, Radway found romance reading to be a relatively siloed and isolating system. The only point of connection for romance readers in Smithton was Dot. Radway found no evidence of book groups, and most readers said they talked to their mothers or other female members of their immediate circle about romance, if at all.[1] Without social media, there were significantly fewer avenues to communicate between authors and readers, and more formal publishing processes made the relationship between authors and publishers much more structured. With the rise in self-publishing and the internet, these communities and new fluid connections between them fostered an evolution in popular romance.

Catherine M. Roach identifies popular romance as a community as well as a genre, comprised of "those who consume the genre of romance stories as readers, produce it as authors, sell it as editors/agents/publishing professionals, and study it as academics. These people all read romance novels but do so in different ways."[2] This first section of our book explores popular romance as a community and how members of the community negotiate that system.

In "Re-Reading Romance: Exploring Practitioner, Reader, and Industry Perceptions of the Genre," Jacqueline Burgess and Gaja Kolodziej explore readers' expectations of the popular romance genre, focusing on readers as consumers. Given the financial success and significance of the romance genre in the global book market, romance writing practitioners are cognizant of their readers' expectations. However, research about romance readers' perceptions and expectations of the genre, and thus how authentic readers feel new books and installments in series are, is still emerging. Starting with Radway's original and contentious study of romance fiction, this research compares the definitions of the romance fiction genre as put forward by scholars specializing in the romance genre and romance writing practitioners. Then, using the follow-up Romance Readers Survey (2021), the comparison is expanded to incorporate a third important stakeholder, the readers, to understand reader perceptions and expectations of what an authentic romance fiction novel is and compromises. Thus, this chapter explores scholar, practitioner, and reader understandings of the romance genre before focusing on readers to understand their perceptions of the romance genre and what they believe to be authentic. The findings reveal that readers' perceptions and expectations of the romance genre are consistent with those of the most recent romance genre scholars and romance writing practitioners.

Ayşegül Rigato's "From Private to Public: #Bookstagram as a Safe Space for Romance Readers" looks at social media's impact on romance fiction communities. One of the most significant changes since Radway conducted her study is the impact of the internet. In the past few years, the Instagram hashtag #bookstagram, where readers of all genres can recommend and discuss their favorite books, has significantly impacted book publishing. It is crucial to look at social media as an influential force in romance consumption to observe how the demographic and the experience of reading romance have changed since Radway's pioneering research.

Rigato argues that pages dedicated to romance books on Instagram create a safe space for readers to build communities through their shared interests. Romance readership has become more public and a wider-reaching community with the impact of social media. The users of romance #bookstagram often "live react" as they are reading, share their favourite quotes, and generate discussions among their followers. For this study, Rigato examines approximately several romance #bookstagram pages, focusing on how the admins engage with the genre, review books, and utilize their public platform to create a safe space to share romance-related content. Through these shared spaces, romance readers make reading a communal experience and challenge the stigmas of romance fiction and its fans.

In "Romance Readers' Perceptions of New Adult Fiction," Josefine Smith explores reader perceptions of New Adult fiction. This chapter uses a quantitative analytical approach to the generic experiences of romance readers for New Adult fiction by looking at preferences for tropes, character development, narrative themes, etc. The "New Adult Fiction" label was first coined by St. Martin's Press in 2009—before it gained popularity—in a writing contest they hosted. It gained popularity by the mid 2010s, and at its core is a grassroots genre supported by its author-fan community.[3] These texts typically focus on feminine adolescence and young adulthood, with their romantic plotlines and female protagonists. Authors began self-publishing texts under this genre label, writing stories that reflected challenges and experiences women face in their late teens and early twenties.[4] Major publishers then picked up these novels because of their popularity and fan base.[5] By 2013, these books were on *New York Times* and *USA Today* bestseller lists. Writer's Digest publishing house even published a book to guide other authors through the writing and publishing process in this genre.[6] NA fiction has emerged as a distinct genre between Young Adult (YA) fiction and Romance fiction. This chapter uses reader perceptions to consider the "complex, temporally evolving interaction between a fixed verbal structure and a socially situated reader" at the subgenre level, the cultural contexts within New Adult fiction, and shape the cultural implications of the genre.[7]

Natalie Duvall and Matt Duvall, in their chapter "Which Women Want What? The Shifting Demographics and Perspectives of Romance Readers," explore how today's readers identify themselves and how they perceive not only their relationship to the genre but the genre's influence on their lives and the society surrounding them. The authors analyze the descriptive characteristics of readers while coding open-response answers to look for emergent themes related to Radway's initial findings. They also draw on the sociocultural perspective of literacy as a social practice to understand the contexts and social purposes that impact romance readers' motivations for reading in the genre.

In "Social Media, Critical Analysis, and Feminist Action: Popular YA's Role in Disseminating Theory Online," Jessica Caravaggio covers young adult romance's presence in virtual spaces. According to the Association of American Publishers, one of the largest data collectors of publishing statistics in North America, young adult fiction (or YA/teen fiction) is one of the only publishing categories currently experiencing significant growth. The YA genre is culturally dominant because of its centering of reader pleasure, but this growth is also due to the fact that popular YA texts like Stephenie Meyer's ongoing *Twilight* series and Sarah J. Maas's *A Court of Thorns and Roses* series take on a life of their own online, as communities of readers produce content of such a magnitude that discussion of these texts influences online culture.

Caravaggio explores online reader communities as a space for feminist analysis and a vehicle for political change. The deployment of feminist theoretical terms online such as toxic masculinity, male/female gaze, and intersectionality brings feminist theory into public forums and gives women and girls outside of academic spaces tools they can use to analyze texts from a feminist perspective. Within these communities, a culture of women engaged in critical feminist analysis is created wherein community members mobilize these terms to deconstruct male-female relations within popular YA fiction, exposing this genre as one that enables women and girls to better explore and understand their own desires for power, sex, and emotional connection. Thus, not only is this chapter immersed in the dynamic field of YA fiction, but it also examines how new ways of reading and new spaces for analysis are emerging in concert with social media platforms, a particularly critical facet to the study of YA fiction in the twenty-first century. This work is made especially relevant by current feminist movements that seek to address sexual violence, reproductive justice, and the misogyny that is a growing presence within these same online spaces: for example, conservative speaker Andrew Tate's rise to fame occurred on TikTok, the same platform that hosts the self-named and wildly popular online reader community "Booktok." Content creation that features popular YA texts can therefore be considered creative emancipatory work on these platforms for the eventual purpose of political emancipatory action.

NOTES

1. Radway, *Reading the Romance*, 96.
2. Roach, Catherine M., *Happily Ever After: The Romance Story in Popular Culture*. Bloomington: Indiana University Press, 2016, 32.
3. Julie Naughton, "NA: A Book Category for Twentysomethings by Twenty somethings," *Publishers Weekly,* July 11, 2014, http://www.publishersweekly.com/pw/by-topic/industry-news/publisher-news/article/63285-new-adult-matures.html.
4. Naughton, "NA: A Book Category for Twentysomethings by Twentysomethings."
5. Deirdre Donahue, "NA Fiction is the Hot New Category in Books," *USA Today*, April 15, 2013, https://www.usatoday.com/story/life/books/2013/04/15/new-adult-genre-is-the-hottest- category-in-book-publishing/2022707/.
6. Halverson, Deborah and Sylvia Day. *Writing NA Fiction*. Cincinnati: Writer's Digest Books, 2014.
7. Radway, "Women Read the Romance: The Interaction of Text and Context." *Feminist Studies* 9 (1983): 54–55.

Chapter 1

Re-Reading Romance

Exploring Practitioner, Reader, and Industry Perceptions of the Genre

Jacqueline Burgess and Gaja Kolodziej

The romance genre is the highest-earning and most popular fiction genre, generating over $1.44 billion USD in revenue and many romance writing practitioners are among the bestselling worldwide authors.[1] For example, Barbara Cartland and Danielle Steel are among the top five selling fiction authors worldwide to date in third and fourth place behind William Shakespeare in first and Agatha Christie in second.[2] The romance genre is thus lucrative and also a vital part of the book market worldwide that outsells science fiction, fantasy, and thriller genres. Given the financial scope and impact of the genre, romance writing practitioners need to be cognizant of the commercial realities of the genre and understand their readers to be successful and appeal to them,[3] and so must approach their writing and publishing with a marketing and commercial as well as a creative mindset.[4] Due to many romance writing practitioners understanding these commercial realities, they were amongst the most prolific adopters of self and e-book publishing so they could more easily and directly reach their audiences to provide them with content and stories that met their expectations.[5] The commercial and popular nature of the romance genre means it is essential for romance writing practitioners to understand reader expectations and perceptions of the genre.

We first reviewed and compared the definitions of the romance genre as put forward by scholars specializing in the genre since Radway's influential *Reading the Romance*,[6] and next by romance writing practitioners. Our research then used Smith and Kollman's 2022 online The Romance Readers' Survey results to compare romance readers' perceptions and expectations of what makes a romance novel authentic to them. This lens of authenticity was informed by branding and marketing research given the commercial realities and market size of the romance genre.

BACKGROUND

Authenticity and the Romance Genre

The idea of authenticity has been used in various disciplines and contexts, but since this research is concerned with the commercial and marketing notions of authenticity, it will draw from the body of work exploring brand authenticity. Romance genre novels are known as narrative brands, and the writing practitioners who create them are human brands like celebrities and athletes.[7] Narrative brands are brands which encompass creative and cultural products such as movie, novel, and television series.[8] Brands that engage in consistent and stable behavior,[9] meets consumer expectations,[10] are deemed by consumers to be authentic.[11] Thus, brand authenticity is built up by being consistent.[12]

Behavior that audiences perceive as being inconsistent reduces their perceptions of a brand's authenticity.[13] For example, readers of a series of romance genre novels use the character development and actions in prior novels in the series to judge the authenticity of character development in new installments in a series. If audiences perceive a narrative brand has an ending or installment that appears to not be consistent with their expectations based on the previous installments in a series, it may be deemed inauthentic and audiences may complain, protest, and boycott the narrative brand in the future.[14] Thus, understanding what audiences perceive as authentic is important to ensure perceptions of inauthenticity of a romantic genre installment in a series is avoided. Also, readers of romance may have expectations about what one should have as part of their narrative, which is built up in their minds through time spent reading the genre.

Audiences can develop intense emotional attachments to narrative brands, particularly their characters, and those who are emotionally attached are known to follow that brand more closely.[15] For example, they might re-read romance genre novels and read them more attentively. The romance genre is known to attract a high degree of intensely emotionally attached readers and fans who engage in this attentive reading.[16] Thus, romance genre readers are well placed to form expectations regarding the authenticity of installments. However, other stakeholders such as writing practitioners and scholars may have different perceptions of the authenticity of a new installment, an ending of a series, or the beginning of a new romance genre series.

Scholars and the Romance Genre

Janice Radway's seminal book *Reading the Romance* has prompted discussion and debate in academic and non-academic settings as the first ground-breaking study that introduced the genre to academia and initiated scholarly interest in it.[17] Radway's book received acclaim and criticism that has given rise to a continued rift in its reception.[18] On one side of the abyss stand scholars that admire Radway's scientific approach and consider her observations valid, even after decades.[19] On the other side, there is another group of scholars that are experts in the genre, and writing practitioners, who unlike those of classical literature, are very much alive, proud of their craft, and therefore offended by Radway's simplifications and generalizations.[20] Taking offence from her writing is understandable as writing practitioners of romance or crime fiction, or any other genre, could hardly feel complimented by having their art called "identical, factory-produced commodities."[21] Through her analysis, Radway argues that not only reading the romance genre is "a profoundly conflicted activity," but also that it is "a profoundly conflicted form.:[22]

Reading the Romance is considered "the single most influential work on the romance novel,"[23] which led to the formulation of definitions of the genre, including this one: "The romance novel is a work of prose fiction that tells the story of the courtship and betrothal of one or more heroines."[24] Regis uses the term "betrothal" because "marriage" is not obligatory. Moreover, while comparing different definitions of romance, she finds certain commonalities such as: "first, love between a heroine and hero; second, the triumphant, permanent, happy ending, usually in marriage; and finally . . . the importance of the heroine."[25] These findings are somewhat similar to Radway's, who names three defining elements of a romance novel as: "a happy ending," "a slowly but consistently developing love between hero and heroine," and "some detail about heroine and hero after they've gotten together."[26] She also analyses common narrative elements of the romance plot structure to identify thirteen plot functions that she calls an "ideal romance." Her detailed and "overly specific" outline led to calling the genre formulaic.[27]

In Regis's opinion, Radway mistakes formula for genre. Furthermore, she compiles her own list of the eight most important ingredients of a romance novel: "(i) a definition of society, always corrupt, that the romance novel will reform; (ii) the meeting between the heroine and hero; (iii) an account of their attraction for each other; (iv) the barrier between them; (v) the point of ritual death; (vi) the recognition that fells the barrier; (vii) the declaration of heroine and hero that they love each other; (viii) and their betrothal."[28] In addition, romance genre novels that do not fulfill all these elements are in her view "near misses."[29]

Although scholars tend to associate studies of the romance genre with *Reading the Romance*, Regis's definition is referred to more often.[30] In fact, it is quoted by the editors of *The Routledge Research Companion to Popular Romance Fiction*, who define romance novels as books that "aim at a broad (mass-market) readership, and center around a love plot that holds the promise of a future with a unified emotional life for two or more protagonists."[31] They use the broader term "the promise of a future" instead of the old-fashioned "happy ending," and touch upon the number of protagonists as "a love plot" may involve more than two.

Looking at the definition through the lens of Joyce Saricks, a librarian and scholar, she names two essential elements of a romance novel: focus on a romantic relationship, and reader's participation.[32] Moreover, in order for a novel to be classified as belonging to the romance genre, Saricks says it needs to be "told in such a way that the reader is involved in the outcome of the Romance; the reader participates on an emotional level and experiences genuine satisfaction at the emotionally satisfying conclusion."[33] In contrast to defining the elements of a romance genre novel as outlined previously,[34] Saricks concentrates on the "experience" of reading romance, and the relationship between the text and the reader.

Therefore, writing practitioners' "tone" is aimed to "draw in" the reader, evoking the feeling of participation in the story, and the underlying theoretical structure of the plot abounds in "engaging details" in order to "attract" the reader. Saricks claims that the appeal of the romance genre "is hard to explain to nonfans and difficult even for fans to acknowledge and verbalize."[35] While readers' resistance to acknowledge they enjoy the genre (the "genre-denial syndrome" as she calls it) can be explained by the social stigma of reading the romance genre, Saricks suggests that the difficulty in verbalization comes from the source of the appeal being based on emotions.

According to Saricks, there are as many definitions of the romance genre as there are its readers, for they construct them based on the selections of romance books they have read. And yet, "there are certain characteristics that all fans acknowledge,"[36] namely their expectation of the plot's outcome to be "emotionally satisfying, and have a happy ending" and their eagerness to read other publications by the same practitioner. However, the romance genre's content is bound to change, for "romance (like all genres) constantly reinvents itself, while maintaining its core identity."[37] This view is supported by the view that genres are "dynamically constituted and re-constituted" participatory constructs,[38] because not only writing practitioners shape genres, but their readers do too.

Writing Practitioners and the Romance Genre

Founded in 1980, Romance Writers of America (RWA) is the largest association of its kind with over nine thousand members.[39] As an active stakeholder in the second and third wave of research on the romance genre,[40] the association has been formulating its own definition of a romance book. In the early

2000s, it changed the wording of an expected ending, and it is no longer necessary to be "happy."[41] Instead, the association substituted the word with "emotionally satisfying" and "optimistic," which are synonyms that represent the progress and evolution of the genre.[42] Hence, the RWA's 2023 *About the Romance Genre* two ingredients that make up a romance novel are:

1. A Central Love Story: The main plot centers around individuals falling in love and struggling to make the relationship work. A writing practitioner can include as many subplots as they want as long as the love story is the main focus of the romance fiction genre novel.
2. An Emotionally Satisfying and Optimistic Ending: In a romance, the lovers who risk and struggle for each other and their relationship are rewarded with emotional justice and unconditional love.[43]

In comparison to Radway's outline in her book, RWA's approach seems very generic and broad,[44] as it leaves decisions on settings and plot structure to writing practitioners.

According to practitioner Mary Jo Putney, there is no other genre that "by definition centers on feelings and relationships rather than on plot or abstract concepts."[45] Nevertheless, RWA's explanation is more specific than Regis's short definition, though "risk and struggle" somewhat refers to "barriers" in her eight-element structure. However, RWA's definition is not the only one formulated by writing practitioners.

In Kate Walker's 2018 *12-Point Guide to Writing Romance,* she provides her own definition of the genre and states that: "A romance novel is the story of a man and a woman who, while solving a problem, discover that the love they feel for each other is the sort that comes along only once in a lifetime—leading to a permanent commitment and a happy ending."[46] Her definition aligns with RWA's, though she uses the term "happy," which RWA abandoned. While Walker insists on permanency and the concept of one true love, promoted by mass culture,[47] she allows second chances and acknowledges widowhood. Just like RWA's definition of the romance genre, the traditional "happy ever after" (HEA) has also undergone a transition and evolved into the term "happy for now" (HFN), which is a decision between the two protagonists to be together and to give their relationship a go without an automatic assumption that it would last "forever after,"[48] Taking into consideration the divorce rate, the fictional reality reflects the reality of readers.[49] Regis too substituted the word "marriage" with "betrothal," because not all relationships end in this way.

Sometimes an "emotionally satisfying" ending can be other than "optimistic." The Romantic Novelists' Association (RNA) in Great Britain understands the genre in a much broader sense, and not only is a happy ending optional, but also the love relationship between the protagonists can be limited to only a part of the plot, instead of its main focus. "Romantic fiction," as RNA calls it, can also portray different stages of love, including "long-standing relationships weathering storms."[50] This explains why the association of Romance Writers of New Zealand (RWNZ) uses "an uplifting, satisfying ending" in the 2023 *The Beginner's Guide to Romance* to differentiate between "love stories" and "romances."[51]

Writing practitioner, Patricia Gaffney, defines the genre the following way: "If a core is a believable story about two people finding and committing to each other for life, if it touches our emotions, if it rings true and makes us laugh, cry, and celebrate the miracle of human intimacy, it's romance."[52] Hence, she asserts like Putney that protagonists' relationships are more important than the plot in a romance book.

In *Romance Fiction: A Guide to the Genre*, librarian and writing practitioner, Kristin Ramsdell, defines a romance book as "a love story in which the central focus is on the resolution of the love relationship between the two main characters, written in such a way as to provide the reader with some degree of vicarious emotional participation in the courtship process."[53] Unlike scholars and other writing practitioners, Ramsdell points out "readers' engagement" in the process of reading and "resolution" of the relationship between protagonists. Hence, a romance book has two main ingredients that can be reduced to an "emotionally satisfying" ending—optimistic or not—and readers feeling like they participated in the story. To some degree, Ramsdell's definitions match Putney's view on the importance of a central relationship and feelings, but in contrast to Putney, Ramsdell refers to readers' feelings.

THE ROMANCE READERS' SURVEY

Survey Questions and Demographics

For the purposes of this paper, we analyzed responses to two questions related to the identity and authenticity of the romance genre. These were:

Q1: What are the three most important ingredients in a romance? The participants were asked to rank in order their three most important ingredients from eleven options provided.
Q2: Which of the following do you feel should never be included in a romance? The participants were asked to rank in order their three most distasteful ingredients from thirteen options provided.

Josefine Smith and Kathleen Kollman conducted The Romance Readers' Survey online. The survey was distributed twice throughout 2020–2022 on social media outlets. Two hundred participants answered both of the above questions this paper focuses on and completed the survey in full save for the final open-ended question. The 200 participants of the survey were predominantly female, aged 35 to 44, resided in North or Central America and had a master's degree or higher educational background. Only six participants had no higher educational background beyond completing high school or a GED. Detailed information on the participants is provided in the following tables. The participants (Table 1.1) roughly align to current demographic understandings of romance readers that found that 82% of the romance genre readers are women and 18% are men, and 45% of all readers of the genre have a college degree and are currently an average age of 42 but are getting younger each year.[54]

Table 1.1 Participant Demographics

Gender of participants	Number
Female	189
Other	4
Gender queer	3
Male	2
Trans man	2
Total	200
Age range of participants	**Number**
18–23	12
24–34	55
35–44	73
45–54	42
55–64	14
65+	4
Total	200
Highest level of education achieved by participants	**Number**
High school graduate	6
Some college	11
Professional license or Apprenticeship	6
Associate degree	7
4-year degree	55
Master's	90
Doctorate	25
Total	200
Location of participants	**Number**
North America/Central America	107
Other	77
Europe	12
Africa	1
South America	1
Pacific Islands	1
Asia	1
Total	200

Survey Questions and Responses

For the two questions we analyzed, participants were asked to rank in order their three most important ingredients of a romance and the three most distasteful ingredients from the options provided. To calculate the results, participants ranked options 1, 2, and 3 and these were allocated 3, 2, and 1 point each respectively to calculate a total score.

Results for Question 1

The option "A happy ending" received the highest score of 273 and was ranked 1st, 2nd, or 3rd by 53% of the participants (Table 1.2). The option

Table 1.2 Results for Question 1

Q1: What are the three most important ingredients in a romance?

Ingredient Options	# of 1st	# of 2nd	# of 3rd	Total Point Score	# of participants	% of participants (Ranked as their 1st, 2nd, or 3rd most important ingredient in a romance novel)
1. A happy ending	75	17	14	273	106	53
2. Well-developed emotional intimacy between the heroine and hero	37	68	14	251	119	59.5
3. A slowly but consistently developing love between hero and heroine	12	22	21	101	55	27.5
4. Lots of love scenes with explicit sexual description	5	15	42	87	62	31
5. Some detail about the heroine and hero after they have finally gotten together	2	3	19	31	24	12
6. Other	2	3	10	19	15	7.5
7. A long conflict between the hero and heroine	1	3	5	14	9	4.5
8. A setting in a particular historical period	1	3	5	14	9	4.5
9. A specific kind of hero and heroine	2	2	3	13	7	3.5
10. Lots of love scenes with little or no explicit sexual description	1	2	2	9	5	2.5
11. Punishment of the villain	0	0	3	3	3	1.25

"Well-developed emotional intimacy between the heroine and hero" received the second highest score of 251 and was ranked 1st, 2nd, or 3rd by 59% of participants. Although more participants rated "Well developed emotional intimacy between the heroine and hero" as an important romance book ingredient than "A happy ending," they generally assigned it a lower rank (2nd or 3rd), which resulted in a lower overall score.

The third most important element of a romance was "A slowly but consistently developing love between hero and heroine," which received the score of 101 and was ranked 1st, 2nd, or 3rd by 27% of participants. According to the participants, the three least important ingredients concerned "A specific kind of hero and heroine" (3.5%), "The inclusion of lots of love scenes with little or no explicit sexual description" (2.5%) and "The punishment of the villain" (1.25%).

Results for Question 2

The ingredients that participants believed should never be included in a romance were ranked by the second question. Among thirteen distasteful options listed in Q2 (Table 1.3), the answer "Rape" received the highest score of 405 and was ranked 1st, 2nd, or 3rd by 83.5% of participants.

Table 1.3 Results for Question 2.

Q2: Which of the following do you feel should never be included in a romance?

Ingredient Options	# of 1st	# of 2nd	# of 3rd	Total score	Ranked as their 1st, 2nd, or 3rd most distasteful ingredient in a romance novel — # of participants	% of participants
1. Rape	89	60	18	405	167	83.5
2. Sad ending	66	39	20	296	125	62.5
3. Adultery	10	31	28	120	69	34.5
4. A cruel hero	9	30	28	115	67	33.5
5. Physical torture of the heroine or the hero	7	28	24	101	59	29.5
6. A cruel heroine	2	7	24	44	33	16.5
7. A weak heroine	3	8	14	39	25	12.5
8. Bed hopping	2	9	12	36	23	11.5
9. A weak hero	3	7	5	28	15	7.5
10. Explicit sex	0	1	3	5	4	2
11. An ordinary heroine	1	0	2	5	3	1.5
12. A hero who is stronger than the heroine	0	0	2	2	2	1
13. A heroine who is stronger than the hero	0	0	1	1	1	0.5

The option "Sad ending" received the second highest score of 296 and was ranked 1st, 2nd, or 3rd by 62.5% of participants. The third most distasteful option for participants was the option "Adultery" with a score of 120 and was ranked 1st, 2nd, or 3rd by 34.5% of the participants. The three lowest scoring answers, meaning they were least distasteful to participants, focused on an "An ordinary heroine" (1.5%), "A hero who is stronger than the heroine" (1%), and "A heroine who is stronger than the hero" (0.5%).

Discussion

The inclusion of a happy ending is often noted in both scholar and writing practitioner definitions of the romance genre.[55] In fact, Saricks observed that readers expect a happy ending and so it is not surprising it was the highest scoring ingredient in Q1.[56] The importance of a happy ending in the survey indicates romance readers expect an authentic romance novel to have one. Authenticity is established by consistent behavior over time that meets expectations.[57] Thus, it would appear that romance readers have established expectations over time that a romance novel has to have a happy ending to be authentic.

Furthermore, it is worth noting the second option: "Well-developed emotional intimacy between the heroine and hero" and the third option: "A slowly but consistently developing love between hero and heroine" highest scoring ingredients would likely be required or at least would help with the construction and set up of "a happy ending." They are also recurrent in writing practitioner and scholarly definitions of constituting elements: RWA's "An Emotionally Satisfying and Optimistic Ending,"[58] "two people finding and committing to each other for life,"[59] "a man and a woman who, while solving a problem, discover that the love they feel for each other is the sort that comes along only once in a lifetime—leading to a permanent commitment and a happy ending,"[60] a promise for the future,[61] and "The evocative, emotional tone draws readers in, and they participate in this love story and read toward the emotionally satisfying, happy ending."[62] Thus, it would appear that to some extent writing practitioners, scholars, and readers' expectations of the romance genre align.

There have been arguments that the ending of a romance does not need to be happy, just emotionally satisfying.[63] However, when ending a narrative, it is essential that the ending offers closure and is consistent with the narrative, mood, and tone of any previous installments in a series or chapters.[64] In short, it must meet readers' expectations, or it will be deemed inauthentic.[65] Given the importance that participants placed upon the ingredients of emotional intimacy and a developing love story, it is hard to imagine what kind of ending would be consistent with those ingredients and be perceived as authentic and not be happy.

Romance practitioners should thus consider the importance of "a happy ending" to their readers' perceptions of authenticity when practicing their craft. A lack of "a happy ending," based on these survey results, could result in the novel not being considered a "true" or authentic romance and provoke negative reactions and perceptions of inauthenticity,[66] especially given how romance readers develop into emotionally attached readers.[67]

Likewise, the top three scoring options for Q2 (Rape, Sad ending, Adultery) that participants ranked as should never be included in a romance would harm the possibility of "a happy ending" and the love story between and the hero and heroine. Nevertheless, it is important to mention the existence of the rape and forgive trope, whose popularity started in the 1970s and decreased in the 1990s, moving later to bondage, discipline (or domination), sadism, and masochism (BDSM) novels and forced the seduction subgenre into romance.[68] Sad endings exist in love stories that are not considered "romances" by some associations of writing practitioners (RWA, RWNZ), and adultery can be mitigated and considered romantic if followed by "a happy ending."[69] Authors, who include what could be considered "a sad ending" should be especially careful to ensure the ending feels satisfying and authentic given the perceptions of the participants of this survey, or consider marketing their books as a different genre to avoid reader findings of inauthenticity.

There was an inconsistency with "A happy ending" receiving the highest overall score (273) but was chosen by less participants (53%) than the second-highest scoring option (251): "Well-developed emotional intimacy between the heroine and hero" with 59.5% of participants. This encouraged us to investigate further and compare participants' choices of options with their demographic data. We found differences concerning age-groups and educational backgrounds. "A happy ending" received the highest score among participants in the following age-groups: 35–44, 45–54, and 55–64. However, for younger participants (age categories 18–23 and 24–34), the option for "Well-developed emotional intimacy between the heroine and hero" received the highest score. Interestingly, the same trend was observed among participants aged 65 or over suggesting that the youngest and oldest participants consider emotional intimacy throughout the novel more important than "a happy ending."

Interestingly, "A slowly but consistently developing love between hero and heroine" received the third highest score among participants aged 24–34, 45–54 and 55–64, which makes it the third most popular ingredient of a romance. Participants aged 35–44 and participants aged 65 or over gave the third highest score to "Lots of love scenes with explicit sexual description," which could be explained by the cultural differences (such as purity) in the times they were growing up or possibly considered part of the story that would lead to "a happy ending." These findings suggest the existence of an age-related trend, with younger participants aged 34 or less choosing "Well-developed emotional intimacy between the heroine and hero" over "A happy ending." However, this may be required for there to be "a happy ending." The results were also screened against participants' education level, but there was no particular trend in the results.

Conclusion

Romance book readers' perceptions and expectations of the genre have not yet been explored through the lens of authenticity. However, given the commercial focus and importance of the genre and its writing practitioners' awareness of commercial realities,[70] understanding these is important to satisfy readers' expectations and increase their writing practitioners' chances for financial success. The romance genre is a "participatory construct,"[71] so strengthening the consensus between the stakeholders is beneficial to all involved. Seventy percent of romance readers discover the genre between the ages of 11 and 18 and 35% have been readers of the genre for more than 20 years.[72] Consequently, many romance readers have established perceptions and expectations about what they expect to be in a romance novel to deem it authentic.

It was found that "a happy ending" was the most important ingredient in a romance novel, and thus a key expectation and factor in readers' perceptions of authenticity.

Emotional intimacy and a well-developed love story were also seen as key expectations and that would lead to "a happy ending." Additionally, a number of elements were considered absolutely unacceptable to be included, with the top three being rape, a sad ending, and adultery. These elements if included would make a romance book inauthentic for readers.

These findings align with scholarly understanding of the genre and are also consistent with writing practitioners' definitions of romance.

However, readers' preferences have been found to vary with age. Middle-aged participants considered "a happy ending" the most important ingredient of a romance, while younger and older participants opted for emotional intimacy. Consequently, younger and older participants did not find a sad ending as distasteful as middle-aged participants.

Readers' views on the admissibility of rape and explicit sex scenes were also found to depend on age, which could be explained by cultural differences of the times they were brought up. However, the top four options chosen in question one are, or would be expected to be part of or lead to "a happy ending." So, although the language may have evolved from betrothed or married to being together as a couple, "a happy ending" still appears to be essential for a book to be considered an authentic romance.

This research contributes to knowledge and scholarship by exploring romance readers', an important genre stakeholder, perceptions, and understandings of authenticity. Future research could explore if there are certain aspects of "a happy ending" that are specifically required for a romance to be considered authentic or if there are other elements of the romance genre that might provoke feelings of inauthenticity outside from those listed in the survey. How practitioners and authors do or do not consider readers' perception of authenticity could also be explored.

NOTES

1. Dimitrije Curcic, October 9, 2022. "Romance Novel Sales Statistics." Wordsrated. Accessed September 17, 2024. https://wordsrated.com/romance-novel-sales-statistics/.

2. Dimitrije Curcic, January 30, 2023. "Fiction Book Sales Statistics." Wordsrated. Accessed September 17, 2024. https://wordsrated.com/fiction-books-sales/.

3. Christine Larson, "Open Networks, Open Books: Gender, Precarity and Solidarity in Digital Publishing." *Information, Communication and Society* 23, no. 13 (2020): 1892–1908. https://doi.org/10.1080/1369118X.2019.1621922.

4. Jacqueline Burgess and Christian Jones, "Investigating Consumer Perceptions of Brand Inauthenticity in a Narrative Brand Ending," *Journal of Product & Brand Management* (2023). https://doi.org/10.1108/JPBM-03-2022-3897

5. Christine Larson, "Open Networks, Open Books."

6. Janice A. Radway, 1991. *Reading the Romance: Women, Patriarchy, and Popular Literature*. University of North Carolina Press.

7. Burgess and Jones, "Investigating Consumer Perceptions"; Russell, Cristal Antonia, and Hope Jensen Schau. "When Narrative Brands End: The Impact of Narrative Closure and Consumption Sociality on Loss Accommodation." *Journal of Consumer Research* 40, no. 6 (2014): 1039–62. https://doi.org/10.1086/673959.

8. Burgess and Jones, "Investigating Consumer Perceptions"; Russell and Schau. "When Narrative Brands End."

9. Julia Guidry Moulard, Carolyn Popp Garrity, and Dan Hamilton Rice, "What Makes a Human Brand Authentic? Identifying the Antecedents of Celebrity Authenticity," *Psychology & Marketing* 32, no. 2 (2015): 173–86. https://doi.org/10.1002/mar.20771.

10. Athwal, N., and L. C. Harris. "Examining How Brand Authenticity Is Established and Maintained: The Case of the Reverso." *Journal of Marketing Management* 34, no. 3–4 (2018): 347–69. https://doi.org/10.1080/0267257X.2018.1447008.

11. Allison R. Johnson, Matthew Thomson, and Jennifer Jeffrey, "What Does Brand Authenticity Mean? Causes and Consequences of Consumer Scrutiny Toward a Brand Narrative," In *Brand Meaning Management* (Review of Marketing Research, Vol. 12), edited by Susan Fournier, 1–27. Emerald Group Publishing Limited, 2015. https://doi.org/10.1108/S1548-643520150000012001.

12. Moulard, Garrity, and Rice, "What Makes a Human Brand Authentic?" 173–86.
13. Kristine Fritz, Verena Schoenmueller, and Manfred Bruhn. "Authenticity in Branding – Exploring Antecedents and Consequences of Brand Authenticity." *European Journal of Marketing* 51, no. 2 (2017): 324–48. https://doi.org/10.1108/EJM-10-2014-0633.
14. Burgess and Jones, "Investigating Consumer Perceptions."
15. Jason Mittell, *Complex TV: The Poetics of Contemporary Television Storytelling*. New York University Press, 2015; Henry Jenkins, *Textual Poachers: Television Fans and Participatory;* Fiske, *Culture, Updated Twentieth Anniversary Edition*. New York: Routledge, 2012.
16. John. "The Cultural Economy of Fandom." In *The Adoring Audience: Fan Culture*, edited by Lisa A. Lewis, 30–49. Abingdon, UK: Routledge, 1991; Jenkins, Henry. *Textual Poachers: Television Fans and Participatory Culture, Updated Twentieth Anniversary Edition*. New York: Routledge, 2012.
17. Radway, *Reading the Romance*.
18. Schell, Heather. "Love's Laborers Lost: Radway, Romance Writers, and Recuperating Our Past." *Journal of Popular Romance Studies* 4, no. 2 (2014): 1–5. https://jprstudies.org/wp-content/uploads/2014/09/LLL_Schell.pdf.
19. Chappel-Traylor, Deborah. "To My Mentor, Jan Radway, With Love." *Journal of Popular Romance Studies* 4, no. 2 (2014): 1–4. https://www.jprstudies.org/2014/10/to-my-mentor-jan-radway-with-loveby-deborah-chappel-traylor/.
20. Schell. "Love's Laborers Lost."
21. Radway, *Reading the Romance*, 11.
22. Radway, *Reading the Romance*, 14.
23. Regis, *A Natural History of the Romance*, 6.
24. Regis, *A Natural History of the Romance Novel*, 14.
25. Regis, *A Natural History of the Romance Novel*, 22.
26. Radway, *Reading the Romance*, 67.
27. Eric Murphy Selinger, "Rebooting the Romance: The Impact of *a Natural History of the Romance Novel*." *Journal of Popular Romance Studies* 3, no. 2 (2013): 1–5. https://www.jprstudies.org/2013/06/rebooting-the-romance-the-impact-of-a-natural-history- of-the-romance-novel-by-eric-murphy-selinger/.
28. Regis, *A Natural History of the Romance Novel*, 14.
29. Regis, *A Natural History of the Romance Novel*, 14.
30. Ann Goris, "A Natural History of the Romance Novel's Enduring Romance with Popular Romance Studies." *Journal of Popular Romance Studies* 3, no. 2 (2013): 1–4. https://www.jprstudies.org/2013/06/a-natural-history-of-the-romance-novels-enduring- romance-with-popular-romance-studies-by-an-goris/.
31. Jayashree Kamblé, Eric Murphy Selinger, and Hsu-Ming Teo, eds. *The Routledge Research Companion to Popular Romance Fiction*. Routledge, 2021, 2.
32. Joyce G. Saricks, *The Readers' Advisory Guide to Genre Fiction*, 2nd ed. Chicago: American Library Association, 2011.
33. Saricks, *The Readers' Advisory Guide to Genre Fiction*, 367.

34. Kamblé, Selinger, and Teo, eds. *Companion to Popular Romance Fiction*. Routledge, 2021; Radway, *Reading the Romance*; Regis, *A Natural History of the Romance*, 2003).
35. Saricks, *The Readers' Advisory Guide to Genre Fiction*, 368.
36. Saricks, *The Readers' Advisory Guide to Genre Fiction*, 388.
37. Mallory Jagodzinski, "We've Come a Long Way, Baby: Reflecting Thirty Years After Reading the Romance." *Journal of Popular Romance Studies* 4, no. 2 (2014): 1.
38. Moody, Stephanie. "From Reading the Romance to Grappling with Genre." *Journal of Popular Romance Studies* 4, no. 2 (2014): 2.
39. Alison Flood, "Romance Writers of America Aims for Happy End to Racism Row with New Prize." *The Guardian*, May 23, 2020. https://www.theguardian.com/books/2020/may/22/romance-writers-of-america-racism-row-new-prize-ritas-vivian.
40. Gaja Kolodziej, "Unforgettably in Love: Uses of the Amnesia Trope in Contemporary Romance." PhD diss., Massey University, 2021. Massey Research Online. http://hdl.handle.net/10179/16476.
41. William A. Gleason, and Erich Murphy Selinger. *Romance Fiction and American Culture: Love as the Practice of Freedom?* London: Routledge, 2016.
42. Kolodziej, "Unforgettably in Love."
43. Romance Writers of America, "About the Romance Genre." RWA.com. Accessed September 21, 2024. https://www.rwa.org/the-romance-genre.
44. Goris, "A Natural History of the Romance Novel's Enduring Romance https://www.jprstudies.org/2013/06/a-natural-history-of-the-romance-novels-enduring-romance-with-popular-romance-studies-by-an-goris/.
45. Mary Jo Putney, "Welcome to the Dark Side." In *Dangerous Men and Adventurous Women: Romance Writers on the Appeal of Romance*, edited by Jayne Ann Krantz, Philadelphia: University of Pennsylvania Press, 1992, 100.
46. Kate Walker, *Kate Walker's 12-Point Guide to Writing Romance*. Straightforward Publishing, 2018: 17.
47. Kolodziej, "Unforgettably in Love."
48. Gleason, and Selinger. *Romance Fiction and American Culture.*
49. Kolodziej, Gaja, "Unforgettably in Love."
50. Romance Writers of America. "About Romance Genre." Accessed September 17, 2024. https://www.rwa.org/Online/Romance_Genre/About_Romance_Genre.aspx.
51. Romance Writers of New Zealand. *The Beginner's Guide to Romance*. Accessed September 17, 2024. https://www.romancewriters.co.nz/about-us/beginners-guide-romance/.
52. As cited in Saricks, *The Readers' Advisory Guide to Genre Fiction*, 424.
53. As cited in Saricks, *The Readers' Advisory Guide to Genre Fiction*, 336.
54. Curcic "Romance Novel Sales Statistics."
55. Radway, *Reading the Romance*; Saricks, *The Readers' Advisory Guide*; Walker, *Guide to Writing Romance.*
56. Saricks, *The Readers' Advisory Guide to Genre Fiction.*

57. Athwal and Harris. "Examining How Brand Authenticity Is Established and Maintained"; Moulard, Garrity, and Rice, "What Makes a Human Brand Authentic?"
58. (*About the Romance Genre,* 2023)
59. Gaffney as cited in Saricks, *The Readers' Advisory Guide to Genre Fiction*, 424.
60. Walker, *Guide to Writing Romance.* 17.
61. Kamblé, Selinger, and Teo, eds. *The Routledge Research Companion to Popular Romance Fiction.*
62. Saricks, *The Readers' Advisory Guide to Genre Fiction.*
63. (Romance Novelist's Association, 2023).
64. Noël Carroll, "Narrative Closure." *Philosophical Studies* 135, no. 1 (2007): 1–15. https://doi.org/10.1007/s11098-007-9097-9; Gerald Prince, *Dictionary of Narratology: Revised Edition.* Lincoln: University of Nebraska Press, 2003; Rebecca Williams, *Post-Object Fandom: Television, Identity and Self-Narrative.* New York: Bloomsbury Academic, 2015.
65. Burgess and Jones, "Investigating Consumer Perceptions."
66. Burgess and Jones, "Investigating Consumer Perceptions."
67. John Fiske, "The Cultural Economy of Fandom"; Henry Jenkins, *Textual Poachers.*
68. Klugman, Ema. "'They Are Like Printing Money': Sex, Rape, and Power in Romance Novels." Unsuitable. Accessed September 17, 2024. https://sites.duke.edu/unsuitable/rape-forgive/.
69. Spencer, Lynn. "Adultery—The Great Romance Taboo." All About Romance. Accessed September 17, 2024. https://allaboutromance.com/adultery-the-great-romance-taboo/.
70. Larson, "Open Networks, Open Books."
71. Moody, Stephanie. "From Reading the Romance to Grappling with Genre."
72. Curcic, "Romance Novel Sales Statistics."

Chapter 2

From Private to Public

#Bookstagram as a Safe Space for Romance Readers

Ayşegül Rigato

Online platforms dedicated to sharing the love of reading started gaining popularity around 2009.[1] Since then, the popularity of literary spheres on various social media platforms has flourished. The bookish[2] communities online can participate in book clubs, "readathons," or hashtag campaigns such as #transrightsreadathon or #sapphicsemptember to connect with readers globally and encourage diverse readership. Among the online bookish communities, the romance fandom has the most digitally active users.[3] With the popularity of the romance genre online, the sales of romance novels are among the highest.[4] This chapter will focus specifically on the romance communities on Instagram, or as fans refer to it, Bookstagram. Instagram has a significant bookish community where users can share reviews and recommendations and discuss any book with other readers globally. Romance bookstagrammers also often share personal stories on how they got into romance or humorous posts in coded language aimed at romance readers only. Additionally, they use their platform to create a communal space where romance readers can make connections and even poke fun at some of the stereotypes associated with romance readers.

Popular romance scholars must acknowledge conversations "outside of academia, particularly in online romance communities."[5] In these communities, there are critiques of the genre, how it can improve, reader and author perspectives, and conversations about the positive impact romance has on its readership. This is not to suggest that the online communities are exempt from criticism. Rhiannon Bury argues that "it is important not to romanticize communities that are formed out of exclusion and/ or marginalization. Within every community, there is a minority who are not always able or willing to engage in the established communal practices."[6] Therefore, my aim is not to suggest that these bookish communities are a utopian alternative but to showcase how they inform people about the genre while addressing some of the issues associated with romance. The unapologetic nature of romance fans online brings a different light to the genre's readership that has been historically shunned by non-romance readers within and outside of academia.

A SENSE OF COMMUNITY AMONG ROMANCE READERS

Engagement within the romance community is not a new phenomenon. Many romance readers have always been active participants in their literary consumption, reaching out to authors and fellow readers even before the popularity of social media.[7] Despite being perceived as passive, romance readers typically take on an active role in their reading and "seek to form bonds" with one another.[8] According to Laura Struve, "romance readers actively seek out other readers in order to share information about books and to discuss and analyze their reading."[9] Through engaging the comment sections of romance blogs, Struve argues that unlike what many romance critics argued, romance readers are not looking for a husband, "they are trying to find a sister of sorts."[10] Janice Radway's pioneering research, *Reading the Romance* (1984), also showcases community building among romance fans. In addition to her analysis of the genre, Radway interviewed several women in Smithton (pseudonym for a suburban town in the U.S.) on what they looked for in a romance novel in order to discuss what drew them to the genre. One of the highlights in Radway's study is the introduction of Dot, the bookstore employee whom the women of Smithton trusted the most with their recommendation. Radway states that Dot initially started recommending romance books because she felt she could be helpful to those looking for trustworthy recommendations for romance books, and she became very popular among her community.[11] Upon first reading about Dot, I distinctly remember being envious of the Smithton women for having access to someone like Dot and having a community of romance readers.

Approximately forty years after Radway's research, we can now find many recommendations accessible to romance readers anywhere in the world. It is debatable how "close-knit" a community can be on social media. However, when it comes to romance, seeing millions of people enjoy similar books certainly removes the "shamed" aspect of the genre and encourages romance readers who might have been hesitant to browse the romance section at the bookstore prior to the massive influence of bookish platforms.

The need to connect with other romance readers often goes hand in hand with the misrepresentation and criticism romance fans often face. Struve argues that many romance scholars "fail to recognize that a reader's choice to read a certain book does not imply the unquestioning adoption of its ideology."[12] The early feminist audience studies have often led with the assumption that romance readers cannot recognize some of the problematic aspects of the genre, or they choose not to. Much criticism of romance fiction and its portrayal of romance readers as uncritical is still prevalent, as romance readers are still encountering the same stigmas today. Early romance scholars, such as Janice Radway (1984), Tania Modleski (1982), and Ann B. Snitow (1979), often place romance readers as passive, and unable to recognize their imprisonment within patriarchy. Additionally, they did not approach the genre from a literary perspective and instead focused on the underlying reasons behind why women enjoyed romance. For instance, Snitow states, "to analyze Harlequin romances is not to make any literary claims for them."[13] Despite examining a few selected works from Harlequin, Snitow makes clear that romance fiction is "not art" and is simply there to "fill a place left empty for most people."[14] Due to her disinterest in the literary aspects of romance fiction, Snitow argues that the fact "that the books are unrealistic, distorted, and flat are all facts beside the point."[15] Instead, her research is more concerned with the hidden reasons women seek this escapism.

Similarly, Radway argues that while romance offers a form of escape for women, it still perpetuates the values that left them dissatisfied in the first place. The romance author and scholar Jayne Ann Krentz criticized this approach, stating that it was insulting to the women who enjoy the genre. Similarly, romance author and scholar Kathleen Gilles Seidel argues that the feminist commentary often sees romance readers as "children with childish reading strategies"; however, "romance readers are grown women, able to distinguish between art and life, the literary and the actual."[16] Seidel and Krentz made these arguments in 1992; however, this stereotype associated with romance readers is still common as the bookfluencers today still respond to similar criticisms. Moreover, when looking at Radway's analysis alongside with some of the other early romance research, their examples consist of Harlequin, Mills & Boon, and the "bodice ripper" historical romances. Jay Dixon criticized this approach, arguing that Radway's treatment of the genre was flawed as Dixon disagreed with Radway's categorization. Radway treats historical and contemporary romances as the same, while the Mills & Boon reader data shows that these categories often have different demographics.[17] Examining romance novels and readers from a generalized lens diminishes the diversity within the genre. In reality, romance fiction has a potpourri of subgenres and tropes that differ significantly.

Early feminist audience scholar Janice Radway was undoubtedly one of the pioneers within romance scholarship. Her work still informs romance research today. However, due to the homogenous group she studied, the results of the study were limited. The romance genre is flexible and changing as it often adapts to its readers' concerns and needs over time. Radway observed that "romance writing and reading continue . . . they are fluid and actively being changed by both writers and readers, [and] that their final effects can neither be foreseen nor guaranteed in advance."[18] By looking at the change in the fandom and the genre, it is safe to say that Radway was correct in her predictions. The readership and the categories of romance have expanded since feminist scholars first started paying attention to the genre.

RISE OF BOOKFLUENCERS

Reading culture has changed significantly in recent years, especially during the early days of the COVID-19 pandemic. Not only did book sales increase by 35% in 2020 alone, but the way we approach reading also changed.[19] While more people got into reading, many readers got into (or got back into) reading romance. According to Book Riot's pandemic reading habits survey, half of the interviewees said they read more romance than before the pandemic.[20] This comes as no surprise since there is no better genre to turn to in economic and sociocultural uncertainty than romance due to its formulaic structure and always guaranteed happily ever afters. The change in reading culture can be observed by looking at the bookish platforms on social media. In the survey conducted by the editors Josefine Smith and Kathleen W. Taylor Kollman, the majority of interviewees stated that they get their recommendations from social media and engage with other readers online. The bookish activities on social media "[contribute] to the broader ecology of online and offline book and reading culture."[21] This shift in the reading culture is most apparent in Gen Z as they are a significant driving force in book sales, particularly in the romance genre, due to their involvement with bookish social media such as #bookstagram and #booktok.[22]

In her research of online literary spheres, Bronwen Thomas argues that with the digitalization of the publication industry, readers are also no longer a passive audience.[23] They are now "interacting with authors, voting online for crowdfunded publishing ventures, . . . engaging in festivals, and mass reading events" and "being addressed, invited to participate and held as figures whose opinions really do seem to matter."[24] This growing reader engagement has given rise to what Bronwyn Reddan refers to as "bookfluencers."[25] Bookfluencers review and recommend books, moderate book clubs, and some get sponsorships and are invited to book-related events as speakers. Although YouTube was at the forefront of online book communities about a decade ago, the shorter format of Instagram and TikTok has become more prevalent in recent years.

Due to social media's focus on aesthetics, being a reader online has been criticized and scrutinized. However, there is something to be said about the success of bookish communities online, as it is now nearly impossible to go into a bookstore without seeing a "#BookTok" or "#Bookstagram" section.

Although we cannot deny social media's fabricated and performative nature, we must still acknowledge its impact on people's engagement with literary works and book sales. If you are wondering how effective online bookish fans can be, Ruby Dixon's success story is a good example. Dixon's alien romance *Ice Planet Barbarians*, initially independently published in 2015, was arguably aimed at a niche audience when first published. However, with its unexpected popularity on social media in 2020, even some readers who do not typically reach for monster romances picked up at least one from the series, and it introduced more readers to the monster romance subgenre. For instance, the bookish YouTuber @bookswithemilyfox is among many who reacted to Dixon's series despite typically not reading or recommending romance novels on their platform.[26] The series' success resulted in Berkley Books (part of Penguin Publishing) publishing Dixon's books in print with revamped covers in 2021. With the digital changes in the literary world, "books 'that had been left to die many years before' have been suddenly brought back to life."[27] Once they are popular online, it shifts trends in the industry and the perimeter of the genre and brings what the publishing houses initially ignore to the forefront for readers to discover.

METHODOLOGY

While there are various research opportunities for online literary spheres, there is a discrepancy among the most often studied. Instagram is one of the popular platforms requiring further research. There are various studies on Twitter, YouTube, or other online platforms such as blogs; however, research on Instagram is "few and far between," mainly due to the inaccessibility of data.[28] However, according to Bronwen Thomas, engaging with individual pages on Instagram still has potential as it highlights the "everyday rituals and private moments of social actors."[29]

My research draws from Thomas to examine some of the accounts of romance fans on Instagram. Qualitative research on selected bookish accounts can give insight into how some of the romance communities operate online. I examine several accounts on Instagram to discuss how they discuss the genre and create an affective space for romance readers. Currently, the hashtag #romancebooks has 3.4 million posts on Instagram, and it is fast growing. My research will focus on these five accounts due to their difference in content as well as the informative and responsive nature. I found these accounts through various searches with the keywords such as *romance books*, *romancelandia*, and *romance reader*. It should also be noted that I used my personal account, therefore the algorithm would have recommended these pages to me due to my engagement with similar content. There are many more bookish accounts dedicated to genre fiction across various social media platforms. My aim is not to suggest that these selected are the sole representatives of romance readers but rather examine few types of content within this vast online community.

The accounts chosen for this research (@romantically_inclined, @toriloves_heas, @talk_about_swoon, @lydia_lloyd_romance, and @yourbookishbff) highlight how romance readers use their platform to respond to some of the stigmas associated with romance and its readership while promoting a diverse range of books for readers who may be seasoned or new to the genre. The romance genre has a long history of dealing with stigma and devaluation. One of the most appealing aspects of romance bookstagram is how community-focused some pages are and how often they use their platforms to encourage fans to be proud of reading romance.

Romance bookstagram is unique in that unlike other bookish groups (e.g., fantasy or horror), romance bookfluencers sometimes feel the need to defend the genre as it has been criticized by non-romance readers for decades. So, in addition to sharing recommendations, reviews, and their emotional journeys in these novels, romance bookfluencers also share responses to some of the criticism and stereotypes and encourage inclusivity within the genre. Doing so, they are fostering a sense of community and connection within romance fandoms, which results in an affective space where romance fans share their passion for the genre.

CASE STUDIES

Figure 2.1   Romantically Inclined Reviews (@romantically_inclined), "Meme Monday (got it right this time)," Instagram, April 17, 2023, https://www.instagram.com/p/CrJDGBaLlFi/?img_index=5&igsh=MTAxbzhxN3kzZ3ZoOA%3D%3D.

The romance industry is known to curate books according to its readership. Most romance publishing houses use "extensive marketing research to calibrate its formulas to the changing tastes of its readers."[30] Therefore, most readers are accustomed to looking for specific recommendations and authors. Radway also observed this during her interviews as many of her interviewees stated they had favourite authors or categories, such as historical or contemporary, that they typically reached for. However, what if you are new to the genre? There is an overwhelming amount of romance books to choose from that have so many different tropes. This is where some of the romance bookfluencers grabbed my attention, as it is relatively easy to find a wide range of recommendations on their accounts, including particular subgenres and tropes.

The narrowed-down recommendations lists are standard among romance bookstagram as many romance readers want to know what they are getting into before diving into a book.

One of the first accounts that drew my attention was Lydia Lloyd's (@lydia_lloyd_romance). Lloyd is an academic in 19th-century British Literature, a historical romance author, and a bookfluencer. Historical romance readers and those looking to learn more about this category might find Lloyd's account very informative as she utilizes her expertise in 19th-century literature when recommending historical romance novels. For instance, before sharing her recommendations of bluestocking heroines in historical romance, she informs readers about the term's history and what it meant culturally within that historical period.[31] In the post, which includes her discussions of several historical romances, Lloyd discusses which types of heroines are historically correct to be called bluestocking by giving specific examples from eight historical romances. Similarly, she addresses different tropes on her account, giving a little historical background and how the theme in question manifests in romance novels. One of the most common tropes, "marrying to settle a debt," might be seen as problematic and a one-sided deal for some. However, Lloyd argues that it is, in fact, "gender neutral" as she encountered many examples where the hero was in financial need as opposed to the heroine.[32] Another observation she talks about is through her discussion of birth control in historical romances. Lloyd states that in many of the books she recommends, heroes are the ones to "take the initiative."[33] Lloyd's romance bookstagram account is very informative about the historical romance genre and where some of these tropes and characters derive from. Additionally, historical romance has been associated with bodice rippers of the 1970s and 1980s, some of which did not age well; however, Lloyd presents a diverse selection of historical romance books that go against their mainstream portrayal, often found in scholarship critiquing the genre. Her selection of what can be considered feminist examples of historical romances provides an alternative narrative missing from the discussion of historical romance within academia.

Another account that curates detailed lists and recommendations is @toriloves_heas. Tori, the admin behind the Instagram account, curates very detailed and specific recommendations for many types of romance fans, whether it is historical, LGBTQ+, contemporary, or paranormal. In addition to the wide range of recommendations, she provides guides for numerous subgenres for readers who may be new to it. Tori also participates in various romance-related hashtags such as #coverlustfriday, which is popular among those who collect paperback romances, or hashtag campaigns such as #transrightsreadalong, which is a read-along that aims to promote LGBTQ+ books among bookish communities. One of the posts pinned at the top of her account is for #transrightsreadathon, which lists twenty romance books with trans characters, in addition to listings of YA, horror, and nonfiction books she compiled after consulting with some of her trans friends.[34] In another curated list, Tori addresses sex work in romance by recommending books with characters who are sex workers. In her caption, she states that what prompted this recommendation list was a judgmental review she saw on Goodreads that shamed one of the characters for being a sex worker and enjoying it.[35] Upon addressing the problematic aspect of that review, she states that "even fictional [people] do not have to live up to your weird, puritanical beliefs about purity, virginity, body count, and sexual expression to deserve happy endings."[36]

Romance has long been described as "porn for women" or "mommy porn." Thus, some of the stigmas associated with the genre come from its treatment of sexuality. Many scholars of romance fiction often focus on the depictions of sex or the sexual dynamics among characters. For instance, Snitow referred to romance novels as "phallic worship," arguing that every contact in romance novels is sexualized.[37] Snitow did not necessarily argue this out of an anti-sex position. However, sex in romance has been a point of scrutiny among scholars. Women have long dealt with the shame of their bodies, sexualities, and desires, and many romance books go against this stigma. Thus, when examining the romance fandom online, the sex-positive outlook among romance readers is more prevalent. In one of her videos, bookfluencer @romantically_inclined argued that "everyone is a feminist until there's sxx in a book," with the caption stating that being pro-women and attacking the romance genre and its readers are contradictory.[38] In growing numbers, the Romance bookfluencers have been taking part in the discussions of sex, purity culture, and the stigmas around women's sexualities, as many claim that romance was what helped them in their healing. The bookstagrammers @swooncast, @yourbookishbff, @sarahinwanderland, and @onlyonebookshelf have a series of collaborative posts titled "I Kissed Purity Culture Goodbye: A Romancelandia Reflection and Call-to-Action," as a counterprotest against those who called for boycotting against "smut" in romance books.[39]

This series of posts discusses religious trauma and purity culture, while each bookfluencer talks about their background with these heavy subjects and how it impacted their outlook towards their sexualities, bodies, and romantic relationships. In addition to discussing their personal journeys, these posts inform about the purity culture and recommend "healing books," which are a mixture of nonfiction, self-help books and some sex-positive romance books. Many of these posts have long, personal, and detailed comments from their followers, also sharing their experiences and how thankful they are for this much-needed discussion. Posts like these also create a space for romance readers to not only connect on a deeper level but also feel safe to share their opinions on stigmatized topics such as sexuality versus purity.

While there is weight and value to the serious side of romance bookstagram, there is also something to be said about how some bookfluencers use humor and "inside jokes" to form similar bonds among one another. For instance, the romance book reviewer and the host of *Up the Smut* podcast @romantically_inclined is among the most well-known bookfluencers among romance bookish platforms. Self-proclaimed "smut reviewer" and "meme queen" @romantically_inclined often shares humorous posts, poking fun at some of the aspects of the romance genre and reclaiming some of the shamed aspects of it, such as the unrealistic depictions of sex or relationships. For example, memes with the caption of "romance math is never needing lube,"[40] or "romance math is no UTIs" poke fun at the always-perfect sex scenes depicted in many romance novels. @romantically_inclined also shares a lot of video content relating to some of the darker romances she typically recommends. For instance, the video with the caption: "Dark romance heroes stalking & kidnapping" with the audio in the background repeating: "but is it against the law though?" has nearly 12K views and the caption states: "It's only against the law if the Stockholm syndrome doesn't kick in."[41] This type of self-awareness is prevalent among romance bookstagram accounts similar to @romantically_inclined. It not only acknowledges some of the criticism the genre receives, but the awareness made clear by romance readers also challenges the notion that they are not able to acknowledge the "problematic" aspects of the genre. Accounts like @romantically_inclined are not trying to glamorize these aspects of romance, but by acknowledging it, they make it clear that they are not "children with childish reading strategies."[42]

Among the typical bookish content shared across platforms such as aesthetically pleasing bookshelves, book reviews, recommendations, favourite quotes and fan art, romance bookfluencers also use the more tongue-in-cheek content of short videos or memes that are not easily accessible to outsiders. This type of content often draws more views as it creates a sense of community with most of the language and humour used in coded language. As discussed, romance readers are often treated as children, not being able to separate fiction from reality or not being able to recognize some of the "toxicity" in romance. Therefore, it is common to see posts on social media critiquing this association with romance readers. One of the videos pinned on @romantically_inclined's accounts addresses how the heroes she loves reading about could not be further from what she seeks in real life. These posts are also typically humorous with memes or short video content, such as with the audio repeating: "What's something that's a [red flag] in real life but that you love in a romance book? . . . Men."[43] Or, at times, romance bookstagram pokes fun at the anti-feminist stereotype associated with romance readers sharing memes with the captions of "Me reading romance novels: Give me a bossy, possessive, jealous alpha male, please / Me in real life: There's not a man alive who can tell me what to do."[44] Romance authors such as Jayne A. Krentz and Robyn Donald discuss the importance of coded language among romance readers in *Dangerous Men and Adventurous Women* (1992), arguing that critics who are not typically romance readers simplify the novels because the coded language in romance is not accessible to outsiders. While recognizing romance novels can be self-care for women, Radway argued that it still perpetuated the problems women were escaping from. To those arguments similar to Radway's, Donald responds with an analysis of the "moody" hero. While a lot of the critiques of the genre interpreted him as a problematic figure, Donald suggests otherwise. She argues that he is made that way as a challenge for the heroine to conquer. Donald states, "his strength is a measure of her power" because no matter how menacing or domineering the hero is, the heroine always conquers him in the end.[45] This type of coded language within the romance genre also reflects in the readers as they use their "insider" position to share their opinions and jokes about the books they read while connecting with others who understand these references. For instance, @toriloves_hea participates in the trend of imagined Instagram accounts of literary characters. She shares her interpretation of well-loved romance heroes' Instagram accounts in her version.[46] The contents similar to Tori's and those reminiscent of inside jokes among friends play a big part in the community aspect of romance bookstagram where readers can create a safe space.

CONCLUSION

There is no denying that romance and feminism have a complicated relationship which continues to this day, however, as Jay Dixon very elegantly put it, "Feminism has many faces. Perhaps romance fiction is one of them."[47] One of the places in which this discussion about feminism and romance fiction happens is among online communities. The romance influencers on Instagram are unapologetic and are not afraid to talk about their favourite romances, respond to some of the criticisms, and create a community among likeminded people. For women on social media, "there is a constant negotiation between the desire to connect and the need to self-regulate."[48]

However, romance bookstagram is one of the spaces in which women might feel less pressured to hide their desires and interests. Although some, if not all, of these romance bookfluencers face some type of judgment and even trolling on the internet, they respond to it with humor or prove those judgments are wrong. For instance, the romance bookfluencer Laura Heath (@elitereading) often shares pictures of her husband kissing or hugging, and she is not the only one sharing her family life on her romance bookstagram. Similarly, author and bookfluencer Stacey McEwan (@stacebookspace) has a series of videos titled "Fictional men vs. my husband," in which her husband clearly participates in the joke. @romantically_inclined has a series of posts, memes, and videos dedicated to the men who send her vulgar, offensive, and insulting comments or messages regularly. One of which has the caption: "When guys start talking shit about romance books being unrealistic," with the photo underneath stating: "You're mad at your wiener, not at me."[49] These videos challenge the stereotype of romance readers being unhappy in their relationships or single because of their "unrealistic" expectations caused by romance novels.

The discussions happening among romance fandoms are valuable and require further research. Many of the past romance scholars tend to focus on the publication of romance or the form and content of the genre while presenting a generalized image of the readers. When looking at online communities in particular, the diversity and the desire to improve the genre are strong among romance fans. The romance author and podcaster Kelly Reynolds discusses being a romance fan and still being able to criticize the genre because she wants it to improve.[50] Similarly, the Smart Bitches and Trashy Books podcast brings up problematic aspects of the particular novels when reviewing while celebrating the good ones and supporting the genre and its readers. This is where academia and the romance readership separate the most, as romance scholars often make assumptions about the genre from a generalized lens, while romance readers can see the problems of certain books but not judge the genre as a whole. In her discussion of fans as tastemakers, Sue Brower argued that "by their activity in relation to the cultural form, they refine and enhance its social image while, as fans, claiming it as symbolic of their identity."[51] Thus, online romance bookish communities have a significant role in restructuring the image of a romance reader and the genre as a whole. Romance bookstagram is one of the online literary spheres where fans can discuss and critique the genre while challenging the image of passive and un-critical romance readers.

NOTES

1. Reddan, "Social Reading Cultures on BookTube, Bookstagram, and BookTok."
2. In *Bookishness* (2020), Jessica Pressman describes bookishness as "creative acts that engage the physicality of the book within a digital culture, in modes that may be sentimental, fetishistic, radical" (1). In the remainder of the essay, I also use this term in relation to literary activities online. I refer to this community as "bookish" rather than "reading" as it involves activities in addition to reading, such as sharing memes, fan art, promoting and buying special edition or collector books and other types of merch (often made by fans).
3. Markert, "Publishing the Romance Novel," 364.
4. Curcic, "Fiction Books Sales Statistics."
5. Young, "Race, Ethnicity, and Whiteness," 524.
6. Bury, *Cyberspaces of Their Own*, 15.
7. Wilkins et al., *Genre Worlds*, 45.
8. Struve, "Sisters of Sorts," 1293.
9. Ibid.
10. Ibid., 1298.
11. Radway, *Reading the Romance*, 46–47.
12. Struve, "Sisters of Sorts," 1293.
13. Snitow, "Mass Market Romance: Pornography for Women Is Different," 142.
14. Ibid.
15. Ibid., 143.
16. Seidel, "Judge Me by the Joy I Bring," 173.
17. Dixon, *The Romantic Fiction of Mills & Boon, 1909–1995*, 34.
18. Radway, *Reading the Romance*, 17.
19. Curcic, "Fiction Book Sales."
20. Brown, "In with the DNF-ing, Out With Real World Settings"
21. Dezuanni et al., "Selfies and Shelfies on #bookstagram and #booktok," 356.
22. Schwartz and Sullivan, "Gen Z is driving sales of romance books."
23. Thomas, *Literature and Social Media*.
24. Ibid., 117.
25. Reddan, "Social Reading Cultures on BookTube, Bookstagram, and BookTok."
26. @bookswithemilyfox, "I read Ice Planet Barbarians . . . and didn't fully hate it?" YouTube, May 26, 2023, https://www.youtube.com/watch?v=cbjVth7yCgs.
27. McGurl, *Everything and Less*, 74.
28. Thomas, "The #bookstagram: Distributed Reading in the Social Media Age," 17.
29. Thomas, *Literature and Social Media*.
30. Brouillette, "Romance Work," 15.
31. Lloyd (@lydia_lloyd_romance), "My theme this week is the bluestocking!" Instagram, March 27, 2023, https://www.instagram.com/p/CqSxbl5LwGF/?img_index=1.
32. Lydia Lloyd (@lydia_lloyd_romance), "Welcome to the second post of my debt- week!!), Instagram, September 6, 2022, https://www.instagram.com/p/CiK2zDYrxSx/?img_index=1.

33. Lydia Lloyd (@lydia_lloyd_romance), "So excited to post this one!!" Instagram, August 30, 2022, https://www.instagram.com/p/Ch4yzQUryzt/?img_index=2.
34. (@toriloves_heas), "it is #transreadathon !!!" Instagram, March 13, 2023, https://www.instagram.com/p/CpuqcxpgvnH/?img_index=1.
35. (@toriloves_heas), "So here I was, scrolling the Goodreads hellscape," Instagram, June 25, 2023, https://www.instagram.com/p/Ct6eF5_L4Wa/?img_index=1.
36. Ibid.
37. Snitow, "Mass Market Romance: Pornography for Women Is Different," 144.
38. Romantically Inclined Reviews (@romantically_inclined), "romance books ARE feminism." March 13, 2023, https://www.instagram.com/reel/Cpu0mv8AkyA/.
39. Kelsey | Bookstagram (@yourbookishbff), "CW: purity culture religious trauma, discussions of sexual content" Instagram, June 6, 2023, https://www.instagram.com/yourbookishbff/?img_index=1.
40. Romantically Inclined Reviews (@romantically_inclined), "the romance math, the rights and the wrongs," Instagram, October 9, 2023, https://www.instagram.com/p/CyLkWJ8r5Bk/?img_index=5
41. Romantically Inclined Reviews (@romantically_inclined), "It's only against the law," Instagram, August 30, 2023, https://www.instagram.com/reel/Cwki6Anyi7u/
42. Seidel, "Judge Me By the Joy I Bring," 173.
43. Romantically Inclined Reviews (@romantically_inclined), "GOD, WOMEN WRITE THEM WELL," Instagram, December 21, 2022, https://www.instagram.com/p/CmcmjdFqHRV/.
44. Romantically Inclined Reviews (@romantically_inclined), "BONUS POST," Instagram, September 24, 2022, https://www.instagram.com/p/Ci5GEt0L26p/?img_index=3.
45. Donald, "Mean, Moody, and Magnificent," 81.
46. (@toriloves_heas), "My personal headcanon is that the blue guys of Not-Hoth would type in all caps like a grandpa," Instagram, December 21, 2022, https://www.instagram.com/p/CmbnPnUrkgw/?img_index=4.
47. Dixon, *The Romantic Fiction of Mills & Boon, 1909–1995*, 194.
48. Nakamura, *Feminist Surveillance Studies*, 222.
49. Romantically Inclined Reviews (@romantically_inclined), "Dedicated to the long DM I got," Instagram, May 23, 2023, https://www.instagram.com/p/CslrAi6LOYF/?igshid=MzRlODBiNWFlZA==.
50. Kelly Reynolds (@boobiespodcast). "it's BECAUSE I'm a romance reader," Instagram, October 19, 2023. https://www.instagram.com/p/CymPBgjv1Ky/.
51. Brower, "Fans as Tastemakers," 163.

Chapter 3

Romance Readers' Perceptions of New Adult Fiction

Josefine Smith

New Adult (NA) fiction emerged in the late 2000s and gained popularity by the mid 2010s, and at its core is a grassroots genre supported by its author-fan community.[1] When a new genre emerges, it suggests a gap in cultural representation. In the case of NA fiction, this new genre reflects the "concrete contests of everyday life" for twentysomethings who are technically "adults" but experiencing the angst and tensions fraught within the coming-of-age process there was a gap in representations of their experience.[2] New Adult fiction explores coming-of-age themes, but the main characters have the autonomy and independence present in adult protagonists of Romance fiction.[3] As popular culture texts are core in the process of cultural production and identify new sites and power systems, it is valuable to explore a new genre to understand the larger cultural implications.[4] This chapter engages in a reader-response, cultural studies approach to participate in this academic exploration by providing a quantitative analysis of results for questions related to New Adult fiction from the survey at the center of this anthology.

The "New Adult Fiction" label was first coined by St. Martin's Press in 2009—before it gained popularity—in a writing contest they hosted. By the early 2010s, novels began to appear that contained the coming-of-age themes present in Young Adult works like *Twilight*, but with more mature subject matter and relationships. Books that superficially might fall in the Young Adult genre began to exhibit plot points involving more mature situations and life experiences. These texts typically focus on feminine adolescence and young adulthood, with their romantic plotlines and female protagonists. Authors began self-publishing texts under this genre label, writing stories that reflected challenges and experiences women face in their late teens and early twenties.[5] Major publishers then picked up these novels because of their popularity and fan base.[6] By 2013, these books were on *New York Times* and *USA Today* bestseller lists. Writer's Digest publishing house even published a book to guide other authors through the writing and publishing process in this genre.[7] NA fiction has emerged as a distinct genre between Young Adult (YA) fiction and Romance fiction.

New Adult fiction has been studied from various perspectives and has been a bit of a conundrum for scholars. Books that can be considered NA fiction float between YA and Romance sections in libraries and bookstores, and Amazon and Goodreads have a "New Adult and College" label, and the label is usually linked to Romance categories.[8] Amy Pattee was the first to write about the genre but situated the texts as an extension of young adult literature.[9] Indeed, in its original inception and early iterations, YA fiction was the "reference point" for NA fiction as a genre.[10] Since Amy Pattee's first paper, Jodi McAlister has thoroughly charted the evolution of NA fiction in the context of the literary marketplace.[11] When approaching any newly developed genre, it is essential to understand that "to best define genres and subgenres, and to account for how they develop, we must understand them as processes, not as static categories."[12] McAlister's work demonstrates the importance of triangulating multiple participants in contemporary genres when studying their cultural, literary, and personal impacts. She charts the paratextual landscape of this genre within the publishing realm, while this chapter explores reader understanding of the genre.

These scholars have looked at early iterations of this genre and the challenge of defining subgenres in a decentralized publishing process. However, there is still necessary exploration about the core of NA fiction. McAlister found that the main unique characteristic is the genre's focalization, in addition to the romantic bedrock of a central love story, and to end happily.[13] That focalization—the focus on the main character's experience and perspective—aligns with the focus on the experience of emerging adulthood, but the central love story situates it firmly as a subgenre in Romance fiction. This genre expands the concept of coming-of-age from an adolescent phenomenon to one that influences young people in their twenties. Though a person's twenties is commonly considered part of adulthood, over the past century it has become a period where individuals form their adult identity, a recently proposed stage named emerging adulthood.[14] Cultural constructions that emerge from this not-quite-adult stage of life include elements of identity exploration such as experimentation, negotiating relationships with authority, and exploring norms of successful adulthood. Themes in NA fiction encapsulate the tension between adulthood and adolescence, particularly for feminine coming-of-age. Those themes are at the core of the plot and character development in the narratives of NA fiction and offer insight into societal expectations for feminine coming of age and so femininity in general. The characters, especially the protagonist, deal with coming-of-age anxieties and do not possess the same level of established identity present in other subgenres of Romance fiction, which represents the experience of more adult characters and readers.[15]

Thus, it is important to also apply popular romance studies to the study of New Adult fiction. NA stories deal with adult characters with developing agency and who do not identify as adolescents. There is a significant body of research establishing the function of romance fiction in our broader gender norms, and feminine identity. Scholar Janice Radway connects reading to popular cultural consumption and meaning/norm-making for women in America. Radway explores how women readers create meaning and negotiate cultural norms when reading romance novels by studying ways readers consume texts and negotiate the messages from the text.[16] This chapter builds from the way she, as a cultural studies scholar, sees reading as a "complex, temporally evolving interaction between a fixed verbal structure and a socially situated reader," which in turn, shape the cultural implications of the genre.[17] I use her survey to explore that relationship at the sub genre level, and the cultural contexts within New Adult fiction.[18]

METHODOLOGY

As discussed in detail in the introductory chapter of this book, the data used in this analysis is from a larger data set collected in the Spring of 2020 and 2023.[19] The study is exploratory, and the data is observational. The results presented in this chapter focus on questions in the survey related to New Adult fiction, questions Q22–Q37. In this section, participants were asked about their understanding of New Adult fiction. The questions were modeled on Radway's questions about romance fiction genre traits and idealized character traits (12–21). Questions Q22–Q37 are a combination of multiple-choice, rank-order, and free-text questions (See figure 1). This chapter will explore the multiple-choice and rank-order questions.

Multiple Choice
22. Are you familiar with the romance sub-genre New Adult?
24. About how many New Adult romances do you read each month?
25. Which of the following best describes what usually makes you decide to read a New Adult romance?
26. Which of the following coming of age storylines in New Adult romances do you read? Check as many as you like.
27. Which of the following tropes are your favorite in New Adult romance?
32. How closely do you think the characters in New Adult romances resemble people you meet in real life?
33. How closely do you think the events in New Adult romances resemble events that occur in real life?
34. How closely do you think the New Adult heroine's reactions and feelings towards people and events resemble women in their twenties?
35. How closely do you feel that the New Adult hero's emotional responses to the heroine resemble the way men in their twenties behave?
Rank Order
28. Please rank the importance of the following ingredients in a New Adult romance.
29. Which of the following do you feel should never be included in a New Adult romance? Please rank the top three with 1 being the most distasteful element.
30. What qualities or characteristics do you like to see in a New Adult heroine? Please rank the top three with 1 being the most desirable quality.
31. How important are the following qualities or characteristics for a New Adult hero? Please rank the top three with 1 being the most desirable quality.
Text
23. Describe the difference between New Adult Romance and other romance fiction.
36. What are your three favorite New Adult romances?
37. What are your three favorite New Adult authors?

Figure 3.1   New Adult Questions

This analysis relies on descriptive statistical techniques to summarize and interpret the data. Measures of central tendency, such as mean, median, and mode, will be computed to highlight any patterns within the responses. The rank-order questions will be analyzed for counts (number of participants selecting each choice) and average.

RESULTS

These result visualizations were generated by Qualtrics. The results are organized by reader's awareness of New Adult fiction, their interpretation of the genre, and questions about how the genre connects to their experiences of the world.

READERS

Of the respondents, 81.5% are familiar with New Adult fiction. Those who answered that they were not familiar with were routed to the next section and did not answer questions related to the genre. The majority (47.9%) of those who are familiar with the genre read 1-2 a month, with 37.9% not reading the genre with regularity. Of those readers, 39.9% chose their New Adult books based on the description, with the majority of the rest based on reading the author before (25.8%) or based on a recommendation from another reader (21.6%). Interestingly, while 69.7% of readers select "first professional job" as their favorite storyline but 45.1% select "Unlikely romance (nerd-popular, wrong side of the tracks, etc.)" as their favorite trope.

Figure 3.2   Familiarity with New Adult Fiction

Figure 3.3   Number of New Adult Fiction per month

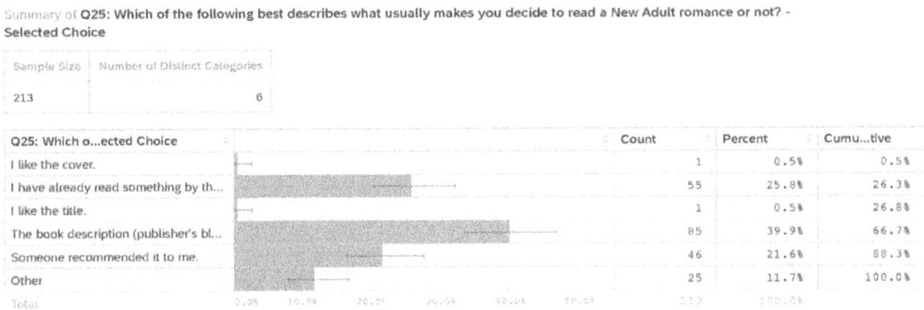

Figure 3.4   Choosing New Adult Fiction Texts

Summary of Q26: Which of the following coming of age storylines in New Adult romances do you read? Check as many as you like. - Selected Choice

Q26: Which o...ected Choice	Checked Percent	Check...Count	Sample Size
First professional job	69.7%	140	201
Graduating college	58.2%	117	201
Senior year of high school/ going to ...	29.4%	59	201
Other	14.4%	29	201
Like a moderate amount	7.5%	15	201

Figure 3.5 Favorite New Adult Storylines

Summary of Q27: Which of the following tropes are your favorite in New Adult romance? - Selected Choice

Sample Size: 204 Number of Distinct Categories: 5

Q27: Which...ted Choice	Count	Percent	Cumu...tive
Sports Romance	36	17.6%	17.6%
Unlikely romance (nerd popular, ...	92	45.1%	62.7%
Student-teacher	4	2.0%	64.7%
Workplace romance	39	19.1%	83.8%
Other	33	16.2%	100.0%

Figure 3.6 Favorite New Adult Tropes

Genre

Respondents ranked the characteristics of NA Fiction. Overall, "Settings/events that support the heroine's coming of age (new school, new job, graduating college, moving)" has the lowest rank score, with "The heroine goes through a coming-of-age process" and "First mature romantic relationship for the heroine" not far behind. Setting is most often ranked first, heroine's coming of age process ranked second, and first mature relationship spread across rank of third or fourth. "Rape" and "Sad ending" were the two top-ranked options for characteristics that should never be included in New Adult fiction.

Summary of Q28: Please rank the importance of the following ingredients in a New Adult romances.

Variable	Count	Average	Median
Settings/events that support the ...	144	4.57	4
First mature romantic relationshi...	144	5.07	5
The heroine goes through a com...	144	5.09	5
A long conflict between the hero...	144	5.28	5
Strong supporting characters	144	5.35	5
Challenging relationships with a...	144	5.67	6
Punishment of the villain	144	5.69	6
Lots of scenes of explicit sexual ...	144	5.82	6
Some detail about the heroine a...	144	5.83	6
Other	144	6.62	8

Figure 3.7 Ranking of New Adult Fiction Characteristics

Romance Readers' Perceptions of New Adult Fiction 51

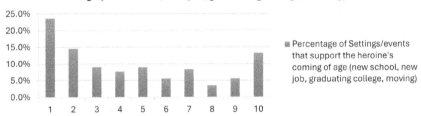

Figure 3.8   Ranking of Setting as New Adult Fiction Characteristic

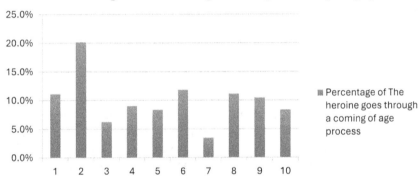

Figure 3.9   Ranking of Coming of Age as New Adult Fiction Characteristic

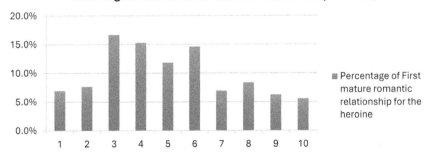

Figure 3.10   Ranking of First Mature Relationship as New Adult Fiction Characteristic

Which of the following do you feel should never be included in a New Adult romance? Please rank the top three with 1 being the most distasteful element.

Variable	Count	Average	Median
Rape	89	1.52	1.0
Sad ending	95	1.85	2.0
Physical torture of the heroine or the hero	55	2.27	2.0
Bed-hopping	18	2.28	2.0
Adultery	50	2.28	2.0
A cruel hero	47	2.66	2.0
A weak heroine	17	2.82	2.0
A cruel heroine	25	2.84	3.0
A weak hero	17	3.00	3.0
Explicit sex	5	5.60	2.0
A heroine who is stronger than the hero	5	6.40	3.0
A hero who is stronger than the heroine	3	8.00	10.0
An ordinary heroine	5	8.80	9.0
Total	431	2.35	2.0

Table 3.1 What should never be included in New Adult Fiction

CHARACTERS

As New Adult fiction characters are central to the genre, so too is understanding reader experiences of those characters. Both "intelligence" and "A sense of humor" had the lowest rank order and the highest selection rate for the most important quality for New Adult fiction heroes. The next most selected in the top three was "kindness." Those were also the most selected within the top two for New Adult heroines, with the other most selected within the top rankings being "independence."

Summary of Q31: How important are the following qualities or characteristics for a New Adult hero? Please rank the top three with 1 being the most desirable quality.

Variable	Count	Average	Median
Intelligence	98	1.78	2
A sense of humor	100	1.80	2
Kindness	76	2.07	2
Protectiveness	46	2.22	2
Other	9	2.22	3
Attractiveness	20	2.45	2
Socially conscious (woke)	40	2.45	3
Bravery	14	2.50	3
Strength	18	2.72	3

Figure 3.11 Ranking of New Adult Hero Characteristics

Romance Readers' Perceptions of New Adult Fiction 53

Summary of Q30: What qualities or characteristics do you like to see in a New Adult heroine? Please rank the top three with 1 being the most desirable quality.

Variable	Count	Average	Median
Other	8	1.63	1.00
Intelligence	105	1.84	2.00
Independence	64	1.91	2.00
A sense of humor	93	1.99	2.00
Feminist	35	2.17	2.00
Kindness	42	2.45	2.50
Assertive	24	2.50	2.00
Strength	31	2.90	3.00
Bravery	23	3.09	3.00
Innocence	7	3.71	2.00
Beauty	5	5.40	3.00

Figure 3.12   Ranking of New Adult Heroine Characteristic

REFLECTIONS

Many participants (44.7%) think that New Adult fiction plot is a little like real life and that characters in the genre are a little (38.5%) like people in real life. A majority also thought that heroes (42.9%) and heroines (55.7%) are somewhat like men and women in real life.

Summary of Q32: How closely do you think the characters in New Adult romances resemble people you meet in real life?

Sample Size	Number of Distinct Categories
143	4

Q32: Ho...l life?	Count	Percent	Cumu...tive
A lot	5	3.5%	3.5%
A moderate amount	43	30.1%	33.6%
A little	55	38.5%	72.0%
Not at all	40	28.0%	100.0%

Figure 3.13   New Adult Fiction Characters and Real Life

Summary of Q33: How closely do you think the events in New Adult romances resemble events that occur in real life?

Sample Size	Number of Distinct Categories
141	4

Q33: Ho...l life?	Count	Percent	Cumu...tive
A lot	6	4.3%	4.3%
A moderate amount	39	27.7%	31.9%
A little	63	44.7%	76.6%
Not at all	33	23.4%	100.0%

Figure 3.14   New Adult Fiction Stories and Real Life

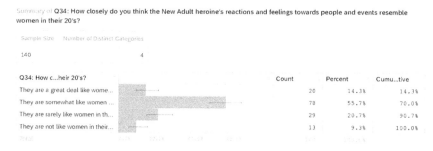

Figure 3.15 New Adult Fiction Heroine's Emotions and Women in Their 20's

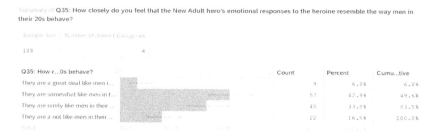

Figure 3.16 New Adult Fiction Hero's Emotions and Men in Their 20's

DISCUSSION

While many of the respondents were familiar with New Adult fiction as a genre, only about 15% of these readers read more than 1-2 a month, and more than a third do not read NA fiction with any regularity. These readers may not have as well-developed sense of the New Adult fiction as a subgenre when compared to avid readers and show a perspective of the broader romance community different from those of someone who is deeply engaged with the subgenre. When filtered by readers who read 3 or more a month, a difference is seen with the role of "Challenging relationships with authority," which jumps to the 4th ranked. This suggests a possible tension of insider and outsider of subgenre romance, and warrants further exploration. Their conclusions about the genre reflect the beliefs of the romance community at large rather than fans of the genre who are well-versed in its nuances.

Setting seems to be the clearest benchmark of New Adult fiction, with the protagonist's coming-of-age process the most common second choice. "First mature relationship" also had a very low average, and seemed to be most ranked third, fourth, or fifth. This suggests that while "First mature relationship" has a slightly lower mean, the protagonist's coming-of-age process is a more common benchmark of the genre. I would argue that the setting of college or a new job, the protagonist's identity development, and a first mature relationship are all facets of a coming of age process which New Adult fiction represents. Like popular romance as a whole, New Adult fiction also prioritizes the happily ever after, as seen by participants selecting a sad ending as one of the least desirable characteristics. "Rape" also ranked low, which is interesting considering issues related to consent are commonly explored in NA fiction, particularly in the stories with college-age protagonists in a college setting.

Readers have slightly different expectations for the heroes and heroines in NA fiction.

Intelligence and sense of humor are important for both the hero and heroine, but the third highest ranked and selected was independence for heroines and kindness for heroes. The fact that innocence and beauty were the least commonly selected and had such a low ranking is very different from expectations for heroines historically.

Interestingly, more participants found that the general character array was only a little representative of real life, but by a smaller margin than question 33. Meanwhile, a higher percentage agree that events represented real life only a little. One reason for this may be the wide range of character experiences (the main character thread for New Adult fiction is the age of the protagonists, so perhaps readers have very divergent communities that are not reflected in NA characters). However, there seems to be more agreement that the plot only reflects real life a little bit. Even with the great diversity in responses to the level of realism for NA characters, many readers answered that heroines of NA fiction are somewhat like women in their twenties. Fewer respondents thought the same for the hero's realism.

The data suggests that coming of age is at the core of New Adult fiction. Given the importance of considering the full genre world for new subgenres like NA fiction, as McAlister demonstrated, this finding should be compared to other elements of this ecosystem. These results must be put in context with qualitative, narrative, and further quantitative study and collated with more concrete author and New Adult fiction reader perspectives.

CONCLUSION AND FUTURE RESEARCH

This genre is still rather young (about twelve years old) and research into its boundaries and cultural implications still has significant ground to explore. This chapter only looks at the quantitative results of this subset of data. Further analysis of the qualitative data would be helpful to better understand how readers think about New Adult fiction. It would also be interesting to only survey engaged fans to compare their experiences. It would also be interesting to run more complex analyses that are outside the scope of this chapter to see if there are any relationships between how readers read general romance and NA fiction, if the answers vary by age-group, and patterns in favorite NA author. Ultimately, New Adult fiction allows popular researchers to explore the representation and norms created for a very specific time of an individual's life in contemporary society. Emerging Adulthood is a stage of development that has only manifested in the 21st century and represents a very different life experience than what existed even 30 years ago. Though a person's 20's is commonly considered part of adulthood, over the past century it has evolved into a period where individuals develop and sharpen their adult identity.[20]

NOTES

1. Julie Naughton, "NA: A Book Category for Twentysomethings by Twentysomethings," *Publishers Weekly,* July 11, 2014, http://www.publishersweekly.com/pw/by-topic/industry-news/publisher-news/article/63285-new-adult-matures.html.

2. George Lipsitz, "Listening to Learn and Learning to Listen: Popular Culture, Cultural Theory, and American Studies," in *Locating American Studies: The Evolution of a Discipline,* ed. Lucy Maddox (Baltimore: Johns Hopkins University Press, 1999), 328.

3. Naughton, "NA: A Book Category for Twentysomethings by Twentysomethings."

4. George Lipsitz, "Listening to Learn and Learning," 316, 319.

5. Naughton, "NA: A Book Category for Twentysomethings by Twentysomethings."

6. Deirdre Donahue, "NA Fiction is the Hot New Category in Books," *USA Today,* April 15, 2013, https://www.usatoday.com/story/life/books/2013/04/15/new-adult-genre-is-the-hottest-category-in-book-publishing/2022707/.

7. Deborah Halverson and Sylvia Day. *Writing NA Fiction.* (Cincinnati, Ohio: Writer's Digest Books 2014).

8. Jodi McAlister, "Defining and Redefining Popular Genres: The Evolution of 'New Adult' Fiction." *Australian Literary Studies* vol. 33, no. 4 (2018): 5, 11.

9. Amy Pattee, "Between Youth and Adulthood: Young Adult and New Adult Literature." *Children's Literature Association Quarterly* 42, no. 2 (2017).

10. McAlister, "Messy Multiplicity: Strategies for Serialisation in New Adult Fiction." *Prequels, Coquels and Sequels in Contemporary Anglophone Fiction.* Routledge, 2018, 144.

11. McAlister, *New Adult Fiction.* Cambridge University Press, 2021.

12. McAlister, "Defining and Redefining Popular Genres," 2.

13. McAlister, "Defining and Redefining Popular Genres," 11, 14.

14. J. J. Arnett, "Emerging Adulthood: A Theory of Development from the Late Teens Through the Twenties," *American Psychologist.* 55, no. 5 (2000). http://dx.doi.org/10.1037/0003-066X.55.5.469.

15. Josefine Smith, "New Adult Fiction: A Feminist Reading of a New Genre," Presentation at the Popular Conference Association, Washington DC, April 18, 2019.

16. Janice Radway, *Reading the Romance: Women, Patriarchy, and Popular Literature*. Chapel Hill: University of North Carolina Press, 1991.

17. Radway, "Women Read the Romance: The Interaction of Text and Context." *Feminist Studies* 9 (1983): 54–55. http://www.jstor.org/stable/3177683.

18. Radway, *Reading the Romance*. Chapel Hill: University of North Carolina Press, 1991.

19. Appendix B.

20. J. J. Arnett, "Emerging Adulthood: A Theory of Development from the Late TeensThrough the Twenties," *American Psychologist.* 55, no 5 (2000): 469–480. http://dx.doi.org /10.1037/0003-066X.55.5.469.

Chapter 4

Which Women Want What?

The Shifting Demographics and Perspectives of Romance Readers

Natalie Duvall and Matt Duvall

In the early 1980's, Janice Radway surveyed romance readers and discovered that many read the genre quietly in their homes, using the books as an escape from modern-day gender inequality. Radway called for female romance readers to bring their social protestations out from these hidden rooms and into the social sphere. Yet nearly three decades later, bestselling romance author Eloisa James still spoke about the criticism she expected to encounter when her colleagues connected her to her non-pen name persona: Mary Bly, Shakespearean scholar.[1]

The romance genre still receives criticism from those in the literary realm, and social stigma is on display through talking points associated with books in this genre.[2] We will explore what changes have occurred for the women, and men, who read romance. Radway projected that romance readers were rebelling against the tenets of the patriarchy, but readers today may have progressed beyond that. Have the demographics of the readers changed in any ways that relate to (or do not) the shifting perspectives of romance readers, and society more broadly, on men, female independence, and the roles of women today? This chapter explores how today's readers identify themselves and how they perceive not only their relationship to the genre but the genre's influence on their lives and the society surrounding them. The authors analyzed the descriptive characteristics of readers as Radway did, by looking for emergent themes. The authors also drew on the sociocultural perspective of literacy as a social practice to understand the contexts and social purposes that impact romance readers' motivations for reading in the genre.[3] This framework situates observable acts of reading and writing within the broader social contexts where such acts occur. Rather than literacy being a binary yes/

no, it is considered as representative of larger power relationships, personal and cultural beliefs, and social purpose. Therefore, the literacy events of writing or reading a text are part of larger literacy practices that inform what is valued within a culture. Using this lens, we can extrapolate from the preferred romance genre elements and tropes to a larger understanding of how and why romance readers engage with the genre and the function it serves for them.

WHICH WOMEN OF THE PAST

When Radway embarked on a journey to discover the cultural intersections of the romance genre and its audience, she found an entry point through a bookstore employee who was seen as a trusted book recommender by many regular romance-consuming customers. Raffaelli details how in the 40 years since that employee counseled consumer purchases, there has been a major shift in how people acquire books.[4] The 1980s saw independent bookstores succumb to chain stores like Waldenbooks, which surged into malls across America at a rate of one new store every week.[5] Then came the book-housing conglomerates Borders and Barnes & Noble. These two mega chains then suffered a massive decline in the 2010s.[6] The cause for their plummeting market share came about in the 1990s, when Amazon arrived on the scene and dramatically shifted how Americans—and the world—purchased books.[7]

So what did these pre-Amazon romance readers look like? Before the explosion of technology that connects us all, for better or worse, Radway interviewed avid romance readers in a Midwestern town of about 112,000 people situated near a metropolitan area with a total population of over 1 million. The readers she interviewed were referred to her by "Dot," a bookstore manager who had a faithful following of romance readers and even published a romance marketing newsletter.[8] Most of Radway's respondents were in their mid-twenties to mid-forties, with an additional quarter of them being in their late forties and early fifties, and nearly nine out of ten of these women had children and were married or widowed/separated. Fewer than half of the women worked. Family income fell mostly in the range of $15,000–$49,000 per year. The median family income in 1980, when Radway's data collection began, was $21,020.[9]

Past these demographics, Radway found these readers shared common feelings regarding their reasons for reading. She noted they read because romance, "gives them hope, provides pleasure, and causes contentment,"[10] which Radway attributed to "vicarious appreciation of the ministrations of a tender hero."[11] The women in Radway's study did not enjoy books with abuse or harm toward the female protagonist. They also disliked too much written sexuality and preferred relationships built through emotional bonds.

Additionally, her survey found that readers preferred a happy woman and an alpha male that demonstrated beta male emotions.

Radway noted that she was surprised by how most of the book readers in her survey aligned to these preferences.

When viewing the favored themes of the reader, and their reasons for those preferences, Radway declared the attraction to the genre as "a temporary but literal denial of the demands these women recognize as an integral part of their roles as nurturing wives and mother... the romance reader in effect is permitted the experience of feeling cared for, the sense of having been affectionately reconstituted, even if both are lived only vicariously."[12]

Forty years later, some might wonder how far those ideas have advanced, if at all. With shifts societally in terms of how books are purchased/consumed, the number of women who work, and views on the roles of both men and women, will these preferences remain the same? Will the same types of women still be reading romance?

WHICH WOMEN OF THE PRESENT

While Radway was able to survey readers who purchased books from a trusted local shop employee, the readers surveyed for this update were found through the use of social media. Radway found her bookstore employee through a colleague's recommendation. The editors of this book found their respondents through social media recommendations, particularly Facebook.

As a tool for data collection, social media provides for a large range of access to diverse individuals. Facebook particularly allows for this, as almost 70% of Americans use Facebook.[13] While this might lead people to think that data collection about romance readers in the modern age might span a larger demographic than Radway's did, it is suspected that this data set is not far removed from that bookstore bubble. Users of social media find themselves in identity bubbles, in which user preferences are used by social media algorithms to create insulated networks where users find themselves interacting with those who share the same preferences.[14] So, despite the seeming differences in data collection between Radway and the present, much of this data could be seen as collected in the same way, since respondents would have been found through a bubble of romance-friendly connections.

In order to expand upon Radway's work analyzing the romance-reading bubble, the authors of this chapter decided to view this readership through literacy as a social practice, with the hope that this framework would not only give an overview of who reads romance in this new century, but how readers of romance are situated in a social world.

LITERACY AS A SOCIAL PRACTICE

While literacy is often viewed as a binary—one is either literate or illiterate—it can also be viewed as a social practice.[15] In this viewpoint, the context in which literacy occurs offers important clues as to how communities view literacy. There is a delineation between observable, objective literacy events (such as reading and writing) and implicit literacy practices (inferred based on connections to beliefs, values, power, and so on). Purcell-Gates and colleagues have advanced a framework (see Figure 4.1) to connect literacy events with literacy practices.[16] This framework views these components as overlapping and interrelated layers. In terms of the literacy practice, the model examines: (1) the context, including power relationships, beliefs, available languages, and more; (2) the social activity domain, or focused action; and (3) the social purpose, or the goal that the literacy practice accomplishes. The literacy event itself is made up of: (4) the text, which includes genre purpose and textual features; and (5) the function, or the communicative intent for reading/writing.

Applying this framework to romance reader demographics, genre and topic preferences, and reasons for reading is one way to reach conclusions about the "Ideological power of this literary form."[17] In looking at data through this framework, the authors used the 194 responses from participants who completed the entire survey; partial responses were not considered. Using these results, as situated in the literacy as a social practice framework, the authors offer the following suggestions of how romance readers view literacy.

Literacy Events

The data provide evidence for what these readers believe does—and does not—make a book a romance. Readers identified the top three elements of a romance (see Figure 4.2) as (a) well-developed intimacy between the heroine and hero, (b) a happy ending, and (c) a slowly but consistently developing love. For romances, a happy ending is a key feature of these texts, and many of these readers would not consider a book to be a romance if it did not have the happily-ever-after conclusion. This finding aligned with Radway's and is a feature that would not have been expected to have changed in the expectations of the genre. One note of interest is that Radway's readers often expected the hero to antagonize the heroine at the beginning and then explain away that resistance later. It is unclear if this is a contradiction or a complement to the third element as found in these current data.

Today's readers also identified which elements would disqualify a book as a romance (Figure 4.3). The top items were rape, a sad ending, adultery, a cruel hero, a cruel heroine, and a weak heroine. These reflect a certain

Which Women Want What? 63

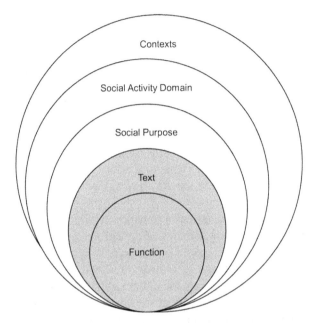

Figure 4.1 A Model of Literacy as a Social Practice. *Note*: Victoria Purcell-Gates, Kristen H. Perry, and Adriana Briseño, "Analyzing Literacy Practice: Grounded Theory to Model," *Research in the Teaching of English* (2011).

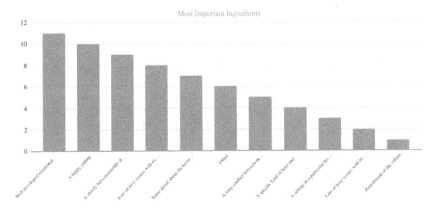

Figure 4.2 Most important ingredients of a romance.

moral perspective on what is and is not acceptable for this genre, and have not changed since Radway's time, with mistreatment of a heroine being an element that would turn her readers away from a book. Most of the remaining findings align with Radway's and show a similar social viewpoint.

One item did stand out in opposition to the earlier data set, though. Contrary to Radway's data, fewer readers identified explicit sex as being problematic, indicating that this element is no longer a disqualifier for many romance readers. It appears there is no longer as much of a stigma attached to descriptions of sex in romance novels. Conversely, rape is now atop the list of elements that readers feel should be excluded. Society in general has become more aware around issues of consent and the importance of healthy sexual representation, which appears to be reflected, and perhaps amplified, among romance readers. The idea that healthy sexual relationships between two willing partners is an important element of a love story shows an expansion of the genre's restrictions, with the acknowledgment that there is a physical component to love as well.

Stemming from what disqualifies a romance in terms of a hero or heroine, there are also expected characteristics of the heroine and hero in a romance novel. The preferred characteristics of a heroine (Figure 4.4) mimic the likable and enviable woman found in Radway's readers' preferences. The top of these traits are intelligence and a sense of humor. It can be noted that these are not necessarily traits stereotypically associated with women in a patriarchal society, especially when the next two preferred traits are considered: independence, and assertiveness. A similar assumption can be made that aligns with the assumption made 40 years ago, that women live vicariously through heroines who do not have to deal with the real-world effects of displaying these traits in what remains, despite some progress, a primarily patriarchal society.

For heroes (Figure 4.5), the same top two traits emerge: intelligence and a sense of humor, which might be indications of a feminist ideal being portrayed in writing. The male stereotype was then flipped, as it was when

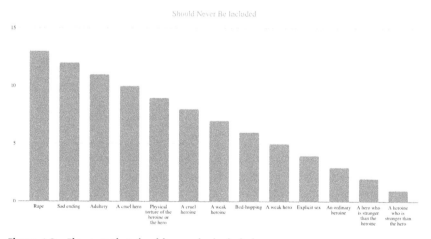

Figure 4.3 Elements that should never be included.

Radway surveyed readers, by showing that readers prefer a man who shows "beta" traits, such as tenderness. However, also like Radway, the stereotypically masculine trait of protectiveness was also at the top of the list. Strength, attractiveness, and bravery ranked in the bottom half. This is an interesting perspective on gender expectations for romance readers, compared with traditional gender expectations in society—particularly since the first two characteristics are identical for heroines and heroes.

It should be noted that there was not enough data available on male/male romances to see if there was a similar preference for the features of the main character and their love interest.

Indeed, a possible direction for future research would be to survey readers about romance without implied gender attributions for the characters. It would also be interesting to examine whether answers to certain questions, such as "hero" and "heroine," would change if alternative descriptions of the characters were used, like "protagonist" and "love interest," that might expand into queer romance fiction.

Radway proposed that her readers read the genre as a form of escapism, using books to get away from the daily expectations they faced as mothers and wives. To see if that reason continued today, the researchers asked questions about the function of reading romance (Figure 6).

The top reason was for relaxation, followed by self-fulfillment ("...just for me. it is my time") and then escape. While Radway's work might have led to an external view that these novels are used for escape or to fulfill experiences that are missing from their real lives, today's romance readers more

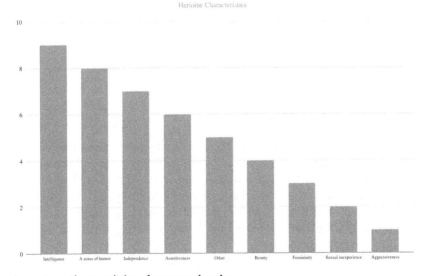

Figure 4.4 Characteristics of romance heroines.

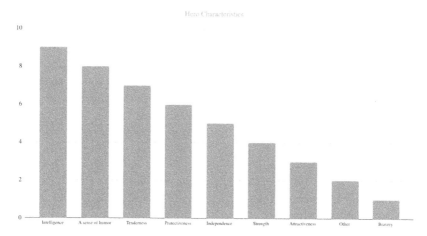

Figure 4.5 Characteristics of romance heroes

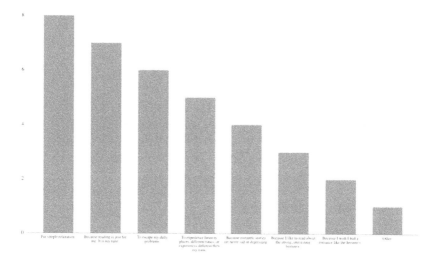

Figure 4.6 Why do you read romance?

strongly view the function of these books as a way to relax or focus on their own enjoyment. This raises a question about whether the social practices of reading romance, particularly the social purpose, has shifted at all or remains the same as it was decades ago. Perhaps what has changed is not that these books, as with most fiction, offer a form of escapism, but rather what it is that the readers are escaping from. Or do women today still feel weighed down by society's expectations of what, exactly, makes a "real woman"? Again, this is an area for future research to focus on these questions more explicitly.

Literacy Practices

Beyond reading preferences, what are some of the implicit literacy practices around reading romance? One interesting result was that the majority of respondents (N=142) said they sometimes or often discussed romances. The primary setting for these discussions was social media (N=85) followed by conversations with friends (N=71). Notably, family relations (e.g., mother and sister) ranked relatively low, with a total of 15 responses. This indicates that one of the social purposes for reading romance is to discuss these books with a community of other readers, which today is often facilitated by the ability to find such a community online. While it is difficult to compare this to Radway's group since they were surveyed pre-Internet, similarities can still be shown in the connection Radway's bookstore clerk made with a community of women shopping for books. What seems to hold true is that there is a distinct community of romance readers, which transcends familial and friendship relations.

The demographics of respondents can also provide some hints about the contexts in which these readers are operating. The majority (N=183) identified as female and are married (N=102). Single and never married was the second highest response (N=59). They also were more likely not to have children (N=109). Again, these demographics reflect those from the previous data collection.

One difference, which is most likely a sign of the changing face of the workforce is in terms of employment and education. Modern readers were primarily employed either full-time (N=125) or part-time (N=25), meaning that 77% of the respondents were employed. Radway noted in her study that Harlequin cited just under 50% of its readership as employed. In terms of education, about one third of her group had some college. 165 of the modern respondents had either a four-year or more advanced degree. So, it appears there has been a shift in the romance reading community that is beyond the trends in society, where the number of women who are employed has remained relatively close to 50% for several decades. It may also be interesting to consider the context for these romance readers in terms of power relationships and available knowledge resources. Traditionally, being female means having less cultural power, but in this group the educational level and household income may provide some leveling of that field. In addition, it appears that these readers are largely cisgender with a slight preference for not having children.

This may help to explain the observable literacy events, such as the reasons why these readers are reading romance. In other words, this particular community of romance readers may objectively say they read romance to relax or for "me time," because their position in the broader society provides them this opportunity.

It would be interesting to find romance reading communities connected in other ways to see if these trends hold true among a broader set of readers.

These results do highlight both explicit and implicit ideas within the network of romance readers, providing insight not just on observable features of these texts but also hidden cultural norms and mores related to reading romance. They tell us about what women want, and which women want it, and how these things have not shifted as much as we might have predicted. At the same time, it may be that there are shifts below the surface that are not as visible. One thing is clear: the romance reading community is still here, and has found new ways to find, recommend, and review romance novels using the advancements in technology to connect with other members of the tribe.

Discussion and Conclusion

In comparing this survey to Radway's research, there has been some shifting in the readership of romance novels. Readers are more likely to be employed and have achieved higher education status. Rather than using romance as an escape from reality, these readers are looking for entertainment and enjoyment. At the same time, the readership remains largely female, with a focus on mostly traditional conceptualizations of romance such as a male/female connection with a happily-ever-after ending.

These elements define some of what it means to be a member of the social group of romance readers. There are norms and expectations to be met, and requirements about what qualifies a person to be a "real" romance reader and what qualifies a book as a "good" romance.

The differences noted, though, provide evidence that this community and the genre are not static. Rather, they are dynamic and subject to change. In some cases, change may be subtle or take a significant amount of time. Other times, a large seismic shift may seem to happen all at once.

One example of this is the explosion of ways for writers to publish their books and connect with readers. There is still a traditional publishing process, with all the gatekeeping that involves for both good and ill. However, writers can now directly connect with their readers via social media, which is one of the major differences between this current survey and Radway's work—in the 1980s, your social network was fairly limited by proximity. Today, we live in a virtually global world where we can connect with like-minded individuals from around the world, uniting over things like affinity for a certain genre of novels. These features can be used to increase representation of diverse perspectives and include marginalized groups in the community. In some cases, representation is an important first step to making a community feel more welcoming and open to new members—and as this survey shows, while the romance community is tight-knit, it is also one that values connecting with new people.

NOTES

1. Mary Bly, "A Fine Romance," *The New York Times*, February 12, 2005.
2. Jennifer Lois and Joanna Gregson, "Sneers and Leers: Romance Writers and Gendered Sexual Stigma," *Gender & Society* 29, no. 4 (2015): 459–483.
3. Perry, 2012. Perry, Kristen H. "What Is Literacy?—A Critical Overview of Sociocultural Perspectives." *Journal of Language and Literacy Education* 8, no. 1 (2012): 50–71.
4. Ryan Raffaelli, "Reinventing Retail: The Novel Resurgence of Independent Bookstores," Harvard Business School, 2020.
5. Ibid.
6. Ibid.
7. Ibid.
8. Janice Radway, *Reading the Romance: Women, Patriarchy, and Popular Literature* (Chapel Hill: University of North Carolina Press, 1991).
9. United States Bureau of the Census, *Money Income of Households, Families, and Persons in the United States* (Washington, DC: US Department of Commerce, Bureau of the Census, 1987).
10. Janice A. Radway, "Women Read the Romance: The Interaction of Text and Context," *Feminist Studies* 9, no. 1 (1983): 62.
11. Radway, "Women Read the Romance," 63.
12. Ibid., 66.
13. Brooke Auxier and Monica Anderson, "Social Media Use in 2021," *Pew Research Center* 1 (2021): 1–4.
14. Markus Kaakinen, Anu Sirola, Iina Savolainen, and Atte Oksanen, "Shared Identity and Shared Information in Social Media: Development and Validation of the Identity Bubble Reinforcement Scale," *Media Psychology* 23, no. 1 (2020): 25–51.
15. James Paul Gee, *Situated Language and Learning: A Critique of Traditional Schooling* (New York: Psychology Press, 2004); Shirley Brice Heath, "What No Bedtime Story Means: Narrative Skills at Home and School," *Language in Society* 11, no. 1 (1982): 49–76; Victoria Purcell-Gates, Kristen H. Perry, and Adriana Briseño, "Analyzing Literacy Practice: Grounded Theory to Model," *Research in the Teaching of English* (2011): 439–58; William H. Teale, "Parents Reading to Their Children: What We Know and Need to Know," *Language Arts* 58, no. 8 (1981): 902–12; William H. Teale, "What Counts? Literacy Assessment in Urban Schools," *The Reading Teacher* 62, no. 4 (2008): 358–61.
16. Victoria Purcell-Gates, Erik Jacobson, and Sophie Degener, *Print Literacy Development: Uniting Cognitive and Social Practice Theories* (Cambridge, MA: Harvard University Press, 2004); Victoria Purcell-Gates, Kristen H. Perry, and Adriana Briseño, "Analyzing Literacy Practice: Grounded Theory to Model," *Research in the Teaching of English* (2011): 439–58.
17. Radway, "Women Read the Romance," 55.

Chapter 5

Social Media, Critical Analysis, and Feminist Action

Popular YA's Role in Disseminating Theory Online

Jessica Caravaggio

The introduction to Janice Radway's *Reading the Romance* poses several questions which she sets out to address in the body of her work: primarily, questions of the market factors, social conditions, and material conditions which inform and create the desire for romance reading.[1] Specifically, Radway questions what "kinds of cultural competencies [...] are learned as a consequence of certain social formations and how those are activated or perpetuated within and through multiple, related genres or discourses," and further, "what competencies prepare certain women to recognize romance as relevant to their experience and as potential routes to pleasure."[2] However, the limitations of a study of romance readers in 1984 include the difficult task of finding and observing these readers, many of whom are isolated in their reading because of their position within heteronormative family structures and because of the shame associated with their sexual expression (especially as the vast majority of these readers are women). Radway herself acknowledges that though "it matters enormously what the cumulative effects of romance reading are on actual readers, [u]nfortunately, those effects are extraordinarily difficult to trace."[3] She furthermore identifies the need for "a place and a vocabulary with which to carry on a conversation about the meaning of . . . personal relations and the seemingly endless renewal of their primacy through the genre of romance" and hopes for a future where "romance writers and readers themselves, as well as feminist intellectuals, might contribute to the re-writing of the romance in an effort to articulate its founding fantasy to a politics that would be progressive for more women."[4] The three issues which serve as roadblocks to a more comprehensive understanding of romance reading and its social and political potentials can thus be synthesized in the following way: readers are segregated from each other, from contemporary feminist discussion, and from scholars and critics. The lack of an easily accessible, largely diverse, and widely populated space or archive for the discussion of romance reading halts the creation of communities of women necessarily interested in female subjectivity and gendered understandings of sex, love, and desire.

I intend to explore the ways in which Radway's visions for the future of romance reader study are realized in the social media reader communities of today by looking specifically at the audience members and creators of TikTok's self-named reader community "BookTok" alongside the *Still Reading Romance* survey data compiled for this collection by editors Josefine Smith and Kathleen Kollman. In order to narrow my focus on this vast community of readers, I address only two novel series discussed on the platform: Stephenie Meyer's Twilight saga (2005–2020) and Sarah J. Maas's A Court of Thorns and Roses (ACOTAR)[5] series (2015–2021).[6] The extreme popularity of these texts means that in analyzing only videos which are made about Twilight, ACOTAR, or both, I am still accessing a wide variety of types of content created by readers. Furthermore, their widespread appeal allows me to understand the general tenor of the BookTok community, as a large portion of BookTok community members consume Twilight and/or ACOTAR videos. This makes such videos good examples of typical BookTok content.[7] While scholars such as Tricia Clasen, Margaret Kramar, and Jennifer Stevens Aubrey et al. have used Radway's work as a theoretical lens through which they comment on fan response to the series,[8] I attempt to understand how new forms of and spaces for fandom can allow scholars to expand on and re-examine Radway's work. Finally, I will draw on the work of feminist theorists as well as reader-response theorists in order to draw connections between the significance of feminist criticism as described by theorists such as Annette Kolodny and Laura Mulvey,[9] and the theory of interpretive communities popularized by Stanley Fish.[10] Ultimately, I argue that social media reader communities are a significant aspect of contemporary romance reading habits. Members of these communities perform engaging feminist analysis of romance texts and therefore participate in feminist consciousness-raising efforts online.

STILL READING ROMANCE SURVEY DATA

The differences between Smith and Kollman's survey and Radway's original survey highlight the changing landscape of the Romance genre, its readers, and gender studies discourses. In several instances, respondents expressed frustration with the heteronormative structure of a survey which asked them about the different "qualities or characteristics [they would] like to see in a hero[/heroine]." One respondent complained that "having different options for heroes and heroines is inherently sexist and excludes queer people." Another pointed out that the "survey was difficult because [they] primarily read romances between partners of the same sex," and yet another noted that they "answered some of [the] questions as hypotheticals, since [they] don't read heterosexual romance." A fourth respondent said that as a queer woman, "so many of the questions ... about 'hero and heroine' did not apply to [them] or [their] reading." These responses indicate not only that as the genre itself has become more diverse, the pool of readers has expanded, but also that there is a greater need for researchers to anticipate and accommodate this diversity in their work. Significant changes like the above example were prevalent in many comparisons with Radway's original research, but few were as striking as the changes in how readers described "who [they] discuss romances with most [often]."[11] Radway's survey provided the following options as answers to this question: "my mother," "my daughter," "my sister," "a female neighbor," and "other (please specify)." This indicates that Radway did not anticipate or expect romance readers would discuss their reading habits with anyone outside of their immediate social circle, and furthermore expected most readers not to discuss their reading habits with anyone outside of their circle of *relatives,* as three of the five options listed include members of one's immediate family. These options are also representative of the expectations of women to remain in the domestic sphere. Smith and Kollman's version, on the other hand, provided the following options: "social media community," "friends," "mother," "sister," and "other."[12] Of the 285 responses to this survey question, only one respondent indicated that they discuss romance texts most often with their mother, ten with their sister, 49 with their friends, and a staggering 132 (over 46% of Smith and Kollman's survey respondents) indicated that they discuss romance novels most often within social media communities. Some respondents specifically named BookTok as that community in later written comments. The changes in these data sets imply that romance reading, once an "intensely private act" (Radway 92), has become incredibly public and increasingly social. Investigating the differences in the ways social media community participants answered survey questions compared to other respondents can illuminate how these participants are affected in their reading and understanding of romance texts through their engagement with online reader communities, and further, what initially draws readers to such spaces.

 The existence of social media reader communities as geographically decentralized spaces resists the isolation of heteropatriarchal family structures and ensures accessibility for most romance readers. Radway's original survey participants, whom she calls "the Smithton women," are comprised largely of married women with children; she specifies that "thirty-two women (76%) in the Smithton group were married at the time of the survey" (56) and that 88% of respondents reported having children. Therefore, Radway's musings on the purpose and effect of romance reading center the stresses and responsibilities of a woman tasked with taking care of her husband, her children, and her home. Radway reports that romance reading enables the Smithton women to escape or "deny their physical presence in an environment associated with responsibilities that are acutely felt and occasionally experienced as too onerous to bear" (93) and also supplies them with "an important emotional release that is proscribed in daily life because the social role with which they identify themselves leaves little room for guiltless, self-interested pursuit of individual pleasure" (96). The ages, marital statuses, and parental statuses of the respondents to Smith and Kollman's survey were more disparate: just over half (58.5%) of respondents indicated that they were or had been married, and less than half (44.5%) indicated that they had children. However, respondents who indicated their participation in social media communities were 10% more likely to be married than those who did not and were 15% more likely to have children. They were also more likely to be older than those who did not indicate their participation in social media reader communities: while nearly 6% of total respondents were persons ages 18–23, none of those respondents indicated that they discuss romances most often within social media communities. In every age category above 24–34, respondents were more likely to participate in social media communities than not. This data implies that while Smith and Kollman's survey does not indicate that the vast majority of romance readers are married women with children—and of course, many contemporary romance readers do not identify as women—it does indicate that social media communities may be largely comprised of readers who share similarities with the original Smithton group. Where Radway purports that romance reading may be a response to the emotional, social, and physical isolation caused by a heteropatriarchal system where women are confined to the home and subject to the exhaustive demands of marriage and parenthood, Smith and Kollman's data suggests that social media communities provide a different way for the needs of readers to be met. Online spaces negate concerns about women being separated from each other because of their confinement to the domestic sphere. Women in online reader communities can participate anywhere at any time, forming communities with people of different genders, ages, races, sexualities, nationalities, religions, classes, and cultures from all around the world and moving away from the isolation of the past.

The Smithton women, should they discuss books with each other outside of their collective interviews with Radway, would still be doing so privately and interpersonally, not publicly. Bringing romance reading *out* of private social circles and into public forums online collapses many of the boundaries of class, race, sexuality, etc. which might otherwise be presented as barriers to diverse and productive discussion and helps to alleviate the "shame" (Radway 90) of romance reading by normalizing the practice. Several respondents indicated that their participation in online reader communities has changed their perception of themselves and their reading in this way:

> "I'm in a romance book club & an online romance community, so (especially during the pandemic) it's a significant part of my 'socializing.' The online one is specifically for smut, and I love how normalized it is."
>
> "Embracing my love of romance, and no longer treating it as a guilty pleasure, has been empowering. I love talking to other romance readers and having not an ounce of shame anymore. I love my stories about awesome women who get happy endings!"
>
> "Having read romance for about 30 years, it's just lovely to see becoming more mainstream or open. I used to never want to admit that I read romances but now with BookTok, I don't feel so weird admitting to it because so many other people are, too."

These responses suggest that not only do readers consume romance novels in order to, as Radway suggests, contend with the stresses and expectations of patriarchal systems, but they also desire to have their perspectives understood and validated by supportive and like-minded communities. Each respondent expresses that prior to their engagement in online reader communities, they self-consciously felt as if their enjoyment of sexually explicit novels was "shame[ful]," not "[normal,]" and/or "weird." The efficacy of these spaces in alleviating shame is no surprise: community engagement as a way to address marginalization and oppression has been encouraged by feminists since before such a term (feminist) existed. In Olympe de Gouges's *The Rights of Woman*, she addresses the Queen of France by saying "[i]t will never be made a crime for you to labour for the restoration of morals, to give to your sex all the firmness of which it is capable. This work is not the labour of a day, unfortunately for the new regime. This revolution will only come to pass when *all women* are struck with their miserable fate, and with the rights they have lost in society" (379; emphasis added).[13] Nearly 200 years later, bell hooks's *Feminist Theory: From Margin to Center* (1984) would describe feminist progress as happening "when groups of people come together with an organized strategy to take action to eliminate patriarchy."[14] Social media reader communities exist as part of an enduring tradition of women gathering in creative community to validate their sisters' experiences as oppressed subjects.

Yet online reader communities are not connected to feminist goals, values, and concerns by their mere existence as spaces where people of marginalized genders and sexualities feel safe in an expression of their needs and desires.

Content creators who post videos on BookTok often directly engage with feminist theories and concepts in their discussions of romance texts, and community members afterwards leave comments on these videos addressing the strategies and conclusions of their peers. It should be noted, however, that neither the dissemination nor consumption of feminist ideas requires self-identification, and also that these topics can exist as a source of reader/audience pleasure. In the next section of this chapter, I will discuss one of these communities in detail to better explain the connections between social media reader communities and feminist consciousness-raising.

INTERPRETIVE COMMUNITIES AND BOOKTOK

In September of 2023, the Canadian Museum for Human Rights published a story by Steve McCullough, the museum's digital content specialist, who addressed the "violent misogyny" that relentlessly targets "women, trans, and nonbinary folks online."[15] McCullough connects increasing misogynistic rhetoric, spurred on by far-right mega-influencers like Andrew Tate, to not only extreme online harassment and abuse but also to instances of physical violence perpetrated by radicalized members of male supremacist communities, such as the 2018 Toronto van attack. The perpetrator of this act of domestic terrorism, who killed eight women and two men, called for a violent "incel rebellion"[16] online.[17] However, some of these same online spaces—social media sites like TikTok, Instagram, and Reddit—are also home to vast and influential communities of readers who largely identify themselves as politically and socially progressive. These readers, who are of diverse ages and genders, are particularly interested in the genre of young adult (YA) fantasy romance fiction, as evidenced by the extreme popularity of Meyer's Twilight Saga and Maas's ACOTAR series. The genre's intense focus on young women's subjectivity is in direct opposition to the misogyny I describe above which seeks to denigrate, humiliate, silence, and violate women and queer people. A culture of readers engaged in critical feminist analysis is created within these communities as community members mobilize feminist theoretical terms such as *toxic masculinity*, *male/female gaze*, and *intersectionality* to deconstruct male-female relations within fictional texts. This activity brings feminist theory into public forums and gives those outside of academic spaces tools to analyze texts from a feminist perspective. Reader-generated content that employs feminist theoretical terms to discuss popular YA fantasy romance fiction can therefore be considered fourth wave[18] feminist consciousness-raising work on these platforms and inspires feminist community formation and activism that resists various forms of misogyny and oppression.

One such community is the self-named "BookTok" hosted on the social media video-sharing site TikTok. Within this community, readers review texts, share recommendations, and make lighthearted jokes about their hobby.[19] Perhaps most interestingly, community members frequently engage in an activity I call *communal reading*. Communal reading occurs when content creators read and interpret texts *with* their audiences, either by using TikTok to post videos which remain on their "page" and are viewable at any time by other users, or by using TikTok's "live video" feature and streaming real-time content which can only be watched by those tuned into the stream. If the former, content creators read a text in sections, posting reaction videos to passages they have read and allowing their audience to follow along and comment. If the latter, creators interpret texts in real time during live events, and their audiences "chat" by posting live comments which are visible onscreen. Communal reading is a method by which content creators engage with audiences and perform textual analysis, but it is also an example of the phenomenon I describe earlier of the continued shift of romance reading from the private sphere into a largely public one. Whereas other creators—and earlier creators on platforms such as YouTube—might perform "readings" by reviewing novels in their entirety, the creators I reference in the examples below literally read (interpret) in public and in real time, allowing other community members to read along with them and collaboratively form interpretations and opinions. We can therefore identify a progression from reading being entirely private, to reading being a private activity that is afterward discussed publicly, to reading being a communal activity where a group of readers interpret a text together.

Communities of readers on TikTok might be considered *interpretive communities* of the kind that Stanley Fish[20] describes in his 1976 article "Interpreting the 'Variorum.'"[21] S. Fish, a reader-response theorist, uses the term *interpretive communities* to describe his theory of how meaning is created. He claims that readers' "predispositions to execute different interpretive strategies will *produce* different formalist structures."[22] These predispositions are not shared by all readers, but are a function of their own cultures, experiences, and educational backgrounds. Therefore, "interpretive communities are made up of those who share interpretive strategies not for reading (in the conventional sense) but for writing texts, for constituting their properties and assigning their intentions. In other words, these strategies exist prior to the act of reading and therefore determine the shape of what is read rather then, as is usually assumed, the other way around."[23] In short, people who are similar for various reasons will read texts similarly, and it is their interpretations which create the meanings they glean from the texts they read. BookTok, therefore, is not a single interpretive community as S. Fish would describe it because content creators from various cultures and geographies necessarily react differently to the same texts, and community members who are also diverse in age, race, location, gender, and experience frequently disagree with content creators and with each other in the comments of videos and live events. However, we can identify similar interpretive strategies being used amongst creators (such as communal reading), a common use of feminist lenses, and a common focus on how women's lives and experiences are represented in fictional texts.

TikTok user Fish (@the.sequel.nobody.wanted) has read both *Twilight* and its sequel *New Moon* alongside their TikTok audience by recording themselves reading each book for the first time and occasionally glancing up at the camera to address their audience. This audience is mostly those who have already read the Twilight Saga, and the comments on Fish's videos reveal the audience's delight in watching Fish's shock, confusion, and bemusement at a text which audience members already know well. They can re-read the series along with Fish because Fish also reads passages they find notable in these videos, commenting afterward with their thoughts on a particular quote or section. This strategy is comparative to the reading practices of literary critics, who close-read by carefully selecting portions of text and commenting on their significance within a larger work. Furthermore, Fish's critiques often have a feminist angle: their videos about *Twilight* and *New Moon* frequently feature their disapproval of the relationship between Bella and Edward, the 17-year-old human protagonist and her 104-year-old vampire love interest, on the grounds of Edward's predation and abuse.

In their videos, Fish consistently argues for Bella's agency, points out Edward's romanticized violations, and criticizes the extreme age gap between the two characters.[24] In a video posted on 24 August 2023, titled "Part 8: Someone get Chris Hansen on this case RIGHT NOW,"[25] Fish is shocked when they discover just how much older Edward is than Bella: "I wasn't expecting that at all. That's criminal. Like he needs to be locked up. He is literally about to walk away in cuffs. 104 years old?" Later in the same video, Fish comments on a passage in which Bella finds out Edward has been sneaking into her bedroom to watch her at night and is embarrassed that Edward has heard her talking in her sleep. Fish turns to the camera and exclaims "[t]hat is not what you should be embarrassed about! That's not what you should be horrified about! You-you should be horrified that he is stalking you, that is a 104-year-old man ... Weirdo, weirdo, weirdo." In "Part 11: My bad thought Bella was actually being reasonable for a second there,"[26] Fish points out that at the end of the book, Edward and his family are "basically kidnapping [Bella]. Taking her away from her family ... and everything that she's ever known. Without her consent." In a video expressing their final thoughts on the novel, posted on 28 August and titled

"Reading this was certainly an experience," Fish explains that they "thought the reason that everyone made fun of *Twilight* was just because people were misogynistic and they didn't want teenage girls to have fun ... Edward is fun when you discard the fact that he's 104." Fish's commenters discuss Fish's interpretations in the comments, many of them agreeing with the identification of Edward as a predator and an abuser despite his portrayal as a sexual innocent; as a 104-year-old virgin, Edward's abusive, predatory, and controlling[27] nature might be otherwise difficult for some readers to identify because of his unwillingness to have sex with Bella. TikTok user Kori Lloyd895 comments, "My parents gave me a copy of this with all the red flags highlighted to teach me about DV." Sara Kirstine writes, "Edward [is] gaslighting her ... like he knows he is designed to attract people so they can't say no." Violet comments, "Edward really exemplifies the past the [GOP] wants to return to." Urbanwitch101 adds, "The less I look at this series as romance books and more as psychological horror the better I think these books are. Bella is a damn victim."[28] Fish, in close-reading Bella's autonomy (or lack thereof), performs feminist literary criticism for their audience, who then continue this work in the comments as they discuss Fish's interpretations.

The commenters work collaboratively to discuss and create meaning, as Fish often responds in turn to their audience members by reacting in agreement to commenters' own interpretations.

TikTok user and BookTok star Connor Padilla (@connor_thebard) is another communal reader, though his texts of choice are those in Maas's *ACOTAR* series. Padilla has read its entirety alongside his TikTok audience and makes videos both commenting on and acting out each chapter in the novel series in a one-man show that features clever video editing, makeshift costumes, and improvised sets. On several occasions, Padilla has hosted live events on his TikTok page where he reads important or climactic scenes in real time. One such live event featured Padilla reading chapters 54 and 55 of the second book in the series, *A Court of Mist and Fury (ACOMAF)*, where the main character Feyre and her love interest Rhysand consummate their commitment to each other by having intercourse for the first time. During these live events, Padilla will read certain sentences aloud, comment on what he is reading, and engage with his audience; viewers comment their own interpretations, express their love of his content, and generally discuss their excitement and passion for the *ACOTAR* series.

Like Fish, Padilla approaches these texts from a feminist angle without explicit self-identification: he champions female independence and fulfillment within the series,[29] and furthermore, uses feminist theoretical terms in his videos. For example, Padilla lovingly nicknames Rhysand "female gaze Dracula," because of his appeal amongst female readers and his bat-like wings. The term *female gaze*, of course, is a derivative of the term *male gaze*, which was originally coined by feminist theorist Laura Mulvey in her 1975 article "Visual Pleasure and Narrative Cinema."[30] In a video posted on 9 May 2023,[31] Padilla directly compares the conditions of women in this fantasy novel to the conditions of women in our own world:

> We discover that our [sexy] court overseer was born in the nightmare court, where women have to navigate a very dangerous patriarchal power structure with very limited options and freedoms, never feeling like they really have autonomy. Squeezing themselves between the extremes of the prized virgin used to advance the men in her life or being a [sexual] object in service to men. Good thing this is a fictional fantasy world and women and femme folk in our society never have to deal with anything like this.[32]

Later in the video, Padilla sums up his remarks by referring to the nightmare court as a "misogynistic hellscape," identifying and engaging with the themes of gender oppression and their impacts which are woven deeply into this series in this and other videos. Padilla's audience, like Fish's, supports his interpretations and adds their own commentary: TikTok user Snooze comments, "the next [big bad evil guy] for feyre to shoot with her arrows is the patriarchy," and community member Klo says, "Rhys is a consent king."[33] They, along with Padilla, interpret the text and its depictions of gender-based power structures by drawing on their own knowledge and experiences as subjects of a patriarchal system.[34]

Both Padilla and Fish cultivate feminist audiences through their interpretations of each series, not only by attracting community members already holding feminist beliefs but also by using methods of literary analysis to persuade readers of the validity of their feminist interpretations. The construction of such a community is significant for various reasons. The first I have already mentioned: participating in these interpretive communities provides readers with a safe and supportive environment within which they can enjoy and celebrate a hobby that is perceived as shameful in other spaces because of its connection to the sexualities and sexual desires of marginalized people. Furthermore, through their interactions with creators and other community members sharing ideas, interpretations, and insights, readers in these communities are able to use this space to explore and better understand their individual desires for power, sex, and emotional connection. Finally, and perhaps most importantly, these communities are spaces of opportunity, where feminist consciousness-raising might be a gateway to feminist emancipatory action.[35] For example, a video by Padilla from 28 August 2023 remarks on the conflict created within Maas's *A Court of Silver Flames* (*ACOSF*), the fifth book in the *ACOTAR* series, when it is revealed that Feyre is carrying a child whose birth will likely kill her:

I have a lot of questions about female healthcare in Prythian ... It's a tale as old as every vertical patriarchal power structure . . . For tens of thousands of years, the High Fae have been ruled exclusively by males, the majority of which have the emotional maturity of a 22-year-old frat boy. Their priority lists have reflected that. These guys didn't think about fucking things, they don't think about—that's why we get the fucking dichotomy of Cassian with his fucking guts spilling out all over the place with Azriel trying to hold them in—oh, we can patch that up, but god, we have to give a c-section to a female, we just don't have the capability! This is why we need more high fae females in power, we need more fem creatures in power in general. Basically, anyone that is non-high fae male, high fae leadership being a fucking boys club for thousands of years [has] led to atrophy and complacency. It's toxic and its fucking dangerous.[36]

Padilla's audience understands that he is passionately advocating (note the many expletives) for changes in their own world, and not in the fantasy world of Prythian, which he recognizes in this and other videos to be a reflection of our own in its representation of, as he calls it, a "vertical patriarchal power structure." User Chel offers her own experience in support of Padilla's statement: "Say it louder for the people in back. From a female who's suffered from a shitty ass medical system, I hope the stars hear ya." User Karla agrees, "love the political rant, because politically speaking this series is . . . something." Note the earlier comment from Violet on a video by TikTok creator Fish about *Twilight*: "Edward really exemplifies the past the [GOP] wants to return to." These creators and their audiences are discussing novels, but they are also very openly discussing their own political realities and allegiances and how those things are shaped by their marginalized identities.

FEMINIST THEORY AND SOCIAL MEDIA READER COMMUNITIES

Social media reader communities, of which BookTok is only one, are representative of Radway's vision for romance reading of the future but can also be linked to the repeated calls for community, reinvention, and recreation made by many other feminist theorists. Audre Lorde's "The Master's Tools Will Never Dismantle the Master's House" (1984) advocates for an interdependency between all women and asks that they "[learn] how to take [their] differences and make them strengths."[37] Laura Mulvey's *Visual and Other Pleasures* (1989)[38] calls upon feminists to "unravel, to question, to reinvent the terrain of popular fantasy in which women's secondary status is sealed by the collective psyche."[39] By unraveling and questioning the popular fantasies on their bookshelves, reader communities are also unraveling and questioning popular fantasies of the kind that Mulvey is referencing.

In "Under Western Eyes: Feminist Scholarship and Colonial Discourse," Chandra Talpade Mohanty insists that "male violence must be theorized and interpreted *within* specific societies, in order both to understand it better and to effectively organize to change it. Sisterhood cannot be assumed on the basis of gender; it must be forged in concrete historical and political practice and analysis."[40] If we can understand the landscape of the internet and social media to be its own kind of "society," then we must understand how "male violence" is performed as well as how "sisterhood" is being "forged" in those spaces.

Perhaps most influential to the creation of this chapter, Annette Kolodny's "Dancing Through the Minefield: Some Observations on the Theory, Method, and Politics in Feminist Literary Criticism" (1980), published only a few years before Radway's *Reading the Romance*, echoes S. Fish's concept of interpretive communities with her claim that readers "appropriate meaning from a text according to what [they] need (or desire) or, in other words, according to the critical assumptions or predispositions (conscious or not) that [they] bring to it. And [they] appropriate different meanings, or report different gleanings, at different times—even from the same text—according to our changed assumptions, circumstances, and requirements."[41]

Kolodny makes this point in order to then argue that the reason women's writing is so often dismissed as "undecipherable, meaningless, or trivial" (accusations which are not uncommonly leveled at texts like *Twilight* and *ACOTAR*)[42] is because, based on the "critical assumptions and predispositions" they have inherited from their positions within patriarchal societies, there is an "incapacity of predominantly male readers to properly interpret and appreciate women's texts. . . . Males ignorant of women's 'values' or conceptions of the world will necessarily . . . be poor readers of works that in any sense recapitulate their codes."[43] This identification of how women read differently is remarkably similar to Radway's identification of romance reading as pleasurable to the Smithton women specifically because of how their lives and experiences as women within patriarchal systems drive them to these pleasurable and escapist interpretations of romance texts. Their husbands are frequently represented as tolerant at best and hostile at worst when confronted with their inability to understand why their wives are so enraptured by romance novels, because they cannot access the "codes" that Kolodny suggests are unique to female readers.

Kolodny calls for men to read more novels written by women—but more importantly, she calls for feminists to embrace "a playful pluralism responsive to the possibilities of multiple critical schools and methods, but captive of none,"[44] because of her recognition that not all women, of course, belong to the same interpretive communities. Deifying a singular feminist ideology and critical method and creating a hierarchy of interpretation would be antithetical to feminist goals and would, to use Lorde's terms, be an attempt to use the master's tools. These "variously focused" criticisms,[45] though, should not inhibit the ability of feminists to "*act* in areas of clear mutual concern." Kolodny ends her essay advocating for a feminist theory that does not confine itself to academia and engages with the ways people "live in the world" and with the ideas, understandings, and interpretations of those people as readers:

> If feminist criticism calls anything into question, it must be that dog-eared myth of intellectual neutrality. For, what I take to be the underlying spirit, or message, of any consciously ideologically premised criticism—that is, that ideas are important *because* they determine the ways we live, or want to live in the world—is vitiated by confining those ideas to the study, the classroom, or the pages of our books . . . to glory in the delusions of "merit," "privilege," and "status" which accompany campus life in order to insulate ourselves from the millions of women who labor in poverty—all this is not merely hypocritical; it destroys both the spirit and the meaning of what we are about.[46]

Importantly, Radway does this work by interviewing the Smithton women and allowing their interpretations to guide her understanding of the affective nature of romance texts. I argue that reader communities, whose members are able to decide for themselves what is trivial, what is meaningless, and what is deserving of belonging to a canon, are engaging in interpretation and analysis that is similarly important to our understandings of romance texts and whose contributions should not be ignored.

CONCLUSION

The connection between social media and contemporary romance reading habits merits further study of social media reader communities. These social media reader communities address the misplaced "shame" of romance reading that Radway addresses in *Reading the Romance*, but more importantly, perform critical feminist analysis using new and exciting interpretive strategies, including the practice of communal reading. This chapter's use of foundational feminist theory is not done for the purpose of validating these strategies but rather to reveal the extent to which the problems of the past (Kolodny's article was published almost exactly 40 years ago as of writing this chapter) continue to persist in the present, and therefore why it is necessary to continue to seek out new interpretive strategies, engage with new forms of community, and to re-examine the work of the past. Social media reader communities present us with new and exciting ways to continue Radway's work in understanding what drives readers toward romance fiction, as well as to understand more generally how feminist consciousness- raising is being performed in these spaces.

NOTES

1. Janice Radway, *Reading the Romance: Women, Patriarchy, and Popular Literature* (Chapel Hill: University of North Carolina Press, 1991).
2. Radway, *Reading the Romance*, 10.
3. Radway, *Reading the Romance*, 17.
4. Radway, *Reading the Romance*, 18.
5. When referencing each series, I will use italics to indicate a single text (ex. *Twilight*) and will not use italics when referencing the complete series.
6. Maas's series was also one of the most common answers to the Smith and Kollman survey question asking what readers' three favorite New Adult Romances were. Fourteen out of seventy respondents who answered this question mentioned the ACOTAR series.
7. A rough estimate of how many videos on BookTok address each book series can be made by reviewing how many videos have been "tagged" with the names of each series. There are also many videos that are tagged with the names of both series and compare the texts seriously or comedically. Tracking the number of tagged videos gives me the ability to confirm Twilight and ACOTAR's popularity in comparison to other texts. As of June 2024, according to TikTok's analytics, the tag "BookTok" has been used roughly 33.8 million times, while the "Twilight" and "ACOTAR" tags have collectively been used about three million times (this does not include related tags, such as character names or the names of other titles in each series). This information indicates that Twilight and ACOTAR content collectively may represent just under 10% of all current BookTok content.
8. Tricia Clasen, "Masculinity and Romantic Myth in Contemporary YA Romance." In *Gender(ed) Identities: Critical Rereadings of Gender in Children's and Young Adult Literature*, edited by Holly Hassel and Tricia Clasen (New York, NY: Routledge, 2017), 228–41; Margaret Kramar, "The Wolf in the Woods: Representations of 'Little Red Riding Hood' in *Twilight*," in *Bringing Light to Twilight: Perspectives on a Pop Culture Phenomenon*, ed. Giselle Liza Anatol (New York: Palgrave Macmillan, 2011), 15–30: Jennifer Stevens Aubrey et al., "The Twilight of Youth: Understanding Feminism and Romance in Twilight Moms' Connection to the Young-Adult Vampire Series," *Psychology of Popular Media Culture* 7 (January 2018): 61–71.
9. Annette Kolodny, "Dancing Through the Minefield: Some Observations on the Theory, Practice, and Politics of Feminist Literary Criticism," *Feminist Studies* 6 (Spring 1980): 1–25; Laura Mulvey, *Visual and Other Pleasures*, 2nd ed. (New York: Palgrave Macmillan, 2009 [1989]).
10. Stanley Eugene Fish, *Is There a Text in This Class? The Authority of Interpretive Communities* (Cambridge: Harvard University Press, 1980).
11. Radway, *Reading the Romance,* 233.

12. In the "other" category, one respondent wrote in that they most often discussed romance texts with their daughter, and seven respondents wrote in that they discussed romance texts most often with their partners.

13. This translation is from Appendix A of Broadview's Mary Wollstonecraft 2001 edited collection. Macdonald, D. L., and Scherf, Kathleen, eds. "Appendix A: The Revolutionary Moment." In *A Vindication of the Rights of Men; A Vindication of the Rights of Woman*, 345–92. Peterborough: Broadview Press, 2001.

14. Macdonald and Scherf, Kathleen, eds. "Appendix A: The Revolutionary Moment, xi.

15. McCullough, Steve. "Online Misogyny: The 'Manosphere.'" *Canadian Museum for Human Rights*. Accessed September 2023. https://humanrights.ca/story/online-misogyny-manosphere.

16. The word "incel" comes from the term "involuntary celibate," a label that (typically male) members of the aforementioned misogynistic communities use to describe themselves because they are unable to find willing sexual partners. The failure to satisfy incels' entitlement to women's bodies is often the impetus behind the violent rhetoric they then espouse toward those of the opposite sex.

17. McCullough, "Online Misogyny."

18. As compared to the second-wave consciousness-raising groups of the 1970s, which Bonnie Moore Randolph and Clydene Ross-Valliere discuss in their 1979 article "Consciousness Raising Groups."

19. Notably, though a majority of content creators and consumers who participate in these communities identify as women, many do not; this means that while Book-Tok and similar spaces are not women-exclusive, they are dominated by discussions of topics and texts which are of interest to (and/or are heavily marketed toward) women. Therefore, even members of the BookTok community who are not women, in order to engage with the dominant culture of the community, must read novels with female protagonists, discuss how these texts represent women's lives and experiences, and largely refrain from blatant misogynistic commentary.

20. Stanley Fish will be referenced in this chapter as "S. Fish" because of the unfortunate coincidence that one of the BookTok creators I reference has the username "Fish."

21. This article was reprinted in Fish's 1980 collection *Is There a Text in This Class? The Authority of Interpretive Communities*. It is this version that is referenced in this chapter's bibliography.

22. Fish, *Is There a Text in This Class? The Authority of Interpretive Communities* (Cambridge: Harvard University Press, 1980), 169

23. Fish, *Is There a Text in This Class*, 171.

24. Scholars such as Ananya Mukherjea (2011), Danielle N. Borgia (2014), Tammy Dietz (2011), Abigail E. Myers (2009), and others draw similar conclusions about *Twilight*'s anti-feminist messaging.

25. This is a reference to the *Dateline* NBC show *To Catch a Predator*, in which child predators are lured and confronted on-camera by the show's host, Chris Hansen. Fish uses this reference to imply that Edward, as a 104-year-old vampire romantically pursuing a 17-year-old girl, is also a child predator.

26. Posted August 25[th,] 2023.
27. Edward's mind-reading ability is another aspect of the control he enjoys over most other people and situations.
28. These comments are from "Part 4: Edward's personality sure is something!" (8/22/23), "Part 7: The cold medicine part really got me" (8/23/23), "Part 8: Someone get Chris Hansen on this case RIGHT NOW" (8/24/23), and "Part 11: My bad thought Bella was actually being reasonable for a second there" (8/25/23) respectively.
29. Scholarship on Maas's *ACOTAR* series is sparse, but Laura Mattoon D'Amore, in her critical text *Vigilante Feminists and Agents of Destiny: Violence, Empowerment, and the Teenage Super/heroine* (2021) also highlights female "empowerment" (29) in the series and identifies Feyre as a "feminist super/heroine" (30).
30. Laura Mulvey, a British scholar, is one of the foundational figures of feminist film theory. The article referenced here is her most famous work. Shohini Chaudhiri, in *Feminist Film Theorists: Laura Mulvey, Kaja Silverman, Teresa de Lauretis, Barbara Creed* (2006), notes of Mulvey and her peers that "the pioneers of feminist film theory in Britain were swiftly overtaking their counterparts in the US and imbibing the stimulus of psychoanalytic and semiotic theory from the Continent" (2). Indeed, Mulvey's incorporation of "psychoanalysis, French structuralism, and semiotics" (8) into film theory shifted the trajectory of both film studies and feminist theory as her ideas took hold in each field. The central argument of "Visual Pleasure and Narrative Cinema" was that "the controlling gaze in cinema is always male" and that "film is structured according to male fantasies of voyeurism and fetishism" (Chaudhiri 31). Mulvey, in this article and later criticism, considers then what the role of the female spectator is and what avenues such audiences have for pleasure.
31. The titles of Padilla's videos are usually replies to comments made by members of his audience. The title of this video is in reply to TikTok user @tiffstokchronicles and reads "Part 16: Replying to @tiffstokchronicles I PROMISE ILL READ FASTER."
32. Padilla, Connor (@connor_thebard). "Replying to @Holly Boone802 CHAPTERS 30 and 31." *TikTok*. August 28, 2023. https://www.tiktok.com/@connor_thebard/video/7272482480081390894.
33. These comments are from a video posted on 2 May 2023, titled "Part 2: Replying to @Abstract I clearly had alot [sic] to say" and a video from 24 May 2023, titled "Part 45: Replying to @moonbeenz THE RING" respectively.
34. Rhysand's own experience as a victim of repeated sexual violence further complicates the way these power structures are represented in the series. In the second book of the series, *A Court of Mist and Fury* (*ACOMAF*), Rhysand reveals that he was victimized by the evil faerie queen Amarantha for a period of fifty years prior to the events of the series' first novel.
35. Fandoms organizing to champion social causes is a phenomenon that Neta Kligr-Vilenchik et al. comment on in their article *Experiencing Fan Activism: Understanding the Power of Fan Activist Organizations Through Members' Narratives* (2012). The article discusses The Harry Potter Alliance (HPA), a group of Harry Potter fans who organize to achieve various "civic and political goals" (2.2).

36. Prythian is the continent on which Feyre and Rhysand live. "High fae" is the name given to the race of faeries which rule over Prythian. Other races of faeries are called "lesser fae." This transcript is from the video "Replying to @Holly Boone802 CHAPTERS 30 and 31."

37. Lorde, Audre. "'The Master's Tools Will Never Dismantle the Master's House.'" In *Feminist Postcolonial Theory: A Reader*, edited by Reina Lewis and Sara Mills, 25–28 (New York: Routledge, 2003), 26.

38. Mulvey's text is the expansion of the previously referenced "Visual Pleasures and Narrative Cinema," which was published in *Screen* journal.

39. Laura Mulvey, *Visual and Other Pleasures*. 2nd ed. (New York: Palgrave Macmillan, 2009): 158.

40. Chandra Talpade Mohanty, "Under Western Eyes: Feminist Scholarship and Colonial Discourses." *Boundary 2* 12 (Spring-Autumn 1984): 339.

41. Annette Kolodny, "Dancing Through the Minefield: Some Observations on the Theory, Practice, and Politics of Feminist Literary Criticism." *Feminist Studies* 6 (Spring 1980): 11.

42. Jessica Sheffield and Elyse Merlo's "Biting Back: Twilight Anti-Fandom and the Rhetoric of Superiority" from *Bitten By Twilight: Youth Culture, Media, and the Vampire Franchise* (2010) identifies a "troubling gendered tendency to represent the (mostly) female *Twilight* fandom as unworthy of entry to traditional fandom spaces" (207). Sheffield and Merlo's use of the term "anti-fandom" is a reference to a collective group of people who identify themselves as those who actively *dis*like the series, and "*mock Twilight*, dismissing its fans as vapid and making little or no effort to engage the source material" (210).

43. Kolodny, "Dancing Through the Minefield," 6, 13.

44. Kolodny, "Dancing Through the Minefield, 19.

45. Kolodny, "Dancing Through the Minefield," 20–21.

46. Kolodny, "Dancing Through the Minefield," 21–22.

Section 2

A REAL MEET CUTE

ROMANCE READING AS SOCIAL PRACTICES

This section opens with "Beyond the Bodice Ripper: What Modern Romance Readers Want Today," a mixed-methods chapter featuring some autoethnography from Joann Stout, a romance author in addition to reader and scholar. In her piece, she discusses how romance is frequently derided as formulaic "beach reads" or "fluff," as well as being assumed to give women unrealistic expectations of heroes that no real man could ever live up to the idea that they reinforce stereotypical gender roles. Yet, the heyday of bodice rippers has long since passed, and modern romances are different in large ways from their counterparts of yesteryear. Modern day romance readers are interested in the perfect blend of reality and fantasy—an idealized version of real life. That desire for a utopic, good triumphs over evil, happily-ever-after ride between the covers has not waned in the past seventy-plus years. If anything, the need has grown, deepened, and certainly become more complex as the landscape of romance writing and reading has evolved. Stout examines the data of what modern readers want, through the lens of redefining what romance is as a genre; analyzing the multiple sub-genres and tropes that have emerged in recent years, including dark romance and erotic romance; and identifying the ways romance has become more inclusive, all with providing her own experience as an author throughout.

"Reading Historical Romance/Reading Romance Historically," by Lise Sanders, asks what the historical foundations for this increased popular and scholarly interest in the romance are, and how we can understand this genre's expansiveness across media forms. In this chapter, Sanders uses the results of the present survey to examine the appeal of the romance, particularly the historical romance, to today's readers. She situates the qualitative data from the survey in a broader Anglo-American historical context, referencing the formative influence of Jane Austen and the Brontë sisters in the nineteenth century, and then turns to early twentieth-century authors such as Ruby Ayres, Ethel M. Dell, and Georgette Heyer, who used historical events and settings to ground their plots.[1] She also explores contemporary examples of the intermedial historical romance and the recent, much-needed attention to underrepresented narratives in historical romances centering BIPOC and LGBTQ+ characters and stories. Sanders argues that deepening our historical understanding of the romance enables us to gain new perspectives on the stakes, significance, and cultural influence of the historical romance in the contemporary moment, through a focus on its complex and diverse audiences.

Anna Michelson, in her chapter "Romance Reading as a Social Activity," takes a sociological approach to romance fiction, starting from the premises that the romance genre is a community and reading is an inherently social act. Her analysis focuses on four key areas in the survey data: pathways to romance reading, discussing romance novels, acquiring romance novels, and entertainment consumption patterns. She explores hypotheses about pathways to romance reading, the discussion of romance, and novel acquisition. The entertainment consumption patterns hypothesis seeks to connect the sociological concept of "cultural omnivores" and interdisciplinary popular romance studies discourse. Cultural omnivores, or consumers who engage with a wide variety of genres, is a consumption trend empirically observed in numerous countries since the 1990s. There is an assumption that romance readers primarily or exclusively seek entertainment through romance reading. Michelson tests this hypothesis and further connects popular romance studies and sociological research on cultural consumption.

"Escaping the Negativity of 'Escapism:' Rethinking Romance Reader Notions of Why They Read" is by Adrea Barra. In this chapter, Barra discusses how Radway identifies two major explanations for why her subjects use romance reading for "escape": a physical/literal escape from family and responsibility and a desire to experience the novel heroine's life and circumstances. Radway emphasizes that this escape is vital to replace the lack of emotional nurturance experienced in their own lives as well as establish time and space for themselves in situations where they have constant relational demands. This leads to guilt in the women, whether over the time, money, or attention they feel they are taking away from their families.

Radway's conclusions, as well as many others who have explored the notion of "escapism," posit the act as damaging and compensatory, indicating that we use popular culture to avoid, change, or imagine away parts of our own lives that are negative or not what we wish them to be.

Through exploring the opinions of today's romance readers, escapism appears to take on very different connotations. Changing demographics of romance readers indicate that there is no need to use the hobby as an excuse to take time for oneself as a justifiable or "educational" pastime.

The now-obligatory "happily-ever-after" is a guarantee of a pleasurable experience, and that is what readers are seeking for various reasons, whether it be for pure entertainment or relaxation, to go along on the emotional rollercoaster, or to feel optimism in the face of macro world problems. This leads to an important distinction from older nations of escapism—romance readers are escaping to not escaping from. The lack of discussion of instrumental escape was notable in the interviews while the emphasis on the couple's journey together and how that makes the reader feel demonstrates the change from Radway's Smithton women. Barra posits that today's readers look for emotional escapism, choosing romance specifically for the particular emotional arc they know will be provided by the genre.

Jessica Kratzer covers the reader experience in "Love, Romance, Sex, and Happily Ever After: A Feminist Exploration of Women Romance Novel Readers." Previous studies have explored romance writing post–*Fifty Shades of Grey* (Birthisel, 2020), negative stigma surrounding romance novels (Cameron, 2020), and romance novels as "mommy porn" (Jankowski, 2020), yet a gap in the research still exists. Kratzer's chapter explores gaps in examining readership. She uses the theoretical lenses of Smith's (2005) Women's Standpoint Theory, which seeks to understand the specific experiences of specific women by focusing on the intricacies of individuals' lives and the norms that affect them. Secondly, she applies Communication Privacy Management (Petronio, 2002) theory, which helps explain the expectations of managing privacy as well as how people create boundaries, rules, and co-ownership in regard to their private information. This study is a qualitative analysis with interviews. The results introduce the emergent themes and use participant quotes to support them, while also explaining the rationale for each theme.

NOTE

1. Ayres and Dell have been little studied; Heyer has received more critical attention in scholarship on the historical romance, particularly in the *JPRS*. For a recent example, see Kim Sherwood, "Pride and Prejudice: Metafiction and the Value of Historical Romance in Georgette Heyer," in *Georgette Heyer, History and Historical Fiction*, edited by Samantha J. Rayner and Kim Wilkins (London: UCL Press, 2021), 75–87.

Chapter 6

Beyond the Bodice Ripper
Why Erotic Romance is Feminist Literature
Joann Stout

We were never a household that shamed sex. There weren't topics I didn't ask about. When I asked my mom what sex was at the checkout lane of a packed grocery story and she said something like, "We'll talk about that later," and I boldly asked, "Is this one of those times when you say that just so I'll stop asking or will you really tell me?"—I was six. One real long walk later, I knew where babies came from. Because sex wasn't something dirty or shameful. It was simply part of life. But this upbringing, where sex and shame were not synonymous, was the exception, not the norm. In America, a country colonized by Puritans, our cultural views on sex have been slow to evolve.

I once had a French woman (a professor of mine) tell me she couldn't understand why American parents would rather allow their thirteen-year-old kids to watch movies steeped in violence and bloodshed than allow them to watch a movie depicting a love scene. She was truly baffled. As a culture, we expect and accept violence and hate and guns as a way of life, but we strive to "protect" kids from sex. This idea of sex being sinful and wrong is all tied up in the idea of purity culture and religion, all connecting back to the forced colonization and population of a country stolen from Indigenous people by extremists.

But this chapter isn't about that, at least, not entirely. This chapter is about why I write romance, specifically erotic romance, with loads of explicit content, and how writing erotic romance is, for me, an act of feminist rebellion. In this chapter, I explore two main questions – 1) what makes erotic romance a unique subgenre of romance, and 2) how do the specific qualities of erotic romance make writing (and reading) this genre an act feminism, all through the lens of autoethnography and my specific relationship and journey with writing erotic romance as a case study for the impact of this genre on feminism.

ME, AS AN AUTOETHNOGRAPHER

Autoethnography is something new to me, something exciting. It is a way to look at the events of my personal past and experiences and use that as a lens through which I can study and share my thoughts about romance, a genre I have loved for twenty years. In this piece, I situate myself as researcher, looking at erotic romance as a genre, but also as subject, and use that position of author, creator, and consumer of content within this genre in order to dig into my understanding of erotic romance writing as an act of rebellion and to share those thoughts with you, dear reader. Through this journey we'll be on together, I will share with you who I am and why I am in a particularly inimitable position to arrange these thoughts for you. Writing romance as a way to push back against patriarchal norms was something I've always done, but until sitting down to reflect upon and to analyze my voyage so far, it wasn't necessarily something I could codify.

I've been studying the genre of romance almost from the first romance book I read, consuming book after book, dissecting them as I went. I remember the first adult romance my mother handed me. It was *Dark Desires* by Christine Feehan.[1] I was sixteen. *Dark Desires* was a watershed moment for me, starting a lifelong love of romance novels that my mother passed on to me directly from her own enduring love of reading romance. Two years later, after having torn through as much of the Carpathian series as I could, I started writing my first paranormal romance at just eighteen years old.

Now, almost twenty years later, I have had the pleasure to see how the genre has evolved and I intimately understand how the world of Romancelandia works. I studied professional writing as an undergraduate and Writing Popular Fiction for my MFA. During this master's program, I also joined a local chapter of the Romance Writers of America organization, and then went on to teach in an MA and then MFA program, both focused on fiction writing. Throughout my years of study, I have met with other authors, readers, bloggers, editors, and industry professionals who share my love of romance. We've had countless conversations on studying and analyzing the genre of romance as a whole, and I've had several meetings with readers, writers, editors, and publishers of erotic romance where we discuss the industry as a whole, as well as defining the genre, marketing it to the right readers, and how to not get dungeoned on distributor websites for having books that contain "adult content."[2] Throughout these conversations, debates, teaching and learning moments, I've developed this overall idea that writing romance is an act of rebellion against patriarchy, which I am now finally able to put into words and share with the world.

Within the confines of the research specifically for this paper, I've analyzed my own writing, as well as my thought process of how and where to explore feminism, queer identity, sexual empowerment, and dismantling the patriarchy in my fiction, but also in my interactions in romance spaces, college and university spaces, and writing spaces. I have also read from researchers and authors both within and outside the romance community, and reviewed the data collected from the 2022 Romance Readers' Survey online by Josefine Smith and Kathleeen Kollman as well as reviews of my own works in order to gauge the experiences and expectations of romance readers. I am curious to see whether this concept of reading and writing erotic romance as an act of feminist rebellion can be seen or quantified outside of my own experiences.

I don't know that being a queer, feminist woman who writes and publishes erotic romance would have been possible fifty years ago, but that's exactly who I am and what I'm doing today. Fifty years ago (even twenty years ago), romance was still too much at odds with feminism, with being queer, and with anything outside of heteronormative narrative of one man and one shrinking violet woman. In fact, in 2005, Romance Writers of America, the premier organization of romance writers in the country attempted to redefine the genre as a love story "between a man and a woman."[3] But as the genre of romance in general, and erotic romance specifically, has evolved in the past twenty-odd years, we, as authors and readers, continue to use the genre to push the envelope, to strive for inclusivity, and to break down the barriers surrounding both gender norms and female sexuality.

SEX SELLS, BUT THAT ISN'T WHY I WRITE IT

In a post–*Fifty Shades of Grey* era, it's clear that sex sells, but that isn't why I write it. When I began writing paranormal romance in my late teens, it wasn't the "behind closed doors" kind where there isn't sex on the page, but the erotic content in the book wasn't the focus. It wasn't until I met my first editor in 2011 that I went from writing paranormal romance to writing erotic romance. He asked me one simple question that changed my life: "Do you write erotic romance?" I can literally draw a direct line of connection from that fateful night in a hotel lobby in Greensburg, PA to this moment right here, writing this piece. I wrote my first erotic romance in the months following this question, and it was published eleven months after that June evening surrounded by my Romancelandia community.

To really understand why erotic romance as a genre is feminist literature and an act of feminist rebellion, we need to first look at how this genre came about, what made it popular, and how that fight of whether or not it was romance had to be won. Erotic romance "emerged in the early 2000s just as e-book technology changed the resource dynamics in the publishing industry."[4] No longer would people have to feel embarrassed reading *Lord of Scoundrels* on the subway, boldly holding the paperback of a shirtless muscled hero and half-ravished heroine for the world to see.[5] E-books allowed people to essentially hide what they were reading, in plain sight. Allowing the erotic nature of erotic romance to be less overt by hiding the explicit half-naked book covers on an e-reader led the way for this genre to be birthed, spawning digital-only or digital-first romance publishers like Loose Id, Ellora's Cave, The Wild Rose Press's Scarlet Rose imprint, and Blushing Books, which focused exclusively on erotic romance.

The erotic romance subgenre was met with resistance within the romance community at first, and there are some within our community that still turn up their noses at the genre. One of the reasons for this is that erotic romance can (and does) include almost all other subgenres of romance (i.e. contemporary, historical, futuristic, fantasy, science fiction, LGBTQ+), which were already distinct genres. This further muddied the waters for calling erotic romance its own subgenre, which then also included multiple subgenres of its own. And the second issue that created so much pushback in the community was the erotic nature of the genre, which was seen by many as vulgar, lowbrow, denigrating to women, and focused so much on sex that it couldn't qualify as a romance. Professional and academic members of Romancelandia agree that a romance must have a central love story and "must end with a 'happily for now' or 'happily ever after' ending."[6] Therefore, any erotic romance that follows those two rules is, by definition, a romance. Erotic romance is a particular subgenre of romance distinct from a spicy or high-heat romance because the sex becomes integral to the plot and character development, and the erotic elements are "the *primary* defining genre of the work."[7] There is no specific formula for how many sex scenes an erotic romance should or must include, but in studying this genre for years, I am confident in saying that if there isn't sex within the first fifty pages of a full-length novel, then it's likely more of a steamy romance than an erotic romance. In an erotic romance, the plot revolves around, is pushed forward by, or is intertwined with the sex, that removing the sex scenes means there's not a cohesive book. This means that you can't get to the end of act one (approximately 40–60 pages into a 350-page novel) without sexual content if it is truly an erotic romance.

Some members of the community feared that erotic romance and its content would "further stigmatize the entire genre" and lead to yet more dismissal of the genre as frivolous and lowbrow.[8] These symbolic boundaries were not only about the content of sex, but also about what constituted a "real" publisher because e-books allowed for small presses, and even independent authors, to publish without the need for one of the major publishing houses. We, as authors, and as readers, legitimized erotic romance as a subgenre by creating, publishing, and buying books within the genre. Even though the debate about what constitutes erotic romance versus steamy romance versus erotica rages on within the community, there are not generally debates about whether erotic romance exists or should exist any longer, thankfully. While e-books started the rise of popularity for erotic romance, the blockbuster success of E. L. James's *Fifty Shades of Grey* trilogy pushed erotic romance,[9] particularly kinky erotic romance, into the mainstream, and the readership numbers, ravenous for more, into the stratosphere. This change pushed me even further into the erotic romance genre. I sat down to write my first BDSM erotic romance, *To Sir*, and took what I was already writing—spicy romances full of erotic content—and kinked things up a notch. This additional pivot not just from erotic romance but into BDSM erotic romance further solidified my exploration of feminism and love and queerness on the page.

SHAME ON ME? NO THANK YOU!

In this paternalistic society, full of the idea that women are not allowed to want sex, not supposed to have needs or desires, but simply subject ourselves to sex for the man's pleasure, it's little wonder that books which centralize a plot line on women's pleasure and sexual agency are met with resistance, with sneers, or leers, or outright outrage. There are literally books from the mid-twentieth century detailing how a wife is supposed to engage in sexual acts simply to keep her man happy, not because she might get any enjoyment out of it. If we *do* enjoy it, we get labeled as sluts. Our views on sex and female sexuality cannot be untangled from our patriarchy, and the ways that patriarchal mores, shame, a strict gender binary, and rigid gender roles are used to control women. Shame is used in our society as a whole as a "key mechanism of social control."[10] I refuse to feel shame surrounding this genre, or the sex within it.

When I'm asked what I write, I proudly say "dirty, dirty romance!" with a grin and a wink, because I embrace the idea that erotic romance is "naughty" or "smutty" in the same way I aim to take back use of words like "slut." As an author, and a woman, and a feminist, I want these words to stop having the negative connotations that currently surround them, that make people sneer or leer. And the only way we get to do that is by reclaiming them, the same way many of us in the LGBTQIA+ community have taken back the term queer. In fact, when I do romance-only book signings (where I know most or all of the attendees will be adults), I give away a giant gummy pecker to one lucky reader. Because displaying it on my table (and sometimes waving it at people and asking if they want to take it home with them) showcases up front to readers what I write, and if it offends the attendees, then I instantly know that my books are not for them. There are still people within the community, who view erotic romance as "soft porn" or "porn for women," which Jennifer Lois and Joanna Gregson would identify as sneers, jeers, or leers.[11] This need to shame us for writing about sex openly stems directly from the patriarchal view that women shouldn't enjoy sex, let alone talk about it, write about it, or celebrate it.

My husband, who often accompanies me to my book signings or public events as my assistant, has often been on the receiving end of comments like "Well aren't you lucky!" and "Do you help her with all the research?" These would be categorized by Lois and Gregson as leers from outsiders (and insiders as well), which they define as thinly veiled, insidious forms of slut-shaming, because comments like these still over-sexualize the author, a professional writer, simply because of the content of their books.[12]

Of course, it's only the women authors who are subject to such treatment. In their analysis, Lois and Gregson found that "Male writers were not only immune from the negative consequences of writing stories with sexual content, they were revered for it."[13] This is very likely because the standards for men are so different from the standards for women, and that translates to romance writing, just like many other aspects of a woman's world. This is another facet of slut-shaming culture. Lois and Gregson write, "Outsiders often expressed their disapproval of romance novels by referring to the books as 'porn for women' and describing them as 'dirty,' 'smutty,' and 'trashy.'"[14] Here, "outsiders" is defined as anyone outside the romance community. Because stigmatization leads to shame, shame is then used as a way to exert control, specifically in this case, shame and control of women writing romance.[15] In their research, Lois and Gregson further noted that the commentary from outsiders seemed to indicate that they viewed female romance writers as "oversexed women who documented their personal sexual experiences and fantasies in their books."[16]

While open-door discussions of sex can be another form of feminist rebellion, because being quiet about sex and sexuality is a facet of the shame that surrounds it, it can often be used in a leering way, which these authors note is actually a form of "mock approval."[17] I've had readers interpret the sexual content in my book as an invitation to share their intimate sexual details with me, in the middle of a crowded room in a book signing when my mother is beside me. While their research was on romance authors as a whole, Lois and Gregson noted: "The more erotic the sexual content, the more cause for shame, and the more need for writers to find others who could help them refute mainstream culture's shaming messages."[18] This research can therefore not only be applied to the genre of erotic romance, but can showcase that the more erotic the content, the more exacerbated the sneers, jeers, and leers hurtled at romance authors. Because the need to control women's bodies and sexualities is so pervasive in our culture, the more erotic the content, the more forceful the push is to shame us. Lois and Gregson contend that the culture of "slut-shaming" romance authors leads to authors having only a few ways to "contest" the shaming. The most effective way was pride, coupled with an acknowledgment of the way we approach shaming women and not men for the same acts. Lois and Gregson state:

> We argue that the subculture of romance writers was instrumental in shaping the emotional counterdiscourse and writers' collective understanding of the sneers, providing them with an "alternative stock of knowledge" (Ronai and Cross 1998, 105) to rebuff the shaming messages. The community's dominant position was not only that they should refute the shaming by directly responding to outsiders' sneering, but that they should do so by pointing out the sexism that gave the slut-shaming messages—and those using them—their power.[19]

Lois and Gregson argue that the ways we successfully manage the stigmas around writing romance and about sex can depend on how the stigma is applied. Many authors interviewed discussed how they used this idea of the double standard against women to combat the shaming messages and shed light on how intertwined the shame surrounding romance is with the patriarchal views of our society.[20] This is another reason for my gummy peckers—I have a lot of pride around what I write.

I want to openly embrace female sexuality to help showcase readers exactly what they will get in one of my books. If the pecker offends a reader, I know they are not *my* reader.

Even within the romance community, not everyone agrees with how we should handle erotic content in our books. Some readers dislike the way I embrace writing about sex and using words like "slut" in positive ways. In fact, some readers are put off by my use of the word "slut" as a term of endearment/slight degradation kink in my highest-selling series, *The K Club Dark Side*. One reader noted that she grew uncomfortable with "too many uses of the word slut..."[21] I was very specific in my use of this word within the series for my main character, who is struggling with her feminism and submission at the same time. This book series, in particular, was particularly telling for my journey with erotic romance. It features a bisexual heroine, who has a difficult time reconciling her sexual need for submitting to a man with her boldly feminist ideals.

Other readers have docked my use of condoms within contemporary BDSM romance, stating that it "diminish[ed] the erotica of the act."[22] However, because I want my contemporary books to reflect the world we live in today, condom use is something I always address. It actually becomes an important character or plot point in several places, especially when I have the female character in the heterosexual encounter be the one to supply the condom, because that sexual agency, that pushback against slut-shaming a woman who carries condoms is part and parcel of writing erotic romance as feminist rebellion.

HOW I USE EROTIC ROMANCE TO REFUTE SHAME, EMBRACE CHOICE, AND EMPOWER WOMEN

Romance as feminist literature is not an entirely new idea or theory. Romance novels have always pushed the envelope, evolving and impacting readers, and society, and then mirroring that change in more novels, in a cyclical fashion. Laura Vivanco's study of approximately 60 romances from Harlequin Mills & Boon Romances in their "Modern" (AKA "Presents") or "Romance" (formerly "Tender") lines published from 2000 to 2007, showed that "many embrace feminist values and disseminate them to an international readership."[23]

In the past fifteen to twenty years since those books were published, the landscape of romance has continued to grow and change, including more diverse voices, more diverse love stories featuring queer characters, BIPOC characters, polyamorous characters, and many characters who identify as feminists, including every one of mine. The idea of femininity and its use by men to disenfranchise and control women requires a rigid gender binary. However, in the fourth-wave feminism we find ourselves in today, gender as a social constructed binary is becoming more fluid and Gen Z has started deconstructing the gender binary entirely.

Simon studied romance fiction and film through a lens of feminism as a reader of the genre, saying:

> Patriarchal attitudes that label anything overtly feminine as somehow lacking, illogical, and irrelevant also taint perceptions of the romance industry, situating the genre in a category of fantasy, fodder, and escapism. This mindset stems from cultural attitudes regarding fictional entertainment, particularly those works created by women for women, as at best fairy tales, and at worst, frivolous works unworthy of serious contemplation—bawdy bodice rippers for the lonely, stay-at-home mom.[24]

However, when we dig deeper into this idea that romance novels are nothing but frivolous fairy tales, as Radway did, we actually find that's not at all how readers view it. In fact, of the readers surveyed, 75.6% said that the events in romance were "a little" or "a moderate amount" similar to real-life events. So, even when we write fairy tale retellings, readers view these books as resembling real-life events 75% of the time. Of the readers surveyed, 57.87% said that they felt the heroine's reactions and feelings toward people and events resembled their own, either a moderate amount or a lot. Conversely, 35.88% of readers said that the hero's emotional responses resembled their partners' responses a lot or a moderate amount. This data showcases that, as in most popular culture, romance novels reflect our society, while also helping to change the narrative in real life. This kind of art imitating life and life imitating art concept helps further the idea that romances, especially erotic romances, can be used for tools to help dismantle patriarchal views and even practices.

Radway studied romance novels from a reader's perspective, and from that outside viewpoint, discusses whether or not authors purposely used feminist demands in their works. She states:

> Furthermore, it cannot be said with any certainty whether the writers who are trying to incorporate feminist demands into the genre have been moved to do so by their recognition of the contradictions within the form itself or by the pressures exerted by developments in the larger culture. What does seem clear, however, is that the struggle over the romance is itself part of the larger struggle for the right to define and control female sexuality. Thus, it matters enormously what the cumulative effects of the act of romance reading are on actual readers.[25]

I can say for certain that I overtly include feminist ideals and views in my books, and I know many erotic romance authors who do the same. In my very first erotic romance, this happened somewhat organically, but it is now something, more than fifteen books later, that I overtly set out to do whenever I sit down to start crafting a new book.

For some women, romance novels are the first time they realize that not only can a woman want and enjoy sexual encounters, but that they can embrace their own sexuality and have agency over their needs and desires, and because of that, it's important that erotic romances portray sex-positive characters, as well as characters who are struggling with their own sexual desires, which many female readers might relate to. Two of my first erotic romance heroines, Layla (from *Love Affair in Times Square*) and Liz (from *To Sir*), both grapple with their sexual sides. As their stories progress, Layla and Liz both learn that rather than shying away from their desires, they should bravely ask their partners to help meet those needs, which is why sex is such an integral part of both of these books, and why they would never work as any other genre except erotic romance. Layla is a mixed-race heroine with a white mother and a Black father, and she constantly faces disapproval from her mother for being too wild. In fact, being too wild, too much, too everything, is the bulk of Layla's backstory:

> What if she ruined this guy's life like she'd almost done to Steven, when his family wanted him to choose between her and them? She'd made the decision and left before he could stop her. She wasn't worth anyone giving up their family for.

What if she ruined her own life this time? Then everyone would see her for the fuckup she was. They'd see she was wild, crazy. Unable to control herself. Just like her parents had said.[26]

Layla's story opens with her returning to her hotel room in Times Square after a long night of working in a law firm and deciding to relieve some tension by masturbating. Partway through the act, she realizes that despite the fact that she is stories above Times Square, she can see directly into the office buildings, and the man sitting behind his desk can *definitely* see her. She continues to pleasure herself to climax without closing the curtains. Opening the book in such a bold way was integral to Layla and Tyler's story, to helping to show Layla that she wasn't always too brazen, too sexual, too much; she just hadn't found the person who wanted to embrace her for who she truly was. I wrote that opening scene while traveling the French countryside by train. Even *I* might have blushed a little bit at that—writing such a blatantly sexual scene in public, because our views on shame and sex are internalized in the same way our patriarchy and racism are internalized. But this was more than a decade ago, and I've written far more explicit scenes since then, and been able to more fully embrace writing erotic romance without stigma or shame.

As a genre, erotic romance pushes the boundaries of what is "socially acceptable," and focuses on how women can embrace their sexual agency, and even pushes back against the idea that monogamy, or single partner, or heteronormativity is the only, or even the best "standard" for a relationship, which makes it one of the most inclusive genres out there. Whereas romances of old perpetuated the stereotype that women needed men to "complete them," modern erotic romances showcase that a woman doesn't need a man to be complete, or to survive, she simply *wants* one (or two, or sometimes more).

As Simon explains in her work studying this genre as a reader that romance novels can be "emancipatory narratives" and that they can be read "as both liberal and radical feminist narratives."[27] Simon analyzes Helena Hunting's *Pucked* which opens with the heroine, Violet, masturbating, stating that the book begins by "slapping patriarchy off the page with Violet, quite literally, taking her sexuality into her own hands. This scene immediately negates Violet's *need* for a man, thus the ensuing story depicts her *desire* for one. These kinds of narratives challenge the gender barriers at the site of ultimate male domination—sex."[28] Simon furthers her argument that it is the "quality of independence and choice present in modern romance," which allows it to "serve as emancipatory rhetoric."[29] I posit that the *writing* of these narratives is just as emancipatory for us writers.

Particularly in erotic romance, authors like myself use the sex in order to showcase independence and choice. What's more is that readers of this genre, while not always in agreement, read it not despite of the sex, but *because* of it. In Kollman and Smith's survey, 41.81% of readers listed "lots of explicit love scenes" as one of their top three required elements in a romance. Initially this high percentage was a bit of a surprise for me, because I absolutely expected that other elements, such as well-developed intimacy between the heroine and hero, a long conflict between the hero and heroine, and a slowly, but consistently developing love between the hero and heroine to be more in demand or ranked as more important for many readers of the genre. The concept of a romance including lots of explicit love scenes aligns with the continued popularity of erotic romance, and also speaks to what a modern romance reader is looking for, which could indicate that the negative associations and shame surrounding explicit sex is slowly changing. At the very least, there has been a shift in this idea that on-page sex is wrong or bad, and that readers (more than 1/3 of them anyway) are actively seeking out this type of physical relationship in their romance novels.

Part of this desire for more on-page sex could be because of the way that a lot of modern romance novels make consent a focus, which furthers the ability to offer women choice, independence, and agency. Erotic romance centers consent most overtly within the BDSM subgenre. While not all BDSM romances are erotic romances, all well-done BDSM romances focus on consent, on the page, so readers can experience those conversations and navigate consent right alongside the characters. This overt use of consent discussion in erotic romances helps further this push against patriarchal views and embraces the concept of an equal partnership, which is a key cornerstone of feminism. While some BDSM themes also include consensual non-consent, dubious consent, Domestic Discipline, and even total power exchange where one character completely cedes control over all aspects of their life to another character, the concept of Consent is King is still apparent. These are characters in a consenting relationship where, in most cases, a submissive woman gives up control of some aspect of their relationship. Domestic Discipline is a very specific type of BDSM relationship (in real life and on the page), in which two people, usually a man and a woman, live in a 1950s-style relationship where the woman is responsible for all of the household duties and she is considered to be in need of a man in order to care for her, to deal with the finances of the household and "keep her in line" in a sense. There is even a term called maintenance spanking in this type of relationship wherein the man will spank his wife just because, to remind her who's in charge and what her role is. However, in today's era, a woman in this kind of relationship is *consenting* to these rules, to these roles, because she *wants* them. In the June Cleaver era, the woman had no such option. She wasn't allowed to not give her consent. In fact, in most states, if a man raped his wife, it wasn't considered rape, because she was his wife, and therefore considered his property. It wasn't until 1979 that marital rape was against the law, first passed in California, and then slowly, state-by-state, laws were enacted until 1993 when finally, all 50 states had laws against marital rape.[30]

Rape is also a theme that is often explored in romance, though it is usually used as part of the heroine's backstory, rather than something that happens "on-page" in the book—as in it's not just alluded to, but readers actually experience the scene with the character. Of those surveyed, almost 68% of readers agreed that rape was one of their top 3 things that should never be in a romance. This even outweighed the percentage of readers (63%) who said a sad ending should never be in a romance. Because rape and sexual assault are at odds with everything a romance should be, yet historically, it was the only way that sex could be portrayed on the page. In the 1980s bodice-ripper height in the romance industry, it was, more often than not, the hero who savagely took the heroine, because his "desire" for her was so intense, it could not be denied, even if she didn't want him. A lot of this stems from a need to subvert censorship and patriarchal views around female sexually that mistakenly believe that a woman cannot enjoy sex. In the late 1970s and early 1980s, in addition to "bodice rippers," these novels were also called "sweet savage romance"[31] books because the men were portrayed as savages who raped or at least assaulted the heroines.

Within the BDSM genre, there are aspects of consent, such as dubious consent, and consensual non-consent (or in very dark romances, complete nonconsent), which are more gray areas, where readers are looking to explore the issues of sexual assault, rape, consent, and desire within the safe confines of fiction. People in the kink community (in books and in real life) support the idea of Risk-Aware Consensual Kink (RACK), wherein the consent given between one person, and another is the crux of the entire relationship. This exploration of consent and rape within the erotic romance genre further positions romances to push for social justice and use what Radway referred to the "critical power . . . buried in the romance as one of the few widely shared womanly commentaries on the contradictions and costs of patriarchy."[32]

This critical power of commentary and exploration of patriarchy is something which I explore in several books. The example that most explores the concept of consent as a key tool of feminism is in *Between Sirs*, where there is an entire consensual non-consent plot point and scene. This book features a ménage à trois throuple with one female lead, Amber, and two male dominants, Nathaniel and Tobias, where Amber wants a faux-kidnapping scene, and to have all her choices taken away from her. During this scene, which Amber has literally begged them for, she finally reaches a limit and uses her safe word to end the scene. In order for Amber to have total and complete control over her sexuality, she first gives it away to Tobias and Nathaniel, and then takes it back using her safe word, because consent is ongoing. Giving her consent to the scene did not mean that she would continue to give blanket consent throughout. Consent can be revoked at any time, and that was what was most important for me to showcase in this scene and book. Readers have called it intense and dark and "escapism at its finest."[33]

In addition to using consent to portray feminist ideals, this book also subverts the notions of heteronormative single-partner relationships. At the end of *Between Sirs*, Amber doesn't marry either hero, and simply having a throuple, where the relationship revolves around three people instead of two is a subversion of patriarchal norms. Many of my books feature non-heteronormative relationships, such as throuples/ménages in both *Gingerbread Photography* and *Between Sirs*, and reverse-harem (one woman with multiple partners, usually men) relationships in *Ruby's Blaze* and *Ruby's Fire*. As a queer woman, I also feature queer main characters in *Awakening Submission, Bound by Submission, Craving Submission, Gingerbread Photography, For Sir, Ruby's Blaze*, and *Queen of Hearts*, all of which push back against traditional heteronormative relationships and mores. Erotic romance is particularly situated to explore these queer characters and relationships because exploring these elements in overt ways both in sexual and nonsexual manners allows me to really examine so many facets of queerness and the queer identity.

Even in my male dominant–female submissive books, the gender roles are often subverted. In *Awakening Submission, Bound by Submission,* and *Craving Submission* the hero, Clayton, is the romance author and teacher and the heroine, Jacey, is the doctor. In *Belle by Night*, the hero, Dean, is a submissive male and a nurse, and Anna/Belle, the heroine, is a preschool teacher and phone sex operator who is a female Domme. Another way I subvert the expectations and norms of patriarchy is with my endings. My characters do always end up together in a committed relationship, as is required in romance. However, this committed relationship only sometimes includes marriage and occasionally includes the protagonists having children, which showcases the evolution of reader expectations and the ability of erotic romance to further change readers' minds that the definition of Happily Ever After can differ from one person (or character) to the next. This kind of freedom of choice is a key element in modern romance.[34]

Romance readers almost always expect a happy ending—either a Happy for Now (HFN) or Happily Ever After (HEA)—but exploring what that definition of "happy" means is not something that was done a lot in romance until recently. In order to have the happily ever after ending, it was pretty much required until recently that the couple get married, and there was usually an allusion to, or inclusion of a child, so much so that they got their own name in the business—a babylogue—where a baby (or at least pregnancy) appears in an epilogue after the couple has gotten engaged or married. Readers still expect that happy ending, but the definition of what that means is thankfully changing, and this change has been pushed in large part by indie authors and the genre of erotic romance. Of those surveyed, 228 out of 287, or 79.44% of readers listed a happy ending as one of the 3 most important ingredients in a romance. Additionally, 85% of readers listed a well-developed emotional intimacy as one of their top three must-haves. Some of this "traditional" thinking about romance, that a Happily Ever After (HEA) ending required the heroine to not only marry the hero at the end but have his baby was an integral part of why the Romance Writers of America organization blew up the Rita Awards (and itself) in 2019–2020—because members judging the books submitted to the contest who didn't see the "married with a baby" ending didn't find these romances to fit an HEA definition. Yet, as romances move away from the idea that a woman has to be married or have children not only to survive but to be happy, we are working to redefine that definition of happy, and happily ever after. This work gives space to the readers out there who might be trying to redefine what happiness looks like for them.

One of my books, *Love Affair in Paris* (previously published as *An Engagement in Paris*), really purposefully pushed back against this "marriage equals an HEA" concept. At the start of this book, Mandy and Julien are already in an established relationship, but are not married, and she is pregnant with their baby. She a professor at a university Julien attends, though he is not actually her student, which takes the student-teacher trope and role-reverses it. The book also plays with the purity of heroines in romance and the way sex will be part of the relationship, as it's clear right from page one that they've already been intimate with each other. It ends with the heroine Mandy and hero Julien getting pacsé, which is kind of the French version of a civil union, though it doesn't entirely have an American equivalent. For the heroine, Mandy, pacsé was a way for her to still be committed and together with Julien but avoid the legally bounding "trap" of marriage as she viewed it.

This really pissed off a lot of readers. People, even within the wonderful world of the romance community, can still have very narrow views of what a romance novel should be. One reviewer said "I hated it . . . the ending could have went in so many directions and she picked the train wreck."[35] Other reviews hated my main character and called the book "horrible."[36] In this book, it was vitally important that Mandy *not* get married. To Mandy, marriage was a cage. A life sentence of making yourself smaller to fit into a relationship with a man who wanted you to be less. The blurb, in fact, tells readers this right off the bat, saying, "Julien needs to get married the same way Mandy needs her freedom. When they find themselves at the impasse of matrimony, one of them will have to compromise what they want and need." In this book, it's Julien, the hero, who compromises *instead* of the heroine. Readers didn't appreciate this role reversal at all, but to me, Julien giving up his need to make Mandy his wife is what makes this book one of my most feminist novels to date. Redefining happily ever after to no longer fit one single narrative is a key way that erotic romance helps further feminist ideals.

CONCLUSION

Erotic romance authors use explicit sex, new definitions of happy, choice, consent, and empowerment in order to subvert patriarchal norms and support feminism ideals. Some critics of romance still insist that it is unrealistic, that it provides readers with unrealistic expectations for a real relationship. Others criticize romance, specifically erotic romance, as trashy, showcasing the wielding of shame as a form of social control, and even calling romance antifeminist in nature. Yet, when we look at the facets of erotic romance from the inside perspective, from studying the genre as a whole, it's clear that both writing and reading it are ways to challenge the patriarchal narrative and, as Radway said, discuss the "contradictions and costs of patriarchy."[37]

The stories we write as erotic romance authors have the power to impact change for a key reason: humans are hardwired for story. Lisa Cron found that when we read (or listen) to a story, the brain centers that light up do so as if the events in the story are happening to us, not as if we are observers of the events.[38] It is through the use of story, of campfire accounts and fairytales, and writings on cave walls, that we learn about the world around us, about the physical, the emotional, the social dangers. Our brains are literally hardwired to use story in order to learn from other people's mistakes, to predict what might happen to us in similar circumstances in real life. So when we talk about using romance, and specifically erotic romance, as a tool to push the needle away from inequity between the sexes, as a means of furthering the cause for equal home and childcare labor regardless of your gender, as a way to dismantle the dangerous system of patriarchy that oppresses everyone (not just women), it's because these stories, these words we use on the page, can influence millions of readers, making an impact in what they believe, how they feel, and give them the freedom to explore (and fight for) a more equitable world. That is the power of romance.

The modern romance novel has a huge task—to redefine feminism, love, romance, relationships, marriage, and even parenting. It is a herculean feat to do even some of this in our works, but the books we write and read these days need to reflect the seismic shift in the collective consciousness about gender roles and the characters we create must embody these modern understandings of what it means to be human, to love, and be loved in return. As an author of erotic romance, it's my job to change the world . . . one feminist romance at a time.

NOTES

1. Christine Feehan, *Dark Desires* (New York: Love Spell, 1999).
2. When a platform makes a book undiscoverable (wont be recommended by the algorithm, wont appear on lists etc.). For a longer explanation, see Sierra Cassidy's description on her website: Sierra Cassidy, "The Amazon Dungeon Pt. 1: What Is the Dungeon & Why Do Books Get Dungeoned?" accessed September 21, 2024, https://sierracassidyauthor.com/the-amazon-dungeon-pt-1-what-is-the-dungeon-why-do-books-get-dungeoned/.
3. Anna Michelson, "Pushing the Boundaries: Erotic Romance and the Symbolic Boundary Nexus," *Poetics* 94 (2022): 6, accessed April 4, 2024, https://doi.org/10.1016/j.poetic.2022.101729.
4. Michelson, "Pushing the Boundaries," 1.
5. Loretta Chase, *Lord of Scoundrels* (New York: Avon Books, 1995).
6. "About Passionate Ink," *Passionate Ink—Some Like It Hot*, December 21, 2021, https://passionateink.org/about-passionate-ink/; Pamela Regis, *A Natural History of the Romance Novel* (Philadelphia: University of Pennsylvania Press, 2013).
7. "About Passionate Ink"; Jodi McAlister, "Erotic Romance," in *The Routledge Research Companion to Popular Romance Fiction*, ed. J. Kamblé, E. Murphy Selinger, and H.-M. Teo (Routledge, 2020), https://doi.org/10.4324/9781315613468.
8. Michelson, "Pushing the Boundaries," 3.
9. E. L. James, *Fifty Shades of Grey* (2012a); *Fifty Shades Darker* (2012b); *Fifty Shades Freed* (2012c); *Grey* (2015); *Darker* (2017); *Freed* (2021).
10. Jennifer Lois and Joanna Gregson, "Sneers and Leers: Romance Writers and Gendered Sexual Stigma," *Gender & Society* 29, no. 4 (2015): 461, accessed June 14, 2023, http://www.jstor.org/stable/43669991.
11. Lois and Gregson, "Sneers and Leers," 480–81.
12. Lois and Gregson, "Sneers and Leers," 466.
13. Goffman, as cited in Lois and Gregson, "Sneers and Leers."
14. Lois and Gregson, "Sneers and Leers," 465.
15. Goffman as cited in Lois and Gregson.
16. Lois and Gregson, "Sneers and Leers," 465
17. Lois and Gregson, "Sneers and Leers," 465
18. Lois and Gregson, "Sneers and Leers," 468
19. Lois and Gregson, "Sneers and Leers," 479
20. Lois and Gregson, "Sneers and Leers," 468
21. Sue, review of *Awakening Submission* by Rachell Nichole, Amazon, October 25, 2019, https://www.amazon.com/Awakening-Club-Dark-Side-Book-ebook/product- reviews/B07QDL1VBW/ref=cm_cr_arp_d_viewpnt_rgt?ie=UTF8&reviewerType=all_reviews& filterByStar=critical&pageNumber=1.
22. RZ, review of *Awakening Submission* by Rachell Nichole, Amazon, July 3, 2019, https://www.amazon.com/Awakening-Club-Dark-Side-Book-ebook/product-reviews/B07QDL1VBW/ref=cm_cr_unknown?ie=UTF8&reviewerType=all_rev iews&filterBySt ar=two_star&pageNumber=1.

23. Laura Vivanco, "Feminism and Early Twenty-First Century Harlequin Mills & Boon Romances," *The Journal of Popular Culture* 45, no. 5 (2012): 1085, accessed August 4, 2023, https://doi.org/10.1111/j.1540-5931.2012.00973.x.

24. Jenni M. Simon, *Consuming Agency and Desire in Romance: Stories of Love, Laughter, and Empowerment* (Lanham: Lexington Books/Fortress Academic, 2017), 18, accessed August 4, 2023, http://ebookcentral.proquest.com/lib/philau/detail.action?docID=5115419.

25. Janice Radway, *Reading the Romance: Women, Patriarchy, and Popular Literature* (Chapel Hill: University of North Carolina Press, 1991), 17.

26. Rachell Nichole, *Love Affair in Times Square* (Philadelphia: Kindle Direct Publishing, 2019).

27. Simon, *Consuming Agency and Desire in Romance*, 40.

28. Simon, *Consuming Agency and Desire in Romance*, 18.

29. Simon, *Consuming Agency and Desire in Romance*, 47.

30. Amanda Kippert, "Can He Rape Me If We're Married?," DomesticShelters.org, accessed August 11, 2023, www.domesticshelters.org/articles/identifying-abuse/can-he-rape-me-if-we-re-married.

31. Radway, *Reading the Romance*, 34.

32. Radway, *Reading the Romance*, 18.

33. J.L. Gribble, review of *Between Sirs* by Rachell Nichole, Amazon, May 18, 2020, https://www.amazon.com/gp/customer- reviews/RVFQZ80NKAP91/ref=cm_cr_dp_d_rvw_ttl?ie=UTF8&ASIN=B07ZK4F5GX.

34. Simon, *Consuming Agency and Desire in Romance*, 47.

35. Nae, review of *An Engagement in Paris* by Rachell Nichole, Goodreads, June 20, 2013, https://www.goodreads.com/book/show/18053720-an-engagement-in-paris.

36. Christina, review of *An Engagement in Paris* by Rachell Nichole, Goodreads, December 7, 2019, https://www.goodreads.com/book/show/18053720-an-engagement-in-paris.

37. Radway, *Reading the Romance*, 18.

38. Lisa Cron, *Story Genius: How to Use Brain Science to Go Beyond Outlining and Write a Riveting Novel Before You Waste Three Years Writing 327 Pages That Go Nowhere* (Berkeley: Ten Speed Press, 2016). you waste three years writing 327 pages that go nowhere. Berkeley: Ten Speed Press, 2016.

Chapter 7

Reading Historical Romance / Reading Romance Historically

Lise Shapiro Sanders

In recent years, sales of romance novels have increased dramatically, supported by a range of media: the *New York Times* began a romance review column in 2020, and a new, younger demographic has gravitated to the genre as a result of streaming series such as *Bridgerton* (adapted from Julia Quinn's book series by Chris Van Dusen for Shondaland on Netflix) and social media such as BookTok.[1] In conjunction with this trend, research on the popular romance has proliferated over the past decade, as evidenced by the peer-reviewed *Journal of Popular Romance Studies* and several important monographs and edited collections. In this chapter, I use the Still Reading Romance survey to examine the appeal of the romance, particularly the historical romance, to a selected cohort of romance readers. I situate the qualitative data from the survey in a broader Anglo-American historical context, referencing the formative influence of Jane Austen, Charlotte Brontë, and Georgette Heyer on the development of romance fiction in the nineteenth and twentieth centuries. Heyer's development of the Regency romance offers particular insights into the cultural significance of the historical romance, especially in terms of the relationship between verisimilitude and fidelity to historical detail on the one hand, and the centrality of the romance plot on the other.[2]

After a brief overview of the evolution of historical romance as a subgenre, I turn to the results of the Still Reading Romance survey and what they can tell us about readers of historical romance today. In my analysis of qualitative responses from readers who identified historical romance as one of the types of romance they read, I focus on three themes: reading for escape, joy, and pleasure; reading as a safe space for self-care and community; and reading to develop empathy and experience different perspectives. In the conclusion, I address several key elements that have begun to transform mainstream publishing and media conceptions of romance in general and the historical romance in particular. These include: 1) the much-needed increase in diversity of representation, with the growing publication of romances featuring BIPOC and LGBTQ+ protagonists and stories; 2) the cross-media flourishing of historical romance, as exemplified by *Bridgerton* and the ongoing adaptation of the lives and works of Austen, the Brontës, and other canonical women authors of the romance, capitalizing on a burgeoning interest in period drama among a younger generation of viewers; and 3) the expansion of the historical romance to enable a move both toward and away from the idea of authenticity and fidelity to historical detail. The rewriting of historical romance has made room for a far greater range of stories featuring nonwhite, queer, bi, gay, lesbian and trans protagonists and centering the experiences of people of color, and has enabled a departure from the constrictions of historical accuracy to facilitate a far more creative engagement with joyful and pleasurable stories that are not bound by the constraints of history.

HISTORICIZING ROMANCE

Scholars have linked the development of the romance to the evolution of the novel in England and the United States, with antecedents including Samuel Richardson's *Pamela* (1740) and Susanna Rowson's *Charlotte Temple* (1791), among many other source texts.[3] Sarah H. Ficke argues that historical romance is "one of the oldest subgenres of popular romance fiction," traceable from ancient Greece through the novels of Sir Walter Scott in the nineteenth century and the swashbuckling adventure romances by authors such as the Baroness Orczy (author of the Scarlet Pimpernel series) and Jeffrey Farnol in the early twentieth century.[4] As Pamela Regis notes:

> Historical romance fiction, with the heroine as the focus of third-person limited point of view, typically depicts a companionate quest set in a society that practices and values dynastic marriage for kinship, political, or economic goals. In many novels, the hero must overcome these dynastic beliefs. Historical romances, which remain popular, return to its once-revolutionary status what historian Stephanie Coontz has called "the radical idea of marrying for love" as the twenty-first-century reader experiences the difficulties of a woman whose striving for companionate marriage is questioned by at least part of the society in which the books are set. Heroines in historical romances often seek and exercise an anachronistically wide-ranging freedom.[5]

At one and the same time, then, the "companionate quest" is a generic feature of the historical romance, yet this quest often exists in tension with the desire to reimagine dominant cultural norms around gender, sexuality, and agency.

Definitions of "the romance"—a term frequently used to signify a variety of fictional modes from short- and long-form prose to visual media, in addition to serving as a stand-in for the romance novel—typically focus on the pivotal role of the love story and the expectation of a "happily ever after" (HEA) ending, sometimes modified in contemporary romance fiction as "happy for now" (HFN). The Romance Writers of America (RWA), the major professional organization dedicated to romance fiction, offers an expansive definition, characterizing the romance novel as involving "a central love story" and "an emotionally satisfying and optimistic ending."[6] However, scholars have often assumed the romance novel, both historically and in the present, to be a form written by and for (cisgender and heterosexual) women, featuring heterosexual relationships between cisgender heroines and the men they love. In her landmark *Reading the Romance: Women, Patriarchy, and Popular Literature* (1984), a study of women readers of romance fiction in a Midwestern US city she termed Smithton, Janice Radway used the term "the romance" to encompass everything from category and series romances to the historical and contemporary romance novels preferred by the readers she interviewed.[7] In *Love and the Novel: The Poetics and Politics of Romantic Fiction* (1998), George Paizis elaborated a working definition of romantic fiction intended to apply to the historical as well as the contemporary romance:

> Its basic ingredients are a private setting, within which a heroine is brought into conflict with a hero, an encounter out of which ensues an affective adventure that ends happily. It is written primarily by women and deals mainly with feminine occupations, preoccupations, emotions and aspirations discussed within a narrative structure which focuses on the heroine's quest for love.[8]

In her 2003 book *A Natural History of the Romance Novel*, Regis similarly framed her argument around a presumed cisgender female protagonist in a heterosexual love story, characterizing the romance novel as "a work of prose fiction that tells the story of the courtship and betrothal of one or more heroines,," although she later replaced the word "heroines" with "protagonists" in an effort to retroactively expand the definition.[9]

A fundamental flaw in much of the historiography of romance scholarship prior to the twenty-first century is the assumption that romances center heterosexual relationships.[10] Although as the editors of *The Routledge Research Companion to Popular Romance Fiction* note, romance fiction is "still the most woman-centered form of popular culture in the western world today," and certainly the vast majority of romance novels (both historical and contemporary) feature straight, cisgender heroines, recent examples abound of romance fiction featuring lesbian, gay, bisexual, trans, queer, and polyamorous characters.[11] Moreover, both historical and contemporary romance novels function as a space for working through multiple modes of affective experience from friendship to love (as well as desire, jealousy, betrayal, and many others), suggesting the value in a more open framework for evaluating what readers value in the romance.

Two of the most frequently cited influences on the evolution of romance fiction in the twentieth and twenty-first centuries are Jane Austen's *Pride and Prejudice* (1813) and Charlotte Brontë's *Jane Eyre* (1847). Austen's six completed novels (as well as her unfinished novel *Sanditon*) are also among the most widely adapted (and parodied) examples of romantic fiction today.[12] The undisputed queen of historical romance fiction in the twentieth century is Georgette Heyer, whose influence on the Regency romance has been extensively analyzed.[13] Inspired by Austen, Heyer kept meticulous notes on details of dress, language, manners, and politics in late eighteenth- and early nineteenth-century Britain, providing a historically attuned foundation for romantic plots set against the backdrop of this period.[14] Stacy Gillis has persuasively argued against a hierarchical model of authorial influence—a direct line from Austen to Heyer—and in favor of a "rhizomatic model of interconnectivities" that can help us to see the ways in which Heyer's work has shaped our reading of earlier authors such as Austen and, I would add, later twentieth- and twenty-first-century writers of Regency romance from Barbara Cartland to Julia Quinn and beyond.[15]

Readers of this volume will undoubtedly be familiar with the historical romance in general and the Regency romance in particular; many have likely seen the most well-known recent example of a Regency romance adapted for the screen, the Netflix/Shondaland adaptation of Quinn's *Bridgerton* series (2020–present). For that reason, following my analysis of the qualitative data on historical romance to be gleaned from the Still Reading Romance survey, I will briefly outline some developments in the recent evolution of the historical romance from 2020 onward—in the years immediately following the circulation of the survey in 2019 and 2021—and offer some suggestions for future research.

READING HISTORICAL ROMANCE: THE STILL READING ROMANCE SURVEY

Methodology

As discussed in the Introduction to this volume, the Still Reading Romance survey was conducted in two stages. In 2019, the first version of the survey was distributed online (through sites including author pages, Facebook, Goodreads, Reddit, and Twitter) by the primary researcher, Josefine Smith, with a total of 130 responses. In 2021, a revised version of the survey was distributed by Josefine Smith and Kathleen Kollman, with additional questions about race/ethnicity, country of residence, and relationship status, and a total of 178 additional responses were received (demographics and other statistical findings are discussed at greater length in the introduction to this volume). Notably, among the 308 respondents, 39 people listed historical romances as their favorite kind of book as a teenager, and one additional reader specified "a mix of historical fiction, historical romance, contemporary fiction, and fantasy" in their response.[16] Furthermore, in reply to the question "What are the three most important ingredients in a romance?" which allowed respondents to rank potential qualities as well as specify their own categories, thirteen respondents identified "a setting in a particular historical period (Romances should be Regencies, Edwardians, about the Civil War, etc.)" as one of their top three elements. From these replies, we can conclude that although historical settings are not necessarily important to a majority of respondents to this survey, they are significant enough to some readers to have shaped their early reading experiences. As we shall see, historical romances are among the most popular of the genres read by survey respondents.

Working with the available data, I analyzed qualitative responses to the final question, which was phrased as follows: "What is one important thing for me to know about how reading romance novels shapes your feelings, opinions and identity?" I sorted the answers to this question to distinguish the answers from readers who read historical romance (232 out of 308, or 75% of respondents) from the answers provided by readers who did not read historical romance but read other genres and subgenres, identified as follows:

a. Contemporary mystery romances
b. Historical romance
c. Contemporary romances
d. New Adult romance
e. Erotica
f. Family sagas
g. Supernatural romance
h. Queer/LGBTQ romance
i. Spy/thriller
j. Other

The way this question was phrased (as a multiple-choice response in answer to the question "Which of the following kinds of romance do you read?" with multiple responses possible) prohibited a more granular approach to the qualitative comments, so it was therefore not possible to separate out only those answers that pertain to historical romance. Although an earlier version of the survey included the question "Which of the following types of romance is your favorite?" readers were not asked to name their favorite types of romance in the final version distributed to respondents.[17] However, since the evidence from the survey suggests that most readers of historical romance also read contemporary mystery romance and contemporary romance, much of what readers value in the romance may well cross these boundaries of genre and subgenre.

Of the 232 respondents who listed historical romance among the categories of romances they read (among whom three respondents listed historical romances as their only romance reading), 104 offered comments ranging from one or a few words to several (five to seven) sentences.[18] This number (over one-third of survey respondents) demonstrates that many readers were inspired to reply with a direct answer to the question "What is one important thing for me to know about how reading romance novels shapes your feelings, opinions and identity?"—although, as we shall see, it also prompted several respondents to critique the question itself and to reframe their answers to illuminate what they value in the romance.

Working with the 104 qualitative comments, I have identified three main thematic areas or discourses: (1) reading for escape, joy, and pleasure (especially for the reward of the HEA); (2) reading as a safe space, for self-care and community; and (3) reading to experience different perspectives and identities, resulting in a deeper sense of empathy and understanding toward others. Respondents also identified the potential of their reading to function as a form of social commentary, and their comments revealed a complex conception of "real life" both informed by and in contrast to the "fantasy" aspects of the romance. In my discussion, I address the notion that the romance offers an escape from "real life," placing these comments in the context of Radway's discussion of the "compensatory" function of romance reading.[19] As respondents' answers to the Still Reading Romance survey revealed, the affective power of the romance functions to sustain readers by offering an alternative space centering optimistic and joyful stories that are often in contrast to their daily lives or that reflect an imagined potential world. Rather than embracing a compensatory model, I argue, these respondents see their reading as developing a care relationship between the self and others, which in turn generates a vision of reenvisioned pasts that have the potential to transform the present.

Discourses

"It's a good way for me to escape"

It has become a truism that romance fiction offers an "escape" to its readers; often, this notion of escapism has been the grounds for critique of the genre as a form of false consciousness or a way of insulating oneself from the "real" conditions of everyday life.[20] Perhaps prompted by the presence of a question on the Still Reading Romance survey echoing Radway's "Which of the following reasons best describe why you read romances?" with the option to rank a range of answers including "to escape my daily problems," twelve respondents used this term or an equivalent phrasing in their replies: "Romance novels provide an escape"; "I read to escape, I don't want to read about more stress"; "the world is very rough, my job deals with world affairs and I constantly have to face the struggles of it all, so having an escape is good." The use of the word "escape" suggests a conscious awareness of romances as offering an experience distinct from the rhythms of daily life. However, several respondents were more precise about what the term "escape" means to them: "There are enough negative things happening in real life. Romance novels help me to remember that love conquers all"; "I get enough sad in my real life, I need an escape and I NEED a happy ending. I'm absolutely fine with tackling tough subjects but deprive me of the HEA and I breathe Fire." Such comments suggest that some readers understand the fictional world (even one that grapples with "tough subjects") to offer an affective experience that is qualitatively different from "real life," and that they find it important to acknowledge the rewards to be found in stories centering love and happiness as a way of navigating the difficult realities of the present.

Indeed, the simple practice of reading for pleasure and fun was noted by multiple respondents:

[Romance novels] are entertaining escapism and while they generally have a formula, the inputs into that formula are always different and fun to read. Reading should be fun.

They are my fun relaxing summer reads typically!

Embracing my love of romance, and no longer treating it as a guilty pleasure, has been empowering. I love talking to other romance readers and having not an ounce of shame anymore. I love my stories about awesome women who get happy endings!

Since discovering romance at the end of 2019, I have become a happier and more curious person.

And they all lived happily ever after! Romance brings me joy.

Reading romance is my escape and I need to know that no matter what the hero and heroine have to overcome there will be a HEA/HFN.

Romance novels are a sure bet that things will work out and be a happy ending in a world where nothing feels like a sure bet.
I read (and write) romance because I love the happy ending!

As well as valuing the HEA on its own terms, several readers specifically observed that romance provides them with hope: "reading romance makes me happy, excited. it gives hope"; "It just feeds that part of me that likes to hope." Others used the term "optimism" to express what they valued in romance reading: "It gives me an optimistic outlook on life"; "Romance provides me with optimism, particularly useful when times are tough or the world seems like a bad place." One reader summed up with the comment, "It always makes me feel better to read a HEA," and a reader who had lost their husband noted poignantly, "[romance fiction] lets me remember happier times before my husband died . . . reminds me that love is real."

In addition to viewing romance reading as a hopeful experience and a way to access a feeling of happiness, several readers explored the concept of escape through the lens of their own and others' experience of sexual orientation and gender identity. One respondent observed, "This survey was difficult because I primarily read romances between partners of the same gender. I find it a more escapist way to enjoy romance outside of my lived experience and I appreciate the way it can shift the dynamics between the characters because it doesn't lean primarily on their sex." For this reader, romance offers insights beyond their own "lived experience" (a point to which I will return shortly) and enabled a deeper understanding of character beyond heterosexual norms. Another reader referenced the experience of being a transmasculine person reading queer (m/m) romance:

> They allow me to step into the place of another character and out of a reality in which I often feel trapped and unhappy. I am a transmasculine person who reads almost exclusively m/m romance, which is a pleasant escape into the mind of a (usually) cis-male protagonist who is desirable to other men, but also to a place where queerness can be normal, unremarkable, and easy. Romance is often a refuge from a world that I feel dislikes me, and that is a great comfort.

This individual's account offers a nuanced and complex understanding of escape, pleasure, and happiness. First, the concept of experiencing a cis-male perspective as a trans man offers a sense of respite from an unsatisfactory reality; the idea of romance as refuge offers a sense of affective sustenance in a world that does not accommodate transmasculinity. Secondly, the respondent's emphasis on the pleasure to be found in reading about a place where queerness can be "normal, unremarkable, and easy" underscores a simultaneous recognition of the insufficient realities of a world where queerness is often rendered nonnormative, too remarkable, and difficult, and addresses the importance of an accommodating space that provides this sense of ease. These aspects of romance as refuge and comfort connect to the idea of romance as a form of self-care and a form of community with others, and enable us to move beyond simplistic conceptions of romance fiction as a form of false consciousness to understand more about the possibilities—both imagined and real—that the form offers to readers.

"Romance Is My Main Form of Self-Care"

As the above quotation underscores (resonating with one multiple-choice answer Radway offered on her original survey to the question of why readers read romance, "Because reading is just for me. It is my time"), respondents in the Still Reading Romance survey noted the importance of reading romance as a form of self-care. In particular, they highlighted three main needs or functions of romance reading as related to the self: safety, community, and learning.

Several respondents suggested they regarded romance reading as offering a safe space. Safety in this context has at least two meanings: the first reflecting the idea of the HEA as an expectation that they knew would be satisfied, and the second suggesting ways in which readers can explore new possibilities for identity and behavior. In the first case, respondents expressed appreciation for the familiarity of romance fictions: "reading romance feels safe. I know that it will have a satisfying ending"; "Reading romance is similar to watching your favorite rom com, or sitcom on TV. It's familiar, it's a warm, safe place that takes you on a rollercoaster for fun with an emotionally satisfying ending." In the second case, respondents noted the importance of the romance as offering opportunities to explore positive aspects of their sexuality as well as to identify negative aspects of relationships:

> [I] think it provides a safe space for people to explore their sexuality and indulge in situations that they are interested in real life.
>
> They help me work through feelings and situatins [sic] I am dealing with in real life in a safe and satisfying way.
>
> Romance novels have helped me to value myself and my own desires/needs in relationships.
>
> Reading some romance novels helps me to see bad behaviours from potential partners to avoid.

The refrain of "real life" returns in these responses, although here it is clear that readers understand fiction as part of a feedback loop—in the sense that reading about fictional situations can have a positive effect on readers' own experiences and relationships in the nonfictional day-to-day world.

A number of readers used the term "community" to characterize one of the aspects of romance reading they most valued:

> I've only recently (within the past six months) come back to reading romance after a 25-year hiatus. I had forgotten how happy a good romance can make me! I am reading voraciously and this has very quickly become an identifying feature—my friends and family make duke jokes (as I read only historical romance) and I've found a great community of fellow readers online.
>
> I feel a part of a fantastic community of people who read romance.
>
> I'm in a romance book club & an online romance community, so (especially during the pandemic) it's a significant part of my "socializing." The online one is specifically for smut, and I love how normalized it is.
>
> Romance has made me value intentional communication, and has made me ask more of all my relationships, which is a good thing that's led to me being more assertive. It's also the basis of increased community with other women, both on and offline.

In the first comment, the respondent's reference to "duke jokes" underscores the popularity of historical romances featuring dukes and other members of the aristocracy, and the ways in which readers of historical romance may seek one another out and signal their shared interests. Like Radway's Smithton readers, such respondents valued the opportunity to connect with other readers of romance, particularly online during the COVID-19 pandemic (when the second version of the survey was circulated).[21]

As the last quoted respondent observes, romance also serves an interpersonal pedagogical function for its readers, illustrating a variety of approaches to communication, expressing emotion, and building healthy relationships as well as deepening their understanding of their own sexuality. One respondent noted, "They gave me more comfort and confidence with sex," while another remarked, "Romance has helped me to have a better understanding of my wants and desires. It's also helped me set boundaries in my personal romantic experiences." A third identified a paradox in their reading of romantic literature, which they acknowledged brought a sense of comfort regarding the absence of romance in their own life: "Strangely enough, it made me feel more confortable [sic] being aromantic. I consume large quantities of romance stories and I feel more acceptance about my identity. I guess I can feel the deep emotions of the characters toward each other despite knowing I will probably never feel it myself." And two respondents specified precisely what they learned from reading romance novels:

It has expanded my cultural knowledge and awareness, consent, body autonomy, feminine strength and celebrating differences.

The Romance genre has taught me a lot, including how to have a healthier relationship with my body, with others; what consent looks like; what it looks like to have a partner that respects you as an equal (and that equality in a romantic relationship is okay to expect and should be expected). They've opened my mind and my worldview, which I'm so grateful for. They are empowering and important. They bring me joy and hope and community in a turbulent, scary world.

These respondents connected their learning about themselves with an expanded understanding of others, underscoring their sense of romance fiction as an empowering and culturally significant form.

Finally, particularly in the case of the historical romance, respondents saw themselves as gaining a deeper understanding of the past through the genre's emphasis on setting and detail, an aspect that supports Radway's argument about the significance of "descriptive detail" in the romances read by the Smithon readers.[22] One respondent remarked, "I learn a lot from romance novels. Both in emotional knowledge and overall knowledge," and another noted, "Romance novels, especially historical romances, make people smarter. I believe it's a different way to teach/learn history that is not dry and will stick with the reader more easily." (As a literary scholar and cultural historian who is also an avid reader of historical romance, I agree!) And one respondent drew a direct connection between romances that question or reinterpret the past and the importance of considering aspects of identity: "Because I read books including characters who either resemble people I know/admire (for contemporaries) or books that actively question the status quo of their setting (historical) I use them as occasions for thinking through issues of gender, sexuality, class, race, etc[.] as they are presented in (romantic) interpersonal relationships." Such comments underscore the active engagement of respondents, as they use the historical romance as an opportunity to think both through and beyond the boundaries of the fictional world, and to shape their own actions and evaluate the behavior of others.

"Reading Romances Has Helped Me Develop Empathy for Others"

Lastly, many respondents singled out the importance of romance novels as offering them the ability to develop a deeper sense of empathy and the ability to understand and embrace different points of view. Comments ranged from the simple "More empathetic" to "it [romance reading] keeps my mind open, makes me more empathic, and gives me a positive outlook." One respondent stated succinctly: "Empathy always wins, because that is what books about love should try to teach us." In addition to framing romance as a site to learn and feel empathy for others, several readers observed that their understanding of society as well as their conception of individuals' feelings and actions were broadened as a result of reading romance: "It gives me a perspective on aspects of society that I may not have direct experience of. [...]"; "I learn how people react differently to things. Or how someone who is considered 'weak' is actually very capable"; "It helps me see different points of view and situations that I haven't dealt with. I think it broadens my horizons and makes me have more empathy and less prejudice." One respondent focused on their increased ability to understand their partner's "feelings about certain situations," while another connected their reading of romance to their reading of literature more broadly, as an opportunity for teaching and learning:

> I treat romance like any other piece of literature. I look for it to show me ideas, concepts and experiences that I may not know myself, I use it as a teaching tool, and I look for big themes, beautiful writing and emotional beats that resonate. I use it to learn more about people but in a way that allows me to indulge in the fantasy of radical joy for everyone regardless of sexuality, race, gender, disability, nationality, age, body type and a myriad [sic] other issues.

This respondent's emphasis on "the fantasy of radical joy" powerfully underscores the liberatory potential to be found in romance fiction. Readers not only see themselves in the romance; they also see others in a new light, in a way that can function as a mode of reparative reading.[23] Rather than simply reinforcing patriarchal, heterosexist and gender-normative societal structures or standing in a compensatory relationship to "real life," romance novels in all their current diversity have the potential to offer a radically expansive and inclusive worldview to their readers, and to underscore the transformative power of fantasy itself to mediate between fictional and nonfictional worlds.

CONCLUSIONS

In her 1969 essay "An Honourable Escape: Georgette Heyer," the writer A. S. Byatt offered an explanation and defense of Heyer's approach to the balance between "romance and reality, fantastic plot and real detail": readers of Heyer "can retreat into this Paradise of ideal solutions, knowing it for what it is, comforted by its temporary actuality, nostalgically refreshed for coping with the quite different tangle of preconceptions, conventions and social emphases we have to live with."[24] Rather than denigrating romance fiction for its engagement with fantasy, Byatt embraces what she terms "good escape literature" for the affective experiences it produces and for the ways in which it enables readers to cope with the everyday.

At first glance, such a characterization might seem similar to Janice Radway's notion of the "compensatory" function of romance fiction in which reading romances "fulfills certain basic psychological needs [...] induced by the culture and its social structures but that often remain unmet in day-to-day existence," or, as she put it in an article published prior to *Reading the Romance*, reading to deny "a present reality that occasionally becomes too onerous to bear."[25] However, as the comments from respondents to the Still Reading Romance survey make clear, romance readers are well aware of the pressures and stresses of daily life (or "real life" in the words of several), and their reading functions as a source of affective empowerment, as a way to claim joy, pleasure, and optimism, to identify a sense of safety and community, and to learn about themselves and others. Interestingly, the Smithton women also characterized their reading as empowering, a fact Radway initially downplayed but later came to recognize as significant (and as an example of her own critical position influencing her interpretation of readers' perspectives).[26] Crediting readers' own accounts enables us to address what is often left out of reader-response criticism, namely "the *pleasurableness* of the pleasure of romance reading" and how the affective experience of reading romance is valued by readers.[27]

Without the opportunity to conduct follow-up individual or small-group interviews, we can only glean so much from the qualitative comments provided as an answer to the question "What is one important thing for me to know about how reading romance novels shapes your feelings, opinions and identity?" Future studies could delve more deeply into the ways respondents embrace, circumvent, or resist this question. To the latter point, three respondents to the Still Reading Romance answered, "It doesn't," with one elaborating: "The material I choose to read is based on my values regarding thing[s] like diversity, what healthy relationships look like [...] the importance of consent and the importance of using condoms [...] All of these values I had before I started reading romance. This informs my reading, not the other way around." Individual or small focus-group style interviews would also provide an opportunity for the interviewer to follow up on certain terms, themes, and questions, and would allow respondents to elaborate on their points at greater length and in depth.

Future reader-response studies focusing on historical romance could also take into account the seismic changes to the romance media landscape just in the last five years. Since the survey was distributed, what we might term the *Bridgerton* phenomenon has brought period drama into the mainstream, alongside intermedial adaptations such as Andrew Davies's *Sanditon* (2019–2023) and Autumn de Wilde's *Emma* (2020).[28] These texts update the Regency romance with a modern sensibility, subverting notions of realism and historical accuracy in period adaptations, and inspiring a new round of scholarship on historical romance and its audiences.[29] This explosion of historical romance across media reflects a long tradition of adapting romance novels to the screen, traceable to some of the earliest film adaptations of novels by Ethel M. Dell, Elinor Glyn, and E. M. Hull, among others.[30] At the same time, the publishing industry has seen a welcome expansion in the past decade, due in part to the rise in self-publishing but also as trade presses embrace a broader representation of characters, plots, and settings. Readers of historical romance can now seek out a far more diverse set of narratives in the work of BIPOC authors including Alyssa Cole, author of the Loyal League series, of which the first installment, *An Extraordinary Union* (2017) features a romance between a Black formerly enslaved woman spy for the Union Army and a white Pinkerton detective, and Adriana Herrera, author of the Las Léonas series, including *A Caribbean Heiress in Paris* (2022) and the forthcoming *A Tropical Rebel Gets the Duke* (2025). Recent publications by authors of LGBTQ+ historical romance such as KJ Charles (the m/m romance *The Secret Lives of Country Gentlemen* [2023]), Alexis Hall (*A Lady for a Duke* [2022], featuring a transfeminine heroine), and Erica Ridley (the Sapphic Regency romance *The Perks of Loving a Wallflower* [2021]), offer alternatives to straight, cisgender narratives of courtship and betrothal. They center underrepresented characters and stories and challenge their audiences to adopt a liberatory relationship to the reading and writing of history. As the Still Reading Romance survey suggests, historical romance remains a vibrant and exciting genre for a diverse population of readers, and further research will undoubtedly help us to understand more about its pasts and presents as well as its potential futures.

ACKNOWLEDGMENTS

I would like to thank the participants in the "Reading the Modernist Romance" roundtable at the 2024 Modernist Studies Association Conference for their insights into romance fiction in the early twentieth century. Thanks also to Viveca Greene for sharing her expertise, and to Kathleen Kollman, Josefine Smith, and an anonymous peer reviewer for editorial suggestions. Lastly, I am grateful to Sheila Greenwald, whose YA novel *It All Began With Jane Eyre* (Dell, 1981) first inspired me to consider the significance of reading romance novels and is truly where this all began for me.

NOTES

1. Elena Burnett, Sarah Handel and Juana Summers, "Even as overall book sales are declining, romance novels are on the rise," *All Things Considered,* NPR, 2

June 2023, https://www.npr.org/2023/06/02/1179850128/even-as-overall-book-sales-are-declining-romance-novels-are-on-the-rise (accessed 5 March 2024); "Books: Romance," *New York Times*, https://www.nytimes.com/column/new-romance-novels (accessed 15 March 2024). For demographics on the increasingly younger romance audience, see Deanna Schwartz and Meghan Collins Sullivan, "Gen Z is driving sales of romance books to the top of bestseller lists," Book News and Features, NPR, August 29, 2022, https://www.npr.org/2022/08/29/1119886246/gen-z-is-driving-sales-of-romance-books-to-the-top-of-bestseller-lists (accessed 5 March 2024).

2. On this point, see Stacy Gillis, "Manners, Money, and Marriage: Austen, Heyer, and the Literary Genealogy of the Regency Romance," in *After Austen: Reinventions, Rewritings, Revisitings*, edited by Lisa Hopkins (Houndmills: Palgrave Macmillan, 2018), 86.

3. Jay Dixon traces the history of English romance novels to the publication of Lady Mary Wroth's *Urania* (1621), connecting the romance to the traditions of amatory fiction, the domestic novel of manners, the Gothic novel, and sensation fiction; and Pamela Regis identifies a number of novels by little-known American women writers in an effort at reframing literary histories of the nineteenth century to include the romance as a significant and under-recognized genre. Jay Dixon, "History of English Romance Novels, 1621–1975," in Jayashree Kamblé, Eric Murphy Selinger, and Hsu-Ming Teo, eds. *The Routledge Research Companion to Popular Romance Fiction*, 27–50 (London and New York: Routledge, 2021); Pamela Regis, "The Evolution of the American Romance Novel," in Kamblé, Selinger, and Teo, eds. *The Routledge Research Companion to Popular Romance Fiction*, 51–71. See also Rachel Anderson, *The Purple Heart Throbs: The Sub-literature of Love* (London: Hodder & Stoughton, 1974); George Paizis, *Love and the Novel: The Poetics and Politics of Romantic Fiction* (Basingstoke: Macmillan, 1998); Pamela Regis, *A Natural History of the Romance Novel* (Philadelphia: University of Pennsylvania Press, 2003).

4. Sarah H. Ficke, "The Historical Romance," in Kamblé, Selinger, and Teo, eds. *The Routledge Research Companion to Popular Romance Fiction*, 118–40. See also Martha F. Bowden, *Descendants of Waverley: Romancing History in Contemporary Historical Fiction* (Lewisburg, PA: Bucknell University Press, 2016); Lisa Fletcher, *Historical Romance Fiction: Heterosexuality and Performativity* (Burlington: Ashgate, 2008); and Helen Hughes, *The Historical Romance* (New York and London: Routledge, 1993).

5. Pamela Regis, "Female Genre Fiction in the Twentieth Century," *The Cambridge History of the American Novel*, edited by Leonard Cassuto et al. (Cambridge: Cambridge University Press, 2011), 855–56, citing Stephanie Coontz, *Marriage, A History: How Love Conquered Marriage* (New York: Penguin, 2005), 15.

6. "About the Romance Genre," Romance Writers of America, https://www.rwa.org/Online/Romance_Genre/About_Romance_Genre.aspx (accessed 25 June 2024).

7. Janice A. Radway, *Reading the Romance: Women, Patriarchy, and Popular Literature* (Chapel Hill: University of North Carolina Press, 1984; rev. ed. 1991). Radway acknowledges that the limited sample size of her study—which consisted of group and individual interviews with sixteen women and a lengthy questionnaire completed by forty-two respondents, on which the Still Reading Romance survey was

based—suggests that "the conclusions drawn from the study. . . should be extrapolated only with great caution to apply to other romance readers" (48). Notably, Radway found that "[t]he overwhelming preference of the group was for historicals" (56).

8. Paizis, *Love and the Novel*, 29.

9. Regis, *A Natural History of the Romance Novel*, 19; Jayashree Kamblé, Eric Murphy Selinger, and Hsu-Ming Teo, "Introduction," *The Routledge Research Companion to Popular Romance Fiction*, 2. See also Regis, "Female Genre Fiction in the Twentieth Century," 849.

10. An important early critique of the heterosexism of "classic romance" appears in Jackie Stacey and Lynne Pearce, "The Heart of the Matter: Feminists Revisit Romance," in *Romance Revisited*, edited by Lynne Pearce and Jackie Stacey (New York: New York University Press, 1995), 19–24.

11. Kamblé, Selinger, and Teo, "Introduction," 1.

12. Regis, *A Natural History of the Romance Novel*, 55; Lisa Hopkins, "Introduction: Looking at Austen," in *After Austen*, 1–15. To be sure, Austen and Brontë were writing novels set close to the time of their publication rather than historical novels: as Regis observes, Austen "set her romances in her own time, contemporaneous with her own life," and thus can be seen as an author of "contemporaries" rather than historicals (Regis, *A Natural History of the Romance Novel*, 126).

13. In the 1920s, Heyer began writing adventure romances set in the eighteenth century, and in the 1930s she shifted her focus to the Regency era (1811–1820, when George IV ruled as regent for his father King George III) with novels such as *Regency Buck* (1935). Kenneth Womack, "Heyer [married name Rougier], Georgette (1902–1974), novelist," *Oxford Dictionary of National Biography*, 23 September 2004 (accessed 28 June 2024). See also Mary Fahnestock-Thomas, ed. *Georgette Heyer: A Critical Retrospective* (Saraland, AL: Prinnyworld Press, 2001); Karin E. Westman, "A Story of Her Weaving: The Self-Authoring Heroines of Georgette Heyer's Regency Romance," in *Doubled Plots: Romance and History*, edited by Susan Strehle and Mary Paniccia Carden (Jackson: University Press of Mississippi, 2003), 165–84; Lisa Hopkins, "Georgette Heyer: What Austen Left Out," in *After Austen*, 61–79; and Samantha J. Rayner and Kim Wilkins, eds. *Georgette Heyer, History and Historical Fiction* (London: UCL Press, 2021).

14. Regis, *A Natural History of the Romance Novel*, 125–27; see also Jane Aitken Hodge, *The Private World of Georgette Heyer* (London: Bodley Head, 1984) and Jennifer Kloester, *Georgette Heyer: Biography of a Bestseller* (London: William Heinemann/Random House, 2011).

15. Gillis, "Manners, Money, and Marriage," 84. Since the 1960s, most major trade presses have established Regency and historical romance lists, including publishers of series romances such as Harlequin (Canada), which eventually merged with Silhouette in the US, and Mills & Boon in Britain, as well as the "Big Five" (Hachette, HarperCollins, Macmillan, Penguin/Random House, and Simon & Schuster) and many smaller publishing imprints. For an early survey of romance writers and publishers, see Aruna Vasudevan, ed. *Twentieth-Century Romance and Historical Writers*, 3rd ed., with prefaces by Kay Mussell and Alison Light (London:

St. James Press/Gale Research, 1994); and for a more recent scholarly discussion of changes to the industry, see Kamblé, Selinger, and Teo, "Introduction," 1–6.

16. Another 30 respondents listed "historical fiction other than romance," and several readers listed "classics" as their answer to this question, with one respondent specifying "classics by women (Austen, Brontë)" alongside other genres.

17. Since a section of the Still Reading Romance survey focused on readers of New Adult fiction, respondents who listed this category were asked to name specific authors and/or titles; however, general romance readers were not explicitly invited to name specific authors or texts. Only one of the respondents who listed historical romances among the categories they read offered their favorite as an answer to this question, noting, "My fav is *Consuelo* by George Sand and *The Thorn Birds* by Colleen McCullough. None offer HEA, are mature and complicated. Both don't fit current romance genre definition."

18. 83 respondents left the answer to this question blank and 45 wrote "N/A" in response.

19. Radway, *Reading the Romance*, 112–13.

20. Radway notes, for example, that "In learning how to read male behavior from the romance, a woman insulates herself from the need to demand that such behavior change" (*Reading the Romance*, 151).

21. For an ethnographic study of novel readers in the UK and Denmark during the early years of the pandemic, see Ben Davies, Christina Lupton, and Johanne Gormsen Schmidt, *Reading Novels During the Covid-19 Pandemic* (Oxford University Press, 2023). In 2020, film historian and textile artist Lucie Bea Dutton created a #georgetteheyerreadalong on Twitter, complementing the #georgetttedaily Twitter (now X); for more, see "Before Bridgerton: how Georgette Heyer re-invented Regency," Penguin UK, 30 March 2022, https://www.penguin.co.uk/articles/2022/03/georgette-heyer-regency-romance-bridgerton (accessed 28 June 2024).

22. Radway, *Reading the Romance*, 193–94.

23. Hannah McCann and Catherine M. Roach, "Sex and Sexuality," in Kamblé, Selinger and Teo, eds. *The Routledge Research Companion to Popular Romance Fiction*, 411–27.

24. A. S. Byatt, "An Honourable Escape: Georgette Heyer," in *Passions of the Mind: Selected Writings* (New York: Turtle Bay Books/Random House, 1992), 239–40.

25. Radway, *Reading the Romance*, 113; Janice A. Radway, "Women Read the Romance: The Interaction of Text and Context," *Feminist Studies* 9, no. 1 (1983), 59. For a related discussion, see Clarke Daniels, "Queering Queer Fiction: From Tragic Narratives to Stories of Queer Joy," Division III Thesis, Hampshire College, 2019.

26. Critiques of Radway's methodology and conclusions are numerous; for a summary and an account of quantitative and qualitative studies of romance readers before and since *Reading the Romance*, see Joanna Gregson and Jennifer Lois, "Social Science Reads Romance," in Kamblé, Selinger and Teo, eds. *The Routledge Research Companion to Popular Romance Fiction*, 340–45.

27. Ien Ang, "Feminist Desire and Female Pleasure: On Janice Radway's *Reading the Romance*," in *Living Room Wars: Rethinking Media Audiences for a Postmodern World* (London: Routledge, 1996), 104, cited in Joanne Hollows, *Feminism, Femininity and Popular Culture* (Manchester: Manchester University Press, 2000), 87.

28. Klaus Bruhn Jensen defines intermediality as "the interconnectedness of modern media," or "communication through several discourses at once, including through combinations of different sensory modalities of interaction." Klaus Bruhn Jensen, "Intermediality," in *The International Encyclopedia of Communication Theory and Philosophy*, ed. Klaus Bruhn Jensen and Robert T. Craig (John Wiley & Sons, 2016), 1–12.

29. See, for example, the essays included the 2023 special issue of the *Journal of Popular Television* on *Bridgerton* edited by Julie Anne Taddeo, among them Amber Davisson and Kyra Hunting, "From Private Pleasure to Erotic Spectacle: Adapting *Bridgerton* to Female Audience Desires," *Journal of Popular Television* 11, no. 1 (2023): 7–25; Amy M. Froide, "The History Behind *Bridgerton*," *Journal of Popular Television* 11, no. 1 (2023): 55–60; and Amanda-Rae Prescott, "After the Duke: Reflections on How *Bridgerton* Has Changed the Period Drama Conversation," *Journal of Popular Television* 11, no. 1 (2023): 61–73.

30. I address these early intermedial romances in my forthcoming book project.

Chapter 8

Romance Reading as a Social Activity

Anna Michelson

This chapter explores how romance reading, often thought of as a solitary activity, has many social aspects. Much of Janice Radway's original *Reading the Romance* study was facilitated by the social ties between bookstore employee Dot Evans and her loyal customers.[1] Though Radway was surprised to learn most of the women did not know each other or talk about romances with each other before her focus groups, it was likely that social connection that got them to participate in the first place. Scholars of literary practices have demonstrated a number of ways that reading is social. For example, reading can encourage ethical reflections about relations with others.[2] Books and their reception are shaped by the context of production.[3] Book clubs can be an important site of sociality.[4] Indeed, discussing a book can even change one's interpretation of its meaning.[5] Aside from Radway, most other early romance studies focused on text analysis or individual reader reception.[6] While these approaches provide essential insights, exploring the social and community aspects of romance reading explores an important dimension of the reading experience. This data set provides an exciting opportunity to better understand contemporary reader practices and how social and technological changes have (or have not) changed the way readers interact with both novels and each other.

More recent romance scholarship has acknowledged the strong community element of the romance genre. Fletcher, Driscoll, and Wilkins's "genre worlds" approach understands romance as simultaneously "a sector of the publishing industry, a social formation, and a body of texts."[7] This approach acknowledges the importance of community, as the genre world is "built on a dynamic of real and imagined sociality."[8] Online forums are an important site of romance community interaction. For example, Greenfeld-Benovitz analyzed the popular Smart Bitches, Trashy Books (SBTB) website as an

129

interactive community.[9] Moody also explores romance through a community participation lens.[10]

The idea of community and social connection is especially important in romance because of the genre's stigmatized reputation. Indeed, research has documented how some romance readers resort to strategies like hiding books or publicly disparaging the genre to avoid association with the genre.[11] Romance authors, too, are subjected to patronizing "sneers" and objectifying "leers" for their association with a genre known in the popular imagination for its lowbrow reputation, female fanbase, and sexual content.[12]

Despite—or perhaps because of—the stigmatized reputation, the romance community is especially proud and protective of its boundaries. Many, such as aca-fan-author Roach, have identified the happily-ever-after (HEA) as a key component of the genre.[13] Indeed, the HEA has long been the constant in a genre that has evolved from almost exclusively traditional heterosexual love stories to a diverse genre that incorporated once-contested classifications outside Gayle Rubin's "charmed circle" of heteronormativity, categories like erotic romance and LGBTQ+ romance.[14, 15] Some feminist theorists such as Lauren Berlant and Sara Ahmed argue that the pursuit of happiness may detract from feminist goals.[16, 17] Regardless, many authors and readers look to the HEA not only for personal enjoyment and comfort, but for political significance in the depiction of happy, triumphant stories for people from historically marginalized groups.[18]

With this background in mind, I was excited to dig into this new dataset. Guided by the overarching questions "How is romance reading a social activity?" and "How do social interaction and community factor into the romance reading experience?," I explored six questions based in four main areas.

1. Pathways to Romance Reading
   a. At what age did respondents start reading romance novels?
2. Discussing Romance Novels
   a. How often do respondents discuss romance novels with others?
   b. Who do readers discuss romances with?
3. Acquiring Romance Novels
   a. How do readers acquire romance novels?
   b. How do readers decide which romance novels to read?
4. Entertainment Consumption Patterns
   a. Do romance readers read books outside of the romance genre?

METHODS

The data was received and analyzed in Excel. The present analysis focuses on the 301 participants who completed at least 20% of the survey. Descriptive statistics were generated for each question that corresponded to a hypothesis. Tables with exact figures are available in Appendix C. While reporting general patterns and percentages is not as rigorous as analytical methods such as regression models, it is in keeping with the way Radway reported her findings and is well-suited to accessibility and general discussion for an interdisciplinary audience. I sought to ascertain general trends rather than identify statistically significant correlations between variables.

Finally, I discuss changes in the institutional matrix of romance publishing and the broader social context of the romance community. I engaged with the write-in responses to the question "What is one important thing for me to know about how reading romance novels shapes your feelings, opinions, and identity?" in order to better understand how contemporary readers found significance in romance reading, especially in relation to community. Focusing especially on those comments that pertained to themes of sociality or community, this qualitative data adds fascinating texture to the statistical patterns and provides more detail about how romance reading is social.

RESULTS AND DISCUSSION

Pathways to Romance Reading

At what age did respondents start reading romance novels? As shown in Table 8.1, a slight majority of respondents (50.8%) became romance readers between the ages of 10-19 (preteen and teen years). 27.6% began reading romance in their 20s and 20% began reading romance at or after age 30.

Table 8.1 Age Began Reading Romance

	Count	Percent
Under 10	3	1.0%
10–14 years	68	22.6%
15–19 years	85	28.2%
20–24 years	41	13.6%
25–29 years	42	14.0%
30–39 years	39	13.0%
40 or older	21	7.0%
N/A	2	0.7%
Total	**301**	**100%**

Comparatively, in Radway's study, 36% of romance readers started between the ages of 10-19, 38% started reading romance in their 20s, and 24% started reading at or after age 30. What might explain readers turning to romance earlier today?

It is not possible to definitively state how these teens and pre-teens came to the romance genre as the present survey did not include those questions (for example, whether a female friend or family member was a romance reader). However, previous research has found that many romance readers are introduced to the genre by mothers, grandmothers, or female friends, suggesting that social ties are important for initially getting people involved in the genre.[19] A combination of social media and less stigma around the genre might let more young people hear about romance novels. In particular, TikTok (BookTok, as the literary corner is known) has been credited with promoting interest in young people's reading, including in romance.

Discussing Romance Novels

One aspect of sociality related to reading is actively discussing books with others. How often do romance readers discuss romance novels with others? As shown in Table 8.2, 70.4% of participants report discussing romance novels with others either "Sometimes" (41.2%) or "Often" (29.2%). An additional 5% reported they "always" discuss romance novels with others, 19.6% of respondents "rarely" discuss, and only 4.3% "never" discuss with others.

With 75% of romance readers discussing romances with others (sometimes, often, or always combined), clearly sociality is an important element of the romance reading experience for many. It is interesting to compare these findings to Radway's original study. Radway was surprised that the Smithton women did not know each other well or discuss books with each other. She noted, "I soon learned that the women rarely, if ever, discussed romances with more than one or two individuals. Although many commented that they talked about the books with a sister, neighbor, or with their mothers, very few did so on a regular or extended basis."[20]

Table 8.2 How often you discuss romance novels with others?

	Count	Percent
Never	13	4.3%
Rarely	59	19.6%
Sometimes	124	41.2%
Often	88	29.2%
Always	15	5.0%
N/A	2	0.7%
Total	**301**	**100%**

Table 8.3 Who do you discuss romances with most often?

	Count	Percent
My mother	5	1.7%
My daughter	0	0.0%
My sister	17	5.6%
My friend(s)	109	36.2%
Social media community	133	44.2%
Other	21	7.0%
N/A	3	1.0%
Blank – Never discuss	13	4.3%
Total	**301**	**100%**

Who do readers discuss romances with today? When write-in responses are considered, 49.8% indicated they discussed most often with friends or family compared to 44.2% who indicated they most often discussed with the social media community (see Table 8.3). If other/write-in responses are not considered, only 43.5% indicated they most often discussed with friends (36.2%) or family (1.7% mother, 5.6% sister). There are some interesting patterns to unpack here. None of the 301 participants selected the "my daughter" option for the person they discussed romance novels with most often. (Though one of the "Other" write-in responses was "husband son daughter" [sic]). This may be a function of the sample's differences in parental status and/or age compared to the Smithton women.[21] The majority of the present sample (54.5%) did not have children, compared to only 12% of readers with no children in Radway's sample.[22] Additionally, only 1% of participants (20/202) from the present sample indicated having an adult child (aged 18 or older), compared to 36% from Radway's sample.[23] Children's ages may be a factor as parents are probably more likely to discuss romance novels with adult children than they are with younger children.

Another interesting finding is that spouse, husband, partner, or boyfriend was the most common type of write-in for the "who do you discuss with" question. Of the twenty-one write-in responses, 71.4% (15/21) involved respondents' partners (spouses, husbands, boyfriends, etc.). While 15 out of the whole sample is only about 5% (15/301), it is notable that this not-uncommon response was not even an answer choice in Radway's original survey. Many of the husbands described in *Reading the Romance* were not entirely supportive of their wives' romance reading, so they do seem unlikely discussion partners.[24] Is this emblematic of a broader change in gender roles and heterosexual relationships? That is certainly possible. It is also important to keep in mind that the sample includes more than just straight women, so the "spouse, husband, partner, or boyfriend" category might well include straight women, queer men, and/or queer women as book discussion partners.

The option to discuss romance novels with the social media community is obviously a new update but one that picks up on what Radway noted was a desire to connect with others: "Through romance reading the Smithton women are providing themselves with another kind of female community capable of rendering the so desperately needed affective support. This community seems not to operate on an immediate local level although there are signs, both in Smithton and nationally, that romance readers are learning the pleasures of regular discussions of books with other women."[25] Radway describes the romance community of the 1980s as "…not an actual group functioning at a local level. Rather, it is a huge, ill-defined network composed of readers on the one hand and authors on the other. Although it performs some of the same functions carried out by older neighborhood groups, this female community is mediated by the distances of modern mass publishing."[26] Arguably, today's romance reading community is mediated through the internet, particularly social media. (See section "Changes in the Institutional Matrix and Social Context of Romance" below for more discussion of community.)

Acquiring Romance Novels

In *Reading the Romance*, participants frequented the same bookstore and received recommendations from Dot Smith. Has the internet changed how people acquire romance novels? What is the main way romance readers today obtain their books? As shown in Table 8.4, the majority (60.8%) of respondents in the current survey most often obtained their novels from "online merchants" such as Amazon or the Barnes & Noble website. Only 4% reported in-store purchases as their most frequent way of obtaining books. A sizable minority (30.2%) most frequently obtained romance novels from the library. Only two respondents from the sample (0.7%) reported obtaining the majority of their romance novels from friends and relatives.

Table 8.4 Where do you get most of the romances you read?

	Count	Percent
In-store purchase	12	4.0%
Online merchant (Amazon, Barnes & Noble, Google Books)	183	60.8%
Author website/Author Direct	0	0.0%
Library	91	30.2%
Fan fiction Website	5	1.7%
Borrow from a friend or relative	2	0.7%
Other	6	2.0%
N/A	2	0.7%
Total	**301**	**100%**

The question did ask about how books were obtained "most often," so these numbers do not capture participants who may occasionally borrow or loan books to others but do not *primarily* do so.

It is also worth noting that zero participants report obtaining their novels directly from authors or author websites. Again, since the question asked about where respondents got "most" of their romance novels, certainly some might occasionally obtain books directly via authors.

However, this poses interesting questions for thinking about community connections and whether/how author-reader relationships translate directly into sales.

How do people decide which romance novels to read? In Smithton, Dot's recommendations and word-of-mouth reviews were an important factor. In the present study, only 16.3% report reading a book because someone else recommended it, compared to the 52.5% that go by an interesting description ("blurb") or the 26.6% who typically choose a book because they have already read something the author and liked it (see Table 8.5). Of the eight "other" responses, three reported "all of the above" as common influences, refusing to specify one over the others. One person indicated they were likely to purchase if a sample of the novel was intriguing. Four people indicated they decided to read romance novels based on reviews and/or podcasts. Question phrasing asked how people "usually" decided what to read, so the data does not necessarily reflect people who occasionally decide to read a book based on a recommendation.

Table 8.5 What usually makes you decide to read a romance or not?

	Count	Percent
I like the cover.	3	1.0%
I have already read something by the author and liked it	80	26.6%
I like the title	1	0.3%
The book description (publisher's blurb or back of the book) sounds interesting	158	52.5%
Someone else recommended it to me	49	16.3%
Other	8	2.7%
N/A	2	0.7%
Total	**301**	**100%**

Entertainment Consumption Patterns

Do romance readers read books outside of the romance genre? As shown in Table 8.6, 64.1% reported reading 1-4 non-romance books per month. This is remarkably close to the 62% who reported 1-4 non-romances a month in Radway's original study.[27] Altogether, in the current survey 82.1% of participants surveyed had read one or more non-romance books each

Table 8.6 How many books other than romances do you read each month?

	Count	Percent
None	53	17.6%
1–4	193	64.1%
5–9	43	14.3%
10–14	8	2.7%
15–19	2	0.7%
20–24	0	0.0%
25 or more	1	0.3%
N/A	1	0.3%
Total	**301**	**100%**

month. Only 17.6% reported exclusively reading romance. This is significant because it refutes the stereotype of romance readers as unsophisticated "univores" who do not engage in varied cultural consumption. In sociology, the language of "univore" and "omnivore" rose to prominence in the 1990s to describe cultural consumption patterns. At the time, cultural omnivores were a new "discovery" that challenged prevailing beliefs that high status consumers exclusively consumed highbrow culture in an effort to signal their high status (for example, eschewing rock and pop music in favor of classical and opera).[28] A plethora of studies, however, have found that upper- and middle-class consumers display omnivorous taste—that is, they expressed preferences for both traditionally highbrow and lowbrow culture.[29] It was low-status consumers, not the upper class, whose preferences were distinguished by univore (unvaried) consumption patterns.[30] By showing that romance readers regularly engage with culture other than romance novels, this finding suggests that romance readers align with mainstream trends in culturally omnivorous consumption.

Changes in the Institutional Matrix and Social Context of Romance

To fully explore potential reasons for the different (or similar) reading experiences of romance readers today, we must look to the broader context and explore changes in the institutional matrix of publishing and the romance community more broadly. *Reading the Romance* provides and in-depth look at the "institutional matrix" of the publishing industry, nothing that book buying is "an event that is affected and at least partially controlled by the material nature of book publishing as a socially organized technology of production and distribution."[31] In the 1980s (and continuing until the 2000s), romance publishing was dominated by mass-market paperbacks, category series from Harlequin and Silhouette, and historicals from Avon.[32]

The traditional publishing industry was disrupted by the advent of the internet and e-book publishing, which gained mainstream traction in the early 2000s. Though this was an industry-wide development, romance readers were especially early e-book adopters.[33] For example, Harlequin was the first major publisher of any genre to make all new releases available in e-book format.[34] E-books and the internet changed the romance reading ecosystem by facilitating small independent publishers and self-published authors. This output, which did not have to go through traditional gatekeepers at the large publishing houses, often pushed the boundaries of what mainstream publishers were willing to print. Small publishers, self-published authors, and e-books all helped usher erotic romance and LGBTQ+ romance into the mainstream by demonstrating to large publishing houses that readers had an appetite for these books. E-book technology also allowed readers to bring romance novels with them everywhere discreetly.

The landscape of the romance community has changed too. When *Reading the Romance* was first published in 1984, the two main organizations with national reach (Romance Writers of America [RWA] and *Romantic Times*) were only a few years old. Radway mentions the nascent RWA in the Conclusion to *Reading the Romance*, saying "Although the movement is still small given the apparent size of the romance audience, not to mention that of the female population as a whole, it is nonetheless significant because it counteracts women's traditional isolation from one another by bringing them together over an issue that concerns them alone."[35] RWA is still an active professional organization geared toward current and aspiring writers. *Romantic Times* was a reader-oriented magazine (and later web forum) that provided reviews, feature articles, and author profiles. Both organizations flourished for nearly forty years before foundering in the late 2010s. *Romantic Times* (by then rebranded *RT Book Reviews* and only digitally published) ceased operations in 2018 when founder Kathryn Falk announced her retirement. RWA still exists but suffered losses in membership and reputation around 2019 and 2020 due to controversies over handling of diversity, equity, and inclusion issues.

RWA and *RT* were important sites of organized community for romance readers and writers. RWA has national reach and local chapters that offer regular in-person meetings.

While one had to demonstrate intent to be a professional writer to be a member of RWA, the organization not only connected writers at all stages but helped authors connect with readers through events like book signings. *RT* was a subscription publication that catered to both readers and writers. Before the internet, *RT* was the main forum for romance readers to keep up with industry news and new book releases, share ideas, and even exchange contact information to establish letter-writing correspondence.

Today, the romance community is arguably less centrally organized than it was in the 1990s or early 2000s. RWA and *RT* are no longer prominent central hubs; community interactions today are more fragmented across different podcasts, blogs, and social media networks. The romance readers in the current survey may or may not have participated in RWA or *RT* events or publications; none mention these organizations by name. However, they do point to new forums, online connections, and emphasize connections not only to romance books but to the romance *community*.

Two participants explicitly discussed the "normalization" of romance novels and indicated they are now more comfortable identifying as a romance reader than they were in the past. Both pointed to online communities (the podcast *Heaving Bosoms* and BookTok) as an important source of normalization. One put it succinctly: "I feel a part of a fantastic community of people who read romance." Several mentioned that shared interests in romance fiction helped them connect with both in person and online communities. One reader wrote, "Reading romance has lead [sic] me to read more often than I used to, and to connect with people who share the same interests (in person and on social media)." Another wrote, "I'm in a romance book club & an online romance community, so (especially during the pandemic) it's a significant part of my 'socializing.'" This is in stark contrast to the Smithton women who, besides their connections to Dot and female friends and family who read, did not speak about feeling part of a larger community.

Furthermore, one participant in the current survey shared how romance helped them explore their own identity:

> I think one of the valuable aspects of the romance genre and community is that they introduce readers to new emotional and sexual concepts in ways that feel both safe and approachable. Romance literature and the related community is how I realized that I'm asexual/aromantic.

Notably, this participant connects their realization about their asexual/aromantic identity not only to the content of romance novels but to the *community*.

Romance novels can provide a kind of indirect support by providing a sense of hope and optimism. A number of participants turned to romance novels for the guaranteed HEA as a source of optimism in an imperfect world. This was especially true for several queer readers who found comfort in romance novels. For example, one participant wrote:

> They [romance novels] allow me to step into the place of another character and out of a reality in which I often feel trapped and unhappy. I am a transmasculine

person who reads almost exclusively m/m romance, which is a pleasant escape into the mind of a (usually) cis-male protagonist who is desirable to other men, but also to a place where queerness can be normal, unremarkable, and easy. Romance is often a refuge from a world that I feel dislikes me, and that is a great comfort.

While this does not explicitly speak about community, it relates to the social nature of romance reading by juxtaposing the pleasures of reading against real world concerns. As another participant says, "Reading romance is like a safe haven for me in a sometimes difficult world."

Some readers said that romance reading shaped their outlook on the world and relations with others. For example, one participant wrote, "It has expanded my cultural knowledge and awareness, consent, body autonomy, feminine strength and celebrating differences." Another participant wrote: "I've been reading romance for over four decades now. There's no way to gauge all the ways it's impacted my psyche, but I believe it's made me strong, compassionate, empathetic and a feminist." Notably, this reader indicates belief in a cause and effect by stating that romance reading "made" her into those things. These quotes illustrate Thumala Olave's assertion that reading is profoundly social in the way it can promote ethical reflection.[36]

For other readers, romance reading did not shape their views; their views shaped their romance reading. "The material I choose to read is based on my values regarding things like diversity, what healthy relationships look like...all of these values I had before I started reading romance. This informs my reading, not the other way around." Another participant similarly stated, "I prefer reading romance novels where the characters reflect my social beliefs, and demonstrate respect for people of all identities."

Another specifically connected their political leanings into their enjoyment of romance novels: "I read romances that reflect the world around me. I want to see realistic representation of our social make-up. I want modern, progressive, left-leaning narratives and characters. I read looking for kindness and hope." This is consistent with previous research findings that romance readers often view the genre in political terms and look to romance for hope.[37]

The social context that today's readers experience is markedly different than that of the Smithton women. Much of Radway's analysis is concerned with whether romance reading upholds the patriarchy. Today, many readers in the community proudly display "Read a Romance. Fight the Patriarchy" merchandise. Whether or not reading romance inherently *does* fight the patriarchy is a separate question; the interesting fact is that contemporary readers widely think it does. For example, one reader wrote, "Romance is one of the few places where the feminine and love is centered and positive and sexuality is accepted and celebrated." This idea, arguably popularized by Jayne Anne

Krentz in the 1990s, was also frequently voiced in previous interviews with romance readers and writers.[38] Another reader emphasized how romance can portray ideal worlds: "These books are important social commentary. I can read books that show how I want society and people to be in the hopes that someday the rest of the world will catch up." Another specified, "*Independently published romance* is often one of the most socially-conscious, equitable, and creative forms of popular culture" (emphasis added).

Here we see how changes in form are related to changes in content—all the technological and social changes that have affected society at large in the last forty years have affected the romance genre.

CONCLUSION

In conclusion, romance reading is a social activity in several different ways. Just over half of participants began reading romance as preteen or teens. Though the present survey did not measure it, other research suggests that many romance readers are introduced to the genre by their mothers, grandmothers, sisters, or other women in their lives. A full three-quarters of participants in the present study discussed romance novels with other people at least some of the time. This direct interaction occurs both in person and online. Though only two participants primarily obtained romance novels by borrowing from friends or family, recommendations from others (both friends and online reviewers/blogs) were a somewhat common factor in decisions about what to read. The majority of participants also report reading books other than romance, suggesting that these readers align with mainstream "omnivorous" cultural consumption patterns. Finally, both the institutional matrix of publishing and the community context of romance have changed. Changes in both form and content have resulted in a more diverse romance landscape, and many of today's readers expressly feel part of a broader community of romance readers.

Romance reading is a social activity, even more so today than it was for the Smithton readers.

NOTES

1. Janice A. Radway, *Reading the Romance: Women, Patriarchy, and Popular Literature*, Chapel Hill: University of North Carolina Press, 1984.

2. María Angélica Thumala Olave, "Reading Matters: Towards a Cultural Sociology of Reading," *American Journal of Cultural Sociology* 6, no. 3 (2018): 417–54.

3. Wendy Griswold, "American Character and the American Novel: An Expansion of Reflection Theory in the Sociology of Literature," *American Journal of Sociology* 86, no. 4 (1981): 740–65.

4. Elizabeth Long, *Book Clubs: Women and the Uses of Reading in Everyday Life*, Chicago, Ill, ; University of Chicago Press, 2003.

5. C, Clayton Childress, and Noah E, Friedkin, "Cultural Reception and Production: The Social Construction of Meaning in Book Clubs," *American Sociological Review* 77, no. 1 (2012): 45–68.

6. See for example Mariam Frenier 1988, Tania Modleski 1984, Leslie Rabine 1988, Thurston 1987.

7. Lisa Fletcher, Beth Driscoll, and Kim Wilkins, "Genre Worlds and Popular Fiction: The Case of Twenty-First-Century Australian Romance," *The Journal of Popular Culture* 51, no. 4 (2018): 997.

8. Fletcher, Driscoll, and Wilkins, "Genre Worlds," 998.

9. Miriam Greenfeld-Benovitz, "The Interactive Romance Community: The Case of 'Covers Gone Wild,'" In *New Approaches to Popular Romance Fiction: Critical Essays*, edited by Sarah S,G, Frantz and Eric Murphy Selinger, 195–205, McFarland & Company, Inc, 2012.

10. Stephanie Lee Moody, "Affecting Genre: Women's Participation with Popular Romance Fiction," 2013 (Dissertation, University of Michigan).

11. Kim Pettigrew Brackett, "Facework Strategies among Romance Fiction Readers," *Social Science Journal* 37, no. 3 (July 2000): 347–60.

12. Jennifer Lois and Joanna Gregson, "Sneers and Leers: Romance Writers and Gendered Sexual Stigma," *Gender & Society* 29, no. 4 (2015): 459–83.

13. Catherine M. Roach, *Happily Ever After: The Romance Story in Popular Culture*, Bloomington: Indiana University Press, 2016.

14. Gayle Rubin, "Thinking Sex: Notes for a Radical Theory for the Politics of Sexuality," Reprinted in *The Lesbian and Gay Studies Reader*, ed, Henry Abelove, Routledge, 1993.

15. Anna Michelson, "Redefining the Romance: Classification and Community in a Popular Fiction Genre," 2022 (Dissertation, Northwestern University).

16. Lauren Berlant, *Cruel Optimism*, Durham, N,C: Duke University Press, 2011.

17. Sara Ahmed, *The Promise of Happiness*, Durham, NC: Duke University Press, 2010.

18. Anna Michelson, "The Politics of Happily-Ever-after: Romance Genre Fiction as Aesthetic Public Sphere," *American Journal of Cultural Sociology* 9, no. 2 (June 1, 2021): 177–210.

19. Radway, *Reading the Romance*, 56.

20. Note: for the parental status question n=202.

21. Michelson, *Redefining the Romance*.

22. Radway, *Reading the Romance*, 96.

23. Radway, *Reading the Romance*, 103.

24. Radway, *Reading the Romance*, 96.

25. Radway, *Reading the Romance*, 97.

26. Radway, *Reading the Romance*, 60.

27. Richard A, Peterson and Roger M, Kern, "Changing Highbrow Taste: From Snob to Omnivore," *American Sociological Review* 61, no. 5 (1996): 900–907.
28. Jordi López-Sintas and Tally Katz-Gerro, "From Exclusive to Inclusive Elitists and Further: Twenty Years of Omnivorousness and Cultural Diversity in Arts Participation in the USA," *Poetics*, 33, no. 5 (2005): 299–319
29. Bethany Bryson, "What about the Univores? Musical Dislikes and Group-Based Identity Construction among Americans with Low Levels of Education," *Poetics*, 25, no. 2 (1997): 141–56.
30. Radway, *Reading the Romance*, 20.
31. John Markert, *Publishing Romance: The History of an Industry, 1940s to the Present*, McFarland and Company, 2016.
32. Markert, *Publishing Romance*.
33. RWR News; Castell, "Up Close and Personal."
34. Radway, *Reading the Romance*, 219.
35. Thumala Olave, "Reading Matters."
36. Michelson, "The Politics of Happily Ever After."
37. Jayne Anne Krentz, "Why Romance?" *Romantic Times*, no #72 (1990): 12–15; see also Michelson 2021 "The Politics of Happily-Ever-After."
38. Michelson, *Redefining the Romance*.

Chapter 9

Escaping the Negativity of "Escapism"

Rethinking Romance Reader Notions of Why They Read

Andrea Barra

When presented with the term escapism, most people think of leisure or habits that allow them to remove themselves from the "real world." These diversions are considered a relief from everyday problems, stresses, or conditions with which the person is unhappy. Scholars have generally labeled escapist activities as compensating for situations or emotions that are missing from the person's life, or they have seen popular culture specifically as a distraction from engaging in serious work or contemplation about the world's *real* problems. While these interpretations may be partially correct, readers of romance novels help us to see that the concepts of escape and escapism can be more complicated than this. Romance readers generally use these terms in a positive way, seeing the hobby as one that helps to generate optimistic feelings and refresh them rather than disengage them from reality. They see this escape as both self-care and the guaranteed ability to experience an emotional journey with a happy ending.

Using responses to the survey conducted for this volume (both quantitative and qualitative) and over thirty in-depth interviews with romance readers,[1] we can begin to expand our definitions of escape and escapism. Compared with Janice Radway's interpretations of her subjects' explanations of what escape meant to them,[2] today's readers feel quite differently about how romance reading is an escapist pastime. Many factors contribute to this change, including demographic shifts, more mainstream acceptance of the benefits of leisure as self-care, and less embarrassment on the part of romance readers for their hobby.

ESCAPE IN RADWAY'S STUDY

Radway's analysis in *Reading the Romance* that is most relevant to this chapter concerns the reasons why the Smithton women enjoy reading romance novels to the extent they do. She emphasizes the issue of escapism as the primary reason for indulging in this type of reading.

> In attending to the women's comments about the worth of romance reading, I was particularly struck by the fact that they tended to use the word escape in *two distinct ways*. On the one hand, they used the term literally to describe *the act of denying the present*, which they believe they accomplish each time they begin to read a book and are drawn into its story. On the other hand, they use the word in a more figurative fashion to give substance to the somewhat vague but nonetheless intense sense of relief they experience by *identifying with a heroine whose life does not resemble their own* in certain crucial aspects.[3]

The first use of the word is escape is the literal or physical escape that the women experienced during the act of reading romance. The choice to eschew duties (completed or not) in the home in order to pick up a book and read was the actual "escape" experienced by the women. When the kids were taking a nap or after the dishes had been put away, it was acceptable for a woman to take time for herself and indulge in reading a romance novel.

The Smithton women feel that not only are they being taken away from their daily routines, but they are also specifically gaining time and privacy for themselves. "Romantic escape is therefore, a temporary but literal denial of the demands women recognize as an integral part of their roles as nurturing wives and mothers."[4] They justify this time "away" by emphasizing the instrumental value of reading as a learning experience, providing information about histories and cultures that are not their own and fighting against the notion of romance as a guilty pleasure or simply insubstantial love stories.

The other way that Radway uses the term escape is to discuss the Smithton women's desire to identify with the main character (presumably the heroine) of the novel. This supposed desire to "be" the heroine has given credibility to the notion that romance readers are experiencing dissatisfaction with their own lives and romantic situations and exorcising it through the act of getting lost in a novel and being a woman who is on a great journey. "[T]hey escape figuratively into a fairy tale where a heroine's similar needs are adequately met. As a result, they vicariously attend to their own requirements as independent individuals who require emotional sustenance and solicitude."[5] Romance, the argument goes, is compensating for the lack of care and nurturing they experience in real life. This argument is compounded by Radway's emphasis on how guilty the women felt about the time, money, and energy they were "wasting" on reading romance.

ESCAPE IN CULTURE

The concept of escape and escapism is threaded throughout the history of popular culture and media studies. Prevailing opinions on the subject are generally negative, emphasizing ideas such as compensation, hedonism, narcissism, passivity, and anxiety. Most research sees escape as negative and compensatory, indicating that we use popular culture to avoid, change, or imagine away parts of our own lives that are negative or unsatisfactory. While there are many definitions of the term escapism, Bolus offers the most succinct (and, I believe, the most popularly understood) one: "the idea that the experience will allow the spectator to "escape" from the pressures and stress of their everyday routines by entering a self-contained, manufactured world that offers respite, if only temporarily."[6]

There are "three views of escape—as an irresponsible excuse to avoid accountability, as an understandable response to society's demand for an overgrown self, and as a temporary and ultimately fallible attempt to evade paramount reality."[7] In this view, our desire to use popular culture to "escape" is to avoid reality and to consciously un-inhabit our own selves for a period of time. It also means, as Radway indicates, that we shun our own obligations and responsibilities for the "better" world we are going to. Escapism is seen then as childlike and immature, with the person who values it not being engaged fully in the real, serious world.

Yi-Fu Tuan, in one of the only full treatments of the concept of escapism, agrees that the social view of escape is not a positive one.[8] As a geographer, he is especially concerned about the spatial and temporal issues surrounding escape. But he also argues that imagination and fantasy are extremely positive aspects of our ability to escape: "Of course, all fairy tales are fantasies; they are alternative worlds, not pictures of the familiar one. And they do offer temporary escape from the dreary reality of daily living. Why not? Escape from one kind of reality may be the only means of making contact with reality of another kind."[9] Denying our imaginations also denies us the possibility of seeing the world in another way, of attempting to create a better society because we've seen it in fiction and dreamed it into being.

Adorno, though not talking specifically about escapism, creates the argument of the "culture industry" which implies an "opiate of the masses" approach to all cultural objects, especially mass-produced ones.[10] Any use of media, then, could be considered escapist in a negative way because it does not challenge the status quo (especially economically) and compensates for real social engagement. In revisiting Adorno's culture industry theory, Gunster argues that mass culture, especially something like romance novels, does exactly what it's supposed to: "Mass culture is filled with objects, events, and practices that are intentionally designed to solicit, accommodate, and attract the fantasies of its consumers. More than any other set of commodities, cultural objects must be ingratiated into the affective and libidinal patterns of their buyers."[11] In other words, the good feelings that popular culture imbues in us simply exist to make us buy more popular culture.

Remarking on definitions of escape in the same year as Adorno, Heilman concurs that it has been accepted as an illegitimate way of dealing with the world—branding the person as dealing in lies and fantasies.[12] He attributes this common understanding of escape to our Puritan heritage that disparages any leisure that takes us away from work. Katz and Foulkes offer a slightly more sympathetic treatment because they believe escape can serve a function for our social roles (either to reinforce or to change them).[13] They also distinguish between spatial/temporal escape (the literal use of media to distance oneself from the rest of the world, like the act of reading or going to the movies) and symbolic escape ("identifying with a star or hero to the point that one loses oneself in a dream which cannot possibly have any feedback to real life").[14]

Hirschman emphasizes the link to anxiety and social dislocation.[15] Those who engage in escapism are those who recognize that their values do not conform to the general population.

Bar-Haim agrees with Hirschman but takes the analysis one step further by attempting to illuminate the link between ideology and popular culture.[16] He sees pop culture as arising in response to ideology (be it religion, capitalism, or politics) and so it expresses our discontent with the ideology. This can, in turn, change the ideology. He sees escapism as the negative part of this process, though never explicitly spells it out—either escape into popular culture is a disengagement with social change or it is an expression of our conscious or unconscious revolt against the ideological system.[17]

Gelder distinguishes between escapism and engagement in reading habits, saying that those who read popular fiction escape the world (it allows us not to be ourselves for a period of time) whereas those who read "literature" engage with the world (it transforms us).[18] He also implies that as readers we believe in or actively inhabit the fantasy that we've escaped to.

Broader discussions of the use of fiction, however, lead us in several directions. Is it merely to entertain and lead us to worlds that are unlike our own? Is it to be perfectly realistic and to fulfill an important function in society? Is some fiction "better" than other fiction in the ways it teaches us about the world? Most would agree that which we consider to be "literature" or even merely good fiction is, at its essence, meant to divert and to evoke a certain set of emotions from the reader. Formula in genre fiction does not diminish its value as amusement and satisfaction; in fact, it may increase it for many readers: "Each James Bond (or Nero Wolfe, or Agatha Christie) novel modulates the basic formula that defines its class, and the reader enters the novel knowing the rules and anticipating a 'good read' within their limits. . . . Readers vote for popular formulas with their money as well as their mouths."[19]

A romance reader might look for a relationship's happy ending, a mystery reader might look for the satisfaction that justice will be served, and a science fiction reader might look for the triumph of defeating an external evil. These are different emotional satisfactions to be sure but fulfill an emotional need in the reader or serve as a distraction during particular global or macro situations.[20] The conventions of genre fiction are decoded only by a savvy reader who understands and appreciates the importance of the formula.[21]

In framing a sociology of reading, Thumala Olave has given the best understanding of the relationship between fiction and escape.[22] It is worth quoting in full here, as it connects directly to the overall argument made below:

> Reading is certainly used to "escape" to alternative, fictional scenarios, as a means to relax and to have fun. However, it is also clear that enchantment does not entail escapism, understood as alienation, false consciousness, or disempowerment. What the data show is that reading and its pleasures help manage physical and emotional pain, understand the self and others, and engage with the world. Rather than an escape from life, reading fiction is a support to it.[23]

What Thumala Olave is rightly pointing out here is that the older ideas of escapism are not precisely how the term is understood in more popular conversation. As will be seen below, the idea of escape is generally believed to be universally understood—so much so that subjects do not feel the need to define or expand upon it. And what they believe about the term is in line with how she explains it here. Academic insistence on the concept belying negative connotations about actions that are compensatory, immature, or fantastical is out of step with the much more neutral (or even positive) ways people speak about what it means to escape through popular culture.

ESCAPE IN ROMANTIC MEDIA

Since Radway, there have been a variety of discussions of escape in romance novels and adjacent types of romantic (or "women's") media. Owen believes that the escapist fantasies of romance appeal to women because of the certainty of economic success that the stories tend to emphasize.[24] This is premised on her notion that heroines always improve their class or social status via the relationship with the hero. This is a fairly astute interpretation; the number of novels that include secretary/billionaire, nurse/doctor, and governess/duke pairings are somewhat overwhelming. Dyhouse agrees that there is a continued appeal of the alpha hero, which includes material success and power as well as a larger-than-life personality.[25] This fantasy of being taken care of and not having to worry about money can certainly be categorized as escapist, especially when heroines begin in precarious monetary situations. Whether or not this makes romance readers numbed to real fights for economic justice, however, is debatable—more likely it could be argued that it reinforces women's understanding of their own economic precarity.

Slightly more sympathetic treatments of escape in romance come from Fowler and Thurston.[26] Fowler argues that romance presents escapist fantasies through the portrayal of positive sexual pleasures, fantasies of power and plenty (materially, like Owen), and distance from the negativities of the real world. Thurston does not necessarily see escape as negative, but she, like Radway, is explicit about its purposes: "Women use romances for escape—to another time or new experience and from the constant demands being made on their time, attention, and energy."[27]

Though escape is not the focus of the study as a whole, Ang's famous 1982 book *Watching Dallas* discusses why people enjoy primetime soap operas. "The term [escapism] is misleading, because it presupposes a strict division between reality and fantasy, between 'sense of reality' and 'flight from reality'. But is it not rather the case that there is an interaction between the two?"[28] Escape is an interplay between fiction and reality to her because it is not either identification or distancing, but a bit of both.

While speaking of romantic comedy movies and their supposed "danger" to women, Guilluy extensively reviews both popular and academic treatments of this parallel women's genre.[29] Escape, to many of her self-proclaimed feminist subjects, is a moment to stop critiquing everything in the world around them and just enjoy something. She also notes an ambivalence "between an escapist, but potentially normative viewing pleasure and a deliberate awareness of the fallacy of the world constructed by the film text."[30] In other words, they know this is not the "real world," but it does not diminish the enjoyment they find in the consumption of the media. Idealism and realism can and do co-exist for consumers of romantic media.[31]

REASONS FOR READING ROMANCE

Data from the survey conducted for this volume gives us insight into current readers' stated reasons for their enjoyment of romance novels. The survey asked respondents to choose their top three reasons from a list of seven possibilities. Of the seven reasons (not including write-in "other" answers), the percentages are seen below in Table 1.

We see that the act of reading romance is mostly prized for its leisure connotations, that is the pleasure of a relaxing hobby (63.8%) and the ability to take time for oneself doing something enjoyable (59.5%). I would speculate that most genre readers of any type would answer in a similar manner. What becomes more relevant to romance reading—and a comparative to Radway's analysis—are the remaining five answers. The next two highest responses are a desire to escape daily problems and to experience faraway places, different times, or experiences different than their own (43.8% respectively). This is followed by the notion that romantic stories are never sad or depressing (39.4%); enjoyment in reading about strong, interesting heroines (20.6%); and wishing for a romance like the heroine's (14.6%).

I was interested in discovering whether reasons for reading would vary among the multiple demographic characteristics of the respondents. Radway's subjects in 1984 did not differ significantly in their demographic profiles. As mostly young, white, high school educated mothers, they represented the generally understood stereotype of the romance reader in the early 1980s. It is unclear whether or not this was a proper representation of that reader, however they were certainly the readers to whom marketing was focused. We know that today's romance readers are a far more diverse group across all demographic characteristics than the assumed reader of the early 1980s.[32] For that reason, being able to link demographics to specific reasons for reading was an advantage of this particular survey.

The data set is not entirely complete, as discussed in the introduction, so I used only categories that were present in both survey distribution cycles. As seen below in Table 2, I focused on age, relationship status (single for any reason versus in a relationship of any kind), parenthood status, income, and highest level of education attained. While these may not represent the

150 Andrea Barra

full population of romance readers (education and income are relatively high overall), they are at least a broader group than Radway's Smithton women.

Table 3 below uses the combined percentages of all top three answers, no matter what the respondent ranked them. Interestingly, when breaking these responses down by demographic categories, very little variety exists. With the exception of one category (income less than $40,000), all age, relationship, parenthood, income, and education subsets had the highest percentages for relaxation and reading as "me time." On the lower end of the responses, in relation to the reasons relating to heroines, the only notable differences are that younger people (age 18–34) and single people were more likely to respond that they were interested in a romance like the heroine's. This is not terribly remarkable as there is likely a significant overlap in these categories. There are no particularly noticeable trends in how different demographics answered these questions at all.

This (lack of) trend stayed similar when I looked at the identified reason for reading ranked number one in each category (Table 4). While there are a few more outliers in this table (21% of those in the $40,000–69,999 income bracket enjoy romances because they aren't sad; 23% of those who have less

Table 9.1 Reasons for Reading by Preference Order

	Relaxation	Reading is for Me	Escape Daily Problems	Faraway Places	Not Sad	Strong Heroines	Romance Like Heroine
First reason	25.5%	19.7%	16.8%	10.6%	14.6%	3.7%	5.5%
Second reason	22.6%	22.6%	13.9%	13.9%	10.6%	11.3%	4.4%
Third reason	15.7%	17.2%	13.1%	19.3%	14.2%	5.6%	4.7%
Total	63.8%	59.5%	43.8%	43.8%	39.4%	20.6%	14.6%

Table 9.2 Survey Demographics

Age		Relationship Status		Children		Income		Education	
18–34	34.2%	Single (all)	35.6%	Yes	45.0%	Less than $40k	17.4%	Up to college (all)	15.3%
35–44	36.6%	In a relationship (all)	64.4%	No	55.0%	$40–69,999k	21.5%	Four Year Degree	27.2%
45+	29.2%					$70–99,999k	17.4%	Master's	45.1%
						$100–150k	19.5%	Doctorate	12.4%
						More than $150k	24.1%		

than a four-year education want to escape their daily problems), the top two reasons remain consistent across the board. It might seem as though varying demographic categories might lean more heavily toward some reasons than others—for instance, we might expect that those who make over $150,000 in income would be less concerned with escaping their daily problems. Those who are single indicated more of a tendency toward looking for a romance like the heroine's but not in overwhelming numbers (only 13% chose it as their number one reason). While some of these did bear out in smaller ways (i.e., those with children were very unlikely to choose a romance like the heroine's), others showed up in what felt like opposite ways (i.e., a full 21% of those making between $100,000 and $150,000 chose "escape daily problems" as their number one reason). The lack of significance in any of these demographic category breakdowns may demonstrate that reasons for reading romance for even current readers are more universal than previously (or popularly) thought.

These data then lead us to consider how today's readers are similar or different from the original study forty years ago. If relaxation and simple enjoyment reasons are so important to today's readers, why was this not the case in the early 1980s? Radway doesn't ignore relaxation, but it is a point made and quickly passed: "Relaxation implies a reduction in the state of tension produced by prior conditions, whereas escape obviously suggests flight from one state of being to another more desirable one."[33] Notable in this quotation is her use of the word "obviously," implying that her definition of escape was universally understood. Radway was certainly much more concerned about the concept of escapism and how romance novels were acting as compensatory reading for emotional gratification and mental stimulation. She also briefly touches on what we would today call "self-care"—a highly touted and accepted concept that usually connotes doing enjoyable or relaxing activities to recover from stress. She interprets her subjects' conversations as indicating that romance reading is "a special gift a woman gives herself."[34] While this "special gift" takes on a feeling of guilt or anxiety for the Smithton women, today's readers appear to be generally immune from that implication.

It is hard to get at the nuance of those ideas via a quantitative question so the qualitative responses, as well as interview data will be discussed in more detail in the sections below.

Suffice it to say, relaxation is clearly a vital reason for current romance readers to engage in this particular hobby. This corresponds with Thumala Olave's research on reading fiction when she notes "the search for relaxation and the comfort of companionship that is observed in the data cannot be fully understood as "escapism."[35] Escape, while not insignificant, is perhaps more complicated than can be captured in a Likert scale.

Radway was also convinced that readers strongly identified with the heroine of the novel and that heroine's journey and eventual happily ever after. As we can see from the survey responses, this identification is not seen as significant to today's readers. Fewer than 10% of respondents indicated either heroine-related response as the number one reason that they read romance. An obvious departure from Radway's time to point out here is that more and more readers are exploring queer romance which may feature more than one heroine or may not feature a heroine at all, making identification a more complicated issue.

But even in the more traditional romances, heroine identification can be tricky. Radway was mostly interviewing women of a particular demographic—one that, at least superficially, was reflected in the books they were reading in terms of age, sexuality, race, and relative class position. While many of these demographics may not have changed in the books as significantly as we'd like, the readers themselves have departed from Radway's subjects' characteristics and what has come to be seen as the "stereotypical" romance reader (young, white, married with young children, middle class homemaker or pink-collar worker).

ESCAPE FOR ROMANCE READERS

What does escape or escapism mean for today's romance readers? The explicit concept of escape was discussed by twenty-one survey respondents in their qualitative answers and by seventeen interview subjects. Many assumed that their definition of escape did not need explanation ("I have found them a wonderful escape"; "It's a good way for me to escape"). Others were more descriptive about what exactly escape, or escapism meant to them, and it is from these that I find a few general trends: escaping with romance means the production of general good feelings, escape into the emotional journey of the characters is paramount, and reading romance is a form of self-care, which feels like an escape from everyday stresses and difficulties.

In Radway's original study, she notes that "romance reading seems to be valued primarily because it provides an occasion for them to experience good feelings. . . . Romance reading provides a vicarious experience of emotional nurturance and [sic] erotic anticipation and excitation."[36] This notion absolutely shows up in today's readers' discussion of why they read, but in a different way than Radway emphasizes. Rather than emotional nurturance and erotic anticipation (not that those aren't important!), there is much more emphasis on the overall happiness that one is left with when reading romance. This is

Escaping the Negativity of "Escapism" 153

Table 9.3 Top Three Reasons (Combined) for Reading Romance by Demographic Categories

	Relaxation	Reading is for me	Escape Daily Problems	Faraway Places	Not Sad	Strong Heroines	Romance Like Heroine
Age							
18–34	52%	58%	48%	48%	35%	23%	25%
35–44	62%	66%	42%	35%	42%	22%	12%
45+	66%	58%	37%	51%	41%	22%	10%
Relationship							
Single (all)	53%	64%	38%	51%	40%	24%	28%
In a relationship (all)	64%	64%	45%	41%	46%	22%	10%
Children							
Yes	62%	68%	42%	57%	43%	17%	9%
No	59%	54%	39%	45%	35%	27%	18%
Income							
Less than $40k	53%	53%	56%	47%	27%	27%	21%
$40–69,999k	62%	43%	40%	43%	52%	14%	24%
$70–99,999k	56%	68%	32%	44%	44%	26%	9%
$100–150k	61%	79%	45%	34%	26%	26%	11%
More than $150k	66%	60%	32%	51%	45%	17%	15%
Education							
Up to college (all)	55%	65%	58%	52%	23%	19%	23%
Four Year Degree	66%	64%	49%	40%	44%	9%	18%
Master's	60%	58%	35%	43%	44%	31%	13%
Doctorate	56%	60%	36%	48%	28%	24%	12%

Table 9.4 Number One Reason for Reading Romance by Demographic Categories

	Relaxation	Reading is for me	Escape Daily Problems	Faraway Places	Not Sad	Strong Heroines	Romance Like Heroine
Age							
18–34	23%	16%	15%	7%	17%	4%	13%
35–44	27%	24%	16%	7%	15%	3%	4%
45+	19%	22%	22%	12%	10%	7%	3%
Relationship							
Single (all)	25%	14%	14%	8%	18%	4%	13%
In a relationship (all)	22%	25%	18%	8%	12%	5%	4%
Children							
Yes	21%	24%	20%	10%	13%	3%	1%
No	25%	18%	14%	7%	15%	5%	12%
Income							
Less than $40k	12%	18%	24%	12%	15%	6%	9%
$40–69,999k	29%	14%	17%	7%	21%	0%	7%
$70–99,999k	18%	29%	18%	9%	12%	9%	3%
$100–150k	21%	29%	21%	11%	8%	5%	3%
More than $150k	32%	15%	13%	4%	15%	4%	11%
Education							
Up to college (all)	13%	32%	23%	6%	6%	10%	10%
Four Year Degree	31%	13%	18%	5%	15%	4%	9%
Master's	20%	19%	18%	12%	19%	4%	4%
Doctorate	32%	32%	8%	4%	8%	0%	8%

connected to the heavy reliance on the happy ever after, which was an explicit reason mentioned by eighteen survey respondents and seventeen interview subjects. Discussing this necessity, Catherine Roach recalls, "Almost universally, authors with whom I talked view the ending as a contract they have with their readers: No matter how wounded the characters are at a book's beginning and how further tortured these characters are by plot conflicts in a book's middle, all will be well by the end."[37]

I believe, however, that the emotional expectation goes beyond just these good or happy feelings generated by the happily ever after. This part of the experience is absolutely mandatory, but it does not encompass the entirety of the emotional journey. If only the ending was important, every reader would be satisfied with every romance novel as the HEA (happy ever after) or HFN (happy for now) is all but guaranteed in today's books.

> Yes, the end result is always the same, as my daughter likes to point out, but it's the journey and the people who make each romance novel unique. (Interview subject P.K.).
>
> That they're all the same. That they're all formulas. That because they're all happily ever afters, everyone knows how it's gonna end. Well, I don't care. A murder mystery, you know someone's going to solve the crime. It's the same thing. (Interview subject R.P.)

Readers want the complete emotional arc with all its ups and downs – from meeting to falling in love to conflict to resolution to declaration of love to, finally, happily ever after. This journey is the emotional experience that readers are seeking. While the enjoyment of the particular shape of the journey varies from reader to reader, each seeks the rollercoaster of emotions that they most prefer.

> I like the way romance makes me feel. It reminds me of that magical "falling in love" time period. (Survey respondent)
>
> So a woman who is happily married does not want to find a new husband. But she does want to revisit the sizzle. Romance is all about that. Remembering that falling in love feeling without risking everything you hold most dear. The long-term relationship, then the friendship, and the deep emotional connection. (Interview subject M.P.)
>
> I read it to enjoy it, experience the journey to love with the characters, to relax and get whisked away elsewhere. (Survey respondent)

If any portion of this emotional process is incomplete or unfulfilling or unrealistic (however defined), the reader is going to leave the book unsatisfied even with a supposed happy ending. The guarantee of the couple ending up together (either for now or forever), the understanding of the romance formula, is what allows the reader to be certain they will have the experience they are looking for. Because there will be no surprise death of a main character or surprise plot twist that will permanently part the couple, a reader is free to experience the ups and downs of the relationship, always secure in the happy ending. Again, this does not mean that every book is going to satisfy every reader, but romance readers are especially adept at finding stories that will get them there (evidenced by the increasing number of romance novels that advertise by tropes so specific as to nearly give away the entire story).

> [R]eading romance feels safe. I know that it will have a satisfying ending. (Survey respondent)
>
> I like the happy ever after. . . . I like the emotional buildup. A good romance novel has that arc. . . . Primarily I'm looking for an emotionally satisfying read. . . If I'm looking for something to affect the way I feel, I read romance. (Interview subject L.K.)
>
> I love seeing characters interact and how they can all fit together in a multitude of ways. Yes, I might know that the end of the romance is a happy one, but I like seeing how that happens! Romance is a genre that focuses on the emotional journey between characters, and that's what I want to experience! (Survey respondent)
>
> You know how it's going to turn out. You don't have to worry that everybody is going to die at the end. . . . It's one of the most basic stories. . . . You know how it's going to turn out, so you have the leisure to explore the settings. You're more focused on the journey than the ending. (Interview subject V.J.)

It is in this way that the true escape happens for the reader, what I term "emotional escapism." Life has no guarantees. A romance novel does. "[It] lets readers experience and express intense emotions unashamedly, granting temporary release from the emotional limits of everyday life."[38]

> Romance has given me a safe space to feel things knowing that everything will be okay in the end. (Survey respondent)
>
> Because since I know a romance will always have a happy ending, I can experience more angst or fear or negativity as part of the plot without the anxiety that something is going to go terribly irrevocably wrong the characters. (Survey respondent)
>
> When I'm reading contemporary when you have a current topic like that, it kinda brings you into the real world and you have no control of the real world . . .

at least in the book. . . . That's kind of a nice feeling because you know in real life it doesn't always work that way. (Interview subject P.M.)

Romance novels are a sure bet that things will work out and be a happy ending in a world where nothing feels like a sure bet. (Survey respondent)

Fekete also found this with her romance readers, noting that "romance novels are valued for their guarantee of enjoyment. Respondents described their books as providing an optimal ratio of predictability and freshness."[39] This perfectly underscores what the appeal is to many dedicated readers. The formula is the hook, the happy ever after is the contract, and the emotional journey is the satisfaction.

In both the qualitative survey responses and the interviews, there is not always a clear distinction between this emotional escapism and general good feelings produced by reading romance, which tended to fall into the self-care category of reason. "Reading romance is similar to watching your favorite rom com, or sitcom on TV. It's familiar, it's a warm, safe place that takes you on a rollercoaster for fun with an emotionally satisfying ending" (survey respondent).

Thirty-one survey respondents discussed overall positive feelings and self-care as reasons for reading romance. Sometimes this was general happiness ("Because a well written love story makes me feel happy and hopeful, and appreciative of the love I see in the relationships around me in real life"; "Mostly, they give me hope and a positive outlook for me [sic] day. They make me happy") or as a way to improve their emotional state ("I think reading romances is a way to boost your mood and mental health. When I started reading more it really helped me with my depression."; "It's gotten me through some tough times in life"). This corresponds with Span's research on readers of "chick lit." She says "My participants, too, reported specific reading practices when sick, to relax after an exhausting day or to complement a particular mood. They would seek a comfort in these situations and consciously choose books from one subgenre or reread individual texts."[40]

This is not to deny that escape from the world is still a desire expressed by respondents, but not precisely in the same way that Radway defined it in the early 1980s. The notion of guilt involved in reading or needing to provide a justification for their reading was absent from both survey respondents' and interview subjects' comments about why and how they read. While using the words "escape" or "escapism" may imply wanting to distance oneself from areas of life where one is unsatisfied, this was not often explicitly stated in either qualitative comments or interviews. This is an element of the problem in using these terms without being able to understand exactly how subjects understand them.

Respondents generally indicated that what they needed escape from was not their own personal relationships and circumstances, but from problems going on in the world. This corresponds with what Fowler (1991) also found in her interviews with readers: "A typical negative reply stated a reluctance to read a novel for 'what you can find in the newspapers' or a more deep-rooted aversion to representations of conflict or alienation."[41] As a survey respondent put it, "the world is very rough, my job deals with world affairs and I constantly have to face the struggles of it all, so having an escape is good."

Both interview subjects and survey respondents expressed some type of desire to not engage with the world for a little while, or to say that real life is often depressing but romance novels are not. Interview subject L.W. said, "I like getting lost in a book, I like books that are uplifting and have happy endings because there is so much unhappiness in the world and I get enough of that reading the newspaper and watching the news. I don't want it in my books. I read for escape." The desired good feelings were often explicit, such as this survey respondent who wrote, "[R]omance is my "convalescent" literature—it's what I read when I'm too tired or stressed to read something that requires more work or might upset me." Several indicated that romance novels had assisted through trying circumstances in their lives, but that type of escape was often instrumental and could have been fulfilled by a multitude of different hobbies. "And those books really, really helped me get through hard times. One time . . . I had a child in the hospital and dying. My child was very, very ill and I sat there reading. . . . And those books got me through it" (Interview subject C.F.). A survey respondent said, "I'm currently going through a heavy family event, and I picked up an old favorite romance book because I knew I could find comfort in the pages."

Likely the same can be said for all genres of fiction. The formula of genre fiction leads to a natural emotional arc. For example, in a mystery or crime novel, there is a criminal event (sadness or anger), attempts to solve the crime (suspense or anxiety), a threat to the main character(s) (fear), and, finally, the perpetrator will be captured and/or punished (relief, happiness, or satisfaction). Though "formula" seems to be a word worthy of derision in the world of fiction, readers understand and appreciate it for the guarantee of an experience that they are looking for. A well-defined genre "comes to the reader with a host of structural predictions, forward memory—anticipation based on past acquaintance with the genre—must work strongly."[42] The romance formula works strongly for readers, not because of any surprise about the main characters' relationship, but because of the emotional experiences it takes to get to a satisfying ending.

As a contrast to Radway's original formulation of the function of escape, it is also necessary to point out that only eight survey respondents discussed heroines in a way that even indicates identification as an important reason for reading. More interview subjects dove into the idea of heroines but that was because it was a question specifically asked in the interview protocol. Even with prompting about heroines, however, interviewees were not likely to indicate that they *identified* with the heroine in any way, though a few did discuss it.

> The readers tend to like the people that they can identify with and they don't always identify with the best of the best of the best because that's not who the regular people are. (Interview subject S.H.)

> When I pick up a book and it's a widow or hero widow, I want to root for that heroine. You know what she's been through and you want her to have her happily ever after. (Interview subject P.M.)

They could articulate which characteristics in a heroine they appreciated or didn't (the idea of TSTL, or "too stupid to live," came up frequently) but it was rare to hear anyone talk about identification per se. Most discussed taking the journey with both characters (dual point of view in romance is a common way of storytelling), enjoyment in watching them grow, and satisfaction about their happy ending.

> So, I like to have women dominating if I can. Not necessarily physically . . . I like to have them finding themselves, finding their sexuality, finding new ways of expressing themselves, new ways of fantasizing, new ways of expression. (Interview subject V. J.)

> It is always aspirational, the heroine should be a little bit better than me but morally achievable so it feels both deserving and attainable in the best stories. It's important to have elements of personal growth and sacrifice or compromise on each character's behalf so their ending feels well-earned and you don't resent the characters. (Survey respondent)

> Romances often focus on the characters and their interaction, and I enjoy reading character-driven stories, where the protagonists grow at the same time as they fall in love. (Survey respondent)

Some respondents did express the desire for a relationship like the characters in romance novels. Again, this was not very common, especially as many were currently in relationships at the time of answering. They were more likely to comment as some above did about wanting to relive the experience of falling in love because they knew they would not do it again in real life. If there was dissatisfaction in their real-life relationships, they did not express it in interviews or the qualitative survey answers. Those not in relationships were more likely to discuss the desire to be partnered but generally not in explicit terms.

> Romance novels are fun to read, but they make me wish I had a partner. (Survey respondent)

> I yearn to be treated like a romance heroine, but realize the reality that these stories are wish fulfillment. (Survey respondent)

> I think when I was younger, I read it for different reasons—to experience romance on some level, to be wistful and to fantasize about what my own love experience might be like. (Survey respondent)

Though speaking more generally (ostensibly not about herself), one interview subject talked in depth about why she believed women were really so attached to romance novels:

> I think it's every girl's fantasy. And I don't think that's changed. I don't care who you are or what kind of career woman you are. In the back of every woman's mind is I want to meet Mr. Right and I want him to love me, and I want to love him and have this great life together. I don't care who you are. Every woman wants that. Every woman wants a different kind of man but at the base of it, every woman wants to find the perfect person for us who we're going to be able to grow old with and be loved. That's really the fantasy. (Interview subject R. P.)

This idea may harken back to stereotypes about romance readers who are obsessed with the fantasy of a perfect partner, but in a way, it was actually a brave response on her part when most readers were (and still are to some extent) extremely defensive about their reasons for enjoying romance. The "fantasy" (which may be a misnomer) of finding someone to love and care for us—or the desire to relive that feeing—is obviously still a strong motivation in the consumption of romantic media whether it's said out loud or not.

CONCLUSION

The ways in which romance readers discuss notions of escape and escapism have evolved over the forty years since *Reading the Romance* was published. This corresponds with the many changes in the romance industry during the same time, including book content, publishing innovations, and reader demographics. The need for readers to escape home and family obligations or feeling guilt and shame over taking time and money for their own happiness was absent from current readers' discussions of their own reading habits. Also absent was Radway's assertion that heroine identification was a strong aspect of the escape appeal. Instead, today's readers escape via notions of self-care, the satisfying emotional journey, and the happily ever after guarantee.

There is more work to be done to fully understand the myriad ways that the terms escape and escapism are used by people in relation to their hobbies and leisure activities. While romance readers are prone to see them in a more positive light, this might not be the same for gamers or sports enthusiasts or TikTokers or even other types of readers. Radway's innovation of in-depth audience study is invaluable to understanding how we navigate, interpret, and make meaning out of the ever-changing landscapes of media and popular culture.

NOTES

1. Andrea Barra, *Beyond the Bodice Ripper: Innovation and Change in the Romance Novel Industry*, PhD diss., Rutgers, The State University of New Jersey, 2014.

2. Janice A. Radway, *Reading the Romance: Women, Patriarchy, and Popular Literature* (Chapel Hill: University of North Carolina Press, 1984; rev. ed. 1991).

3. Radway, *Reading the Romance*, 90, emphasis mine.

4. Radway, *Reading the Romance*, 97.

5. Radway, *Reading the Romance*, 93.

6. Michael Peter Bolus, *Aesthetics and the Cinematic Narrative: An Introduction* (New York: Anthem Press, 2019), 120.

7. Heidi Slettedahl Macpherson, *Women's Movement: Escape as Transgression in North American Feminist Fiction*, Atlanta: Editions Rodophi B.V., 2000: 19

8. Yi-Fu Tuan, *Escapism* (Baltimore: The Johns Hopkins University Press, 1998).

9. Yi-Fu Tuan, *Escapism*, 148.

10. Theodor W. Adorno, "Culture Industry Reconsidered." *New German Critique* 6 (Autumn 1975): 12–19.

11. Shane Gunster, "Revisiting the Culture Industry Thesis: Mass Culture and the Commodity Form." *Cultural Critique* 45 (Spring 2000): 58.

12. Robert B. Heilman, "Escape and Escapism: Varieties of Literary Experience." *The Sewanee Review* 83, no. 3 (Summer 1975): 439–58.

13. Elihu Katz and David Foulkes. "On the Use of the Mass Media as 'Escape': Clarification of a Concept." *The Public Opinion Quarterly* 26, no. 3 (Autumn 1962): 377–88.

14. Katz and Foulkes, "On the Use of the Mass Media as 'Escape,'" 384.

15. Elizabeth Hirschman, "Predictors of Self-Projection, Fantasy Fulfillment, and Escapism," *The Journal of Social Psychology* 120 (June 1983): 63–76.

16. Gabriel Bar-Haim, "Popular Culture and Ideological Discontents: A Theory." *International Journal of Politics, Culture, and Society* 3, no. 3 (Spring 1990): 279–96.

17. See also Serazio's 2019 discussion of the "stick to sports" narrative.

18. Ken Gelder, *Popular Fiction: The Logic and Practices of a Literary Field.* New York: Routledge, 2004.

19. Cynthia Whissell, "The Formula Behind Women's Romantic Formula Fiction." *Arachne* 5, no. 1 (1998): 103.

20. See Stougaard-Nielsen's 2022 analysis of reading crime fiction during the Covid 19 pandemic.

21. Gelder, *Popular Fiction.*

22. María Angélica Thumala Olave, "Reading Matters: Towards a Cultural Sociology of Reading." *American Journal of Cultural Sociology* 6, no. 3 (October 2018): 417–54).

23. Thumala Olave, "Reading Matters," 418.

24. Owen Mairead, "Reinventing Romance: Reading Popular Romantic Fiction." *Women's Studies International Forum* 20, no. 4 (July–August 1997): 537–46.

25. Carol Dyhouse, *Heartthrobs: A History of Women and Desire.* London: Oxford University Press, 2019.

26. Bridget Fowler, *The Alienated Reader: Women and Romantic Literature in the Twentieth Century.* London: Harvester Wheatsheaf, 1991; Carol Thurston, *Romance Revolution: Erotic Novels for Women and the Quest for a New Sexual Identity.* Chicago: University of Illinois Press, 1987.

27. Thurston, *Romance Revolution,*132.

28. Ang, Ien. *Watching Dallas: Soap Opera and the Melodramatic Imagination.* New York: Routledge, 1985): 49.

29. Alice Guilluy, *'Guilty Pleasures': European Audiences and Contemporary Hollywood Romantic Comedy.* New York: Bloomsbury Academic, 2022.

30. Guilluy, *Guilty Pleasures,* 230.

31. Dyhouse, *Heartthrobs.*

32. Romance Writers of America. "About the Romance Genre." Last modified 2017. https://www.rwa.org/Online/Romance_Genre/About_Romance_Genre.aspx.

33. Radway, *Reading the Romance,* 90.

34. Ibid., 91.

35. Thumala Olave, "Reading Matters," 435.

36. Radway, *Reading the Romance,* 105.

37. Catherine Roach, *Happily Ever After: The Romance Story in Popular Culture* (Bloomington, IN: Indiana University Press, 2016), 166.

38. Mary F. Rogers, *Novels, Novelists, and Readers: Toward a Phenomenological Sociology of Literature* (Albany, NY: State University of New York Press, 1991), 12.

39. Maleah Fekete, "Confluent Love and the Evolution of Ideal Intimacy: Romance Reading in 1980 and 2016," *Journal of Popular Romance Studies* 11 (May 2022), 217.

40. Madeline Span, "Caring for the Self: A Case Study on Sociocultural Aspects of Reading Chick Lit," *Journal of Popular Romance Studies* 11 (June 2022), 11.

41. Bridget Fowler, *The Alienated Reader: Women and Romantic Literature in the Twentieth Century* (London: Harvester Wheatsheaf, 1991), 144.

42. Eric S. Rabkin, *The Fantastic in Literature* (Princeton, NJ: Princeton University Press, 1976), 55.

Chapter 10

Love, Romance, Sex, and Happily Ever After

A Feminist Exploration of Women who Read Romance Novels

Jessica M. W. Kratzer

INTRODUCTION

My introduction to romance novels didn't start that differently than many women. One of Birthisel's romance author participants referred to *Fifty Shades of Grey* as a gateway book that got nonreaders or former readers to start reading romance novels.[1] Birthisel also noted that one of the romance authors in her study had countless readers admit that *Fifty Shades* was the first romance book they'd read, and they began consuming many romance novels since. So, it seems that I am among friends when it comes to my introduction to romance novels.

As a sex and communication scholar, most people assumed that I read *Fifty Shades of Grey* when it was first published in 2011.[2] The timing was not fortuitous for me because I had never read a romance novel (that wasn't Young Adult), and I had just given birth and started a new tenure-track job. There was no time to read a "fun" book much less get into a genre I wasn't familiar with. After each release of the three books and the first two movies, students, colleagues, and friends would ask if I had either read the books or watched the movie(s). I felt like an inadequate sex communication scholar due to my lack of knowledge regarding the *Fifty Shades* trilogy. In 2018, I decided that it was finally time to see what all the popular culture rage was about.

I read the whole series: *Fifty Shades of Grey*, *Fifty Shades Darker*, and *Fifty Shades Freed*, as well as two books from Christian's perspective: *Grey* and *Darker* (a third book has since been published called *Freed*).[3] I didn't just like the books, I loved them! I know that people have been critical of the writing and relational issues between the main characters,[4] but I still loved it. Reflecting back, my love of the book was not just the book itself but it was the awakening of my interest in . . . no, that doesn't encapsulate it . . . my love of romance novels. I was 38 years old, which meant that I fell into the romance-reading age range of 35–54.[5] However, most readers discover this genre between the ages of 11–18,[6] so I was definitely delayed in comparison to others. My consumption of romance novels has increased over the past several years and I've also embraced audiobooks, which offer the flexibility to multitask: folding laundry, listening to a romance novel; walking the dogs, listening to a romance novel; doing a puzzle, listening to a romance novel.

Not only did reading *Fifty Shades of Grey* awaken my insatiable reading of and listening to romance novels, it also opened an academic door for me in the kink community. After reading these books, I proposed an edited collection about the series that was published in 2020.[7] I have two chapters in that collection and another chapter about the kink community in another edited collection.[8] My scholarly work continues to evolve, and that first romance novel allowed me to explore a great deal of sex and communication research. My interest in romance novels has evolved more and increased my "fun" reading exponentially, guided me on a new path in my scholarship, and led me to wanting to know more about the effects these novels have in women's lives. According to Catherine Roach,

> If we think about the community interested in genre fiction romance as a large whole, we can divide it into four sub-communities: (1) fans, (2) romance writers, (3) industry professionals, and (4) academics; or those who consume the genre of romance stories as readers, produce it as authors, sell it as editors/agenda/publishing professionals, and study it as academics.[9]

I can be categorized in two subcommunities related to romance fiction: fan and academic. I not only get to be a fan/consumer but also to combine my favorite hobby with my work by conducting research about romance novels. The current study is the next step in my scholarly evolution. The purpose of this study is to explore the experiences of women who read romance novels to learn from their stories and experiences with the books, the storylines, and how they may influence aspects of their lived experiences.

LITERATURE REVIEW

Romance novels are a widely sought commodity, which makes them an interesting and vast area for scholarship. In this section, I'll review the current trends in romance, perceived problems with the genre, perceived benefits of the genre, and Women's Standpoint Theory.

Current Trends in the Romance Genre

Romance has been, and continues to be, a top-selling genre. According to Curcic, romance novels are the highest earning genre of fiction, generating over $1.44 billion in revenue.[10] Between May 2022 and May 2023, over 39 million printed novels were sold. This showed a positive growth of 52% from 2021–2022.[11] Romance novels constitute over 33% of paperback books sold. According to *The Economist*, sales of romance novels in Britain have risen by 110% in the past three years so this isn't just a trend in the U.S.[12] Specific authors are very popular among readers with two accounting for 80% of total unit sales in the romance category as of 2023: Colleen Hoover's novels account for over 48% and Emily Henry with 32%. Lucy Score follows with 4% and Ana Huang with 3%. Other well-known authors such as Nicholas Sparks, Nora Roberts, and Julia Quinn account for 2% each. These authors have specific niches in the romance genre, which include love stories with intimate scenes that are culturally normative (e.g., oral sex, penetrative sex). Therefore, it may be surprising that the *Fifty Shades of Grey* series is the best-selling romance novels series of all time having sold over 150 million copies. The first book in the series, *Fifty Shades of Grey*, is also in the top ten of the best-selling audiobooks of all time.[13]

Romance novels are easier to get through e-readers, online library accounts, and apps like Kindle Unlimited and Audible. This allows readers to carry their reading with them more conveniently, makes reading more accessible, and makes it easier to access niche genres.[14] According to erotic romance author Chloe Carson, "The eBook changed everything by creating a kind of public privacy. People can read whatever they want, whenever and wherever they desire. Even the act of buying is anonymous."[15] This allows readers to read any romance subgenre they want in the presence of others due to the privacy offered by e-readers.

The romance genre consists of many subgenres and tropes that allow readers to consume their favorite types of stories. Some of the most common romance subgenres are contemporary, erotic, historical, paranormal, LGBT+, comedy, suspense, sports, and more.[16] Some of the most common tropes are marriage of convenience, forced proximity, enemies to lovers, friends to lovers, meet-cute, second chance love, fake relationship, opposites attract, billionaire, etc. These tropes can be found listed on websites like Evie Alexander's that has an article listing 150 different romance novel tropes.[17] However, Radway's seminal study revealed that the two most important parts of a romance for her participants was the happy ending and the hero and heroine's love story.[18] Social media is another place where readers and authors can post about their favorite genres. For instance, TikTok fans of romance novels have partitioned romantic fiction into categories like #enemiestolovers, #friendstolovers, #academicrivalstolovers, #spicytok, #smuttok, #forbiddenlove, #forced proximity, #billionaireromance.[19]

Problems with the Romance Genre

Objectification

Romance novels have been continually criticized since their surge of popularity in the 1970s.[20] Regis discusses the many perspectives of why scholars of the past have found romance novels to be void of feminism and female agency.[21] Greer was a leader of the movement to criticize romance novels claiming that they enslave women.[22] "The traits invented for [the hero] have been invented by women cherishing the chains of their bondage."[23] Romance authors incorporated more sexual agency for the heroines in the 1980s, yet similar critiques continued.

Other claims support Greer's idea of bondage where the heroine in the story never has or yearns for female friendship, further bonding herself to the hero of the story;[24] and the heterosexism of the storyline where the heroine is only interested in the hero, motherhood, and monogamy.[25] Many critiques claim that women in the novels become submissive and subservient in order to find their happiness, which further fantasizes the structures of patriarchy.[26] For instance,[27] claims that women read romance novels because they aren't finding what they want in real life and use these stories to fill the void.

Cranny-Francis (1990) claims that these novels focus on the passivity and powerlessness of the heroine. Radway encompasses the sentiments of these scholars well. She states, "the story permits the reader to identify with the heroine at the moment of her greatest success, that is, when she secures the attention and recognition of her culture's most powerful and essential representative, a man. The happy ending is, at this level, a sign of a woman's attainment of legitimacy and personhood in a culture that locates both for her in the roles of lover, wife, and mother.[28]

Mommy Porn

There is an ongoing argument about whether or not romance novels, especially erotica, are pornography. According to Jankowski, many journalists framed it "mommy porn" as a "quick and catchy phrase with which to define a community."[29] "As is often the case with women-centric texts, though, because *Fifty Shades* was a cultural spectacle created by and cheered on by women (not to mention that it dealt with expressions of female sexuality), it was widely derided, and often dismissed as "mommy porn."[30] Carson makes it clear that outsiders, those not interested or part of the romance novel community, are the ones calling these novels mommy porn or smut. Even with these monikers, romance novels are different from porn because the focus of the medium is different.[31] Carson clarifies the differences between porn and erotica:

> In erotic romance, sex is necessary for the plot of character development; without it the story wouldn't make sense. To qualify as a romance, a book must have a Happily Ever After (HEA) for the two main characters. Erotica focuses on a single person's sexual journey and doesn't need to have an HEA. In sexy romance, there's a lot of sex but it's not inherent to the plot; this genre may also use less graphic language than erotic romance. On the other end of the spectrum, porn focuses exclusively on sex and lacks a well-developed narrative.[32]

This distinction clarifies the ongoing discussion about the difference between romance novels and porn. Within popular romance studies, erotic romance must utilize eroticism and sexuality integrally in the plot and is entwined with the overall love story.[33] While there are problems with romance novels, there are also benefits.

Benefits of the Romance Genre

Social

Romance novels are so popular that people arrange book swaps, book clubs, and an interviewee on an NPR show talked about playing BINGO with the most loved and loathed tropes in the genre.[34] Facebook groups are created to discuss books and series and to support authors. TikTok has had a big influence on romance novels because it gives people an outlet to share their thoughts.

According to Holpuch, people on TikTok share book recommendations with the hashtag #BookTok, which has become very influential in publishing.[35] For instance, in June 2021 Ruby Dixon's self-published series, *Ice Planet Barbarians*, went viral on TikTok. The author has since republished the series with Berkley Books.[36]

Educational

Women have also used romance novels as informative to their sexual education and communication in romantic relationships. Lawrey et al. found that the women in their study used *Fifty Shades of Grey* to learn about various forms of sexual expression and it helped them explore their own sexual desires. The same study found that when their partners knew they were reading *Fifty Shades of Grey*, they were curious, which led to discussions about trying sex acts described in the book.[37]

Noland discusses the practical use of romance novels, using *Fifty Shades of Grey* as an exemplar of self-help around sexual communication.[38] She offers a four-step "recipe" for how romance novels can be used to follow the self-help formula. Noland notes that women may or may not want to do the sex acts that they read, but what they really want is the open communication about sex that many romance novels feature. This is similar to what Regis said about freeing women to explore. "The [romance] genre is not about women's bondage, as the literary critics would have it. The romance novel is, to the contrary, about women's freedom. The genre is popular because it conveys the pain, uplift, and joy that freedom brings."[39]

Ansley argues that historical fiction romance novels bring historical knowledge to its readers because the authors do their research on the time period and events. Readers of historical romances learn facts about the time periods of the stories. For instance, readers "can tell you in detail about the courtship rituals, gaming clubs, fashions, and hobbies of both sexes in London during this era."[40] Indeed, authors will often include a note in the book that documents their research and identifies the aspects of their story that are factual.

Agency

Many scholars argue that romance novels do not objectify the heroine and have positive effects on readers. According to Kolmes and Hoffman, romance novels are structured in a way that keeps the heroine from being purposively objectified. They argue that "part of the appeal of romance novels is that they provide a place for readers to engage in a fantasy that *cannot* become objectifying."[41] Within this framework, part of the fantasy is that as they read, they "are *totally* safe from even the possibility of being objectified in a harmful way, or at all."[42]

Span states that chick lit is not only read for entertainment but it allows readers to see themselves in the characters and assemble the characters and their behaviors based on their lived experiences.[43] Therefore, readers have the opportunity to see themselves in the characters, which can help them address issues in their personal lives such as overcoming heartache. Span's participants used reading as an act of self-care that affected them long after they finished reading because the novels make them feel good. Women's agency is important to explore through theory as well.

Women's Standpoint Theory

Women's Standpoint Theory seeks to support the understanding of specific experiences of specific women by focusing on the intricacies of individuals' lives and the norms that affect them. This theory's critical focus seeks to shed light on feminist issues that affect women. According to Smith, the proper term for what she seeks to examine is women's standpoint and prefers this terminology because she believes that it focuses more on the specific experiences of specific women rather than feminist standpoint, which she argues focuses on the universal woman.[44] For example, feminist standpoint has "implicitly reproduced the universalized subject and claims to objective truth of traditional philosophical discourse, an implicit return to the empiricism we claimed to have gone beyond."[45] Therefore, feminist standpoint focuses more on the universal, or generalized woman, rather than focusing on the intricacies of individual women's lives and how the relations of ruling affect them. It is important to note that women's standpoint theory is very similar to feminist standpoint and some scholars who discuss Smith's women's standpoint consider it to be further theorizing of feminist standpoint.[46] I have decided to distinguish Smith's version because of the methodological flow to her use of women's standpoint by using four ways to understand and connect aspects of a phenomenon together. To explain this further, Smith's work will be broken down into four parts: actualities of people's lives, social organization, texts, and relations of ruling.

First, Smith argues that, as researchers, we need to begin with the actualities of people.

Similar to feminist standpoint, people's lived experiences are important. The actualities of people refer to individual's lived experiences, where those lived experiences take place, and that individuals engage in these experiences every day and night.[47] Smith is interested in the active lives of people including what they do in their everyday living. This is where individuals are located and this is where research should begin. Continually, Smith also believes that the researcher is situated in the research in a way that his/her participation is an active form of knowing and discovering, therefore the researcher can become part of the actualities of the participants' lives.[48] Specifically, the researcher should find out what people *do* in their daily lives and learn what their experiences are. Romance novels are part of the lived experiences of many women, and Radway noted this stating that romance novel critics "do not take account of the actual, day-to-day context within which romance reading occurs,"[49] and in fact she herself was not a regular romance reader. This emphasizes the importance of daily lived experiences.

Second, we should focus on how activities in a person's life are coordinated and embedded in social relations. According to Smith, "individuals are there; they are in their bodies; they are active; and what they're doing is coordinated with the doings of others."[50] This focus is called social organization which refers to how the of actualities of people's lives are coordinated by the social and cultural structures. This means we want to know how the activities in people's lives are coordinated as part of the social world. All individuals are situated in the actualities of their own lives and in relation to the lives of others.[51] Examples of social organization include considerations of scheduling of activities in people's lives, services available and times it is available, physical context (e.g., place where activities take place), and other ways in which limitations and parameters are created.

Third, we should focus on how text mediates much of the social organization in our lives. Text may be material, or symbolic, and bridges together the actualities of our lives and the ruling relations.[52] Text as a material object includes reading words or "images that can be and may be read/seen/heard in many other settings by many others at the same or other times."[53] Writing the social allows the researcher to isolate parts of social organization that are embedded in the actualities of people's lives.[54] Text as symbolic includes discourses that set standards for how people should live (e.g., religion, culture). Texts can help researchers learn how participants gained knowledge for certain values, morals, or rules under which they live their lives. Romance novels are a text that can help us learn about those who read them but also can be representative of cultural norms. For instance, Radway finds that romance novels are ruined by their endings because the characteristics that make the heroine unique are stripped away through her marriage to the hero.[55] These endings make her story, and her existence, dependent on a man.

Finally, we should pay close attention to the relations of ruling. This emphasizes the importance of power, culture, and the issues associated with the social organization, with less focus on individual emotions. Relations of ruling refer to the hierarchical power in society and are influenced by both the social organization and texts that influence individuals' daily lives. Smith's emphasis on the ruling relations focused on the cultural norms under which people live out their daily lives. The actualities of individuals' daily lives are constrained by the ruling relations, which set limits to what people can and cannot do. Again, Radway notes that the cultural norms for women are apparent in romance novels. She states that reading romance novels "gives the reader a strategy for making her present situation more comfortable without substantive reordering of its structure rather than a comprehensive program for reorganizing her life in such a way that all needs might be met."[56] This continues to be a reflection of the relations of ruling in our culture. With an understanding of Smith's women's standpoint, a discussion about how to use it as a method of analysis is discussed in the next section. The purpose of this project was to explore the experiences of women who read romance novels through a feminist lens. Data was collected to address the following research questions.

RQ1: Why do women read erotic romance novels?
RQ2: How do women use what they read in romance novels?
RQ3: Who do women tell about their reading genre preference and habits?

METHODS

Participants

Twenty-eight women were recruited using snowball sampling. I posted a recruitment script on my Facebook page and several friends shared it with their friends, book clubs, and Facebook groups. All demographics were collected verbally and participants used their own terminology to identify themselves in each category. Therefore, some demographics have several descriptors provided by the participants. Women ranged in age from 24-56 with an average of 35 years old. Twenty-six participants were white (93%) and two were black (7%). Participants identified as heterosexual/straight (n=20; 71%), bisexual (n=2; 7%), and one participant (4%) for each of these identities: pansexual, asexual/straight, queer, bi-curious, and still processing. Relationship status ranged from married (n=20; 71%), engaged (n=1; 4%), boyfriend (n=6; 21%), and single (n=1; 4%), and all participants practice monogamy. Eleven participants have children that range from 1-28 years old.

All participants had college degrees: associates (n=1: 4%), bachelor's (n=12; 42%), master's (n=10; 36%), and doctorate (PhD or JD) (n=5; 18%). Household incomes ranged from $24,000-$350,000 with an average of $143,000 (one participant did not report). Thirteen (46%) participants report being of the Christian faith (Christian, Catholic, Episcopalian), 1 Buddhist (4%), 1 Jewish (4%), 2 atheist (7%), and 11 (39%) reported none. The following was reported for political orientation: democratic/liberal (n=19, 68%), republican (n=2; 7%), middle (n=4; 14%) independent (n=1; 4%), democratic socialist (n=1; 4%) and one (4%) participant reported none. Pseudonyms were used to maintain confidentiality.

I asked each participant to share with me their favorite recommendations, which could include their favorite authors, books, series, Facebook groups, etc. to share with the other participants. As a gift for participating in my study, I combined all of the recommendations from the participants and emailed it to them (separately as to not breach confidentiality). Participants were happy to share their favorite books, series, and authors, and voiced their excitement about receiving a list of new recommendations after the interviews. See Appendix D for the list of recommendations.

Data Collection

All interviews were conducted using a semi-structured interview protocol and were audio recorded through Zoom. Interviews lasted between 46-122 minutes for a total of 2,064 minutes (34.4 hours) and an average of 74 minutes. Zoom was used because it was convenient and gave participants the option to use video so it felt more like a conversation for both of us. All but one participant chose to use the video option. This also gave participants the option to be in a space most comfortable for them to be interviewed, which Creswell and Creswell describe as a natural setting.[57] Theoretical saturation occurred at around the 20th interview but in order to be additionally thorough, and because there were so many women interested in participating, I conducted 28 interviews.

Data Analysis

The first step of data analysis were conducting interviews with participants. Interviews were transcribed using the Office 360 transcription option in Word. A thematic analysis was used to analyze the data into themes. Three steps were used to analyze the interview data. I took notes, or memoed,[58] during the interviews and on subsequent review of the data. I used Lindloff and Taylor's method for data management, reduction, and conceptual development of organizing data.[59] First, I used data management to read through the transcripts and make note of potential themes and useful quotes. These were all copied and pasted to another document in chunks of data. Second, I used data reduction to whittle down the themes to the most prominent. Finally, I chose the quotes that best fit the themes and subthemes using conceptual development. The next step was using women's standpoint theory as an application and tool for analyzing the data.

The second part of data analysis included applying Smith's women's standpoint as a methodological tool.[60] This approach allowed me to apply the four steps of women's standpoint theory to analyze the emergent themes found in the thematic analysis. The four parts of women's standpoint discussed previously (actualities of others, social organization, texts, ruling relations) can be considered steps to understanding a phenomenon. Specifically, I began by collecting data from individuals (actualities of others). During this process I conducted interviews where I asked questions about the social organization, or how these individuals "do" the phenomenon being examined (e.g., How do women use what they read in romance novels?). I also had to consider the texts surrounding the individuals. For example, what cultural texts, related to gender, or other norms, exist that may help or hinder the participants' experiences of reading romance novels. Finally, social organization and texts come together to form the ruling relations which constitute how power relations act through these mechanisms. The ruling relations are the mechanisms that surround us socially and culturally.

Validation Strategies

Creswell and Creswell suggest using at least two validation strategies in qualitative research.[61] First, direct quotes from participants were used in order to highlight the rich, thick descriptions of the participants' experiences. This allows the reader to see some of the comments that led to the creation of the themes. Second, clarifying the bias that I, the researcher, brought to this study. The main influence is that I love reading romance novels so it is easy for me to see the benefits of this hobby, therefore I needed to be conscious of being critical of the data as to not only look for themes that support my opinions of this phenomenon. Additionally, I would like to add a reflexivity statement that explains other aspects of my potential influence on the data.

Reflexivity

Of the 28 interviews, I knew 11 participants in some capacity. While this can negatively affect some research, the participants were very open to all of the questions and answered the most personal of questions without hesitation. This may be for a few reasons. First, almost all of the participants that I know are through past proximity and we have not been in touch for many years. This level of separation allowed us to become less familiar with each other so they are comfortable answering personal questions and yet familiar enough to know that they can trust me with confidentiality. I informed participants of my previous research in sex and communication in order to give them background information and to let them know that I am very open to hearing about their personal experiences. I did not ask many sex-related questions, but there is a stigma related to reading romance novels, and letting the participants know that I am not only open to hearing about their varied experiences and preferences, but that I am also an avid romance novel reader, made the interviews feel more like fun conversations. I think this made the interviews more relaxed, which allowed the participants to be more open with their comments.

FINDINGS

The romance community has its own set of terms and acronyms that are important to know. Below are the most common romance novel terms used by participants in this study: HEA (Happily Ever After), FMC (Female Main Character), MMC (Male Main Character), TBR (To Be Read), DNR (Did Not Finish), POV (Point of View).[62]

Through this analysis, three major themes emerged. The first major theme, Escape, has three subthemes: Not Reality, Happily Ever After, and Reflection. The second major theme, Ladies' Choice, has three subthemes: Bringing Sexy Back, Read Porn Like a Lady, and Female Agency. The third major theme, Communication, has two subthemes: Social Media and Friends.

Below are excerpts from the interviews that represent the themes. Pseudonyms are used to maintain participant confidentiality.

Escape

The first major theme that emerged is Escape. This theme addresses the first research question: Why do women read erotic romance novels? Most women either directly or indirectly mentioned using romance novels as an escape of reality. Escaping into novels happened in a few different ways for participants. The subthemes of Escape are Not Reality, Happily Ever After, and Reflection.

Not Reality

Participants in this study wanted a way to escape real life and enter a world that isn't real. They liked being able to immerse themselves into a story that ends well. For instance, Polly said "But like when I'm reading a fantasy romance like I'm not reading for the intellect I'm reading just because I want to escape, for fun." Zara similarly states that she wants to read something light that will bring joy to the characters. She said, "Reading is kind of like my escape, so I'm not looking for something educational. I hate reading nonfiction. I hate reading something educational. I want kind of an escape that's easy to get into, usually kind of light and fluffies." Sadie said, "I read them because I think it's just a fun escape. Same reason I watch like romantic movies. It's just something to make you happy that feels good, that you don't leave and you're thinking ohh shit, the world sucks." Reality is messy and for many participants, it was nice to escape into something else in order to decompress. Ada talks about how reading romance helps her feel better when dealing with reality.

> There's just like something universal about romance stories that we just enjoy and we love, that it doesn't matter the time the place. . . . There's just something universal about finding love and finding joy that I think really speaks to women. And then also, you know, it allows us to escape our kind of maybe mundane lives, right. Like I am currently potty training a 2 year old. In no universe is that a fun task . . . but like I know, like I can go listen to my book for an hour and like, feel better.

Another aspect of escaping from reality is enjoying the happy endings that many romance novels provide.

Happily Ever After

One aspect of escape is the desire to read books with happy endings, which indicates the additional desire of predictability. The stories may be different, and the ways in which the characters navigate the stories may also be different, but the most desired end result for the participants was a happy ending. Finding joy in the stories allows readers to bask in the happiness of the characters' experiences and how they find their happily ever after. Quinn reads many genres, but she wants a HEA when reading romance.

> It's the conflict and it's the feeling that it all works out in the end. I get mad if there's not a happily ever after. . . . The real world is difficult enough. I don't need your real-life bullshit. Like, give me all the happily ever afters that I can get because that's what I need to believe in when I'm losing myself in this.

Similar to Quinn, Jayla started reading romance novels and now she almost solely reads romances with happy endings. This is quite a lot considering that she reads around 300 books each year. Jayla said, "So then I started reading rom coms and I'm like ohh, I really like these. So now that's all I read. And I mean, I'll tell you the reason I read them is because I do like the predictability of knowing that there is happily ever after." The women in this study enjoyed being able to escape reality and enjoy a happy ending, but they also reflected on how escaping into romance novels affects them.

Reflection

Another form of escapism is self-reflection, which manifests itself in a few ways. First, some participants found that they experience personal growth from reading romance. For example, Iris said,

> I think there is this like inherent human need to connect with others and I think romance novels, as cheesy as it is, like you're seeing all these different ways of like connecting with somebody and of like, learning more about yourself and growing. As like a partnership and it's something that I think almost everybody can relate to. Not a lot of people enjoy feeling alone. I don't know. I feel like it's a very, like, natural human feeling to want connection and to want to feel like you're not alone. . . . I guess I can really only like talk to what, how the books make me feel, which is empowered. I feel like I've become more confident and more like ok with my sexuality and with how I express it because of the books that I've read and the experiences I've had through that.

Nora found that she could learn about relationships through romance novels. She said,"You see, like this perfect couple in a book and you're like, oh, that's what I strive to be. So it's kind of like looking up to them for advice and then also what not to do. And some couples and stuff."

The second way this subtheme manifested is that participants wanted to see characteristics of themselves in the FMC. For instance, Tess said, "I like reading women who are like characters who are not helpless characters who are like I guess, in the same way like though I see kind of myself, which is weird to think about. I'm like not afraid to like embrace sexuality."

Third, some participants talked about getting to feel the romance again when it's new. Romance novels allow them to reexperience those feelings through the stories. For example, Uma talks about reliving the feelings of having a crush.

> I like the romance novels just because, like, I've heard actors be like, Oh yeah, I love acting because it takes me to a whole other world. I got to be a different person for a little bit. And that's kind of like how I feel with romance novels. . . . You get to be someone else, you get to experience those butterflies all over again and like, kind of feel like you're sitting there at the slumber party talking about your crushes.

Brynn had a similar enjoyment of romance novels. She enjoyed inserting herself into the story as the FMC.

> Because I started so young, I really can't remember exactly what kind of drew me into it. In particular, I just liked boys and whatever, you know. [I would] self-insert the character the author had made for, you know, its readers. If I could place myself in that spot where I was experiencing whatever the, you know, male lead was providing to that character. Kind of make me feel good. . . . And of course the happy endings are always feel good.

Escapism was the main reason why women in this study wanted to read romance novels. Their escape allowed them to suspend reality, enjoy a happily ever after, and see characteristics of themselves in the FMCs they read.

Ladies' Choice

The second major theme that emerged was Ladies' Choice. This theme addresses the second research question: How do women use what they read in romance novels? Romance novels often have, at a minimum, a romantic interest, maybe some sexual tension, various forms of sex, and more extreme, or, as the romance novel community has coined, dark romance. Three subthemes emerged in relation to sex and agency in romance novels: Bringing Sexy Back, Read Porn Like a Lady, and Female Agency.

Bringing Sexy Back

The participants agreed that romance novels that have sex scenes often, by default, increase their libido. In return, some participants mentioned that it has improved their sex lives. Much of this comes in the form of information, and communication. Having their partner notice that romance novels increase their libido, partners being willing to try new things, and getting to know your body and what you like, were experiences that many women in this study had. First is an example of some participants' partners noticing that romance novels get them in the mood. For instance, Kali said, "Yeah, absolutely it gets my mind going, right. And I think in some ways that's a big part of it. My partner will be like, oh, you've been reading your books again haven't you. Or he'll say you should read that book more, right. Like clearly this is working."

Some participants had partners who were "shy" when it came to talking about sex so they would try new things with their partners while in the moment. For example, Xia said, "I have tried things that have gone great or very poorly. I think I have definitely like normally it's more of a like just slip this in. But that's just because he gets uncomfortable like talking about it. Yeah, but he's fine to do . . . he goes with it." A few other participants were open to talking with their partners by sharing excerpts from books to insinuate their desire to have sex. For example, Billie sends her partner screenshots throughout the day.

> But I will sometimes, like if there's something that's like, super steamy, I'll just . . . screenshot and send them a little clip and be like hey babe, want to try this tonight. And so it's less of a talk about, it's more of a sending over like little quips throughout the day of interesting things, and then at night time he'll be like OK, so like this. And so it's not a conversation, it's just a, you know, thought generator.

Other participants read romance novels so often that they aren't sure if the books increase their sex drive of not because they are always listening to books with sex scenes. Orla stated,

> Not particular. Like I said, I read a lot in general and so like . . . it probably does have an effect, but I don't really think about it because I read so often that I don't really at this point have like the context. Like ok, if I'm not reading regularly, like, what does that look like for my sex drive and all those things?

While some participants weren't sure how romance novels affect their sex drive because they've not taken a break from reading to see if there is a change, other participants have noticed a change. A few participants mentioned learning more about their sexuality and learning language from romance novels to use when talking about sex. Specifically, Abigail said,

> Starts to give you like language and ideas around like having these discussions. Because no one really teaches you any of this . . . and on top of that, depending on who you're around like, no one really wants to talk about [sex]. . . . Depending on where you're at, like, you're very dependent on like your resources are just what you have available, and I think the beautiful thing about romance is like you have a phone. If you have a store and you like you can have that availability and you can learn more advocacy and, like more bodily autonomy and like sexual freedom and pleasure around that, because like the possibilities are there on page and again like the language is there. So you can start to just kind of formulate like what would I like to try and then how do I have this discussion about it, you know because sex is all about, like communication and actually saying what you want, and that was such a struggle for me for the longest time was like, not even knowing what I wanted and then how did I even like . . . formulate the words to say that you know . . . I think that's pretty awesome.

Read Porn Like a Lady

When comparing sex scenes in romance novels to that of video porn (e.g., PornHub.com), most women stated that they are not the same for a few reasons. A few women mentioned a meme that they've seen that says "I don't watch porn. I read it like a lady." They found this humorous even if they didn't view romance novels as a form of pornography. Most women said that romance novels are different from pornography. Some agreed that it was similar due to the explicit scenes but that it was exactly the same. Almost all of the women mentioned that the major difference is that women want to read about the relationship and emotional connection between the two characters. For example, Violet said,

> Probably the way they're written, because I feel like sometimes porn is like, just super cheesy. . . . I don't think I've ever read a book where it's like page two and it's like there already [having sex]. I'm sure there is like on Kindle, but like books like I can really remember and like really enjoy . . . a buildup and then like, you know the intimacy happens and then you have like. Ideally my ideal book is like happens like on page 100 and then you the rest of the story goes on and it happens again like page 200. It's like you have more of like a timeline versus I think like on Pornhub it's like you got 30 minutes. So, I'm more into like a story and then like the reward of like the intimacy scene.

Other women talked similarly about how porn is made for the male gaze whereas romance novels are written for the female gaze. Laine stated, For reasons that I really can't even explain, I don't watch porn. It's just never been something that's interesting to me. I couldn't even tell you what. But I've always loved romance and even like erotica. And so I think a lot of women maybe feel the same, that they're just not visual creatures. In that same way, but you still have the human instinct to be interested in that kind of stuff, but it's just traditional porn is not the format that I think works for all women, or maybe even most. I wouldn't be surprised if [romance novels], you know, it's scratching like a very human itch in a way that feels just feel better to women."

Similarly, Yalena discusses women wanting an emotional connection with the characters. She also mentions fan fiction, which is an important genre because the writer can take characters that the reader already likes and is familiar with, and can add more romance, sex, etc. in order to keep the story going or enhance different aspects of the former story.

> More of like the emotional connection because you're, like, getting to know these characters. And like, there's a world building respect and it's, by the time, like the actual romance part kicks in, you already have like a connection. . . . I feel like women need typically appreciate more of, like that connection and like the understanding because it's . . . like so popular for like the fan fiction stuff. And it's that same thing. It's like, these are characters that you already have a connection to, that you're already emotionally connected to, so I feel like it's that same concept.

Most of the women thought reading romance novels was different from porn due to the relational aspects. This study also explored how social media and friends create a community of readers.

Female Agency

As readers, women have the autonomy and the choice to select what they want to read, and many are choosing romance. The concept of choice alone is feminist because women are making decisions for themselves about what they enjoy, what turns them on, and how they want to use their time. Orla said,

> Women who are reading it are choosing to read what they want, and they're choosing to read things that, like, are sexy to them and that are appealing to them. And so I think as long as they have that, that agency, they are, I would say it's a net positive. . . . When women have the agency to pick the things that they're reading and they're able to like make those decisions, I think, overall coming out positive just for helping women like express their sexuality.

Not only is there agency when it comes to choosing what women want to read, there is also the idea that romance novels are very basic to the human experience. Most people want to experience intimate relationships and, as Charlotte states, romance novels give us that.

> I mean, romance novels are literally the documentation of lived experiences. And really they attempt to distill them down to, like, their truest form right like, nothing happens in that book except for two people falling in love and then they put a plot around that. And so it's like they're distilling human relationships down in, I think that that allows them to be so flexible and also like move with the times and that's why you get so much romance reflected in like, whatever's happening in the world and that in itself is like truly feminist.

Cultural expectations are forced on women, and they seek representation that shows women with power. Romance novels give women the opportunity to interact with stories that highlight strong women, which can help them to see themselves as strong as they make choices throughout their lives. Gianna had an experience like this.

> At least 90% of the romance, all those I read, there's a woman CEO or there's a woman taking charge of her life, there's a woman that she's single by choice or she's motherless by choice. I love that. I love that. That brings that perspective in because I was raised where you get barefoot and pregnant by the time you graduate high school. You don't get higher education. My mom wasn't, she pushed education. That's why I have a master's degree. But I was raised with family that that's you know, you don't achieve things, you just help your husband achieve things. And I feel like a lot of romance novels are not like that.

In addition, women with disabilities may have more difficulty either participating in sex acts or even getting motivated to want to participate. Reese has a disability that has affected her desire and has used romance novels to help her decide if she's in the mood.

> So I think it's going to be interesting dating someone reading these books because it is harder, especially with disabilities too, it's harder to get in the mood and I think these books will be interesting, that because it's again, it's giving you a safe, quiet space to decide am I into this today or not? Do I feel good?

The women in this study have the agency to choose to read romance novels and those novels are often based on the most basic of human experiences.

They get to read about strong women making choices for themselves while simultaneously making the choice to read romance.

Communication

Communicating with others about hobbies is common and the women in this study stated a few ways in which they talk about romance novels. This theme addresses the third research question: Who do women tell about their reading genre preference and habits? Three subthemes emerged in relation to communication: Social Media and Friends.

Social Media

Many participants talked about being in Facebook groups for specific authors, books, and/or series. Only a few of them stated that they actively communicate with others because they prefer to read comments and recommendations from others posts. Therefore, the use of social media among these participants was mostly to get recommendations for new books to read. For instance, Zara said, "Mostly just like Facebook groups, but not, I guess I don't engage in a lot of discussions in them. I'm more just kind of watch for recommendations and that kind of thing." Other participants, like Maeve says below, really enjoyed staying connected with stories and characters through Facebook groups.

> I'm on their Facebook group and it's crazy just how much depth these authors have to go in to make it all believable . . . consistent. And then you get . . . all of these fans who want to talk about all of it. So . . . I can get sucked into their, you know, Facebook chatter for a long time. But then the authors come on and . . . they talk about the world and give you a little bit of a guide and a timeline. And this and that and so. It is hugely rabbit hole-ish. . . . I really enjoy those kind of things maybe because it make takes that next next level escape of this is something totally different and I can learn about it and, you know, it's fascinating to me.

The women also used social media as a way to connect with other people who also enjoy them. It was a way to find a community of people with similar interests and to make friends. Holland stated, "So that's what makes it popular, too, is almost like the community with it, like, because like, a lot of these women that I follow on TikTok, they're like making friends through it." Another participant, Evie, talked about not feeling judged when asking for recommendations in Facebook groups.

> There is a whole community that does not judge. . . . I'm like, hey, I'm looking for this specific kind of, you know, with this, this . . . there is no judgment. Everybody wants, you know, to like share the love speak. That's what I'm learning so much of is people are like so excited to give recommendations and I think that's really fun.

Many women connected with the romance novel community through social media but several also discussed them with their friends.

Friends

Several participants had friends that they texted or talked to about the novels they read. Similar to the social media experience, women enjoy having a community of romance readers. For Charlotte, she thought she was alone in enjoying romance novels. "I wasn't telling anybody and then when I mentioned it . . . like everyone was like, oh my gosh. And they wanted to talk about it. I was like this is awesome, yeah. And it's like having a community then that I just didn't think I'd have." Community was an important aspect to talking about romance novels, even if it was only to get recommendations.

Participants shared recommendations and some of them were in book clubs or would buddy read with someone else but most found that difficult because they consume at different rates or have different interests than their friends. For instance, Faith talks about trying book clubs but it didn't work for her.

> You know, I have tried to do that with a couple of friends and what I have found is that it is for one, I jump around so much in books that it's harder for me to like, I've tried three times to have a book club and either I can't get enough interest on a single book. . . . Everybody reads at a different pace, and everybody has different tastes in reading. . . . I find it's less stressful and more fun for you to go it alone. Now I will ask recommendations from friends.

However, a few participants were very active when it came to talking with friends about romance novels. For instance, Winnie stated,

> I have a couple of my new friends I've made. We actually met at a book convention last year and so we have like an online text group chat that we talk in. One of my friends, we actually meet monthly at a coffee shop and either we'll start our book there together or we'll just talk about it in the coffee shop and then go home and read separately. I run two other book clubs.

There were also participants who made friends at work who had similar interests and would either share recommendations, or like Demi, would also talk about the books when it was convenient.

> My coworkers . . . the girls there, they all read. . . . We would just, like, talk about the books, you know, it's just something we would do on the side because we'd eat with a book in our hand. Like, hey, did you read this book or have you seen this book out, you got any good book recommendations?

The women in this study were very interested in getting recommendations and having a community of friends who also liked reading romance novels. Even if many of them didn't participate in organized groups, knowing that other women also enjoy reading romance was enough to make them feel like part of a community.

DISCUSSION

This section is used to discuss the application of women's standpoint theory to the emergent themes. The themes mentioned above can be applied to Women's Standpoint Theory in several ways. First, we must consider the actualities of women's daily lives. The women in this study had busy lives with 26 (93%) working outside the home and two participants (7%) working inside the home. All but one participant was in a romantic relationship of some sort and 11 participants had children. This doesn't consider their other responsibilities that may include maintaining their home, caring for pets, making meals, running errands, etc. that come with being active people. The actualities of these women's lives include a lot of "doing" for others and themselves, while also making time for their hobby of ready romance novels.

Additionally, these women also enjoyed seeing relationships develop in the novels they read. Relationships are a key component to life, whether it be family, friends, coworkers, or neighbors. Women wanting to read about relationships, people coming together, couples overcoming relational obstacles, and women reaching their goals in important. The participants often saw something in themselves when reading the strong, smart, courageous, independent women in the romance novels. And, for some participants, the novels helped them learn to communicate better and overcome some of their own obstacles. Therefore, romance novels can be part of the actualities of women's lives both as a hobby and a reflection of themselves as strong, capable people.

Second, we must consider the social relations, or the social organization of how women's lives are coordinated by the social and cultural structures. This is where we see how women are able to balance their lives and include reading romance novels into the structure of their daily lives. For example, many women talked about connecting with friends by discussing romance novels and/or sharing recommendations, but they also interacted with people via social media such as TikTok's BookTok.[63] Women are also busy, dynamic people with a lot of responsibilities. Sometimes sex with partners isn't at the top of their priorities in a day and can be dampened by busy schedules and stress. The women in this study discussed how romance novels have potentially influenced their sex lives for the better by increasing their libidos, giving them sex acts to try, and/or giving them language on how to talk to their partners about their desires.

Third, we must consider how text, such as symbols and standards for living in a particular culture. This may also include values, morals and rules. For this study, we can see how our culture and the consumption of romance novels may influence participants' experiences related to sex. For instance, in the theme "Ladies' Choice," we see that the cultural norm of viewing pornography is greatly associated with male pleasure and the male gaze. The women in this study discuss how our culture suppresses a wider discussion about romance novels because they are not for the male gaze, therefore making them less culturally valuable. However, the participants noted that, while there are distinct differences between pornography (e.g., Pornhub) and romance novels, they also can enhance one's libido similarly to pornography.[64]

Other texts include social media, where many women in this study go to discuss romance novels, characters, storylines, theories, and to get recommendations. Social media is a dominant cultural text that helps people connect with others who have similar interests, therefore allowing these women to find a community surrounding their enjoyment of romance novels. Finding a community of others gave the participants a space to remain connected to their favorites novels, series, characters, and authors in a way that we didn't have before social media.[65] These communities have allowed women to see that they are not alone in their enjoyment of reading romance novels.

Finally, the relations of ruling emphasize power, culture, and issues associated with the social organization of our lives. When we look at those with power, we see the influence of our patriarchal system and how it degrades the things women enjoy and find important. Whereas, for example, men are not degraded, but instead elevated, when going to athletic events, wearing players' jerseys, becoming emotional over wins and losses, and being passionate about it.

However, women's consumption of romance novels, which is also consumed fiercely, is deemed culturally less significant. Women having agency and enjoying things that men disapprove of is a long part of our cultural history but the women in this study are putting pressure on that norm.

The social relations of daily organization and the oppressive cultural norms for women make women want to escape and enjoy something that is unlike reality. They chose to escape reality and enjoy the happy endings in the novels they enjoy. Echoing Span's conclusions,[66] participants also used the novels to reflect upon themselves, and found agency in their choice to read romance as well as through the larger romance reader community. Consuming and enjoying romance novels that are centered around female agency and pleasure, continues to move women's needs and desires out of the cultural shadows.

CONCLUSION

This study adds to the current romance novel research, but there are ways in which it could be expanded in future scholarship. For instance, the methodology could be expanded. Qualitative work offers the benefit of getting detailed responses from participants, which is necessary information for understanding a phenomenon. However, a parallel quantitative study would broaden the knowledge already gained. Quantitative studies allow scholars to get generalizable data from a larger number of participants. It is important to recognize the value in both large, quantitative data sets and qualitative data that include women's detailed experiences. The combination of the two will help scholars more fully understand the influence of romance novels in our culture.

Additionally, this study is also limited to a mostly white population so interviewing women of color, women in the LGBTQ+ community, and men who read romance novels would give us more valuable information about romance novel consumption, preferences, and influence. A strength of this study is that it has shown that romance novels are important to women. Future research could focus on the cultural value of romance novels in order to understand more about women and this phenomenon. This study is a stepping stone to shedding light on romance novels as an important cultural artifact and valued component of women's culture.

In this chapter, we have expanded our knowledge on the lived experiences of women who read romance novels. The participants in this study placed great value on reading, enjoying, sharing, connecting, escaping, and learning from romance novels, which highlighted how these novels are woven through the fabric of their lives.

NOTES

1. Jessica Birthisel, "Erotic Romance Writing in a Post–*Fifty Shades of Grey* Landscape," in *Communication in Kink: Understanding the Influence of the Fifty Shades of Grey Phenomenon*, ed. J. M. W. Kratzer (Lanham, MD: Lexington Press, 2020), 53–76.

2. E. L. James, *Fifty Shades of Grey* (New York: Vintage Books, 2012).

3. *Fifty Shades of Grey* (James, 2012), *Fifty Shades Darker* (2012), *Fifty Shades Freed* (2012), and two books from Christian's perspective: *Grey* (James, 2015), *Darker* (James, 2017), and *Freed* (James, 2021).

4. Birthisel, 2020; Lawrey, J. A., A. McLuckie, B. J. Mulberry, E. K. Mullins, A. R. Shuler, and J. M. W. Kratzer, "Communication, Kink, and Sexual Education: What Young Women Learned from *Fifty Shades of Grey*," in *Communication in Kink: Understanding the Influence of the Fifty Shades of Grey Phenomenon*, ed. J. M. W. Kratzer (Lanham, MD: Lexington Press, 2020), 77–96.

5. D. Curcic, "Romance Novel Statistics," *Wordsrated*, October 9, 2022, https://wordsrated.com/romance-novel-sales-statistics/.

6. Curcic, "Romance Novel Statistics," 2022.

7. J. M. W. Kratzer, ed., *Communication in Kink: Understanding the Influence of the Fifty Shades of Grey Phenomenon* (Lanham, MD: Lexington Press, 2020).

8. J. M. W. Kratzer, "Kinky People's Perceptions of the *Fifty Shades of Grey* Trilogy," in *Communication in Kink: Understanding the Influence of the Fifty Shades of Grey Phenomenon*, ed. J. M. W. Kratzer (Lanham, MD: Lexington Press, 2020), 9–28; Lawrey et al., 2020; J. M. W. Kratzer, "Kinky Access: Information Provided to Young Adult Kinksters by 'The Next Generation' Groups on Fetlife.com," in *Young Adult Sexuality in the Digital Age*, ed. R. Kalish (Hershey, PA: IGI Global, 2020), 194–209, https://doi.org/10.4018/978-1-7998-3187-7.ch011.

9. C. M. Roach, *Happily Ever After: The Romance Story in Popular Culture* (Bloomington: Indiana University Press, 2016), 31–32.

10. Curcic, 2022.

11. Jim Milliot, "Romance Books Were Hot in 2022," *Publishers Weekly*, January 13, 2023, https://www.publishersweekly.com/pw/by-topic/industry-news/bookselling/article/91298-romance-books-were-hot-in-2022.html.

12. "Sales of Romance Novels Are Rising in Britain," *The Economist*, March 6, 2023, https://www.economist.com/britain/2023/03/06/sales-of-romance-novels-are-rising-in-britain.

13. David Talbot, "Best-Selling Books of All Time," Wordsrated, October 11, 2023, https://wordsrated.com/best-selling-books-of-all-time/..

14. C. Carson, "'People Are at Their Most Vulnerable When They're Naked Together': The Rise of Erotic Romance," *Salon*, January 4, 2014, https://www.salon.com/2014/01/04/people_are_at_their_most_vulnerable_when_theyre_naked_together_the_rise_of_erotic_romance/.

15. Carson, "'People Are at Their Most Vulnerable'," para. 15.

16. L. Murphy, *The Ultimate Guide to the Romance Genre and Romance Tropes*, She Reads Romance Books, 2023, https://www.shereadsromancebooks.com/romance-genre-and- romance-tropes-guide/.

17. Evie Alexander, *150 Romance Novel Tropes*, Evie Alexander, 2023, https://eviealexanderauthor.com/150-romance-novel-tropes/..

18. Janice A. Radway, *Reading the Romance: Women, Patriarchy, and Popular Literature* (Chapel Hill: The University of North Carolina Press, 1991).

19. Sales of romance, 2023.

20. Pamela Regis, *A Natural History of the Romance Novel* (Philadelphia: University of Pennsylvania Press, 2007).

21. Regis (2007)

22. Regis, 2007

23. Germaine Greer, *The Female Eunuch* (New York: McGraw-Hill, 1970), 176.

24. Susan Ostrov Weisser, "The Wonderful-Terrible Bitch Figure in Harlequin Novels," in *Feminist Nightmares: Women at Odds*, ed. Susan Ostrov Weisser and Jennifer Fleischner (New York: New York University Press, 1994).

25. Ganguly, K, "Alien[ated] Readers: Harlequin Romances and the Politics of Popular Culture," *Communication* 12 (1991): 129–50.

26. Rabine, Leslie W, *Reading the Romantic Heroine: Text, History, Ideology*. Women and Culture Series (Ann Arbor: University of Michigan Press, 1985).

27. Dubino, Jeanne, "The Cinderella Complex: Romantic Fiction, Patriarchy, and Capitalism," *Journal of Popular Culture* 27 (1989): 103–18.

28. Radway, *Reading the Romance*, 84.

29. S. M. Jankowski, "Mommy Porn for the Suburban Wife," in *Communication in Kink: Understanding the Influence of the Fifty Shades of Grey Phenomenon*, ed. J. M. W. Kratzer (Lanham, MD: Lexington Press, 2020), 107.

30. Birthisel, Erotic Romance Writing in a Post–*Fifty Shades of Grey* Landscape, 54.

31. Carson, "'People Are at Their Most Vulnerable'".

32. Carson, para. 5.

33. Jodi McAlister, "Erotic Romance," in *The Routledge Research Companion to Popular Romance Fiction*, ed. J. Kamblé, E. Murphy Selinger, and H.-M. Teo (Routledge, 2020), 212–28.

34. E. Burnett, S. Handel, and J. Summers, "Even as Overall Book Sales Are Declining, Romance Novels Are on the Rise," radio broadcast, NPR, June 2, 2023, https://www.npr.org/2023/06/02/1179850128/even-as-overall-book-sales-are-declining-romance-novels-are-on-the-rise.

35. Amanda Holpuch, "A Messy Relationship with Romance Novels," *The New York Times*, August 14, 2023, https://www.nytimes.com/2023/08/09/sports/hockey/hockey-romance-booktok-explainer.html.

36. Madison Nankervis, "Diversity in Romance Novels: Race, Sexuality, Neurodivergence, Disability, and Fat Representation," *Publishing Research Quarterly* 38 (2022): 349–63, https://doi.org/10.1007/s12109-022-09881-6.

37. Lawrey, "Communication, Kink, and Sexual Education".

38. Carey Noland, "Self-Help in Kink: A Critical Look at Erotic How-To," in *Communication in Kink: Understanding the Influence of the Fifty Shades of Grey Phenomenon*, ed. J. M. W. Kratzer (Lanham, MD: Lexington Press, 2020), 114–31.

39. Regis, 2007, xiii.

40. Laura Ansley, "Townhouse Notes: Let's Talk About Romance Novels," *Perspectives on History* 59 (2021): 3.

41. K. Kolmes and M. A. Hoffman, "Harlequin Resistance? Romance Novels as a Model for Resisting Objectification," *The Journal of Aesthetics and Art Criticism* 79 (2021): 39, https://doi.org/10.1093/jaac/kpaa004.

42. Kolmes and Hoffman, "Harlequin Resistance? Romance Novels as a Model for Resisting Objectification," January 1, 2021: 39

43. Megan Span, "Caring for the Self: A Case Study on Sociocultural Aspects of Reading Chick Lit," *Journal of Popular Romance Studies* 11 (2022).

44. Smith, Dorothy E. *Institutional Ethnography: A Sociology for People*. Lanham, MD: AltaMira Press, 2005.

45. Smith, *Institutional Ethnography*, 8.

46. Smith, *Institutional Ethnography*.

47. Dorothy E. Smith, *Writing the Social: Critique, Theory, and Investigations* (Toronto: University of Toronto Press, 1999).

48. Smith, *Writing the Social*.

49. Radway, "Women Read the Romance: The Interaction of Text and Context," *Feminist Studies* 9, no. 1 (1983): 54.

50. Smith, *Institutional Ethnography*, 59.

51. Smith, *Writing the Social*.

52. Smith, *Writing the Social*.

53. Smith, *Writing the Social*, 7.

54. Smith, *Writing the Social*.

55. Radway, *Reading the Romance*, 215.

56. Radway, Janice A. *Reading the Romance: Women, Patriarchy, and Popular Literature*.Chapel Hill: The University of North Carolina Press, 1991, 215.

57. John W. Creswell and J. David Creswell, *Research Design: Qualitative, Quantitative, and Mixed Methods Approaches*, 6th ed. (Thousand Oaks, CA: Sage, 2023).

58. Matthew B. Miles and A. Michael Huberman, *Qualitative Data Analysis* (Thousand Oaks, CA: Sage, 1994).

59. Thomas R. Lindlof and Brian C. Taylor, *Qualitative Communication Research Methods*, 4th ed. (Thousand Oaks, CA: Sage, 2019).

60. Smith, *Institutional Ethnography*; Smith, *Writing the Social*).

61. Creswell and Creswell, *Research Design*.

62. Additional terms: https://joreadsromance.co.uk/romance-glossary/.

63. Holpuch, "A Messy Relationship with Romance Novels."

64. Carson, "'People Are at Their Most Vulnerable'".

65. (e.g., Holpuch, 2023).

66. Span, "Caring for the Self."

Section 3

UNDER THE COVERS

TEXT ANALYSIS

The book's final section drills down more with individual texts, applying results from both Radway and the present study to explore how a variety of novels exemplify certain genre trends and connect with segments of the romance readership.

To start, Kathleen W. Taylor Kollman argues in "Coming of Age and Coming Out: The Intersection of New Adult and Queer Romance" that the new survey should have anticipated the popularity of and need to include LGBTQIA+ romance more prominently, especially as the process for coming of age in NA fiction mirrors and aligns with the coming-out process for people in their late teens and early twenties. She also sees gaps in romance scholarship failing to recognize that LGBTQIA+ romance is not a new phenomenon, even if it has become more prominent lately, and uses E. M. Forster's Edwardian novel *Maurice* (published posthumously in the 1970s) as an example of one of the first M/M romance novels. Kollman compares that both with Casey McQuiston's wildly popular *Red, White & Royal Blue* as well as the eight-point romance novel template developed by scholar Pamela Regis.

In "Getting Love Out of the Margins: Race, Disability, and the Idea of a Happy After for Marginalized People," Trinidad Linares uses close readings of Jenn Bennett's *Grave Phantoms* and Chloe Liese's *Always Only You* to discuss how romance novels can uplift readers who identify with marginalized characters and why this is important to popular culture and society. Many books centering marginalized characters rest on trauma porn, where the narrative concentrates on their pain and lack of agency as entertainment for the dominant audience. In line with this, writers often depict these characters as sexless or thwarted in their desires. In Bennett's and Liese's books, characters not only have sexual desires, but they act upon them without a disastrous ending. These books normalize the reality that marginalized people can have healthy relationships by providing a glimpse into their established coupledom countering the overwhelming number of tragic endings and negative stereotypes in mainstream stories about people of color or with disabilities. Other genres can learn from romance on how to better treat their marginalized characters because romance does not dwell on the degradation of its protagonists. Romance has the ability to puncture popular fiction's false grand narrative that marginalized people are incapable of agency or experiencing happiness, thus, benefiting all members of society.

Louise Schulman-Darsy's chapter, "Mr. Darcy as the Perfect Book Boyfriend" covers the popular character from *Pride and Prejudice*, looking at the impact that TikTok has on his representation in popular culture. The term "book boyfriend" has been around since the 2010s but exploded on BookTok (a hashtag on TikTok regrouping especially romance readers). It defines the "perfect boyfriend" in romance books. BookTok has a big impact on the male characters in new and young adult romance books. Schulman-Darsy argues that Fitzwilliam Darcy not only is a book boyfriend, but the original one, and TikTok drastically changed romance readers' reading habits and their interaction with Jane Austen's text.

Sara Partin and Josefine Smith explore the romantasy phenomenon in their chapter, "Reading Romance and Erotic Literacy." While fantasy fiction is no stranger to sex, contemporary, "new adult" fantasy novels are indulging the erotic in ways that have become even more meaningful to female readers since COVID-19, the overturning of *Roe v. Wade*, and the #MeToo movement. Sex is everywhere in the twenty-first century: social media, television and film, the news, as a form of work, and in fiction, and readers must consider the ways in which sex, both as an act and as a gendered construct, intersects with race, class, disability, nationality, and caste. The authors analyze how fans of Sarah J. Maas's ongoing New Adult, fantasy romance series *A Court of Thorns and Roses* (ACOTAR) interpret sexual expression in the series and contemporary culture.

Finally, Christina Babu explores reimagined works in "Retellings and Re-readings—Romance, Representation, and Reimaginations in *Self-Made Boys: A Great Gatsby Remix*." *Self-Made Boys*, by Anna-Marie McLemore, is a novel exploring transgender representation. The book re-imagines F. Scott Fitzgerald's classic *The Great Gatsby* through the lens of a transgender protagonist, challenging traditional gender norms and bringing attention to the experiences of the transgender community. The author looks at transgender representation, class inequality, and self-acceptance using queer ecologies as a methodology, along with textual analysis. As more works in the traditional literary canon fall into the public domain, it is interesting to consider how many classic novels might receive a treatment positioning marginalized characters—and romance—at their centers.

CONCLUSION

Through these fifteen chapters, as well as our framing material, we hope that readers, scholars, romance fans, and authors alike will observe the ever-changing landscape of this popular genre in all its forms and learn more about how audiences interact with texts and each other. As the romance community becomes more decentralized and its members use online networks to connect individually on a global scale, readers are taking the experience of reading to be a community behavior, interacting with each other in real and virtual spaces, and being critical consumers and artists by demanding more inclusivity, more and better representation, and a greater emphasis on the empowerment of characters without the baggage that historically stereotyped the genre as lacking a positive effect on women's real lives. As of this writing, it has been over forty years since Radway first surveyed her participants, and as you will see here, the landscape of romance has dramatically changed in the interim.

Chapter 11

Coming of Age and Coming Out

The Intersection of New Adult and Queer Romance

Kathleen W. Taylor Kollman

A recent article from *The New York Times* indicates that LGBTQA+ romance novels have lately gone from "a quiet presence" to being "prominently displayed at independent bookstores and on the shelves at Walmart."[1] As of this writing, there are nearly 8,000 books shelved on Goodreads as LGBT romance.[2] Goodreads users have also created a more curated list of the top ten best such novels in the New Adult subgenre.[3] The sixth book on that list was written over a century ago, which calls into question the perception of queer romance as being a new phenomenon or a fad. In fact, this classic novel has much in common with one of the most popular examples of queer romance of the twenty-first century, and both have the distinction of detailing young men in new adulthood navigating the process of experiencing true love at the same time as coming out to important people in their lives. For far too long, LGBTQA+ romance's contributions to the New Adult subgenre (and vice versa) have not been well documented, but the intersection of these two genres is an important one in the field of romance studies. Readers respond enthusiastically to stories of people voicing their identities while simultaneously moving from youth to adulthood and combining these two important events in one's life with also finding love makes for a compelling combination of literary tropes. Janice Radway's *Reading the Romance* almost exclusively focused on novels featuring characters past young and new adulthood, and the couples in all the books her participants read were heterosexual. This chapter (as well as others in this book) seeks to shed light on areas that were not acknowledged anticipated by either Radway or her contemporaries. Herein, I aim to highlight the importance of uncovering dismissed or unacknowledged romances that were not within the recognized heteronormative romance world.

METHODOLOGY AND THEORETICAL LENSES

This chapter will take a textual analysis approach to looking at two novels—written over a hundred years apart—that stand as significant works in the history of LGBTQA+ romantic fiction. Furthermore, these two novels could easily both be called New Adult romances, as the characters involved are all in their early adulthood and through their coming out develop a more firmly established adult identity. In both cases, one half of the romantic pair embarks on a coming-out process, articulating their sexuality to either part or all of their social circle (or the world at large), as well as to themselves. As such, this chapter's standpoint is also rooted in queer theory, with grounding in the work of Eve Kosofsky Sedgwick.[4]

SCHOLARLY CONTEXT

LGBTQA+ Romance and New Adult Romance Scholarship

Both LGBTQA+ romance and New Adult romance have not been studied enough. This collection offers some redress to both, however, including Josefine Smith's contribution, "Romance Readers' Perceptions of New Adult Fiction," and Christina M. Babu's "Retellings and Rereadings—Romance, Representation, and Reimaginations in *Self-Made Boys*: A Great Gatsby Remix." The 2016 collection *Romance Fiction and American Culture: Love as the Practice of Freedom?* is one of the earliest examples of research material dedicated to LGBTQA+ romance, in the form of chapters by Elizabeth Matelski ("I'm Not the Only Lesbian Who Wears a Skirt") and Len Barot ("Queer Romance in Twentieth- and Twenty-First Century America").[5] Two of the most influential pieces of romance scholarship from its earliest days (*Reading the Romance* and *A Natural History of the Romance Novel*) make no mention of it at all, even though LGBTQA+ romance novels did exist prior to the publication of those books.

Pamela Regis: Background

Seminal scholar Pamela Regis is an English professor whose scholarship has focused on early American literature, Jane Austen, poetry, and—most relevant to this present collection—popular romance fiction. With *A Natural History of the Romance Novel*,[6] Regis wanted to engage in elements of romance fiction analysis that *Reading the Romance* does not.[7] Where Janice Radway's work is concerned with audience reception of, engagement with, and enthusiasm for romance novels, Regis focuses instead on the content of the works themselves. Form is key for Regis, while as a cultural studies scholar, Radway is more concerned with what people do with the works once published. Certainly, this is an oversimplification of two very key texts (Radway's *Reading the Romance* and Regis's *A Natural History of the Romance Novel*, because certainly both books do a bit of analysis of content and reception). However, this distinction in general focus is one way to categorize and differentiate the two and best summarize their contributions to popular romance studies.

Regis's book covers a lot of ground and includes feminist interpretations of romance novels, a history of the genre from 1740 onward, and a full hundred pages on romance novels in the twentieth century, a nice lead-up to present scholarship that moves the conversation forward into the current century. However, there is an element absent from Regis's discussion when she defines and codifies the expected generic conventions of the romance novel, and that is where I hope to enter the discussion and expand upon her analysis.

E. M. FORSTER'S CONTRIBUTIONS TO LGBTQA+ AND NEW ADULT ROMANCE

In *A Natural History of the Romance Novel*, Regis devotes an entire chapter to E. M. Forster's 1908 novel *A Room with a View*, calling it "the ideal romance novel."[8] Regis makes this assessment even though she calls it Forster's "only novel that ends happily" and "his only romance novel,"[9] all despite critics finding fault with the unconvincing nature of the central couple's elopement.[10] This criticism is often set down to Forster being gay and having such ambivalent feelings about heterosexual love and marriage that the ending feels rushed, hurried, half-baked, and not as exciting as the lead-up to the ending. But I would argue with Regis's assertion that *A Room with a View* is Forster's only romance novel with a happy ending; he wrote and published another, which came out years before Regis's book.

Regis devotes six full pages of her book to dissecting *A Room with a View*'s plot and success adhering to romance novel tropes—believably and well—but never once does she mention Forster's novel *Maurice* (written 1913, published posthumously in 1971, and featured on the aforementioned Goodreads list of best New Adult LGBTQA+ romance novels). *Maurice*, in fact, has been lauded for giving readers "a rarefied view of queer possibility: a happy ending for gay men, with the book's protagonist, the wealthy and well-educated stockbroker Maurice Hall, finding love with the young groundskeeper Alec Scudder."[11] Yet for Regis it is as if it never existed.

The main plot points of *A Room with a View* and *Maurice* are incredibly similar, when boiled down. In the earlier novel, the naïve-but-curious Lucy Honeychurch goes on an Italian holiday with her much older cousin, Charlotte, who is deeply overprotective of her charge's reputation. Lucy meets the mercurial and proto–"manic pixie dream boy"[12] George Emerson, whose joie de vivre is unlike anything Lucy has ever encountered. George steals a kiss from Lucy in a field of violets, much to Charlotte's chagrin, and the two are forcibly separated for the remainder of the vacation. Upon returning to her home in the English countryside, Lucy becomes engaged to the much wealthier and more socially appropriate match, Cecil Vyse. Cecil is a wealthy man of leisure who treats Lucy like a beautiful inanimate object, however, and the two of them have almost inverse chemistry. Ultimately, Lucy breaks her engagement and, with the blessing of George's father, elopes with George, alienating the rest of her family in the process.

Maurice, comparatively, follows a similar pattern. The title character, Maurice Hall, first falls in love with a classmate at Cambridge, Clive Durham. Clive is unwilling to physically consummate their relationship, but he is remarkably similar to George in terms of opening up a new world of philosophical possibility to the more analytical and introverted Maurice. A significant point where the two novels diverge, however, is that Clive effectively turns into Cecil, becoming staid, boring, and—the death knell to his relationship with Maurice—heterosexual, at least outwardly. Maurice does meet his "true" George, however, in the gamekeeper Alec Scudder. With Alec, Maurice is able to have a relationship that is a match physically as well as emotionally, and the only issue is one that also plagued Lucy and George: Alec is not of Maurice's social and cultural rank. The disparity here is far greater than Lucy and George's economic differences, though, and Maurice must give up a lot to remain with Alec, particularly during a time period in which homosexuality was still criminalized in the U.K. After wrestling with the repercussions, Maurice ultimately determines that a closeted life in higher society is not worth the pain of hiding or not having Alec in his life, and he throws off the bonds of convention to reunite with his true love.

According to Regis, romance novels must follow a basic plot template of eight points: first, the novel must depict "the initial state of society in which heroine and hero must court," then comes "the meeting between heroine and hero," followed by "the barrier to the union of heroine and hero," a depiction throughout of "the attraction between the heroine and hero," a "declaration of love between heroine and hero," "the point of ritual death," "the recognition by heroine and hero of the means to overcome the barrier," and an ending which includes "the betrothal."[13] *A Room with a View* contains each of these points. For the first, readers meet Lucy and Charlotte at the start of the book and quickly understand the time period and time of society (both within their family and their socioeconomic class) that they are trying to adhere to.

Charlotte represents the staid ideology of the Victorian era, while Lucy represents the more progressive Edwardian era, but otherwise the two women are products of their culture. George enters their lives as both families are staying at the same Italian *pensione*, and the barrier to their union is the interference of Charlotte to preserve Lucy's reputation. Charlotte presumes that, simply because George stole a kiss, Lucy is in danger of being compromised, and the further implication is that George is not a suitable match for Lucy based on his demeanor and economic status.

George and Lucy's attraction is made palpable by their kiss (an action which is repeated when George and Lucy are reacquainted in England), the two at various points declare love for each other, either directly or to their family members. The point of ritual death is a moment Regis defines as being "the moment in a romance novel when the union of the hero and heroine seems completely impossible" and can be "marked by death or its simulacrum," such as "fainting or illness."[14] In other romance circles, this plot point is sometimes referred to as the "black moment," and Regis states this comes in *A Room with a View* when "[n]ear the Loggia one Italian stabs another," with the dying man seeming to reach out to Lucy as he falls; Lucy faints in response.[15] Of course, George rescues her from this moment, which further cements their relationship. The final two points come with Lucy breaking her engagement to Cecil, followed by her admitting her love for George to his father. The final point, the betrothal, culminates in Lucy and George's elopement.

All the exact same points are present in *Maurice* as well: readers first see the society and pressure Maurice lives in, with the limitations he and Clive must endure to have any semblance of a relationship. The problems associated with being an openly gay man in Edwardian England are their barrier, and it is here when the role of the secondary protagonist is switched from Clive to Alec.

The attraction between Alec and Maurice is a slow burn; Maurice first only knows the other man as the gamekeeper, Scudder, not even learning his first name. But in the throes of his angst over losing Clive, Maurice has almost preternaturally summoned Alec to his room one night, as if both men have been signaling their mutual interest subconsciously until it is no longer in question. Alec puts a ladder up to Maurice's window and enters his room, asking "was you calling out for me?" and then stating emphatically "I know" of Maurice's longing for him. The text then merely euphemistically describes Alec as "touch[ing] him," but the implication is clear.[16]

The declarations of love between Maurice and Alec are fraught and not wholly joyful, unfortunately, at least early in their relationship, but they are well-defined. As they discuss whether or not they can somehow stay together, Alec casually mentions that the two "love each other," and Maurice does not deny this but insists it is not an "excuse to act silly."[17] Earlier, Maurice and Clive had professed love to each other with much less practicality and angst, and yet their relationship was doomed. Maurice admits to Clive that he loves Alec, and their ultimate commitment to one another cements the relationship firmly, even if the declarations of love are not as passionate as they are between Lucy and George in *A Room with a View*.

The black moment or ritual death is more allegorical and contained in Alec's intention to leave England. Due to Maurice seeming to be willing for him to go alone, it appears the two will be separated indefinitely. Instead, Alec and Maurice have their "means to overcome the barrier" by agreeing to stay together, the social perception of their sexual orientation and class differences no longer as important to them as keeping each other. And although Maurice and Alec could not have been legally engaged or wed during the early twentieth century, it is clear they intend to live as a married couple; hence the "betrothal" moment is fulfilled.

Pamela Regis's book was published twenty years before this present volume was conceived, and in the intervening years, LGBTQA+ romance fiction has exploded in popularity. This phenomenon is covered more comprehensively in other chapters in this book, but it is key to note here that not only was this neither true in 2003 when *A Natural History of the Romance Novel* was released nor in 1984 when Janice Radway conducted her study for *Reading the Romance*. It certainly was not the case when Forster wrote *Maurice* or when it was published after his death, although LGBTQA+ fiction did exist; it was simply not classified alongside romance novels with largely heterosexual female audiences. In fact, when updating Radway's survey for this collection, greater inclusivity of romance fiction beyond heterosexual couples was not included, partly to maintain consistency with the earlier data. If a new survey were designed, however, a full overhaul should warrant integration of much more precise and inclusive categories. Thus, it is not my purpose to call out Regis or Radway for any oversights on their parts but merely to point out how far LGBTQA+ romance fiction has come since not only Forster's lifetime but also even the last twenty years.

RED, WHITE & ROYAL BLUE AS LITERARY DESCENDENT OF *MAURICE*

Maurice is a clear antecedent to works like Casey McQuistin's 2019 novel *Red, White & Royal Blue*. McQuistin (who describes themselves as nonbinary, bisexual, and uses they/them pronouns, per their profile on the *Out* magazine 2023 "Out 100" list[18]) is the author of three LGBTQA+ romance novels, as well as a short story and a forthcoming fourth book, due out in 2024. While McQuiston writes in *Red, White & Royal Blue*'s author's note that the political rom-com was inspired by their reaction to the 2016 election,[19] the structure and setup is as if *Maurice* replaced much of its angst with a modern sensibility that does not assume complete social ruin for coming out as being in a same-sex relationship. Christine Larson and Ashley Carter cite this novel as "likely the first gay romance novel" to hit the *New York Times* bestseller list, achieving this honor in June of 2019, and "it was far from the last."[20]

Like *Maurice*, *Red, White & Royal Blue* still follows Regis's eight romance plot points, and the novel ends fully happily for its two male protagonists, Alex and Henry. First, readers see the initial state of society: Alex is the son of the sitting U.S. President and Henry is a prince of England. They have already been acquainted prior to the events of the novel, but do not particularly like each other. Alex and Henry's later meeting is really their first in a way, as they are now grown men and have a stronger initial connection. Their barriers are multifaceted and include the fact that while Alex is more open about his bisexuality, it is still not widely known, and Henry is not at all open about being gay. Furthermore, the couple is concerned not only about their own individual sexualities but how the media, their families, and even international politics will affect their union. There is a depiction throughout of their attraction, however, and the two have multiple steamy scenes together. Their love is declared in several ways, but perhaps most romantically through emails and text messages, since they live in different countries and are only able to connect in person intermittently. Henry frequently sends Alex poetry and regales him with interesting historical tidbits, which serves to further emotionally seduce Alex. The point of ritual death occurs when someone hacks into theses texts and emails and leaks them to the press, which is something they ultimately overcome when it is clear that their families are more supportive of the relationship than they initially assumed. While Alex and Henry do not get engaged by the end of the novel, they do agree to give up their political lives to live together and work on nonprofit social justice endeavors, which is tantamount to Regis's final plot point for a romance novel that ends happily ever after.

But *Red, White & Royal Blue*, as contemporary as it is, still includes an element that is also present in *Maurice* and which some critics and readers may be surprised is still necessary in twenty-first-century LGBTQA+ fiction: in both books, characters come out (in different ways and to different numbers of people) as queer. Coming out might be seen today by allies and members of the LGBTQA+ community as necessary and perhaps something that should not cause as much internal angst and external conflict as it is portrayed in some literature and media narratives, especially those of the twenty-first century. Research does suggest that coming out happens at an "increasingly younger age,"[21] and, on the average, "disclosing sexual identity (being 'out') yields wellness benefits for lesbian, gay, and bisexual (LGB) individuals."[22] However, due to a variety of factors including geographical location, social stigma, heteronormativity, family support and lack thereof, political climates, religion, and multiple other intersectional identity markers and standpoints, coming out presents different issues. For many members of the LGBTQA+ community, coming out has appreciable benefits to one's mental and physical health, but Nicole Legate et al. found that is strongly determined by someone's level of support in their personal and professional lives.[23] Furthermore, for individuals without strong support systems, coming out at all—or coming out at a young age or while enduring unsupportive situations—can be actively deleterious.[24] In fact, whether the risk is real or not, "Perceiving a social context as controlling in nature may be a barrier to disclosure for LGB individuals and a risk factor for concealment."[25] Nicholas Guittar found, too, that in recent years, young LGBTQA+ community members may also feel it is helpful to not come out with an identity but instead an affinity (e.g., "I like men" or "I like women" instead of saying "I am gay").[26] In this way, coming out with an affinity can be a strategy seen as "a less risky way to express sexual difference in a heteronormative society."[27]

Concealment of one's sexual orientation, affinity, or identity is also not uncommon, even in recent years, due in part to the nature of the coming-out act. It is not something one can do and be done with but is instead a process to be completed every time a member of the LGBTQA+ community meets a new acquaintance or coworker. As Roberto Baiocco et al. found, the "life stories [of LGBTQA+ community members] were characterized by fluctuating moments lived between certainty/uncertainty, revelation/concealment, denial/non-denial (i.e., 'blocked identity' vs. assertive-agent identities), and acceptance/non-acceptance (i.e., aware vs. fearful identities)."[28]

To summarize much of the research on the coming-out process, it is indeed a process not an event, it is fraught with social and political implications, it is not always something someone does in youth or early adulthood, and while it is indeed overall less dangerous now in many societies than it was in earlier eras, it is still not without risk to one's physical and mental safety. Thus, coming out is undertaken with extreme care and caution in many cases. Furthermore, representation matters to both members of marginalized communities as well as people for whom literature and other forms of fiction are their only exposure to such people; in research conducted by Jessica E. Black and Jennifer L. Barnes, it was found that exposure to fiction— especially young adult fiction—positively raised readers' "empathic concern, integrity, and moral agency," as well as "moral self via empathic concern."[29] There have also been other studies conducted that indicate a positive correlation in empathy and opinion formation when audiences consume literature and media with a variety of plots and themes, including issues and identities readers or viewers previously saw as controversial.[30]

New adult fiction, defined more thoroughly elsewhere in this collection,[31] includes periods of life where characters find themselves at turning points. Unlike the *bildungsroman*, which is defined as "coming-of-age," the period just past or at the end of one's teenage years is less about a specific rite of passage or initial self-discovery and more about blossoming more fully into an adult identity. The liminal period between young adult and new adult is one in which a character may think they know who they are, but the new adult journey is where they endure a further trial toward self-actualization (at least for the first quarter of their lives). Coming out as queer may be part of the *bildungsroman* process, to be sure, but it is sometimes more prevalent in New Adult fiction. In both YA and NA literature, both partners in the relationship may not be in the same place at the same time in their coming-out journey. In *Maurice*, Alec is ready to live his life as openly as possible with Maurice, whereas Maurice dithers about with this option, at times even going so far as to try to seek conversion therapy. Maurice (unlike Clive) knows he is gay, but he is not yet certain he wants to embrace it. Alec is already there, and this difference is part of their conflict.

In *Red, White & Royal Blue*, Alex already knows he is bisexual, and while Henry seems fairly certain he is gay, the public coming-out process for the two of them is fraught with social and political ramifications: Alex is part of the American first family, and Henry is the grandson of the British queen. While Maurice may face prison for being openly gay, part of his quandary is also the socioeconomic difference between himself and Alec. For Alex and Henry in McQuiston's novel, the lovers are at least similar in social standing, yet that almost makes things more difficult. Alex and Henry are not just common young men; their families are in the news media constantly, and their affair is leaked to the tabloid press. Alex's mother, as the U.S. President, even needs to determine whether a full acknowledgment of her son's relationship constitutes an international crisis, politically, despite the allied nature of the two nations.

Arguably, the political nature of Alex and Henry's relationship and the socioeconomic issues in Maurice and Alec's relationships are merely allegories for the coming-out struggle. An out queer person in their twenties may find themselves falling in love with someone who is not quite as comfortable with revealing this part of themselves to more than just their partner, and that is a very realistic, relatable phenomenon for readers of New Adult LGBTQA+ romance fiction. The "black moment" may not merely involve something external that threatens to pull the lovers apart but may stem from an internal struggle in one or both partners as to what this relationship means for their personal identity.

JANICE RADWAY'S ORIGINAL SURVEY AND THE PRESENT DATA

The new data from the current survey still fills in some important gaps from Radway's original version while not deviating altogether from her initial questions. For one thing, the current survey could be distributed much more widely and internationally, thanks to the internet and social media. Still, for future researchers looking to specifically widen the scope, definition, and inclusivity of romance fiction, a simple language update might have been helpful. By continuing to use the terms "hero" and "heroine," the current survey perhaps prevented some potential respondents from finishing filling it out, on the assumption that this closed set of terms is meant to disparage their reading genre or even exclude their own identity, when that was certainly not the intention.[32]

Amazon publishes an annual Top 20 Romance Books of the Year, and for 2023, this list includes one novel—*Dragged to the Wedding*, by Andrew Grey[33]—that features a same-sex pairing.[34] In the Top 100 Best Sellers in New Adult and College Romance as of January 2, 2023, the Top 20 also includes a same-sex pairing (*God of Fury*, by Rina Kent).[35] Both lists include subgenres of everything from fantasy to mafia to hockey romances. Furthermore, Larson and Carter point out that innovations in digital publishing have opened up the romance genre in particular to greater experimentation and allows "marginalized voices or practices [to] become amplified, institutionalized, and legitimized," although they also caution "that new structures may create new types of marginalization, permitting only limited expansion of historically underrepresented voices in a phenomenon known as 'pinkwashing.'"[36] It is also feared by readers and creators in the queer romance community "that queer romance might prove to be yet another short-term publishing trend, liable to fade away or come and go, such as vampire romance and other well-worn tropes."[37] These factors and concerns may be why the mainstream lists include a token amount of LGBTQA+ fiction even as the audience for these works is extensive and shares their book recommendations with enthusiasm.

Still, while even greater representation of more sexual identities on these lists would be nice, it is important to note that it is present here even in lists that appeal to broad audiences of romance readers. Thus, future research based on Radway's original survey should indeed be updated to include these multiple identities, pairings, and forms of representation, even if Larson and

Carter temper their notice of these expanded offerings with a fair amount of caution that the trends may not hold. LGBTQA+ people will continue to exist, regardless of the proliferation of queer romance, and the voices of those who read and produce queer romance should still be better represented in romance criticism and scholarship. Furthermore, recent book bans on "themes about L.G.B.T.Q. life aimed at children and young adults" means that representation is more important than ever to support the community and its allies.[38]

CONCLUSION

Ten years after the publication of *A Natural History of the Romance Novel*, Pamela Regis gave a talk at the Popular Culture Association conference to revisit the work; this was subsequently published in the *Journal of Popular Romance Studies*. Regis is humble and funny throughout this talk, at one point citing as her first principle of literary critical ethics the notion that "[t]he most modest work of fiction, including romance fiction, is a greater accomplishment than the finest work of literary criticism."[39] This perspective suggests that not only that writing fiction is a noble undertaking but also that judging and analyzing others' work is still somehow not as pleasurable an activity as consuming romance fiction. This is particularly true because romance fiction is a genre built on providing readers with joyfully embodied feelings, which even the best literary criticism fails to do. Regis goes on to describe the various approaches one can take with doing a close reading of a romance novel, regardless of the era of its composition or application of other methods of analysis, such as trying to gauge reader response. With a novel written during the early American period, for example, a reader might have enjoyed learning about complex legal issues that they might also face in real life—which also might be of interest to current scholars of American studies or American history—but ultimately the readers were most likely interested in the work in the end due to its conclusion that "still arrive[s] at happiness."[40] She also points out that in her aforementioned eight elements, these "can occur in any order, be doubled or tripled, and more than one element can be manifested in a given scene or bit of action."[41] The example she uses in much of this talk— *Emily Hamilton*, written by Sukey Vickery in 1803—includes many historical details that speak to women's legal and social subjugation during the early nineteenth century. And yet, Vickery is still able to give us happy endings for her protagonists. Although nowhere in her talk does Regis discuss LGBTQA+ romance, the very fact that there is an acknowledgment that romance fiction of earlier eras is sometimes capable of allowing its couples to live happily ever after, even in environments hostile to women, indicates that members of any marginalized group have always still been able to flourish in love—at least on the pages of romance novels—for as long as the genre has existed. As women have made substantial gains in being seen as a participating as full citizens in most societies (albeit with periods of backlash), so now we see that the romance genre is opening up to depicting the fact that members of the LGBTQA+ community have also been able to navigate the space between oppression and happy romantic love. Therefore, expanding the bounds and definitions of the romance fiction genre to acknowledge this fact is, in some ways, a form of artistic and critical activism that further inculcates empathetic responses in readers both within the community and those allied with it.

As Regis closes her talk, she asks those in attendance and her fellow panelists what the "challenges" the field faces are, what its "tasks" are, and, finally, "Where do we go from here?"[42] I would say one great place to go would be to start seeking out historical works like Forster's *Maurice* and more obscure variations thereof, for their examination is just as important as lesser-known romance novels depicting heterosexual relationships. Furthermore, McQuiston is not the only person writing LGBTQA+ romance today, and treating popular works of the current decade with equal respect and enthusiasm is similarly vital an endeavor. Since *Red, White & Royal Blue*'s success, other works released by major publishers have been similarly hits with audiences, such as "Alexis Hall's male-male *Boyfriend Material* in 2020, Lana Harper's sapphic *Payback's a Witch* in 2021," among others.[43] A future scholar may also wish to fully reframe Radway's survey to only focus on LGBTQA+ romance, for example, or only romance featuring people of color. By targeting specific readerships and fandoms, scholars can get a fuller and clearer picture of the state of the genre in the twenty-first century.

NOTES

1. Elizabeth A. Hall, "'I Just Want Something That's Gay and Happy': L.G.B.T.Q. Romance is Booming." *New York Times.* https://www.nytimes.com/2022/03/30/books/lgbtq-romance-novels.html.

2. "LGBT Romance Shelf," Goodreads, https://www.goodreads.com/shelf/show/lgbt-romance.

3. Best LGBTQ Contemporary Romance Novels for New Adults," Goodreads, https://www.goodreads.com/list/show/164978.Best_LGBTQ_Contemporary_Romance_Novels_for_New_Adults.

4. I write about male LGBTQ+ identity and my reliance on Sedgwick's work at more length in my book chapter, "'Getting Bi': Darryl Whitefeather as Bisexual Bellwether." In *Perspectives on Crazy Ex-Girlfriend: Quality Post-Network Television*, edited by Amanda Konkle and Charles Burnetts (Syracuse University Press, 2021),

which I provide a brief history of gay and bisexual male characters in a variety of media genres.

5. Elizabeth Matelski, "I'm Not the Only Lesbian Who Wears a Skirt," and Len Barot, "Queer Romance in Twentieth- and Twenty-First Century America," In *Romance Fiction and American Culture* (Routledge, 2017), 71–88; Len Barot "Queer Romance in Twentieth- and Twenty-First Century America" In *Romance Fiction and American Culture* (Routledge, 2017), 389–404.

6. Pamela Regis, *A Natural History of the Romance Novel* (University of Pennsylvania Press, 2003).

7. Janice Radway, *Reading the Romance: Women, Patriarchy, and Popular Literature*. (Chapel Hill: University of North Carolina Press, 1991).

8. Regis, *A Natural History*, 99.

9. Regis, *A Natural History*, 99.

10. Regis, *A Natural History*, 99–100.

11. Manuel Betancourt, "A New Novel Reinvents E.M. Forster's Classic Gay Love Story 'Maurice.'" *New York Times*. https://www.nytimes.com/2021/07/06/books/review/alec-william- di-canzio.html.

12. Sakshi Sharma, "The Male Version of the Manic Pixie Dream Girl Has Arrived. But Is the Bar Too Low?" *Elle India*, May 4, 2022. https://elle.in/male-manic-pixie-dream-girl-arrived/.

13. Regis, *A Natural History*, 30.

14. Regis, *A Natural History*, 14.

15. Regis, *A Natural History*, 101.

16. E. M. Forster, *Maurice* (Avarang, 2023), 185–86.

17. Forster, *Maurice*, 224.

18. Raffy Ermac, "Casey McQuiston," *Out Magazine*, October 17 2023). https://www.out.com/out100/2023/storytellers/casey-mcquiston.

19. Casey McQuiston, *Red, White & Royal Blue* (St. Martin's Griffin, 2019), 419.

20. Christine Larson and Ashley Carter (1–2).

21. Nicolas Guittar, "'At First I Just Said "I Like Girls": Coming Out with an Affinity, Not an Identity," *Journal of LGBT Youth* 11 (2014): 403.

22. Nicole Legate, Richard M. Ryan, and Netta Weinstein, "Is Coming Out Always a 'Good Thing'? Exploring the Relations of Autonomy Support, Outness, and Wellness for Lesbian, Gay, and Bisexual Individuals," *Social Psychological and Personality Science* 3, no. 2 (2012): 145.

23. Legate et al., "Is Coming Out Always a 'Good Thing,'" 145.

24. Legate et al., "Is Coming Out Always a 'Good Thing,'"150.

25. Legate et al., "Is Coming Out Always a 'Good Thing,'" 150.

26. Guittar, "'At First I Just Said 'I Like Girls,'" 388.

27. Guittar, "'At First I Just Said 'I Like Girls,'" 388.

28. Roberto, Baiocco, Fau Rosati, Altomare Enza Zagaria, and Jessica Pistella. "Telling My Life: Narratives of Coming Out in LGB People between Certainty/Uncertainty and Revelation/Concealment." *Journal of Gay & Lesbian Mental Health* 27, no. 4 (October 2023): 458.

29. Jessica E. Black and Jennifer L. Barnes, "Fiction and Morality: Investigating the Associations Between Reading Exposure, Empathy, Morality, and Moral Judgment." *Psychology of Popular Media* 10, no. 3 (2021): 159.
30. See in particular Hoewe and Sherrill, whose work goes into the conceptions of parasocial relationships and narrative transportation.
31. See Chapter 3, "Romance Readers' Perceptions of New Adult Fiction" by Josefine Smith.
32. This issue was brought up by several survey participants.
33. *Dragged to the Wedding*, by Andrew Grey.
34. Amazon.com, "Best Romance Books of 2023," https://www.amazon.com/best-romace-2023/b?ie=UTF8&node=17296235011.
35. Amazon.com "Amazon Best Sellers: Best Sellers in New Adult & College Romance," https://www.amazon.com/Best-Sellers-New-Adult-College-Romance/zgbs/digital- text/6487838011; *God of Fury*, by Rina Kent.
36. Christine Larson and Ashley Carter, "Love is Love: Reverse Isomorphism and the Rise of LGBTQ+ Romance Publishing." *New Media & Society* (December 2023): preprint, 3.
37. Larson and Carter, "Love is Love," 18.
38. Elizabeth Harris, "'I Just Want Something That's Gay and Happy': L.G.B.T.Q. Romance is Booming." *New York Times.* https://www.nytimes.com/2022/03/30/books/lgbtq- romance-novels.html.
39. Regis, "Ten Years After *A Natural History of the Romance Novel*: Thinking Back, Looking Forward." *Journal of Popular Romance Studies* 3, no. 2 (2013): 3.
40. Regis "Ten Years After" 5.
41. Regis "Ten Years After" 7.
42. Regis "Ten Years After" 9.
43. Larson and Carter, "Love is Love," 2.

Chapter 12

Getting Love Out of the Margins

Race, Disability, Sexuality, and the Idea of a Happy After for Marginalized People

Trinidad Linares

In this chapter, I will do a close reading of romance series that follow marginalized couples beyond the start of their relationship using a number of popular romance scholars who belong to the same or similar minority communities. My argument is people with oppressions deserve a happy ending and a positive future, even in fiction, which is why I chose romances that checked in after the regular happy ending. At the Researching the Romance Conference at Bowling Green State University in 2018, which makes reference to Janice A. Radway's *Reading the Romance* in its title, I presented a survey on the limited representation of Asian American men in romance novels written after 2000. Afterward, I mentioned how impressed I was that Jenn Bennett's *Grave Phantoms* (2015)[1] had an epilogue that covered the relationship after the characters were married. Another conference attendee commented dismissively, "Oh, yes. That used to be a trend." I did not respond to the woman because I do not always feel safe responding to white women as a woman of color (WOC), especially to someone who had more seniority in the field. As Dwight Conquergood remarks, "Subordinate people do not have the privilege of explicitness, the luxury of transparency, the presumptive norm of clear and direct communication, free and open debate on a level playing field that the privileged classes take for granted."[2] This chapter is inspired by that exchange and is a response to something that I see as a problem within Romancelandia. Of course, white able-bodied heteronormative couples have happily ever afters. They are the dominant group. When it happens to marginalized couples, it is monumental.

In this chapter, I analyze several novels in which marginalized couples get their happily ever after and beyond, as readers are given glimpses into their continued happiness through an epilogue or later books in a series. Race, sexual orientation, and able-bodiedness matter when talking about romance, because representation matters not only for members of the marginalized communities represented, but also for readers from other communities. Books are windows as well as mirrors, so I discuss why white able-bodied straight women romance readers like those who participated in Radway's research would find value in reading about minority communities. These representations could be instructive without being didactic for readers in dominant groups. American society is nowhere near equitable, so although representation cannot do all of the work, let us not disregard the work that it does do. Romance novels are accessible. They are in libraries, which allow patrons to have both digital and paperback copies. They can be bought in stores and online. As book banning, state and government policies, and hate crimes are currently affecting many of the marginalized communities in the romance books presented, this is the best time to read them and share them with others.

I selected books that center marginalized characters from different communities as full- fledged members of their communities and families. The aforementioned *Grave Phantoms* presents the story of an Asian American male hero in an interracial relationship during the time of anti-miscegenation; *Always Only You* (2020), by Chloe Liese, presents the story of a disabled heroine who forms an equitable partnership that lasts into the future;[3] and Alexis Hall's *Husband Material* (2022) explores queer futurity through the story of a gay couple.[4] Despite the fact that the romance books cover different oppressions, they all show what happened to the couple after they committed to each other and their relationships developed further. These views of long-term relationships refute the idea that people with oppressions do not deserve to be loved or have a future, which is what romances have traditionally espoused.

LITERATURE REVIEW OF MARGINALIZED IDENTITIES IN POPULAR ROMANCE

Race specificity matters in romance novels, and my analysis relies on the work of several scholars who have addressed this in their work. Erin S. Young's "Race, Ethnicity, and Whiteness" differentiates the representation of Asian Americans in comparison to other minoritized groups like Black and Native Americans, whose experiences are often conflated because of racism.[5] In comparison to other men of color (MOC) who have been represented as hypersexualized in popular culture, Asian American men have been presented as hyposexualized. This allows us to then see the implications of Bennett making Chinese American Bo the hero of *Grave Phantoms*. Young acknowledges that while depictions of interracial relationships between a person of color (POC) and a white person have been problematic, well-written representations can offer insight to these lived experiences.[6] *Grave Phantoms* eschews stereotypical tropes and uses casual and legalized racism as barriers to Bo's love with Astrid, a white woman. Bo's Asian American masculinity is a welcome departure from the aggressive white heterosexual masculinity Jayashree Kamblé documents in "Heterosexuality: Negotiating Normative Romance Novel Desire."[7] In Kamblé's "White Protestantism: Race and Religious Ethos in Romance Novels," she covers the value given to whiteness in terms of procreation, which is the reason for anti-miscegenation laws.[8] Jonathan A. Allan's "Gender and Sexuality" suggests that while Bo's characterization seems a contrast to the heroes in Radway's research, his more caring type of masculinity was something she mentioned as a flaw of the hero even though she saw it as valuable to the hero's makeup.[9] I use Young, Kamblé, and Allan in my analysis of Bo as he navigates his relationship with Astrid in California in 1929, when interracial relationships were discouraged and interracial marriages were illegal because of the fear that interracial children would contaminate the white populace.

The novel *Always Only You* shows that disabilities integral to Frankie, the heroine, do not prevent her from forming equitable partnership and having a future. In "Disabled Sexuality, Incorporated: The Compulsions of Popular Romance" Emily M. Baldys contends that representation of disabled people in popular romance can be meaningful to both disabled and nondisabled readers, but argues there needs to be a shift from the trope of rehabilitation to a better representation of chronically disabled people.[10] Frankie's disability in *Always Only You* is a permanent state and acknowledges the lived reality for many disabled people. Ria Cheyne's "Disability Studies Reads the Romance" points out the ways that romance can challenge negative stereotypical views on disability by stressing that disabled characters have the right to be loved and have sex.[11] Liese does not shy away from descriptions of sex and desire between Frankie and her able-bodied boyfriend Ren. Sandra Schwab's "'It is Only with One's Heart that One can See Clearly': The Loss of Sight in Teresa Medeiros's the *Bride and the Beast* and *Yours Until Dawn*" points out how gendered disability representation in romance does not favor a disabled heroine, instead she must be the helper to the disabled hero.[12] *Always Only You* challenges the patterns in Schwab's research by having a heroine who is disabled, but is capable of helping others.

To contextualize my reading of *Husband Material,* I turn to scholarly work on gay and M/M romance. Kacey Whalen's master's thesis entitled "A Consumption of Gay Men: Navigating the Shifting Boundaries of M/M Romantic Readership," one of the most comprehensive works on the subject to date, details the complicated history of queer representation when straight women have been both the writers and the audience.[13] Hall's *Husband Material* rejects the male/male (M/M) tropes that mimic heteronormative relationships and instead presents a gay relationship developing from a queer community. Jonathan A. Allan's chapter "Slashing and Queering," in his book *Men, Masculinities, and Popular Romance*, covers slash fiction and bromance to provide some context for what makes a homosexual popular romance novel different.[14] In addition to Allan and Whalen's work, I also incorporate Kamblé's overview about how romance heroes became antisocial to perform heteronormativity and the growth of gay visibility in romance novels. This is relevant to my discussion of how Luc and Oliver, the gay couple in *Husband Material*, negotiate their long-term relationship when society often views queer relationships as disposable.

I argue in this chapter that epilogues to romance novels and mentions of characters in later books that assert the continued happiness and togetherness of the couple after the standard happily-ever-after ending are especially significant when included in books where the heroes and/or heroines are from marginalized communities. Marginalized characters in fiction are rarely guaranteed love or a happy ending beyond living by the end of the story. Even in romances, if such characters exist, they are consigned to the background as a helper or beneficiary of the protagonist's kindness, but destined to end the story alone. Epilogues and continuing character storylines, however, are mostly dismissed or ignored by romance scholars, as evidenced by the throwaway comment I received at the Researching the Romance Conference. Except for Nicole M. Jackson's article on Black romance writer Alyssa Cole,[15] no other scholars touch upon how important an epilogue can be for minority characters. Jackson posits that such epilogues could actually be seen as beginnings, indicating a future for the characters, their family, and community. My scholarship extends Jackson's argument and shows how this idea can be applied to more than one minority community and type of story extension. In addition to romance scholars, I also turn to academics who document the historical, medical, and legal aspects of these oppressions to better ground my literary analysis of enduring marginalized relationships.

SITUATING MYSELF AS A MINORITY READER AND SCHOLAR

I am an immigrant, an Asian/Asian American mother, a Pinay, with some health issues, and a straight woman (in a queer relationship). My experience falls in line more with Homi Bhabha's term "hybridity" rather than intersectionality, because I acknowledge I have both oppressions and privileges. Some of my struggles happen independently of those oppressed identity markers, and I can experience joy in being who I am. My excitement at seeing

Asian American/Asian representation in a book has often been curtailed upon seeing words such as "poignant," "generational struggle," and "triumph of the spirit" in the backcopy or promotional quote. To have a book with an oppressed character experiencing never-ending horrors solely based on their identity with no sense of agency, is more of a fantasy than marginalized characters being able to love and form relationships that last.

I read romance novels long before it even occurred to me that there was a possibility someone with an intersectional/hybrid identity like me could be a protagonist in a romance novel. As a child, I received a box of Dell romances from the late 1970s and early 1980s. In college, I had an internship with Dorchester Publishing, which published Leisure Books and Love Spell. I wrote the back-cover copy for *McLaren's Bride* by Debra Dier, read their books, and ran a contest. I presented for the romance track for the national Popular Culture Association. My other romance presentations have been for the Literature/Film Association Conference 2016, the Midwest Popular Culture Conference 2020, the International Association for the Study of Popular Romance Digital Forum 2020, the Wayne Pop 2020 Virtual Conference, and the Bowling Green State University Latino Issues Conference 2021, as well as the aforementioned Researching the Romance Conference 2018. In 2021, I was briefly a book reviewer (with a focus on LGBTQIA+) for Tallon Lake, which was to be an online romance magazine. My romance interests are not limited to books or the West and instead are driven by looking at representations of marginalized characters. I thought I loved romance, but I have come to find that the discussion of the subversion of power dynamics is itself sexy and compelling, which makes the genre of romance in its various mediums a great vehicle for analysis.

RACE: *GRAVE PHANTOMS*

Even in this century there are books like Lori Wick's *Bamboo and Lace* that are a literary version of yellowface.[16] Recently, however, more writers of color (Asian [especially Southeast Asian/Desi] and Black female writers) like Sonali Dev and Alyssa Cole have changed the landscape somewhat. Black women and Asian men have faced discrimination in dating sites and representation in media.[17] Some Black women authors with this dating experience, who are sometimes also fans of either Korean pop music (K-Pop) or Korean dramas (K-Drama), have published books through online publishers centering themselves and Asian men. Reader recommendation sites like Goodreads have brought attention to these books, thus creating a market.[18] Now public libraries have these books in their digital offerings. Online publishing as well as the continuation of popularity of the Hallyu Wave may have pushed some mainstream publishers to finally allow this representation. In the *Ripped Bodice State of Racial Diversity in Romance* 2021 report, racial representation was still low.[19]

Grave Phantoms is a novel set in the 1920s, yet the discrimination it depicts is incredibly relevant today. The current attacks on APIDAs (the umbrella term that includes Asian Pacific Islander and Desi Americans) have risen over 330% as a result of fears over COVID-19 and the 45th American president's hateful rhetoric toward Chinese/Chinese Americans, but have received limited mainstream news coverage.[20] The scientific community has been studying and validating the very real effects of this discrimination.[21] Romance novels can remind readers that APIDAs are people and deserve to live. The Smithton readers' belief "in fiction's rendering of the material world" is not limited to white women in the 1980s.[22] In readers' negotiation with text, they can accept that part of it is real even if it contains fantastic or supernatural elements.

I am detailing all sorts of legal discriminatory practices because many are still in play. Current laws like SB 264 in Florida, which prevents Chinese nationals from buying homes and suggesting that they are a threat to national security are just new versions of the Alien Land Law enacted in 1913 that kept Japanese immigrants from owning land.[23] Discrimination sees Asian people as foreign invaders—even if they are born in America or are half-white—not individuals. Additionally, history is filled with examples in which laws targeting one Asian group were then applied to others. For instance, the Page Act of 1875 restricted the immigration of Chinese women on the assertion that they were all prostitutes.[24] This became general public perception of Asian/Asian American women and is the root of the popular American stereotype that all Asian women are sex-starved, will happily have sex for money, and are basically identical. Young stresses that Asian or biracial Asian heroines in romances have traditionally not been allowed to achieve "the genre's narrative goal of the conventional gendered victory—typically afforded to white heroines" and are instead presented in racialized/sexualized stereotypes like "the dragon lady."[25] Unlike other racial groups, where both the men and women are represented as more overtly sexual than their white counterparts, the hypersexualization of Asian women has led to the emasculation of Asian men.

Bennet set *Grave Phantoms* during a time period when so many of the laws curtailing Asian American rights were aggressively enacted, especially in California. Generalizing based on the genre's formulaic nature, Radway remarks, "There is little need for that reader to attend the nuances of any particular novel to understand the nature of the story."[26] However, I would argue that these nuances matter when you are talking about oppressed minorities, especially in certain points in history. The author of *Grave Phantoms* is a white woman who understands this and decisively proves that it is possible for people from dominant groups to also tell these stories if they do them with respect and thorough research. In her acknowledgments, Bennett thanks:

> John Jung (author of several fascinating books about the history of Chinese immigrants in America), the National Women's History Museum, the Bay Area Radio Museum, the Shaping San Francisco Museum history project, the University of Washington's Civil Rights and Labor History Project, the National History Project, the National College in Mexico City, radio historian John F. Schneider, and Professor Tak-Hung Leo Chan.[27]

Bennett does not go into full detail about which resources she used for which specific sections of her novel, but it is clear that she spoke to people who are not only knowledgeable about the Chinese/Chinese American community, but are also part of that community. She dedicates the book to Mary Tape. Seven decades before the Supreme Court Case *Brown v. Board of Education*, Mary Tape successfully fought the San Francisco school board for her daughter's right to go to public school in the *Tape v. Hurley* case only to have her children end up in segregated a Chinese school, yet it later allowed Chinese children access to public schools in San Francisco.[28] With her dedication, Bennett is signaling support of the Asian American struggle. Bennett's *Roaring Twenties* novel series centers around a Swedish American family, the Magnussons. *Grave Phantoms* features Astrid Magnusson and Chinese American Bo Yeung, who is the second-in-command of the Magnusson family's bootlegging business. Kamblè comments that "romance encapsulates the responses that economic and political policies have evoked in the British and American public" and the romance hero is often the way that the romance tries to work out uncomfortable contradictions."[29] Although he is not a Magnusson or white, Bo is in a favored position as hero. The novel starts with letters between Bo and Astrid, establishing their long-standing companionship. Bo has grown up with the Magnusson family since he was hired in his youth by Astrid's older brother Winter, creating an almost fictive kinship. Jackson explains, "Fictive kinship is the practice of valuing without distinction bonds between two people as familial, regardless of their actual blood relationship."[30] The Magnussons keep a room for him in their Pacific Heights mansion despite the fact that Bo has an apartment in Chinatown. Bennett, in a few short descriptions, shows that—even though the Magnussons were also immigrants—white immigrants had opportunities denied to Chinese immigrants that were influenced if not mandated by race laws toward Asians, and Bo's relationship with them gave him some benefits in a segregated city.

When she returns from college, Astrid's grown-up view of Bo does objectify him: "[T]he elegant sheen of his finely muscled arms seemed almost risqué. Virile."[31] Romance authors usually describe white men this way, but this bucks against the desexualized view of Asian American men that has dominated in the media for years. Celine Parreñas Shimizu, who studies Asian American sexuality in media, opposes ameliorating the racialized asexuality of Asian/Asian American men through espousing a toxic hypermasculinity, as a way to reclaim a non-white manhood. Instead, she suggests that looking at how relationships with Asian/Asian American men can bring understanding to "one's ability to oppress and at the same time experience subjugation."[32] She argues that we can take advantage of racialized masculinity, where the privilege of gender is countered by the oppression of race, to uncover attributes not found in white patriarchal society. The hero's tenderness created by racialization is what Radway's readers see as the flaw in the hero: "his exemplary masculinity is tempered by the presence of a small feature that introduces softness into the overall picture."[33] Ironically, it's this flaw that endears the heroine to him. Allan acknowledges that Radway sees the value of this flaw before there were critical studies on masculinity.[34] Bennett espouses this as an attribute, not as a flaw when she depicts the first time Bo and Astrid have sex and Bo tells her, "'I need to be in charge now. You've got to let go and give me the reins. You've got to trust me.'"[35] Bo's version of manhood rejects toxic masculinity and is into mutual fulfillment rather than simply a man's pleasure.

Radway pointed out that the reader "can read the story as a realistic novel about what might plausibly occur in an individual woman's life without having to face the unknown."[36] Readers must engage with Astrid as the female protagonist when she feels horrible about the racism Bo has encountered, considers how to best defuse a discriminatory situation, and thinks about their future:

> And then there were the deepest worries. The ones about class and race, and how he could not legally marry her. That if she got pregnant, their children would be under similar restraints. Where would they go to school? Would he take them to Dr. Moon if they got sick. Would they get treated with the same indignities he'd faced? Or would it be worse for them because they wouldn't be accepted in either community?[37]

Bennett spells it out for the readers because she realizes that many of them might not have had to think about these issues. Young contends that thoughtful depictions of interracial relationships can provide the "opportunity to address lived realities and celebrate the freedom of choosing whom to love."[38] American history is full of real instances that mirror what Bo and Astrid experienced. There were real dance halls where white women mixed with Asian American men.[39] They faced legal and personal challenges in getting married and starting families.

Not only do readers learn about the discrimination through Astrid witnessing white racists' treatment of Bo, but also through the point of view of Bo himself. Through Bo, readers can learn what it is like to live in such a body. Bo is strong, but when he is injured, he has to rely on Astrid's help to get him to a doctor in Chinatown because he cannot go to a regular hospital. Segregated hospital facilities existed in San Francisco during that time. Chinese immigrants were charged a hospital tax for services they would never be allowed to use when they entered the country. In the meantime, the Board of Health condemned the hospitals the Chinese created for themselves and repeatedly refused to recognize Chinese physicians as doctors.[40] This hurt-comfort scenario buoys the romance story while giving a nod to the grim reality of attaining medical care as an Asian American.

Even when Bo and Astrid realize they want to build a future together, they have to figure out what is possible. Young asserts, "We need more diverse novels . . . with protagonists whose racial identities are fully developed and not made symbolic."[41] Marriage laws create a distinct barrier. Bo's friend Sylvia Fong hands him a newspaper clipping about Washington state:

> The only state in the West that will allow different races to marry. They talk about how couples are getting around laws in other states—a Caucasian woman claimed to have Filipino blood in order to marry her minister in Nevada. But you don't have to lie in Washington to get a license. . . . Whether they honor that license is another story.[42]

As couples would come up with a plan to marry, laws would change around them. For instance, the *Roldan v. Los Angeles County* case allowed Filipinos to marry white people because they were classified differently from Japanese and Chinese people, but then a few weeks later, the state legislature amended the state's miscegenation statute to include Filipinos.[43] Even when one Asian group might be allowed a certain right, laws can be changed to lump them in with other groups. Rick Baldoz states, "The absence of clear-cut consistent definitions about racial classification gave local bureaucrats and state officials wide latitude in determining boundaries of exclusion, since they were free to interpret statutory meanings in line with prevailing community prejudices."[44] That's partly why Sylvia adds the end comment about honoring the license. Not only can states ignore the rights given in other states, but the laws can easily change to discriminate further. Additionally, states updated anti-miscegenation laws, using both racial and national labels, to expand the types of Asian Americans they could discriminate against.[45] Upon learning which groups were newly facing discrimination from other states, states would add those groups to their own laws. All these laws are important to document because they affect Bo and Astrid's future.

In the epilogue, we learn that Bo and Astrid are married and have had two children in the ten years after their relationship started. Despite the challenging laws, their relationship has not only continued, but they have grown into a settled family. Astrid is a radio broadcaster. Her family's company changed to a more legitimate fishing company and incorporated Bo's last name. Most of her family is celebrating Chinese New Year with her and Bo. They even had a float in a parade. Admittedly, this a highly positive ending, but Chinatowns could not have survived without some goodwill from white businesses. Jackson notes, "Epilogues in romances can take many forms and serve many functions. At their core, they can cement the fulfillment of the couple's major internal and external conflicts and the realization of the HEAs [happily ever afters], often by jumping ahead into the future."[46] Yet, the joy of marriage and children are tempered for people of color, as Jackson herself acknowledges in her article, because in a white-dominant America safety is not guaranteed. We see this as Astrid talks about not moving her children around for another radio job, showing how interracial families had to be careful even if they had financial means. One of the goals of anti-miscegenation laws was to curtail the production of mixed-race progeny because they were seen as a danger to society. Here the Yeung family has a little girl named May and a little boy named Ty. Kamblè states, "The advent of a new generation is an ideal conclusion for a white romance."[47] By describing May and Ty as happy and beautiful children, the author is lifting them up to be equal to white children. Bennett did not note how she landed on the date of 1939 for her epilogue, but in 1939 a California court case determining the estate of Allan Monks brought out the fact that his wife Antoinette Giraudo was of mixed race, which should annul their marriage under the anti-miscegenation laws of Arizona where they were married.[48] This court case would be part of the many court cases used to ultimately help decide *Loving v. Virginia* in 1967, the case that ended anti-miscegenation laws and allowed interracial marriage. Bennet cannot change Bo and Astrid's fate because of the time they live in, but she foreshadows the big future win created by many interracial couples fighting for their right to love one another. Young reminds us, "[A]s scholars, we must think more critically about how the genre has been and continues to be racialized, as well as the unique opportunities the genre affords in addressing and healing racial trauma."[49] *Grave Phantoms* details real obstacles that white supremacy has created for Asian Americans and presents an Asian American hero that resists stereotypes to fight against the continuous waves of anti-Asian hate.

DISABILITY: *ALWAYS ONLY YOU* AND THE BERGMAN BROTHERS AND SISTERS SERIES

Romance novels have had a history of positing that "love cures everything." Thankfully, more contemporary novels have normalized disability and a number of them have combined disability and race to create characters with intersectional identities. Anna Richland's *His Road Home*, Alisha Rai's *Swipe Right*, Alyssa Cole's *Can't Escape Love*, Helen Hoang's novels, and Talia Hibbert's Brown Sisters series are just a few of the novels out there. While she and her partner Ren Bergman are white, I focus here on Frankie Zeferino in Liese's *Always Only You* because she has both physical and mental disabilities. The entire Bergman Family Series covers couples where one or both partners have a disability. Liese's depiction of Frankie Zeferino also makes a great point of analysis because since *Always Only You* is the second novel in the series readers can witness the development of her relationship with Ren after they get together and even after they are married.

Frankie's brash voice starts the novel by criticizing her romantic interest in caps no less: "REN BERGMAN IS TOO DAMN HAPPY."[50] Frankie rants and raves about Ren, a hockey player on the team for which she handles the publicity. She takes pride in being a grump. We see her personality before she admits she has Autism Spectrum Disorder (ASD). Frankie's expression of her feelings refutes the stereotype that people with ASD are emotionless and robotic. She also shows limitations like understanding the social conventions of sarcasm, but being able to discern its utilization by others in real life. Frankie's cane, which is a mobility device, is an expression of her style and a weapon. She uses her cane against a drunk hockey player trying to come on to her. Radway declares that romance does not encourage the reader "to view the fictive analogues of real human activity in a new or unusual light."[51] However, the way Liese introduces Frankie shows she is disabled and creative with a sense of agency.

One popular pattern in romance, identified by Schwab, is for the heroine to see the hero's "inner wound and to heal it."[52] In the romance genre, disability is gendered as male while the heroine shows her value as carer. Schwab notes, "Impaired heroines tend to be much rarer. In these cases, disability is often used to emphasize the female's vulnerability and (uber-) goodness."[53] One disability would already keep a character from being a romantic lead, unless she was cured, but to have both would have been inconceivable in the past.

In *Always Only You*, Frankie is centered as the heroine and expresses W. E. B. Du Bois's "double consciousness" in practice as she describes her awareness of other people's treatment of her: "My whole life I've either been a puzzle or a predicament."[54] Frankie's descriptions of her childhood and early adulthood show her difficulty navigating situations she didn't fully comprehend and trying to placate others. Like most medical research, research on autism has focused on white male subjects so the masking that girls and women go through was understood much later.[55] Masking is mimicking the social behavior of others to appear neurotypical and can also be considered "compulsory able-bodiedness."[56] Frankie's adherence to her strict Italian Roman Catholic grandmother's rules about behavior actually delayed her autism diagnosis because she appeared neurotypical.

Frankie is apprehensive about her future with Ren based on her past experiences: "[M]y sensory limits, my unexpected emotions, my easily tired body, my unfiltered mouth, are part of the package deal with me, and apparently they wear out their welcome."[57] Frankie's restating how she is perceived by neurotypicals may be the "redundancy and overzealous assertion [that] perform important and particular function[s]."[58] Frankie's concerns are valid because American society still sees people with disabilities as burdens, not as people who can form equitable relationships. Sarah Smith Rainey explains, "The cultural script for relationships in which one person is physically disabled and the other is nondisabled is one of despair and pity. This script is enforced by portrayals of care burden on television, in film, and by the questions and comments of friends, family members, health care professionals, and strangers."[59] To validate Frankie's feelings of guilt, Liese provides details about Frankie's family dynamics and previous relationships. Her meltdowns angered her sister, her mother saw her as fragile, and her grandmother considered her a source of social embarrassment.[60] Frankie was accepted when she could conform her behavior to others' expectations, but her physical and mental health needs could not be hidden indefinitely. One of the breakthroughs in their relationship occurs when Frankie realizes Ren is a neurotypical who also performs for others:

> [Ren] "I've learned that things go better for me when that's what other people see."
>
> [Frankie] "But that's not all there is, is it? What most people see is . . . incomplete."[61]

Frankie's realization that there was more under Ren's placid façade makes her more interested in him because from her own experiences she understands what is behind that behavior. The surprise twist then is not that disabled people are also fully human, but that everyone performs acts of "normal" to meet certain expectations from different members of society.

When she finds out that Ren's younger sister Ziggy has autism and has trouble communicating with her parents, Frankie steps in to support Ziggy. She's displaying a variation on fictive kinship and also exemplifying the role of nurturing heroine.[62] Frankie's agency shows how the autistic community can fill in the gaps when parents and other family members don't understand.

Frankie's disabilities do not keep her from having sexual desires and acting on them. In fact, in this novel, Ren is the virgin and Frankie initiates the first kiss between them. When Ren talks about her virtue, Frankie quips, "I lost my virtue in the tenth grade."[63] Long before their friendship starts, Frankie is attracted to Ren and fantasizes about his body. Michael Gill notes, "sexual ableism operates by constructing individuals with the label of intellectual disability as being unable to live and act in sexually deliberate ways."[64] Because *Always Only You* is split between Frankie's and Ren's point of view, the reader is able to witness their desire for one another. Not only are Frankie's desires normalized, but Ren's attraction to Frankie's disabled body is not presented as a perversion. In one instance, she playfully pokes him in the butt with her cane when he notices she is checking him out. Cheyne asserts that romance challenges sexual ableism by "[d]epicting disabled heroes and heroines in satisfying sexual relationships and as erotic agents."[65] Before Ren and Frankie have vaginal intercourse, they already had manual and oral sex. Romance novels have had a tradition of focusing solely on vaginal intercourse, in spite of the fact that oral and manual sex are part of common heterosexual sexual behaviors. Focusing solely on vaginal intercourse in the narrative gives the assumption that "[o]ther ways of expressing sexuality and sexual intimacy are either ignored completely or viewed through a heternomative lens in which other forms of sex are perverse, unsatisfying, or pathetic."[66] Therefore, by highlighting a number of instances of manual and oral intercourse, Liese is cripping the heternormative sex in her novel. She is normalizing that intimacy for a couple is not solely dependent on a penis penetrating a vagina. Thus, a disabled person can have both heteronormative and non-heteronormative sex, even in the same relationship. Admittedly, these descriptions are now easier to elide along with the main heteronormative sex scene because there are more graphic descriptions of what couples do together in current novels.

Although *Always Only You* is the book that focuses on the development of their relationship, the couple's after story exists in the other books of the series, challenging Frankie's original fears and the ableist attitudes in popular culture. In *Ever After Always*, Frankie joins Ren's family on vacation and forgoes the strenuous activities.[67] In *With You Forever*, Frankie spends Christmas with the Bergman family.[68] Axel, the romantic protagonist of *With You Forever,* is also autistic, but he and Frankie have scant interaction, showing that disability is not always enough of a commonality for friendship. In *Everything for You*, Ren's brother Oliver has a shower chair in his shower for Frankie's use and refers to her as his "soon to be sister-in-law."[69] At the end of *Everything for You*, Frankie and Ren are getting married. *If Only You* starts with Frankie and Ren's wedding, although they are not the featured romantic couple in this novel. At this point, Frankie has gone to law school and is now an agent for Ren and his teammate Seb.[70]

We see that even though she is a side character now, Frankie is quite a forceful agent and her marriage with Ren is a happy and supportive one. She has continued acting as a big sister to Ziggy and is now exerting her influence as an aunt to Ren's niece. At the end of *If Only You*, we learn that Frankie is pregnant and the Bergman family is excited about it. Able-bodied women become pregnant in romances all the time, but disabled women usually don't have this right. Gill states, "When it comes to intellectual disability and motherhood, it would seem that mothering is only qualified by assessments of supposedly measurable intellect and assumed ability to take care of the offspring."[71] Based on Gill's research of how society and the law has treated disabled women who want to reproduce and be mothers, society views women as the parents who could profoundly affect the genetics and behavior of the children, so families and the government have tried to dissuade disabled women from getting pregnant or even sterilized them against their will. Thus, it is no small feat to show Frankie happily pregnant and supported as Ziggy, another autistic woman, looks at her with love at the end of *If Only You*.

When Radway researched and wrote *Reading the Romance*, large publishing houses and mass-market publishing were the norm and there were fewer self-published romance novels. She noted, "Because the shift to professional production has reduced self-storytelling substantially, there is no sure way to know whether the narratives consumed by an anonymous public are in any way congruent with those they would have created for themselves and their peers had they been able to buy them."[72] With the advent of online publishers and digital books, there has been a change in the landscape. Liese published the original paper copies of the Bergman series herself. I used the print copies as my source so my citations for the novels only have Liese's name, year, and title of the book. Penguin Random House publishes the e-book under its Berkley Romances imprint. Liese is autistic like her heroine and she wanted to write a #OwnVoicesStory.[73] By using beta readers, Liese ensures that her work is more polished than many self-published romances, and thus is garnering the publishing industry's attention and a place on the shelves of public libraries. Yet, works less polished than Liese's have also found fans online, suggesting that the romance audience are interested in stories about marginalized characters who are not represented in mass-market books. Radway's research showed that "what is perhaps crucial to the ideal reading experience is that the woman's success and particular feelings of worth, power, and satisfaction it engenders in her as well as the reader who vicariously shares her life."[74] Readers may be more open to identities different from theirs in a genre convention they know well. Autistic women may not be diagnosed until adulthood.[75] Therefore, it is also possible that Liese's readers are also women with autism. David T. Mitchell and Sharon L. Snyder's lament about disability representation in fiction is that, "while stories rely upon the potency of disability as a symbolic figure, they rarely take up disability as an experience of social or political dimensions."[76] The combination of *Always Only You* and mentions of Frankie in the later books show that disabled people are worthy romantic partners, they are very much their own person, and they are capable of long-lasting relationships. Cheyne elucidates, "Romance novels with disabled heroes or heroines require the reader to enter into an imaginative engagement with a world where disabled people love and are loved—happily ever after."[77] The Bergmans' accommodations in certain situations for Frankie are an example of equity, not infantilization. The depictions of some of the Bergmans or their partners as disabled provide the feeling of community or family to counteract the social segregation of people with disabilities. Frankie's disabilities are not a metaphors, but contextualized as a lived experience.

SEXUALITY: *BOYFRIEND MATERIAL* AND *HUSBAND MATERIAL*

During the time of Radway's research, all mass-market romances were heteronormative. However, that does not mean the interest in M/M romance among women readers is new. Guy M. Foster points out that straight women's interest in M/M romance has its antecedent in slash fiction, where heterosexual women took male characters from media and created a relationship between them in fan fiction.[78] Whalen chronicles how self-publishing in the digital era paved the way for slash fiction to turn into M/M romance novels.[79] This is similar to the increase of representation in mainstream romance novels after the rise in self-published romances with POC and disabled characters.

Even though the audience of romance readers is becoming more diverse or at least willing to read more diverse material, straight white women readers are still the main demographic according to *Still Reading the Romance* editors' data and the publishing industry. In fact, in 2020, the *Telegraph* had an article entitled, "Why is so much gay male romance fiction marketed at straight women?"[80] The article mused that a romance between men allowed women to enjoy romance with no chance of women being objectified. Whalen's research found that the lack of heroines was a selling point for M/M romance readers and at least one key reason was the guarantee "to not see women forced into traditional roles that other novels have a history of forcing them into."[81] These romances then may seem more equitable and with no chance of an abused heroine.

Kamblé's survey of Harlequin Mills & Boon novels in the U.S., Canada, and Britain during the 1970s and 1980s found that the rise of the alpha hero was a response to the gay pride and rights movements happening in these countries:

> The romance hero at this time is not only physically imposing but also emotionally remote and humorless, qualities associated with traditional masculinity. He is socially isolated as well, having no close friendships with men, and his relationships with women outside his family are completely sexual in nature. In other words, this hero seems impervious to homoerotic overtures and incapable of platonic friendships with women—an ideal antidote to the worry that some eligible bachelors might not want a woman at all.[82]

In this light, the hero's behavior was not only a backlash to the feminist movement, but was also an attempt to undercut any possibility of homosexuality or bisexuality. Kamblé also notes that this agenda with Orientalist leanings resulted in the uptick of sheik novels during this time as well to obfuscate the connection between straight white men and patriarchy.

In the preceding decades, changing views about gay rights and more acceptance about gay visibility (possibly combined with Islamophobia) made mainstream publishers abandon this type of hero. By the early 2000s, there are even gay couples in the subplots of a few mainstream romance novels.[83] Not to oversimplify the challenges the LGBTQIA+ community has faced and is still facing, it is still a feat to go from the fear of any suggestion of homosexuality, no matter how slight, in the 1980s to presenting a gay couple at the center of the romance story, not in opposition to it. Allan states, "Unlike slash, wherein the fantasy is for seemingly straight men to become a romantic unit, and unlike bromance, which cannot include sexuality, the popular romance introduces us to characters who are by and large gay and who are seeking the stability of a monogamous relationship."[84] Then romance presents its general body of readers, like the Smithton women, a perspective they don't know in a genre they intimately know, which makes them more amenable to it. Why not tropes about coupling and hope to make readers empathetic toward gay characters instead of a barrage of traumatic events where the character has no agency?

Senior editor Mary Altman used the success of the New Adult M/M romance *Red, White & Royal Blue* to make publisher Sourcebooks Casablanca to publish Alexis Hall's *Boyfriend Material*.[85] Hall uses a pseudonym to write queer romances. Unlike Liese, he finds the "own voices" problematic because of the expectations it creates.[86] For him, the work should carry more weight than the author's identity. Additionally, marginalized writers have been pigeonholed to only write about their community. Hall self-published the Spires series, and now Sourcebooks Casablanca is reprinting it.

Luc O'Donnell and Oliver Blackwood start their relationship in *Boyfriend Material*. Oliver is a straitlaced barrister, even if his views are progressive on many issues like the environment and animal rights. Luc criticizes him for being uptight and having a heterosexual circle of friends. Luc's friend group is queer. Priya is a lesbian with a college professor girlfriend. The James Royce-Royces are married gay men who have the same name and decided to hyphenate it. Tom is bisexual. Bridget is the token straight girl in Luc's queer group and one of the nonlawyer friends in Oliver's straight group. Luc is openly gay, but the tabloids' coverage of his behavior as the son of formerly famous singers has adversely affected his dating and work life. Oliver needs a partner for his parents' upcoming anniversary celebration. The two pretend to date each other as a public relations move. Since they are fake dating, they tend to be brutally honest with each other, therefore drawing attention to each other's personal issues that provide a start for recovery from trauma. In a relatively quiet ending, Luc and Oliver admit they do love each other and agree to work on being better together.

When *Husband Material* starts, they are over two years into their relationship. Luc and Oliver are in a more equitable relationship with a sense of established domesticity. Oliver is going to therapy to work on personal issues Luc made him aware of in *Boyfriend Material*. Since Luc is in a better place, he's able to be more supportive of his friends and partner. Having an entire book about a relationship after extended time allows for a detailed look at a relationship beyond coming out and getting together. Luc can notice that he and Oliver have: "neuroses in different places."[87] The ability to closely view your partner over time and have an understanding of their inner workings plus how it is different from yours is an important aspect of a relationship. Oliver can also read Luc so Luc's internal monologue shows his realization of Oliver's awareness. Then Luc must carefully decide how to respond. The ordinary daily life and inner life needs to be explored for marginalized couples whether or not it intersects with their oppressions.

Western popular media, especially television shows, view protagonists entering a relationship as the end of the story, with the couple's sex life as a casualty. The couples of *Grave Phantoms* and *Always Only You* reject this trend by providing glimpses of affection and obviously pregnancies in their extended storylines. *Husband Material* challenges negative stereotypes about homosexuality with tender sex scenes. Unlike sex scenes in the beginning of courtship, which can be exploratory or purely physical, Luc and Oliver use sex as part of their method of care and often after reconciliations. Luc confesses, "[E]ven after two years of relationshipping and self-care and emotional development, it still scared me how vulnerable sex could make me feel."[88] They have sex after Luc has a run-in with the ex who sold his story to the tabloids. Another affectionate time that leads to sex happens when Luc comforts Oliver, who is having body issues. Heather McCann and Catherine M. Roach note, "sex can function as a way to draw the reader into the larger romance narrative."[89] The meaning behind sex in a relationship can just become richer and be an indicator of the relationship's progress. When m/m romances are written for the heteronormative gaze the focus is on domination and assigning gendered roles to the couple, with anal penetration to replace vaginal penetration and marking one partner physically as the effeminate bottom.[90] Neither *Boyfriend Material* nor *Husband Material* focus on anal penetration. Hall writes against m/m[91] sex as a base or aggressive act, but rather as an equal partnership. Both Allan and Eric Murphy Selinger emphasize that Radway did not entertain any homoerotic reading of the hero, but rather focused on him as a carer for the reader through his care of the heroine.[92] In this way, *Husband Material* then presents us with two nurturers and sex as a method of care.

Husband Material is based on the framework of Richard Curtis's *Four Weddings and a Funeral*. In Curtis's film, there is one lone gay couple who attend weddings they can never have and then one partner dies. Just like Mindy Kaling used her Hulu adaptation of *Four Weddings and a Funeral* as a way to grapple with the source material using race and nationality, Hall's version works through what it means when a committed gay couple can actually get married. Luc and Oliver can observe how commitment can be different for different people in the LGBTQIA+ community through the relationships of their friends. Priya is in a throuple with two women. Even Bridget's marriage is queer because she marries Tom. The James Royce-Royces have adopted a child. Luc's ex-boyfriend, Miles, has a showy queer wedding in an abandoned railway tunnel that had been converted into a bar with a drag king officiating. All these changes prompt nonconformist Luc to propose to Oliver.

When Luc's coworker Alex, who is the son of landed gentry, finally marries his upper-class girlfriend, Luc and Oliver witness an über-traditional wedding. In talking about heterosexual romances, Kamblè asserts that, "though the inevitable happy ending has been regarded as a way to indoctrinate readers to accept patriarchal marriage, in actual fact the narrative can work to remind them that the conclusion is unusual, quite a departure from the norm."[93] Luc's response is similar to what Kamblè is describing for heterosexual woman looking at the expectations of tradition. He remarks derisively, "It was the way that everyone else took it for granted that this was . . . universal somehow. That we were all united in this single idea of what marriage was and should be."[94] Luc is horrified that Oliver also has no problem in being part of this and actually enjoyed it over Miles's wedding, which causes them again to reassess their wedding and marriage expectations. Hall puts Luc and Oliver's arguments to good use, showing readers that having new options does completely free marginalized characters from all societal oppressions. Luc is still the narrator in *Husband Material*; however, Oliver can express his views more because the familiarity they now have and how much time they spend together in their long-term relationship. Oliver admits he feels alienated by queer iconography and questions its use for consumerism. Since both men are educated, their arguments cover a fair amount of queer history even though this is not a historical novel. Knowing the historical struggles of your community does not necessarily provide neat answers for personal problems. These sticky subjects that were hard to broach when they were just dating are now completely appropriate in a long-term relationship. This is where the value of a relationship story can really shine. What is in it for the straight female reader? Eva Y. I. Chen provides a possible answer: "Pleasure is produced when the old fixed boundaries are eroded and new possibilities are tried on."[95] A dedicated gay couple planning to get married has some of the tropes in the romance genre creating a similar, but different effect that revitalizes the genre for the reader.

The ending in *Husband Material* mimics the ending of the original *Four Weddings and a Funeral* film, with the couple not marrying, but committing to each other. Yet, it is also about queer futurity to not choose the same-sex version of a traditional marriage. Unlike the straight couple that just finally gets together at the end of *Four Weddings and a Funeral*, Luc and Oliver have been working through their relationship together for over two years, thereby rejecting the stereotype in mainstream romances that gay couples are more fickle than heterosexual couples. Hall might be also subverting the genre by meshing the states of happy for now with happy ever after while rejecting the marriage state. José Esteban Muñoz states, "Indeed, to live inside straight time and ask for, desire, and imagine another time and place is to represent and perform a desire that is both utopian and queer."[96] In the end, Luc and Oliver choose each other over the marriage because they feel getting married would destroy the love they have. This is the freedom to love that Jackson and Young mention. Oliver declares, "You are the truest thing I have ever dared choose for myself. And we are the only thing I've ever had that I haven't let other people define for me."[97] For very repressed Oliver, who enjoyed Alex's wedding, to say this is monumental. His ability to live within the rigid confines of society makes him an effective barrister, but it also has negatively affected his personal life. Because of his love for Luc, Oliver takes the leap outside of the restrictions he has adhered to and finally loves himself. He bucks the tradition and the guilt from his parents' manipulation that make him conform to society's heteronormative wishes.

Oliver chooses to see a future with Luc outside marriage. By having his main characters chose queer futurity, despite some couples in their queer community choosing more traditional avenues, Hall is saying the LGBTQIA+ community has multiple futures and they can choose what future works best for them.

CONCLUSION

Selinger points out Radway's analysis was limited by the small number of the Smithton group and their particular subgenre.[98] Since the white women of Smithton group focused primarily on historical romance, there are ways in which her analysis would not be relevant, especially on different subgenres dealing with one or more oppressions. The Smithton group could still be seen as a template because readers may read different subgenres, but clearly the overarching happy ending of the genre is at least one reason they read the genre. Additionally, as we have seen from the effect of self-publishing, an investment of numerous readers in a subgenre can elevate it to mainstream publishing.

Reading a romance with marginalized characters is not activism, but a well-written romance can provoke thought because reading is not a passive act. Having an after section whether it is an epilogue, mentions in other books of the series, or a sequel book can make readers grasp the burdens of oppressions and view marginalized people in a more well-rounded way. More dominant readers choosing these texts increases publishers' and libraries' investment in them at the very least.

Marginalized characters in romance have the freedom to express desire and other emotions (e.g., sarcasm), laugh, enjoy sex, love, be loved, have agency, and be promised a future without the focus on victimization. Young is right. Representation matters. Most fiction sees all these categories of oppression as sites of trauma. Romance says these sites of difference could be ways to have a conversation and do not devalue people. With these stories that provide a check-in after the original happy ending, the end goal for those marginalized could be more than about basic survival, but having a future where they are really thriving.

NOTES

1. Jenn Bennett, *Grave Phantoms* (New York: Berkley Sensation, 2015).
2. Dwight Conquergood, "Performance Studies: Interventions and Radical Research," *TDR: Drama Review* 46, no. 2 (2002): 146.

3. Chloe Liese, *Always Only You* (2020).
4. Alexis Hall, *Boyfriend Material.* (Naperville, IL: Sourcebooks Casablanca, 2020).
5. Erin S. Young, "Race, Ethnicity, and Whiteness," in *The Routledge Research Companion to Popular Romance Fiction*, ed. Jayashree Kamblé, Eric Murphy Selinger, and Hsu-Ming Teo (Abingdon, Oxon; New York, NY: Routledge, 2021), 511–28.
6. Young, "Race, Ethnicity, and Whiteness."
7. Jayashree Kamblé, *Making Meaning in Popular Romance Fiction: An Epistemology* (New York: Palgrave Macmillan, 2014), 87–130.
8. Kamblé, *Meaning in Popular Romance Fiction*, 131–56.
9. Jonathan A. Allan, "Gender and Sexuality," in *The Routledge Research Companion to Popular Romance Fiction*, ed. Jayashree Kamblé, Eric Murphy Selinger, and Hsu-Ming Teo (Abingdon, Oxon; New York, NY: Routledge, 2021), 428–53.
10. Emily M. Baldys, "Disabled Sexuality, Incorporated: The Compulsions of Popular Romance," *Journal of Literary & Cultural Disability Studies* 6, no. 2 (2012): 125–41.
11. Ria Cheyne, "Disability Studies Reads the Romance," *Journal of Literary & Cultural Disability Studies* 7, no. 1 (2013): 37–52.
12. Sandra Schwab, "'It is Only with One's Heart that One Can See Clearly': The Loss of Sight in Teresa Medeiros's *The Bride and the Beast* and *Yours Until Dawn*," *Journal of Literary & Cultural Disability Studies* 6, no. 3 (2012): 275–89.
13. Kacey A. Whalen, "A Consumption of Gay Men: Navigating the Shifting Boundaries of M/M Romantic Readership" (Master's thesis, DePaul University, 2017).
14. Jonathan A. Allan, *Men, Masculinities, and Popular Romance* (London and New York: Routledge, 2020).
15. Nicole M. Jackson, "Freedom's Epilogue: Love as Freedom in Alyssa Cole's Historical Novellas," *Journal of Popular Romance Studies* 11, no. 1 (2022): 1–12.
16. Lori Wick. *Bamboo and Lace.* (Eugene, OR: Harvest House Publishers, 2009).
17. Emi Kolawole, "Black Women Face Prejudice Every Day. I Don't Need It in Online Dating, Too: Asian Men Don't Fare Well on Dating Sites, Either," *The Washington Post*, 2015, ProQuest, https://www.proquest.com/blogs-podcasts-websites/black-women-face-prejudice-every-day-i-dont-need/docview/1722816140/se-2 ; Sofi Papamarko, "Why Black Women and Asian Men Are at a Disadvantage When It Comes to Online Dating," ProQuest, March 21, 2017, https://www.proquest.com/blogs-podcasts-websites/why-black-women-asian-men-are-at-disadvantage/docview/1879536737/se-2; Joanna Schug et al., "Gendered Race in Mass Media: Invisibility of Asian Men and Black Women in Popular Magazines," *Psychology of Popular Media Culture* 6, no. 3 (2017): 222–36.
18. Felicia, "Fans of Interracial Romance Discussion," *Goodreads*, https://www.goodreads.com/topic/show/18070597-lovers-of-black-women-asian-men-books. Accessed October 22, 2023.
19. Leah Koch and Bea Koch, "Empty Promises: The Owners of the Ripped Bodice Bookstore Say Diversity Efforts in Romance Publishing Still Lag." *The Publishers Weekly* 268, no. 10 (2021): 80.
20. Kimmy Yam, "Anti-Asian Hate Crimes Increased 339 Percent Nationwide Last Year, Report Says," *NBC News*, January 31, 2022, https://www.nbcnews.com/news/asian-america/anti-asian-hate-crimes-increased-339-percent-nationwide-last-year-repo-rcna14282. Accessed October 22, 2023; Ráchael A. Powers, Kacy Bleeker, and Crystal

Alcalde, "Anti-Asian Hate Crime in U.S. National News: A Content Analysis of Coverage and Narratives from 2010–2021," *Race and Justice* 13, no. 1 (2023): 32–54.

21. Katarina Wang et al., "Asian American Women's Experiences of Discrimination and Health Behaviors during the COVID-19 Pandemic," *Journal of Immigrant and Minority Health* 26, no. 2 (2024): 421–25; Chunyan Yang, "Influences of Prepandemic Bullying Victimization and COVID-19 Peer Discrimination on Chinese American Adolescents' Mental Health during the COVID-19 Pandemic," *School Psychology* 39, no. 1 (2024): 20–30.

22. Janice Radway, *Reading the Romance* (Chapel Hill: University of North Carolina Press, 1984), 188.

23. Brendan Farrington, "Florida Sued for Restricting Chinese Citizens, Other Foreigners from Buying Property," AP News, Accessed October 18, 2023, https://apnews.com/article/florida-chinese-citizens-property-law-4aeecc7a9470d03726658f1ef7b1d1f1; Mark Howland Rawitsch and Lane Ryo Hirabayashi, "Keep California White," in *The House on Lemon Street: Japanese Pioneers and the American Dream* (Denver: University Press of Colorado, 2012), 129.

24. Madeline Y. Hsu, "Race and the American Republic," in *Asian American History: A Very Short Introduction* (Oxford: Oxford University Press, 2017), 34.

25. Young, "Race, Ethnicity, and Whiteness," 522.

26. Radway, *Reading the Romance*, 196.

27. Bennett, *Grave Phantoms*, Acknowledgments.

28. Judy Yung, "Mary Tape, an Outspoken Woman: 'Is It a Disgrace to Be Born a Chinese?'" in *Unbound Voices: A Documentary History of Chinese Women in San Francisco* (Oakland: University of California Press, 1999), 171–76; Heather Thomas, "Before Brown v. Board of Education, There Was Tape v. Hurley," *Headlines & Heroes*, The Library of Congress, May 5, 2021, https://blogs.loc.gov/headlinesandheroes/2021/05/before-brown-v-education-there-was-tape-v-hurley/.

29. Kamblé, *Making Meaning in Popular Romance Fiction,* 23.

30. Jackson, "Freedom's Epilogue: Love as Freedom in Alyssa Cole's Historical Novellas," 7.

31. Bennett, *Grave Phantoms*, 10.

32. Celine Parreñas Shimizu, *Straitjacket Sexualities: Unbinding Asian American Manhoods in the Movies.* (Stanford, CA: Stanford University Press, 2012). 4–5.

33. Radway, *Reading the Romance*, 128.

34. Allan, *Men, Masculinities, and Popular Romance*, 432.

35. Bennett, *Grave Phantoms*, 210.

36. Radway, *Reading the Romance*, 207.

37. Bennett, *Grave Phantoms*, 229.

38. Young, "Race, Ethnicity, and Whiteness," 524.

39. Rhacel Salazar Parreñas, "'White Trash' Meets the 'Little Brown Monkeys': The Taxi Dance Hall as a Site of Interracial and Gender Alliances between White Working Class Women and Filipino Immigrant Men in the 1920s and 30s." *Amerasia Journal* 24, no. 2 (1998): 115–34.

40. Nayan Shah, *Contagious Divides: Epidemics and Race in San Francisco's Chinatown* (Berkeley: University of California Press, 2001), 70–1.

41. Young, "Race, Ethnicity, and Whiteness," 526.
42. Bennett, *Grave Phantoms*, 291.
43. Rick Baldoz, *The Third Asiatic Invasion: Empire and Migration in Filipino America, 1898–1946* (New York: NYU Press, 2011), 1.
44. Baldoz, *The Third Asiatic Invasion*, 9.
45. Deenesh Sohoni, "Unsuitable Suitors: Anti-Miscegenation Laws, Naturalization Laws, and the Construction of Asian Identities." *Law & Society Review* 41, no. 3 (2007), 597.
46. Jackson, "Freedom's Epilogue," 6.
47. Kamblé, *Making Meaning in Popular Romance Fiction*, 141.
48. Roger D. Hardaway, "UNLAWFUL LOVE: A History of Arizona's Miscegenation Law." *The Journal of Arizona History* 27, no. 4 (1986), 380–82.
49. Young, "Race, Ethnicity, and Whiteness," 526.
50. Liese, *Always Only You*, 1.
51. Radway, *Reading the Romance*, 197.
52. Schwab, "'It is Only with One's Heart that One Can See Clearly,'" 276.
53. Schwab, "'It is Only with One's Heart that One Can See Clearly,'" 276, Note 2.
54. Liese, *Always Only You*, 30.
55. Ashra Piterman, "Autistic Women and Masking: The Road to Closing the Gender-Based Gap in Autism Spectrum Disorder Diagnoses." *ProQuest Dissertations Publishing*, 2022; Alana Whitlock, et al., "Recognition of Girls on the Autism Spectrum by Primary School Educators: An Experimental Study." Autism Research 13, no. 8 (2020): 1358–72.
56. Baldys, "Disabled Sexuality, Incorporated: The Compulsions of Popular Romance," 127.
57. Liese, *Always Only You*, 189.
58. Radway, *Reading the Romance*, 196.
59. Sarah Smith Rainey, *Love, Sex, and Disability: The Pleasures of Care* (Boulder, CO: Lynne Rienner Publishers, 2011), 2.
60. Liese, *Always Only You*, 155.
61. Liese, *Always Only You*, 101.
62. Radway, *Reading the Romance*, 127.
63. Liese, *Always Only You*, 145.
64. Michael Gill, *Already Doing It: Intellectual Disability and Sexual Agency* (Minneapolis: University of Minnesota Press, 2015), 147.
65. Cheyne, "Disability Studies Reads the Romance," 40.
66. Sarah Smith Rainey, *Love, Sex, and Disability*, 144.
67. Chloe Liese, *Ever After Always*, 2021.
68. Chloe Liese, *With You Forever*, 2021.
69. Chloe Liese, *Everything for You* (2022), 262.
70. Chloe Liese, *If Only You*, 2022.
71. Gill, *Already Doing It*, 108.
72. Radway, *Reading the Romance*, 49.
73. Liese, *Always Only You*, Acknowledgments.
74. Radway, *Reading the Romance*, 184.

75. Sarah Bargiela, Robyn Steward, and William Mandy. "The Experiences of Late-Diagnosed Women with Autism Spectrum Conditions: An Investigation of the Female Autism Phenotype." *Journal of Autism and Developmental Disorders*, vol. 46, no. 10 (2016): 3281–94.

76. David T. Mitchell and Sharon L. Snyder, "Narrative Prosthesis and the Materiality of Metaphor" in *Narrative Prosthesis: Disability and the Dependencies of Discourse* (Ann Arbor: University of Michigan Press, 2000), 48.

77. Cheyne, "Disability Studies Reads the Romance," 41.

78. Guy M. Foster, "What to do if Your Inner Tomboy is a Homo: Straight Women, Bisexuality, and Pleasure in M/M Gay Romance Fictions." *Journal of Bisexuality*, vol. 15, no. 4 (2015), 510.

79. Kacey A. Whalen, "A Consumption of Gay Men," 11.

80. Nakul Krishna, "Why is so much gay male romance fiction marketed at straight women?" *The Telegraph.co.uk*, Apr 12, 2020. ProQuest, https://www.proquest.com/newspapers/why-is-so-much-gay-male-romance-fiction-marketed/docview/2388653121/se-2.

81. Whalen, "A Consumption of Gay Men," 19–20.

82. Kamblé, *Making Meaning in Popular Romance Fiction*, 95.

83. Kamblé, *Making Meaning in Popular Romance Fiction*, 124.

84. Allan, *Men, Masculinities, and Popular Romance*, 83.

85. Madison Nankervis, "Diversity in Romance Novels: Race, Sexuality, Neurodivergence, Disability, and Fat Representation." *Publishing Research Quarterly* 38, no. 2 (2022), 354.

86. Alexis Hall, "FAQ: About Me." *Alexis Hall*, Alexis Hall, quicunquevult.com/faq/faq-about-me/?Display_FAQ=12085. Accessed 30 Oct. 2023.

87. Alexis Hall, *Husband Material* (Naperville, IL: Casablanca Sourcebooks, 2022), 381.

88. Hall, *Husband Material*, 32.

89. Hannah McCann and Catherine M. Roach, "Sex and Sexuality," in *The Routledge Research Companion to Popular Romance Fiction*, ed. Jayashree Kamblé, Eric Murphy Selinger, and Hsu-Ming Teo (Abingdon, Oxon; New York, NY: Routledge, 2021), 413.

90. Kacey A. Whalen, "A Consumption of Gay Men," 37–39.

91. m/m (male/male).

92. Allan, "Gender and Sexuality," 432–33; Eric Murphy Selinger, "Rereading the Romance." *Contemporary Literature* 48, no. 2 (2007), 311.

93. Jayashree Kamblé, "Female Enfranchisement and the Popular Romance: Employing an Indian Perspective" in *Empowerment versus Oppression: Twenty-First Century Views of Popular Romance Novels*, ed. Sally Goade (Newcastle, United Kingdom: Cambridge Scholars Publishing, 2007), 170.

94. Hall, *Husband Material*, 241.

95. Eva Y. I. Chen, "Forms of Pleasure in the Reading of Popular Romance: Psychic and Cultural Dimensions," in *Empowerment versus Oppression: Twenty-First*

Century Views of Popular Romance Novels, ed. Sally Goade (Newcastle, United Kingdom: Cambridge Scholars Publishing, 2007), 38.

96. José E. Muñoz, *Cruising Utopia: The Then and There of Queer Futurity* (New York: New York University Press, 2009), 26.

97. Hall, *Husband Material,* 414.

98. Selinger, "Rereading the Romance", 313.

Chapter 13

Retellings and Re-readings—Romance, Representation, and Reimaginations in

Self-Made Boys: A Great Gatsby Remix (2022)

Christina M. Babu

Romantic literature has enchanted countless readers from various times and cultures, with each author and reader bringing their own unique interpretation to the concept of romance. It's important to recognize that portrayals of love and intimacy in romantic literature have often been predominantly heteronormative. However, there is a growing shift toward inclusivity, embracing a wider range of romantic relationships and diverse representations of love. This chapter seeks to explore a different facet of romance—that between queer characters facing multiple intersectionalities of class, race, and gender. Since it focuses on queer characters, queer readers would also make up a large part of the readership.

Janice Radway's famous book *Reading the Romance: Women, Patriarchy, and Popular Literature*, revolutionized the study of popular culture and gender dynamics. In this book, Radway explored how women engaged with romance novels as a form of escapism and empowerment within the constraints of patriarchal society. Radway conducted ethnographic research in the 1980s, interviewing women readers in the Midwest United States about their reading habits and preferences. She found that many women turned to romance novels not only for entertainment but also for emotional fulfillment and a sense of control over their own desires and fantasies. *Reading the Romance* found that these novels offer women a space to negotiate and resist dominant cultural norms. Radway's work inspired further research into popular culture, media consumption, and gender studies, and it remains influential in academia today.

Radway's initial research focused on understanding why women read romance novels and how these novels functioned in their lives. However, her analysis is through a clearly heteronormative lens, as it directly focuses on straight couples and indirectly includes only straight women. By considering new sociocultural dynamics and shifts in literary trends, this collection also addresses the need for more inclusive methodological approaches. While Radway's early work employed ethnographic research methods such as interviews and participant observation, any developments in research methods, including the incorporation of digital ethnography or mixed-methods approaches, could highlight the gap between her past practices and the current need for diversity. Additionally, Radway's research did not consider readers and works outside the United States, further underscoring the necessity to expand beyond her heteronormative framework.

This research paper aims to examine the transgender representation in popular literature through the lens of a transgender protagonist Nicolas Caraveo in the novel *Self-Made Boys: A Great Gatsby Remix* by Anne Marie McLemore. The novel is a reimagination of the classic *The Great Gatsby* by F. Scott Fitzgerald, which talks about love and romance during the times of the American Dream. *Self-Made Boys* adds a slight twist to the tale through its queer non-white representation—the narrator, Nick Caraveo, is trans and of Mexican heritage, and it is revealed later that Jay Gatsby is also trans. Apart from these two, there are other queer and non-white characters in the novel as well, which give it an interesting perspective for the readers. The author Anna-Marie McLemore identifies as nonbinary and is of Mexican American heritage. The novel was released in 2022, but it is set in New York in the 1920s. By this study, the author is trying to understand what life might have been like for queer non-white characters in America, when it was establishing itself as the world capital of splendor, freedom and opulence. This chapter discusses McLemore's depiction of the non-white queer community in the rural and urban parts of New York, and how they deal with their identities in both these spaces by doing a close reading of *Self-Made Boys: A Great Gatsby Remix*. The reason for choosing this as a primary text was because it is a highly representative text that came out quite recently, so not much scholarship has been done on it.

Heterosexual communities need to understand queer and trans communities better to overcome the existing prejudices and stereotypes. One way to do this is to advocate for more representation of queer characters in popular culture, so that the readers get some insight into their lived experiences. Given the overlap between coming of age and LGBTQA+,[1] books like *Self-Made Boys* are great to show representation and inclusivity. This chapter addresses the thematic concerns in the novel like: 1) how the deconstruction of gender impact identity, (2) how a trans reimagination of

Retellings and Re-readings- Romance, Representation and Reimaginations 237

a popular text (*The Great Gatsby*) affects the readers, and how it has dealt with intersectionalities like race, class and gender and 3) how a queer person would look at life during the period of the American dream, when the landscape was undergoing such drastic changes? This chapter tries to answer these questions.

GENDER: CAN WE ONLY HAVE BINARY IDENTITIES?

From the very beginning of the novel, the protagonist Nick narrates of a change. He begins with a reference to a change in his identity: *"Ever since my parents helped me become Nicolás Caraveo,"* a becoming of sorts.[2] Nick looks at his new identity as a medium to do things he wasn't able to do before as a woman, like look after his parents financially or provide the needed support. His situation is different from his cousin Daisy, who has a man, Tom Buchanan, to back her up. Since Nick has become a man, he feels that he has an added responsibility toward his parents—both for their acceptance and his role as the "man of the house." His roles changed when he started identifying as a man. While it did give him better opportunities in the new and evolving continent of America, can he truly erase his past identity of being assigned female at birth? I want to ask, had the situation been reversed, would he have fared better or worse? Jodi Kaufmann, in their article, discusses a specific case where they had interviewed a male-to-female transsexual named Jessie, in which they ended up erasing her identity through deconstructing her gender.[3] Kaufmann refers to the first recorded sex-reassignment surgery in the 1920s, and considering *Self-Made Boys* is also set within that time period, it provides an interesting and contrasting experience. But then again, one is fiction and the other is a person's lived experience. Is it alright to erase their humanness and just consider transsexual persons as data and statistics to help us study? What about the experiences they've been through, that have shaped them? The subject of Jodi Kaufmann's studies on transsexual representation, Jessie, became very upset with the author's analysis, feeling that her identity had been lost.[4] Through their research, Kaufmann tries to understand how trans representation can emancipate gender from the heteronormative ideas it is encased in, at the same time making Jessie feel seen. But identity is a very complex and fluid thing, particularly in the case of transsexuals.[5] *"Papá had always been one to give advice, even back when he thought I was a girl. But last winter I had told him and Mamá that I was a boy."*[6] This makes me wonder if some level of heteronormativity will always remain in gender, at least for the foreseeable future. Nick's family knew her as a girl initially, then as a boy. But these are not the only two identities possible for a transsexual person.

The relations among the characters are highly gender specific—male-presenting Nick is expected to behave in an "appropriate" way by Tom Buchanan (as in turn a blind eye toward his affairs, which is considered to be very masculine) while Daisy and Jordan are expected to be more feminine and interested in things like jewelry, parties, and clothes. The intersection of queer theory and political ecology would help us understand these characters better, because Anderson et al. have compiled a series of viewpoints ranging from performativities, anticapitalist activism etc. through the mesh of the queer, psyche, and the oikos.[7]

One interesting thing though, is the fashion of the times that binds the transsexual Nick and the cis-het Daisy together: both have to use the "Symington side lacer" to appear less curvy, in keeping with the trends of the times.[8] Daisy says, *"All the girls with chests like mine wear them. And I see no reason a boy like you can't use one for your purposes."*[9] Nick is trying to be a particular kind of man, and Daisy is trying to be a particular kind of girl, albeit using the same means. Nick is very much aware of the male fashion of East Egg, but he is not that comfortable experimenting with his new clothing. For the time being, he tries to cling on to the secondhand clothes he brought from home. Along with changing her Latina appearance, Daisy has qualms as she introduces Nick as a friend rather than as a family member to her fiancé, thus cutting off the familial tie.

In some instances, a character's racial identity changed as well. Nick Carraway becomes the Americanized version of Nick's last name Caraveo. *"But here, you forget the family name. You're Nick Carraway."*[10] The American dream was all about opportunities for everyone who worked hard, but people like Tom and others were still prejudiced, and haven't moved on from the master/slave mindset. So, people like Nick had to become someone they were not in order to be given a fair chance at life.

"I help my mother with the cooking all the time.... I didn't just stop when I changed my name and my clothes."[11] Nick might have changed his name and gender, but he still carries some attributes associated with his assigned gender at birth. But in other areas related to women like fashion and makeup, he is clueless and to an extent, uncomfortable. But the representation of transsexuality in its multiple forms helps to emancipate the idea of gender from the typical heteronormative constructs, and it increases the significance of the sex-gender misalignment plot for the identity of a transsexual person.[12] Kaufmann's analysis of transsexuality as "a feeling of difference" would help us to understand the characters of Gatsby and Nick, rather than just subjecting them to the binaries of sex and gender and how they confirm those.[13] Up until now, normative readings have considered trans people as deviants from the "normal," but Kaufmann argues for a representation that brings in both aspects simultaneously—trans bodies that deconstruct gender while also maintaining

the individuality of the human within them. Having a binary between the narrative and the body only reduces the chances of trans representation.

Kaufmann also invokes Deleuze and Guattari to try a different approach for the reading of trans characters- the double articulation of expression, and later the double articulation of content.

Bittner et al. discussed the representation of trans identities and gender studies and how it could be brought into a classroom setting. One method they recommend is bringing more trans literature to the young audience through the multiple avenues available in the publication industry to increase the discussion on trans characters.[14] This can help the readers understand and educate themselves on the difference between sex and gender, understand the lives of the trans community and the usage of correct pronouns. By doing this, the readers would also understand their own identities better. The available body of literature shows a notable lack of queer characters and trans/ queer authors. But *Self-Made Boys* fills this gap. There is also a pressing need to include more diverse identities, which again, the primary text has managed to do, with the help of racial identities like Latinx (Nick and Daisy) and Jewish (Martha Wolf).

Bittner et al.'s study provides a framework for the representation of queer characters in *Self-Made Boys*: trans characters are finally in the limelight of a story arc that is not restricted to depicting surgery, violence, and trauma of trans characters.

Cole's work also tries to identify problems in the representations of sexuality and queerness in the available body of literature, which tends to alienate people who don't conform to a particular identity.[15] But the genre of queer reimagined literature can help provide the space for the lived experiences of queer characters and readers. It could also lead to the potential shift in literature (including fairy tales) that challenges the existing heteropatriarchal ideologies.[16] Cole notes a steady increase in the rise of queer characters in YA novels, while the characters themselves are becoming more diverse and inclusive. The newer literature also focuses on coming to terms with whatever they identify as.

The Impact of Reimagined Characters on Readers across Race, Class and Gender

Mexican. Working class. Trans and queer. Nicolas, Daisy, and Gatsby are all these identities and more, trying to explore their own American Dream in the city of New York. In *The Great Gatsby*, all these characters were cis-het and white but in the reimagined version of *Self-Made Boys*, the author explores a marginalized community most people tend to overlook—the working-class Latinx community in the America of 1920s. When America was running after its dream of wealth and splendor, what was the working class doing? They were the real hands behind the dream, the ones who worked as butlers and servants while the wealthy could have a gay merry time in their gardens, lavishing their wealth away. Daisy and Nick are not from privileged backgrounds in *Self-Made Boys*—their working-class background gives us a deeper insight into the way they deal with the city and the white people around them. Daisy and Nick deal with their lives differently. While Daisy tries to pass off as rich and white, Nick does not try to hide the fact that he's Mexican and non-white. His trans identity though, is a different matter. It made sense to hide his identity, considering he was around people like Tom Buchanan who focused on being masculine. Not everyone could be as accepting as his parents, and revealing his trans identity could have greatly jeopardized his life and career. For Daisy, revealing her identity as a Latina could mean losing out on Tom's financial backing.

The racial mindset is heavily ingrained in Tom via his parents—*"But they can't see one of them sitting on their furniture."*[17] Tom's comments speak volumes about how they see the "others," especially people of Nick and Daisy's heritage. The sense of entitlement is also very clear when he says that the whites have always been ruling that country, and that won't change just because colored people have now started to have money. Tom claims to be free of this prejudice, but then he comments that Nick is honest, unlike the others (of his race) in the very next chapter. Nick has no choice but to remain silent at the blatant racism in order to make use of his arrival in the city and the sacrifices his parents have made for him.

It is hard to imagine that they are still adolescents, Daisy is eighteen (Nick is seventeen and Gatsby is also close in age to them), but Tom expects her to behave like a grown woman, someone fit to be the wife of a wealthy man like Tom Buchanan. Casual remarks like *"We men know what's important, don't we, Nick?"* are thrown around by Tom, which make Nick very uncomfortable because of his hidden identity.[18]

"Boys like us always know one another about a thousand years before anyone else knows us, don't we?"[19] The moment where Nick recognizes Jay as a fellow transsexual is a moment of vulnerability for both of them: Nick finally feels seen in ways he wasn't before, while trusting the other to keep his secret. And thus, we have the meet-cute of the two protagonists. If in *The Great Gatsby* they were merely friends, in the reimagined version *Self-Made Boys* they are two trans persons trying to find their place in the world. The book was aimed at young adult audiences, many of whom might be queer. This brings us to the discussion of other works that have been aimed at young, queer audiences, and their reception. Scholars Bittner et al. have looked at the history of representation of queer and trans characters in their research, and how such characters can be used in a classroom setting to bring awareness about gender equality and social justice.[20] In that aspect *Self-Made Boys* would make a great comparative study along with *The*

Great Gatsby in school/university spaces because of the representation and the themes discussed, and to bring a contrast to the work of Fitzgerald for the contemporary audience. Martha Wolf's character is a new addition (there is no character like this in *The Great Gatsby*) who is a source of comfort for both Nick and the lesbian readers. For the readers she represents the lesbian community, and for Nick who is struggling to adapt to a new place, she is a wonder because she is unapologetic about herself and her preferences. In their work, Bittner et al. have tried to bring in the theoretical perspective of trans and queer character analysis in children's and young adult literature. Their research, primarily intended at educators, social scientists, and parents of queer children, argues that rather than focusing on the number of queer representations in young adult fiction, it is important to look at how they are represented (like their authenticity, diversity, and different kinds of lived experiences) and how representations can be improved in the future. The body of literature that was available during their research largely focused on the storylines following an overarching plot of eventual gender confirmation via means like surgery or coming out to their parents/peers to gain acceptance into the queer community after an experience with violence or trauma. In *Self-Made Boys*, we already know from the beginning that Nick is out to his family, and his parents have accepted him, so the story does not focus much on his identity crisis and eventual acceptance. Instead, he ends up meeting more people from the queer community who are open about themselves.

Browne's work on reimagining queer death in young adult fiction tries to understand queer misery and the connection between queer characters and death in the literary representations. In most of the examples considered by the author, it was almost as if the same-sex relationship deserves a punishment by death, which creates a subconscious association between queerness and death among the readers.[21] Is the death of a queer character mandatory to develop the plot further? Browne feels that the discourse around queer death helps the readers to understand their own mortality. For queer readers, death then becomes associated with not following the "norms" of the society, and the realities in store for their future. The death of queer characters has different impacts on queer and non-queer readers. In non-queer readers, death serves as a reassurance of the stability of their sexuality, while for the queer readers it means impending doom, as if the universe expects them to die sooner or later, or for the good of the larger narrative. The reason why we are discussing queer death is because *Self-Made Boys* is not free from it. Jay Gatsby died in *The Great Gatsby* (movie), and Gatsby's character has a death in this novel as well. But it is not to fulfill some higher purpose, and it is not to punish his queerness or the attraction he feels for Nick. In the reimagined version, Gatsby fakes his own death with the help of Nick, Daisy, and Jordan, and is "reborn" while still retaining his identity as a trans individual. Even his death was not orchestrated because of any identity crisis, it is to begin a new life for himself and the other queer characters, away from people like Tom Buchanan. The readers of this novel would now realize that a trans character does not always have to die, and they do deserve a happy story arc. *The Great Gatsby* might have been written to show death as a sacrifice for love, but *Self-Made Boys* shows death for a rebirth, a new life.

QUEER LIVES AND THE AMERICAN DREAM: A CHANGING LANDSCAPE

Nick narrates about his cousin Daisy, *"It was the possibility of such wealth that had lured my cousin away from Wisconsin in the first place"*[22] New York City has a powerful pull with its glamour and wealth, and it is not easy to resist it. What does the city as a space mean for a queer, working class individual? As students of cultural studies and queer ecologies, it is important to understand the intersections between queerness, ecologies/spaces and how both of them interact with areas like ecopsychology and vice versa. One of the principal points raised by Anderson et al. is this: how do we see the world around us and how does that affect the way we deal with patterns of dominance in the world? How do we appreciate the queerness of the ecosystems?

They use theorists like Adrienne Rich, Isherwood, and Kushner to support their arguments. Wealth is an important part of domination. People who have money dominate those who don't. And for those who don't, seeking/acquiring wealth often becomes an important part, like it becomes for Daisy. Initially, she desires wealth to support her family in Fleurs-des-bois, but wealth also gives her a sense of security in the form of *"an emerald ring, the promise of an eventual New York engagement."*[23] This speaks volumes about the social, economic, and political relations among the characters, especially in light of their queerness.

"They call us brownettes." She led me away from the station's bustle. "Us girls of light-brown hair and intermediate coloring."[24] Daisy tries to cover up her ancestry by any means necessary, feeling that she might be exposed for her "inferiority" in front of the Buchanans, which also explains her need to gain more wealth, to put her on equal footing with them. Nick, Daisy, and several of the supporting characters come from a background of slavery, and during the time of the American Dream they have to also navigate coexisting with their former white masters. But according to Daisy, *"No one looks at anybody anymore. They're too taken with themselves."*[25]

The American Dream might have been a splendid and glamorous adventure for many, but the toll it took on the environment is not small. The American Dream tilted the resource distribution of the world. The rich like Jay Gatsby and Tom Buchanan get to flaunt it excessively (Nick describes Gatsby's house as a 'castle-cathedral' in chapter II), while the people who helped to create it suffer in poverty (the people living in outskirts of the city, like the Wilson family or the host of servants Gatsby and the Buchanans employ). Something that I could not help noticing was this: the second chapter ends with Nick saying that he was glad Daisy was here, and Daisy responds that she's glad to be "here" as well. The spatiality of "here" is different for both of them, while Nick is glad that his cousin is "here" with him (the acceptance, helping him get settled down), but Daisy's response sounds more like she's glad to be "here" at East Egg, among all the wealth and glamor. Even among the wealthy, the "old money" scorned the "new money." According to Tom and Daisy, the way a person talks can easily show if they were old money or new money. *"You say pardon, you sound like an amateur. Like you're putting on airs."*[26] Tom thinks that Gatsby reeks of new money, and Daisy is desperate to come across as old money by introducing Nick as the son of her mother's maid, while in reality her mother was a seamstress all her life. *"If people like us wanted to make something of ourselves in a world ruled by men as pale as their own dinner plates, we had to lie."*[27]

Daisy feels that as a woman in 'high society' it was very important for her to have a debut, which is the American version of a European affair that focuses on the display of wealth. She is still not engaged properly to Tom, even though she has gotten a ring from him. But no matter how much wealth/extravagant gifts he showers her with, she is not satisfied because those are not enough to cement her place as a high society girl or to gain acceptance from the Buchanan family. And soon, our main item of contention is introduced —the necklace that Tom gifted Daisy at one of the parties, worth a fair fortune, which is now supposed to be at the bottom of the ocean.

Nick introduces himself as *"I am Nicolás Caraveo of Beet Patch, Wisconsin, of the Beet Patch Caraveos,"*[28] in an attempt at grandeur in front of a stranger (who later turns out to be Gatsby) but from the start Nick is honest about his family and the kind of history they have in America. But for the first time after coming to East Egg, it is at Gatsby's party that he sees more people like himself—other colored (and wealthy) openly queer people. In that sense, we could look at Gatsby's galas as a sort of modern Pride event. Initially Nick is mistaken for waitstaff, but that is because of his outfit, not the color of his skin. Even in the office, he is not thought of as an employee in the beginning. But he is quickly introduced to the four main things that contribute to the American Dream: steel, railroads, automobiles, and the movies.[29] *"There's more money in selling dreams than in all the wheat futures in the world,"*[30] says Nick's employer, and that seems to be the guiding principle behind the emergence of the American dream. There is another reference to dreams, when Gatsby speaks of his first encounter with Daisy. He says both of them were "dream-filled."[31] Their dreams coincide with the American dream, yet they are very distant from it because both of them are pulling off characters they are not. And immediately, Gatsby begins dreaming of a life with Daisy and wants to be worthy of her. But is it Daisy he yearns for, or the idea of a grand lavish lifestyle with a woman beside him? Gatsby aspires to be everything that Daisy represents, to be called worthy of her. This becomes the main driving force for his pursuit of wealth and his own version of the American dream. In his opinion, he feels like Daisy has become the woman she has always dreamt of becoming.

The hustle and bustle of the city is in contrast with nature and the main characters also interact a lot with it. Then, can nature be queered? Sandiland challenges the notion that queerness is against nature by investigating the articulations of the natural world and nature.[32] They question how queer people can learn from the environment and how queer studies can contribute to the field of environmental studies. They have tried to queer the ecological community by discussing how the field of queer ecologies impacts the environment processes and the way humans interact with it. Nature and spatiality have a huge role to play in *Self-Made Boys*—there is a stark contrast between West Egg and East Egg. Jay Gatsby and Nick live in West Egg, while Daisy and Tom Buchanan live in East Egg (the more affluent part of the city). Gatsby uses his wealth to create lavish gardens and parties in West Egg, all to impress Daisy.

The divide between West Egg and East Egg is also present in their relationship because Daisy is on the other side, and no matter how much Gatsby tries, he can only look at her from afar. The parts of the city they live in also represent their aspirations—for Daisy, life in East Egg means parties, wealth, grandeur, and her dearest friend, Jordan Baker. But for Nick, West Egg is a relief from the hustle and bustle of East Egg, a quiet life amidst his gardens alongside his neighbour Jay Gatsby. But Gatsby has created an Eden for Daisy inside Nick's house which can be considered as one of the first instances of the intersection of queerness and ecologies. Then Nick and Daisy visit the vast and opulent gardens on Gatsby's property, with Nick (the youngest in the group) acting as a chaperone for the other two.

Nick's idea of the American dream is quite different from Daisy's: *"A quiet life is a lofty dream in itself."*[33] Daisy is a romantic at heart, with lofty dreams and imaginations, while Nick is clearer on the difference between what he deserves and what he actually might be able to get. Gatsby is also a romantic, and this is the reason Nick believes Gatsby is better off with Daisy even though he has already begun to fall for him. For someone who claims to be unromantic, it is Nick that orchestrates the reunion of Gatsby and Daisy. Daisy's idea of romance is slightly different: while a lot of men have fallen for her, she has rarely fallen back for any boy except Gatsby. The fact that

Daisy admits she hasn't caught feelings for any "boy"becomes part of the story later, when she comes out about her relationship with her best friend Jordan Baker. She had only wanted to be married to a man like Tom so that she could secure the lives of herself and her family. Ironically, she says, *"Daisy Fay was gay again, as gay as ever,"* which could be a reference to her sexuality,[34] but considering the times, it could also mean she was happier again.

Looking at things from the perspective of the environment, the American dream was an example of unequal distribution of wealth: the rich can flaunt their wealth however they want, while the poor have no choice but to struggle in poverty. The income inequality is huge, which also corresponds to the way the different classes are treated. The coal mining in Ash Heaps causes it to become an eyesore for the wealthier classes, while they do not think about the lives of the people that live there. The rich people like Gatsby and Buchanan live in posh parts like West Egg and East Egg, while Buchanan's mistress lives in Ash Heaps—money is a key factor that is able to provide accessibility to nicer neighborhoods. This becomes a generational cycle that becomes difficult to escape. Nick did manage to do it, even while being trans. But he is also an exception rather than the rule. This might not have been possible in those times had Nick transitioned from a male to a female. The American dream could also be seen as an ecological crisis, with the increased coal mining, deforestation, and artificial gardens with exotic flora to support a few opulent lifestyles. The contrasts are stark; for the rich, the American dream meant wealth and a life of leisure, while for the poor, it was more work and disproportionate benefits. If a few use up all the resources what are the next generations supposed to do?

Sandilands talks about reproductive futurism, the idea that humans are supposed to leave behind resources for the future generations which is supported by the ideas of inheritance and possessive individualism.[35] But it is not just humans that need resources, other species deserve them too. Queer ecologies interpret the idea of a future where all species coexist harmoniously (both human and nonhuman). Queer ecology is one of the few disciplines which sees the presence of multiple genders, desires, and forms of erotic expression and the ways in which we can express these connections with our interactions with the environment. The gardens which are so adored by Nick, Daisy, and Jay can be seen as an aspirational form of the queer community—a space where multiple species of plants coexist, much like how different identities would, in an ideal world. The gardens could also become a metaphor for love, because it is an artificially created space that is neither "inside" nor "outside," a clandestine space where lovers could meet up without prying eyes. However, gardens could also symbolize colonialism and the global trade exchanges of plants across the world, considering the history of America as a settler-nation. The gardens in *Self-Made Boys* witnessed both the reciprocity and the changing nature of romantic relationships—from Jay/Daisy to Jay/Nick—and they were little pockets of greenery in the middle of a city that was seeing rapid industrialization, and bore a testimony to the extravagant yet environmentally degrading lives led by the wealthy.

CONCLUSION

This analysis unpacks the deconstruction of gender and the impact on identities, trans reimaginations of popular characters/texts and how they are dealt with across intersectionalities of gender, class and race, and how a queer person deals with life with respect to the American dream, and navigate the ever-changing landscapes of the city and the environment they interact with. While this chapter was valuable in terms of reading a reimagined text from the perspective of cultural studies and queer ecologies, there were many things that fall beyond the scope of this study, and there are some limitations that need to be addressed. I focused only on one text with this kind of representation. Future research and scholarship in this field should look at more texts or even have a comparative study between several texts/media. This study opens up several new avenues of research. For example, one could look for more reimagined stories across other minorities/oppressed groups, or even change the narratives around conventionally heteronormative storylines/themes, and this discussion could be bought into academic circles and the general public. Overall, this could also erase the social stigmas surrounding queer/trans people of color. The analysis of this text would have an impact on both queer and heterosexual readers, and it would also impact policymakers, romance fiction authors, publishing houses, and practitioners of queer ecologies and cultural studies. This could improve the lives of the queer and trans community on an individual level and help to make their stories more visible. Finally, I conclude by urging more and more authors from the trans and queer communities to bring out books with such representation so that we can free gender from the heteronormative shackles it is bound to. It becomes all the more beautiful if they do it through romance, because after all, "love is love."

NOTES

1. See further detail in Kollman chapter, "Coming of Age and Coming Out: The Intersection of New Adult and Queer Romance" in Section 3 Chapter 1 from this volume.

2. Anna-Marie McLemore, *Self-Made Boys: A Great Gatsby Remix*. Feiwel & Friends, 6 Sept. 2022, I.
3. Jodi Kaufmann, "Trans-Representation." *Qualitative Inquiry*, vol. 16, no. 2, 30 Oct. 2009, 104–15, https://doi.org/10.1177/1077800409350699.
4. Jodi Kaufmann, "Trans-Representation." *Qualitative Inquiry*, vol. 16, no. 2, 30 Oct. 2009, 104–15, https://doi.org/10.1177/1077800409350699.
5. (Kaufmann).
6. (McLemore, *Self-Made Boys,* I).
7. Jill E. Anderson, Robert Azzarello, Gavin Brown, et al. "Queer ecology: A roundtable discussion." *European Journal of Ecopsychology* 3, no. 1 (2012): 82–103.
8. (McLemore II)
9. (McLemore II)
10. (McLemore VIII).
11. McLemore XII).
12. (Kaufmann).
13. Kaufmann, Trans-representation. *Qualitative Inquiry, 16*(2), 113
14. Robert Bittner, Jennifer Ingrey, and Christine Stamper, Queer and Trans-Themed Books for Young Readers: A Critical Review." *Discourse: Studies in the Cultural Politics of Education* 37 (6): 948–64. doi:10.1080/01596306.2016.1195106.
15. Cole
16. Cole
17. (McLemore IV)
18. (McLemore IV)
19. (McLemore VI).
20. (Bittner et al).
21. Katelyn R. Browne, "Reimagining queer death in young adult fiction." *Research on Diversity in Youth Literature* 2, no. 2 (2020): https://sophia.stkate.edu/rdyl/vol2/iss2/3
22. (McLemore I)
23. (McLemore I).
24. (McLemore I).
25. (McLemore I).
26. (McLemore V).
27. (McLemore IV).
28. (McLemore V)
29. McLemore VIII).
30. McLemore VIII).
31. McLemore IX).
32. Catriona Sandilands, "A Very Queer Nature: On Queer Ecologies, Gardens, and Flourishing Multispecies Practices." *Sydney Environment Institute*, 1 Jan. 2018, www.academia.edu/49663781/A_Very_Queer_Nature_On_Queer_Ecologies_Gardens_and_Flourishing_Multispecies_Practices. Accessed 22 Apr. 2023.
33. (McLemore XII).
34. (McLemore XIII).
35. Catriona Sandilands, "A Very Queer Nature: On Queer Ecologies, Gardens, and Flourishing Multispecies Practices"

Chapter 14

Mr. Darcy as the Perfect Book Boyfriend, or the Impact of BookTok on Male Characters in Romance Books

Louise Schulmann—Darsy

Since the 2010s and the development of readings communities—starting with BookTube in 2010, and now with BookTok—romance is more popular and "acceptable to read" than it ever was. Pamela Regis talks about a "romance formula"[1]: Two people meet, they fall in love, something prevents them from getting together, then they overcome it to be with each other, and get to live a happy ending. Have you ever heard of Rhysand,[2] Edward,[3] and Christian Grey?[4] What do they all have in common? All of them can be referred to as "book boyfriend," meaning that despite being three very different people, they all meet a common set of criteria that makes them the "perfect" fictional boyfriend. On top of that, they all allow Regis's romance formula to come true, revealing themselves as the one true love of the female main character. This chapter will attempt to give a tangible definition of the concept of book boyfriend.

This idea of making the main male character attractive to appeal to women readers is as old as romance books; Mr. Darcy[5] being a good example of that. When it comes to romance, making the main male character attractive and likable (by the end of the book) is something vital. This is where the concept of the book boyfriend comes into play. Book boyfriends and the set of characteristics associated with them fit almost every main male character in contemporary romance books. This leads to an interesting question: who inspired this description? Where are those standards coming from? Throughout an analysis of contemporary representations of Mr. Darcy and engagement with the survey's results, this chapter argues that the main character from *Pride and Prejudice* is the blueprint of today's book boyfriends.

THEORETICAL FRAMEWORK

Because this chapter engages with survey results that are in conversation with Janice Radway's *Reading the Romance*, it will extensively delve into its content. Comparing the similarities between the results and Radway's analysis of them to the responses to today's survey will allow us to see if readers' reading habits have changed, and what do the current answer tells us about today's romance readers. This chapter attempts to connect those results to the character of Mr. Darcy and his perception and representation on social media and contemporary retellings of *Pride and Prejudice*.

Pamela Regis and her concept of "romance formula" have been mentioned in the introduction. Regis's theoretical framework in *A Natural History of the Romance Novel*[6] provides a crucial foundation for comprehending the inner workings of romance literature and understanding patterns within the stories. Indeed, by delving into her scholarly insights, one gains a deeper understanding of the intricate mechanisms that drive romance narratives, including the essential elements that contribute to their structure, dynamics, and appeal.

Something that cannot be ignored is the importance of *Pride and Prejudice* in Regis's book. Indeed, she even deems Austen's novel "the best romance novel ever written" and dedicates an entire chapter to it.[7] This is of interest here, as it proves that the canon work has a lot of impact on the romance genre, even though the representation that most people have of Mr. Darcy today is one that is shaped by the diverse contemporary adaptations and rewritings of his character. Something interesting to note is that Regis's definition of a "sentimental hero" closely relates to the concept of book boyfriend, as the two concepts share a lot of similarities.

THE ROLE OF BOOKTOK IN THE CONCEPT OF BOOK BOYFRIEND

Due to the relatively recent popularity of the term "book boyfriend," there has been little work done on the concept as a whole. The term became popular with the explosion of BookTok. BookTok is a subcommunity on the social media app TikTok that focuses on books and literature. Creators make videos reviewing, recommending, discussing, and joking about the books they read. They are "celebrating their love of books and reading, making reading cool again."[8] It has become a massive phenomenon—#BookTok cumulates 189.4 billion views as of October 2023—since the last four years. It exploded during the 2020 worldwide lockdown, where people started to read more: "BookTok is a TikTok subculture where book lovers discuss the books they can't stop talking about."[9] Even though these books range in genre, romance is by far the most popular one; the #romancebooks hashtag on TikTok counts six billion views as of October 2023. An article from the *Times* reports that "TikTok has helped heat up the romantic fiction genre with booksellers […]. Publishers have attributed the rise—to levels not seen since the 2011 release of EL James' *Fifty Shades of Grey*—in part to the genre's popularity on the TikTok platform. The #romancebooks hashtag has had billions of views on the platform, making it the biggest subgenre within the BookTok community."[10] This results in the genre being promoted to a younger and wider audience, as "BookTok is still mainly used by a younger demographic and these readers are looking for modern, fresh romance fiction that reflects the world we now live in."[11]

The *Still Reading Romance* survey results highlight the significant role of social media when it comes to romance novels. In fact, 134 out of 303 participants aid that they discussed romance the most with a "social media community."[12] Discussing romance with friends came second, with 109 participants picking this option. This emphasizes the profound impact of social media on romance discussions, creating a safe place for individuals to openly engage in conversations about the genre without fearing judgment. Furthermore, it showcases the influence of social media on reader engagement. One respondent even stated: "I don't seek out New Adult romances or any of their storylines. I only read one if it's recommended, usually by someone on social media."[13] While the survey doesn't specify the particular social media platforms used for discussing romance, the fact that nearly half of the respondents chose "Social Media community" as their preferred discussion space reflects how prevalent social media is when it comes to reading romance, and therefore, to their expectations.

WHAT IS A "BOOK BOYFRIEND"?

The relationship between readers and their book boyfriends is explored by Sarah Hassen in her article "New Tools for the Immersive Narrative Experience." Even though she does not give an actual definition of the concept in itself, she theorizes that throughout the concept of book boyfriend, romance readers are a very good example of Matt Hill's theory of hyperdiegesis, which he defines as "the creation of a vast and detailed narrative space, only a fraction of which is ever directly seen or encountered within the text, but which nonetheless appears to operate according to principles of internal logic and extension."[14] Hassen states that romance readers "form a special relationship with the hero of these books, as if he was a character in their own lives. […] This intense emotional connection and fantastic escape, enriches the lives of these readers."[15] This emotional connection can also be reflected in the extensive online presence of the concept of book boyfriend.

Indeed, it is clear that the concept of book boyfriend mainly exists online, and as such, is defined mainly by social media users. As the author of the blog *She Reads Romance Books* Leslie simply puts it "Book boyfriends are the heroes in romance books who display characteristics and qualities that would make them ideal boyfriends in real life."[16] However, even though it existed before BookTok, it is on this sub-platform that the term became really popular. As of October 2023, the #bookboyfriend cumulates 2.8 billion views, and the #bookboyfriends 761.9 million views. This online enthusiasm also results in interactions that have an impact on readers' daily lives, as pointed out by Hassan: "[Readers] show up at romance conferences with nametags stating who their 'book boyfriend' is. They join online forums for fans of specific characters and authors. They fantasize about what their 'book boyfriend' would look like. They spend weeks debating which model or actor should portray the lead character. This intense emotional connection and fantastic escape, enriches the lives of these readers."[17] A popular expression when it comes to reading romance is "Boys in books are better," so popular in fact that it is marketed on memes, stickers, or bookmarks. The #bookboyfriendsdoitbetter has 428.2 million views and the #bookboysarebetter 21.2 million views on TikTok (as of October 2023). The message that is conveyed is that because boys in books are fictional and therefore perfect, they do it better than real men. The concept of book boyfriend is the impersonation of this quote, as the blogger Lizz puts it when defining the concept: "I think this all started because, really, boys in books are just better. You don't have to clean up after them, listen to excuses, and they don't forget your birthday. A Book Boyfriend is the guy in the book with whom you want to end up. He is dreamy and makes your heart beat a little faster."[18] Another interesting fact is that the concept of book boyfriend is close to the idea of a "man written by a woman." This idea is developed by Trica Clasen, who states that "Because young adult literature is largely a feminine space, it's not surprising that definitions of masculinity more closely align with what Craig might call the "woman's man."[19] Indeed, because the book boyfriend was written by a woman (that knows exactly what women expect from a partner), the book boyfriend is perfect and de facto "better" than real men.

Something to note about the concept of book boyfriend is that the idea of tropes does not matter. Regardless of the trope, the definition of book boyfriend and the expectations that go with it remain the same. It extends beyond tropes: it is about other parts of the representation, such as the love of the readers for this category of characters, or the comfort that can be found in well-known patterns in romance. Even though all male characters are different, they follow the same blueprint: they are, for the reader, better (and arguably more attractive) than a real man. Therefore, just like romance has a formula,[20] we could argue that book boyfriend does too.

In the most literal use of the term, a "book boyfriend" is the main male character of a romance book, and the boyfriend of the main female character, but because he is so perfect, he also becomes the "dream" boyfriend of the reader (by omission). The book boyfriend comes with a predefined set of characteristics when it comes to his physical appearance and his personality. Physically, he is tall, rich, good looking (sharp jaw, dark hair most of the time, and muscular), and very good in bed. Emotionally, he is kind, generous, sensitive, respectful, and protective, is madly in love with the heroine, but has a very heavy past/traumas. Despite his heavy past and flaws, he makes the heroine always feel safe, even when they are not together yet. This feeling of safety is a big part of what defines a book boyfriend. All those characteristics lead to very romantic or heroic acts proving their unfailing devotion to a particular woman and playing an active role in her happy ending. Generally, before meeting the woman, he was a playboy. To the reader, he appears vulnerable and displays raw emotions. The survey reflects the interest of readers for emotions: among 288 answers, 163 participants included "tenderness" in their top three characteristics they liked to see in a hero, while 100 opted for "protectiveness."[21] This description quite literally fits almost every main male character in contemporary romance books. Wanting a protective hero, therefore reinforcing the feeling of safety, is interesting here, as it also shows how romance reading habits and preferences transfer to real life. It can be argued from the survey results, with more than half of the respondent's selecting "tenderness" and nearly half choosing "protectiveness," that these traits may not be commonly found in real-life men. Consequently, individuals seek out these characteristics in romance novels, reflecting the definition of a book boyfriend as demonstrated by the significance attributed to these traits in the survey.

The notion of a male archetype in romance literature is far from recent. Indeed, for Radway, masculinity is central to the romance novel. In *Reading the Romance*, Janice Radway explores this concept and highlights several ideas that can be associated with today's concept of book boyfriends. She writes: "His exemplary masculinity is always tempered by the presence of a small feature that introduces an important element of softness into the overall picture."[22] She further notes that in the romance novel, "every aspect of [the hero's] being, whether his body, his face, or his general demeanor is informed by his maleness."[23] In *A Natural History of the Romance Novel*, Regis defines several types of heroes, one of them being the sentimental hero. She characterizes the sentimental hero as "Still strong, virile, manly ("a lion among men"), but he is wounded physically, psychically, or emotionally. The heroine must heal him."[24] She argues that healing the hero is a central component to the heroine's journey and of the love story between the two main characters. Those characteristics listed by Regis not only match the definition of a book boyfriend, but they also match the description that can be made of Mr. Darcy. Indeed, no matter in what medium (Austen's book, social media, cinematic adaptations, or modern retellings) he is described, and perceived by the audience as such. Masculinity represented through the female gaze of female authors (83% of romance authors are women[25]) is interesting to explore through the character of Mr. Darcy, as it can be argued that he is "the blueprint" when it comes to the archetype of book boyfriends and of several romantic heroes.

This leads to some interesting questions: who inspired this description of the book boyfriend? Where are those standards coming from? It is possible to argue that Mr. Darcy is the prototype of today's book boyfriends, and that those contemporary male characters reflect the standards he is setting in the novel, both as a character in himself and in the dynamic of his relationship with Elizabeth. However, the argument here lies on the character of the modern cinematic Mr. Darcy (meaning the 1995 BBC adaptation with Colin Firth and the 2005 movie with Matthew Macfayden) instead of the character of Austen's book. Due to social media, the popularity of Mr. Darcy as a book boyfriend can be mostly attributed to the movies, as Patsy Stoneman summarize it: "Although modern readers still accept Darcy (that is Jane Austen's Darcy from the novel) as a prototype hero of romance, we prefer the version of Darcy enacted by Colin Firth [...] when he emerges, wet shirt clinging to his manly body, from his swim in the lake."[26]

MR. DARCY AS A BOOK BOYFRIEND

Indeed, if it can be easily argued that Mr. Darcy's description in the book is one of a book boyfriend, it is the modern cinematic version that is more popular on social media, therefore inspiring the archetype for today's book boyfriends. The representation of Mr. Darcy in modern cinema is heavily inspired by how the character is described in the book. Having the definition of the book boyfriend in mind, it is easy to see how Mr. Darcy fits in with it. He is written by Austen as being physically attractive, who describes him as a "fine, tall person, handsome features, noble mien; and the report which was in general circulation within five minutes after his entrance; of his having ten thousand a year."[27] As we can see here, Darcy checks all the boxes of the physical attributes of a book boyfriend: he is tall, handsome, and rich. He is attractive to the readers because he meets these specific qualities. The men at the assembly judge him to be "a fine figure of a man,"[28] while "the ladies declared he was much handsomer than Mr. Bingley."[29] As the readers get to know him, they realize that he also checks all of the emotional boxes of the definition: he has big flaws (his pride) but is devoted to only one woman, Elizabeth, and is indeed contributing to her happy ending not only by marrying her but also by saving her family from scandal. It is this heroic action that makes Elizabeth start to realize that he might not be the rude character that she though he was, and that she might have feelings for him: "She began now to comprehend that he was exactly the man, who, in disposition and talents, would most suit her."[30] On top of that, Mr. Darcy is synonymous with safety, which is, as discussed previously in this paper, one of the major characteristics of a book boyfriend. Indeed, Darcy represents several types of safety, not only for Elizabeth, but also for the entire Benett family. As Regis notes: "Darcy is wealthy; his regard can guarantee a subordinate's security […]. Marriage to him means untold wealth and the security that it brings."[31]

Today, one of the most active places where people are talking about *Pride and Prejudice* in reference to its different adaptations is TikTok, and especially BookTok. The book and the character of Mr. Darcy are very popular on the platform: the #Mrdarcy cumulates 611.4 million views and the #PrideandPrejudice 1.8 billion, as of October 2023. On it, a lot of people will recommend the book as a classic that absolutely needs to be read, or as their favorite romance book, calling Mr. Darcy "the blueprint"[32] for all other fictional men. Despite being promoted largely on TikTok when it comes to the last four years, this belief is widespread online, as we can see from this quote from newspaper ran by students: "The name "Mr. Darcy" is now a stand-in for the ultimate fictional romantic interest."[33]

However, since the explosion of BookTok, more than a belief, it became a concept. Interestingly enough, when recommending the book, people often use images or quotes from the 2005 movie adaptation. This leads to people being encouraged to read the book based on the ideas of Mr. Darcy in the cinematographic adaptation. TikTok is a platform based on short video clips and images, often promoting something with "edits." An edit is a short (generally under one minute) compilation of brief clips or images from a TV show or movie, often accompanied by music or a popular sound, to promote that content. *Pride and Prejudice* is no exception—the #Prideandprejudiceedit counts 98.1 million views and the #Mrdarcyedit 19.6 million views as of October 2023. An interesting phenomenon that can be observed is that some people are using some clips from the 2005 movie or from the BBC adaptations in order to promote the book.

BookTok is a particular audience that has been shaped by the concept of the book boyfriend and by the short format of edits. All of that leads them to expect something else from the character of Mr. Darcy than the representation of him that is provided in the book. Those expectations are resulting in what is called a fanon representation. A fanon can be defined as "a false image of canon, a wish-fulfillment fantasy […]. Fanon is not an inferior interpretation of canon in this light, but a fantasy based on the needs of individuals writers rather than the reality established by shared source text."[34] In shorter terms, fanon is used to define commonly accepted ideas among authors and readers even if they are not actually expressed in the canon work. A good example of the impact of a fanon representation is the idea of making Mr. Darcy more romantic and even erotic than he is in the book. This idea is not only reflected in the modern cinematographic adaptations, but also in twenty-first-century retellings of *Pride and Prejudice*. Furthermore, because people are coming into *Pride and Prejudice* with this idea of Mr. Darcy as THE romantic character, it can sometimes create disappointment when they read Austen's book for the first time. Indeed, compared to the movies and retellings, this character is way colder, stale, and not as romantic. On top of that, contrarily to the cinematographic adaptations, the reader does not actually know Mr. Darcy other than by the eyes of the narrator, as Cheryl Nixon points out in her analysis of the representation of Mr. Darcy in the 1995 adaptation: "Unlike the film, the novel does not express Darcy's continued emotional struggle; when he or Elizabeth are separated, the reader learns nothing of his thoughts or actions. While the novel leaves the reader, like Elizabeth, uncertain of Darcy's emotions, the BBC adaptation allows no such questioning of the relationship."[35] Interestingly enough, as Hopkins notes in her article about Mr. Darcy's representation through the female gaze, it is only the representation of Mr. Darcy who changes: "all changes tend in the same direction: to focus on his feelings, his desires, and his emotional and social development."[36] These quotes are very representative of the expectations of twenty-first-century readers, especially those from BookTok, who anticipate encountering the fanon version of Mr. Darcy they've grown fond of as a book boyfriend.

THE EROTIZATION OF MR. DARCY

The desire to encounter the fanon and more erotic version of Mr. Darcy results in countless modern retellings, as Meyer summarize it: "There is an ENDLESS number of those erotic stories existing around the love story of Darcy and Lizzy."[37] As priorly established in this paper, romance is a genre that is written by women for women. This leads to Mr. Darcy's representation being directed toward the female gaze. Through the combination of the twenty-first-century expectations influenced by social media and cinematic adaptations, Mr. Darcy is depicted in a more romantic and, at times, erotic manner to cater to the female-focused audience. The author Lisa Hopkins, who explains the role of the female gaze on the different adaptations of *Pride and Prejudice*, puts it very simply: "these adaptations are unashamed about appealing to women—and in particular about fetishizing and framing Darcy and offering him to the female gaze."[38] Even though some people, such as Sue Birtwistle (the producer of the 1995 BBC adaptation), think that Mr. Darcy is already an erotic character in Austen's book, his character is even more eroticized in twenty-first-century cinematographic adaptations and retellings. In an interview on the official A&E Television website, Birtwistle stated that "*Pride and Prejudice* is simply the sexiest book ever written. . . . Darcy staring at Elizabeth across a room is exciting, and Darcy and Elizabeth touching hands the first time they dance is erotic."[39] While this analysis makes a lot of sense, especially thinking about the time that Austen wrote her book in, where sexuality was still very much taboo, and erotic representations had to be very metaphorical or tamed, twenty-first-century romance does not have those restrictions. This leads to a fanon representation of Mr. Darcy, derived from the expectations of readers and BookTok users. The fact that Mr. Darcy is being eroticized makes him fit even more into the concept of a book boyfriend.

These expectations also resonate with a significant aspect of twenty-first-century contemporary romance: the prevalence of explicit sexual content, often referred to as "spicy scenes." The survey demonstrates well the importance of those scenes when asked what the three most important ingredients in a romance were, out of 288 answers, 121 included "Lots of love scenes with explicit sexual description," while only 10 answered "Lots of love scenes with little or no explicit sexual description."[40] This demonstrates that what readers like about love scenes is the fact that they are explicit. In addition, this can be seen in the results of a different question from the survey, that reveals readers' interest in erotica. Indeed, when asked what kind of romance they read, 145 readers chose erotica as one of their choices.[41] On the contrary, to the question, "Rank what you watch most often when you watch movies. Please rank the top three with 1 being the most common,"[42] pornography or erotica only got selected 2 times.

The female perspective holds significant importance in women-written erotic content, as opposed to content geared toward the male gaze, such as conventional adult films. This is reflected clearly in the results of those questions. It can be argued that this is because the focus is primarily on the woman's desire and experiences within the narrative, as pointed out by Meyer: "Female erotica is written for women by women. Female erotica involves sex, but the main focus lies on the relationship in which sexual encounters take place. The hero finds full satisfaction in his female partner and her pleasure."[43] This aligns with the argument made by Radway that while romance novels often contain explicit sexual content, the primary focus is not on graphic depictions of sexual acts but rather on the emotional and psychological aspects of intimacy and desire. Radway suggests that romance novels provide a safe space for women to explore their own fantasies and desires within the context of a fictional narrative. This idea and the survey's results is interesting because it ties to the concept of book boyfriend. Indeed, not only of the characteristics of the book boyfriend is that he must be good in bed, but another one is the fact that he is in love with the female character, almost to the point of adoration. It makes sense that those feelings apply to the bedroom, leaving the female character sexually satisfied. This also ties down with the idea of the book boyfriend giving to the reader what they might not have in real life, such as equal consideration of their desires and guaranteed sexual pleasure. Radway states that "the romance novel's emphasis on female pleasure suggests that the heroine is entitled to have a fulfilling sexual relationship,"[44] reflecting the genre's potential to challenge traditional gender norms and promote women's sexual autonomy.

This omnipresence of erotic content in modern romance, and in this case in *Pride and Prejudice* modern content can be referred to as "a harlequinization." It is Deborah Kaplan that is at the origin of this idea, as she reflects on Austen's legacy: "Jane Austen as one of the mothers of the Harlequin or Silhouette novel? This genealogy should amuse many of Austen's admirers, who know her novels to be much more culturally and linguistically complex than the mass-market romance. And yet, recent popular representations reveal a distinct trend: the harlequinization of Jane Austen's novels. If Austen is one of the ancestors of the paperback romance, recent films of her work are not the heirs of this popular form."[45] Directly coming to mind here are the cinematographic adaptations of *Pride and Prejudice*. In those adaptations, the viewers get to know a more romantic and human Mr. Darcy, which is at the origin of their fanon representation. Some physical intimacy is added, such as Mr. Dary in a wet shirt, or physical contact between Elizabeth and Mr. Darcy.

Mr. Darcy's infamous hand flex after helping Elizabeth in the carriage in the 2005 movie adaptation is very popular online. As Hannah Kerns, a journalist, simply puts it: "It is a truth universally acknowledged (or, at least, it should be) that the hand flex in *Pride & Prejudice* (2005) was a cultural reset."[46] This hand flex is very important when it comes to the humanization and erotization of Mr. Darcy. It is the first time that his feelings for Elizabeth, and that the impact that she has on him, is acknowledged. Throughout the movie up to this point, Elizabeth and Darcy have maintained an openly hostile relationship. In their initial encounter, Mr. Darcy deems her as "barely tolerable," and she makes a point of proving to him that she barely tolerates him either.[47] However, as time passes, they gradually discover shared interests and common ground. This particular moment beautifully illustrates Darcy's reluctant yet burgeoning affection for her. His feelings are taking over, leading to this physical reaction. This is also the perfect representation of Mr. Darcy as a book boyfriend: he has flaws—that the reader and Elizabeth are aware of—but he also cares about her and displays emotions and vulnerability. This shows that the producer was aware of the audience of the movie—mostly women—and shows the impact of a scene that is shot with the female gaze in mind. Kerns simply puts it as: "Although the film was directed by Joe Wright and the hand flex was improvised by Macfayden, it's the epitome of embracing the female gaze and running with it."[48] Additionally, both cinematographic adaptations add a kiss at the end, which is a level of physical intimacy that the reader never gets to see in Austen's paper version. When it comes to which version of *Pride and Prejudice* adaptation is more popular on BookTok, the 2005 one is a clear winner. This can be explained by the fact that the two cult romantic declarations—"I love you most ardently" and "You have bewitched me body and soul" appeal even more to Mr. Darcy's romantic side, making him fit into the book boyfriend category even more. Those two iconic declarations and the hand flex scene are heavily used in TikTok edits as part of the #Prideandprejudice, #Prideandprejudiceedit, #Mrdarcy and #Mrdarcyedit.

The same phenomenon can be observed with the wet shirt scene. Indeed, the viewer gets to discover the closest thing to Mr. Darcy's naked body: a scene where he appears with a wet shirt. This heavily adds to the erotization of his character in a way that is absent from the book because it relies solely on the female gaze and on visual elements: "We now live in a world that relies heavily on visual images, which is part of why "Colin Firth in a wet shirt" signifies passion and desire in *Pride and Prejudice*."[49] Mr. Darcy's wet shirt is even deemed as a popular culture icon by some, such as Imke Licherfeld, who dedicates an entire book chapter to explaining its importance. She states: "The character of Fitzwilliam Darcy gets eroticized through the scene and sweatshirt, and his body becomes the focus of the viewer's attention. [...]. Mr. Darcy emerged as the very type of brooding romantic hero, a model of ideal maleness."[50] This emphasizes that this representation of Mr. Darcy is what the idea of Mr. Darcy as a book boyfriend draws from. He is the ideal man and partner, with emotions, directed toward the female gaze.

All of this is intricately connected to what is often referred to as the "Mr. Darcy Complex." This concept can be described as follows: The "Mr. Darcy Complex" is the belief that contemporary women often compare real-life men to the romantic ideals established by fictional literary figures like Mr. Darcy, unwittingly setting unattainable expectations for every man they encounter, resulting in frequent disappointments. Gislind Rohwer-Happe dedicates a whole article to said complex, where she defines it as "the truth is so well fixed in the minds of the female readers of *Pride and Prejudice* that they can only consider Mr. Darcy as the rightful object of their affections and would whole-heartedly agree that only Mr. Darcy will do!"[51] It is easy here to make connections to the idea of book boyfriend, and to Mr. Darcy being the blueprint for it. Just like a book boyfriend, the "Mr. Darcy Complex" rests on the idea that because he is so perfect and holds-up to every standard a woman could wish for (by the end of the story), only him would do. Rohwer-Happe summarized it really well when she wrote "Let's face it, whenever any woman says, 'I love Jane Austen' what she is really saying is, 'I love Mr. Darcy' and he is the standards by which all men I know are doomed to be judged."[52] This quote is interesting because it shows that the "Mr. Darcy complex" is being convinced that Mr. Darcy is everything that one could hope for, exactly like a book boyfriend. It can be argued that the two attractiveness to Darcy's original appeal by their performances (more romantic and more directed toward the female gaze than Austen's book).

Because Mr. Darcy was so well written as that romantic hero who unconditionally loves Elizabeth Bennett and so well adapted with added romanticism, he becomes the prototypical book boyfriend for not only the rewritten versions of *Pride and Prejudice*, but also for all the book boyfriends. His character, and to some extent, Rochester's as well, is beloved by the Book-Tok community and among twenty-first-century readers.[53] They are revered as the archetypal figures that have laid the foundation for the modern-day beloved book boyfriends, exemplified by characters such as Garrett Graham (*The Goal* by Elle Kennedy), Brenan (*It Happened One Summer* by Tessa Bailey), Jamie (*Outlander* by Diana Gabaldon), and Joshua (*The Hating Game* by Sally Thorne) among many others. These contemporary book boyfriends share common characteristics: towering stature, affluence exceeding that of the female protagonist, romantic actions to win the heart of the main character despite their initial disapproval her. Furthermore, they often possess brown hair, sharp jawlines, and an unwavering devotion to the heroine, even before the commencement of their romantic involvement. In this regard, they can easily be compared to Mr. Darcy, making it easy to see how he can be considered "the blueprint" when it comes to the definition of book boyfriend.

The importance of today's book boyfriends based on Mr. Darcy cannot be overlooked. For example, when asked what was something important to know about how reading romance shaped the participants' feelings, opinions and identity, one of them answered: "I started reading more mature and explicit romance novels when I was starting our high school and I feel like it really altered my perception of men and sex growing up […] I want "the man that was written by a woman" type guy. I've come to understand that the perfect romance that I read about in books isn't really a thing, but I guess I still kinda hold out hope just in case."[54] This is really interesting because it shows how much the idea of "a man written by a woman" is implanted into readers' minds when it comes to their expectations.

These expectations are fitting the character of Mr. Darcy, as he was indeed written by a woman, and produced (in cinematic adaptations) toward the female gaze.

PRIDE AND PREJUDICE MODERN RETELLINGS

Romance, especially chick lit, is still often made fun of, or criticized as being trashy or a waste of time, not serious and even anti-feminist, as pointed out by both Radway and Regis. Regis opens her book with a preface named "The Most Popular, Least Respected Literary Genre"[55] and states that "More than any other literary genre, the romance novel has been misunderstood by mainstream literary culture."[56] In her book, Radway acknowledges that romance novels have often been marginalized and dismissed by literary critics, who view them as lacking in complexity or literary merit.[57] Those two opinions about romance's dismissal as a serious genre are still valid today, as pointed out by one of the survey's answers, where the reader states that "[she is] not ashamed that romance isn't "real literature." I don't think that I am any less intelligent because I only read romance." This shows that by most people, romance is still considered a non-serious genre, even though readers are aware that it is not. Despite being called trashy or a "guilty pleasure," romance novels generate over $1.44 billion in revenue,[58] making romance the highest-earning genre of fiction. Contemporary retellings, whether of popular Greek myths, or literature classics, are very popular. This trend can be attributed to the demographic most engaged with these retellings, typically aged between 19 and 25. This age-group, having been exposed to fan fiction during their younger years, finds parallels between retellings and the fan-created narratives they are familiar with. As argued by Betsy Rosenblatt and Rebecca Tushnet, "At their core, retellings seem to be a more formal version of fanfiction, paying homage to a certain work as a whole."[59] Jane Austen is among the most popular authors when it comes to contemporary retellings. This can easily be attributed to her widespread recognition and the enduring popularity of *Pride and Prejudice*, which remains the third best-selling romance novel of all time, with a staggering thirty million copies sold.[60]

Rohwer-Happe develops the following theory: if there are so many retellings of *Pride and Prejudice*, it is because of the "Mr. Darcy Complex." She writes: "It is therefore not surprising that a character so attractive to women as well as the complex he causes have become recurring if not notorious topics in contemporary fiction and especially in Chick Lit, with about 200 novels available at the moment [in 2015] that features the name of Mr. Darcy in their title."[61] As of today, using the same Goodreads search as her, approximately 1427 novels incorporate the name of Mr. Darcy in their titles. This comparison not only underscores the enduring popularity of the character but also highlights the continuous expansion of this popularity. The love story written by Jane Austen, with the additional massive impact of cinematic adaptations incorporates more explicit and passionate elements that cater to today's readers and their expectations in terms of romance books.

In order to examine the idea of Mr. Darcy as the original book boyfriend, this chapter examines four modern retellings of *Pride and Prejudice*; two of them taking place in the twenty-first century and two of them taking place in Austen's original setting. This examination aims to analyze and compare the depiction of Mr. Darcy in those retellings compared to the fanon one. *Pride and Papercuts*[62] is set in the contemporary twenty-first century, where Mr. Darcy is transformed into Liam Darcy, a CEO who no one likes (except for his extroverted sister) owing to his cold and reclusive nature. *Eligible*[63] also takes place in the twenty-first century and features Darcy as a neurosurgeon and Elizabeth as a journalist, both constrained by their circumstances in Cincinnati, the story's backdrop. *Unequal Affections*[64] initially began as a fanfiction before being published by Audible (online audiobook and podcast service that allows users to purchase and stream audiobooks and other forms of spoken word content), and it maintains Austen's original Regency-era setting. However, it takes an imaginative approach to the story, exploring an alternative scenario: what if Elizabeth had agreed to marry Mr. Darcy during his first proposal, despite her lack of affection for him? The last novel, *Mr. Darcy Takes a Wife*[65] explores the passionate and sensuous aspects of Elizabeth and Darcy's marriage, commencing their journey from where the book and film concluded—on their wedding night. This novel is marketed as "*Mr. Darcy Takes a Wife*: The sexiest Austen-inspired novel that has readers talking." These diverse rewritings were deliberately selected to examine whether the portrayal of Mr. Darcy remains consistent across different adaptations.

Those four books are among the most popular on BookTok when it comes to contemporary *Pride and Prejudice* retellings recommendations. All of them have been well received, as can be seen from their Goodreads (the world's largest site for readers and book recommendations, where people evaluate and comment on the books that they read) and Amazon ratings. *Unequal Affections* currently has a score of 4.08/5 out of 5,014 ratings on Goodreads and of 4.5/5 out of 2,439 global readings. The audiobook is included in the Audible membership, making the book accessible for free to everyone that owns a membership. *Mr. Darcy Takes a Wife* has a current score of 3.41 out of 11,613 ratings on Goodreads and scores at 4.1/5 out of 1,401 global reviews on Amazon. As for *Pride and Papercuts*, the numbers are a little bit lower, but still pretty good: 3.65/5 out of 3,406 ratings on Goodreads, and 4.2/5 out of 1,050 global writings. Staci Hart maintains an active presence on BookTok, where she introduces her book as a spicy reinterpretation of *Pride and Prejudice* with the catchphrase "Mr. Darcy with a spicy twist" (@ stacihartwrites). *Eligible* is the book that has been reviewed the most, but it has lowest ratings, despite being popular on BookTok. It scores an average of 3.6/5 on Goodreads, out of 89,478 ratings and a 3.9/5 out of 12,723 global reviews on Amazon. It is part of a bigger project—"Austen Project"—that published modern retellings of Austen's books written by famous contemporary romance authors.

Pride and Papercuts takes place in today's society. Laney Bennet and her brother Jett work at Wasted Words—a bookstore/bar that is undergoing a new marketing campaign. Since Laney does all their social media and current marketing, she is heavily involved with the new launch. Liam's Darcy company is the one in charge of that new launch. At the contrary *of Unequal Affections*, the change of universe is complete: not only is the story taking place during the twenty-first century, but it also takes places in New York. If the family names remain the same, the first names change: Fitzwilliam becomes Liam, and Elizabeth becomes Laney (short for Elaine). The Bennet sisters are transformed into brothers, almost all already married, and the loyal Jane becomes Jett, the protective brother. *Eligible* also takes place in twenty-first-century society: the story takes place in Cincinnati, where Jane and Elizabeth are coming back to take care of their father that suffered from a stroke. Almost all the names and characters are kept the same, the biggest change to the plot being that the storyline of Lydia and Wickham never happens, and Bingley becoming "Chip." Both of these retellings address contemporary social issues such as technology, social media, and the impact of modern society on relationships and communication, while humanizing Mr. Darcy and giving the reader what the original story is "missing": non-metaphorical romantism and erotization. Both authors acknowledge the fact that it is heavily inspired by *Pride and Prejudice*. For example, Hart keeps some very interesting details from the original speech that Darcy makes about not wanting to dance with Elizabeth. *In Pride and Papercuts*, Liam says: "Georgie, I'm going to say this once—Laney Bennet is perfectly tolerable. But she's not like us. She's not the kind of girl I would ever ask to dance, especially not in a bar to a Lionel Richie song. Ever. Do you understand?"[66] In Austen's book, the content is pretty much the same; as Darcy says: "She is tolerable; but not handsome enough to tempt me; and I am in no humor at present to give consequences to young lady who are slighted with other men. You had better return to your partner and enjoy her smiles, for you are wasting your time with me."[67] It is very easy here to see how the content is similar: in both books, Darcy refuses to dance with the main female character and calls her "tolerable." In *Eligible*, Darcy initially comes across as discourteous in his first meeting with Elizabeth as well, engaging in unkind conversations about her at the party they both attend: "In a friendly tone, Chip said, "In your first year here, you didn't find any lady Buckeyes who met your exacting standards?" "I can hardly think of anything less tempting," Chip chuckled. "Someone told me Jane's sister Liz is single, too." "I suppose it would be unchivalrous to say I'm not surprised." Darcy answered."[68]

On the other hand, if both *Unequal Affections* and *Mr. Darcy Takes a Wife* are taking place in Austen's universe, they are offering a closer look at Mr. Darcy's character, as the reader get regular chapters or parts of chapters narrated from his point of view. This provides readers with a deeper understanding of the character, offering a level of insight that surpasses both Austen's original work and cinematic adaptations. In those narratives, readers are privy to Mr. Darcy's innermost thoughts and emotions, further solidifying his portrayal as the original book boyfriend. This intimate perspective aligns perfectly with the emotional qualities expected of a book boyfriend.

The double narration is something very common in contemporary romance. This attitude is reflected in the survey's results. Out of 280 answers, 132 participants said that they preferred to read romance novels that give the point of view of both the heroine and the hero.[69] The chapters written from the point of view of the book boyfriend allows the reader to realize their internal struggle and their love for the heroine. In three of the four books, the reader gets to see his internal struggles and his deep feelings for Elizabeth, but also his friendship with Bingley. All of that is giving him a more "human" side, a side that readers can relate to. Mr. Darcy is not this distant character that they only know through Elizabeth's eyes or the viewer's eyes, but a character that they can understand, making him more appealing.

In all four books, Mr. Darcy is depicted in an erotic manner, highlighting his desire for Elizabeth. The narratives also underscore his prowess as a passionate lover and his strong masculinity. For example, in *Pride and Papercuts*, Liam is described as "made of velvet and stone, of strength and desire."[70] In *Mr. Darcy Takes a Wife*, Elizabeth is stunned by Darcy's masculinity: "Because she had felt of his body in full cry, and therefore appreciated the ampleness of his . . . credentials, Elizabeth had harbored a certainty she would not be taken unawares when she saw them. Yet, she could not help but stare."[71] Both of these aspects align him with the characteristics of a book boyfriend.

WHY MR. DARCY?

Despite being mostly written by women for women, the romance genre has a complicated relationship with feminism; as some scholars consider the genre reductive in their representation of women, and even antifeminist. Indeed, Radway points out the romance's emphasis on relational identity (the heroine regains her identity only through union with the hero) as being patriarchally restrictive: "The romance does deny the worth of complete autonomy. In doing so, however, it is not obliterating the female self completely. Rather, it is constructing a particular kind of female self, the self-in-relation demanded by patriarchal parenting arrangements."[72] Because the romance emphasizes identity secured through heterosexual union with a man, it seems tailor-made to enforce the traditional female role of dependent wife, discouraging alternatives. It can rightfully be argued that *Pride and Prejudice* and all of the retellings are falling right in this category. However, the concept of book boyfriend also rests on the fact the hero loves the heroine deeply, listens to her, and values her as a partner. This claim is backed up by Clasen, who writes that "A final theme of deviance from hegemonic masculinity in YA contemporary romance is the general value of love and romance in the lives of the male protagonists. They are unabashedly romantic and unafraid of commitment."[73]

Mr. Darcy is the perfect example of this, and it can be argued that this is why he is still so popular today. Darcy can be considered the original book boyfriend because he values Elizabeth for what she is and does not only see her as a woman and a (potential) wife but also as an equal, worthy of all his attention, which is a unique feature of his character that cannot be found to that extent in any other Austen characters. In the 2007 movie, Mr. Darcy is portrayed as deeply romantic, which can be seen in the two monologues where Darcy professes his love to Elizabeth and appears to put his love for her above everything else.

Voiret summarizes it pretty well: "*If Pride and Prejudice* can be described as the most popular of Austen's production, it is because it most expresses this longing for a caring, attentive, respectful and equal partner."[74] This desire to see couples develop a relation as equals is also reflected in the survey's results. When asked what the three most important ingredients in a romance were, 247 out of 288 answers included "well-developed emotional intimacy between the heroine and hero" in their top three.[75] Clasen writes that because romance is a largely a feminine space, "The men would be more sensitive, and understanding [...] and that romance would be something they value above all else may very well be a reflection of the desires of female audience."[76]

Yet, even to this day, the enduring allure of Darcy and of *Pride and Prejudice* persists. The explanation is rather straightforward: the themes addressed in Austen's novel are timeless and universally relatable. Darcy's character continues to captivate women today, which explains the continued success of any adaptation of the story. Voiret explains the phenomenon by the fact that "The narratives then, provide to the viewer the pleasure of a story in which a man helps his female companion to express those qualities that for too long have been associated with the masculine—mastery, assertiveness, will, enthusiasm—and which, to an often-unacknowledged degree, many of our contemporaries still find distasteful in a woman."[77]

When asked something that was important to know about how reading romance shaped the participants' feelings, opinions and identity, one of them answered: "The Romance genre has taught me a lot [...] including what it looks like to have a partner that respects you as an equal (and that equality in a romantic relationship is okay to expect and should be expected). They've opened my mind and my worldview, which I'm so grateful for. They are empowering and important."[78] Darcy's character is presented as appreciating and loving Elizabeth for her true self, encouraging her to develop those qualities. In *Pride and Papercuts*, Liam keeps pushing Laney, telling her that she is talented enough for the marketing competition and giving her advice to make her propositions better. In *Unequal Affections*, Darcy loves the fact that Elizabeth reads so much and encourages her to read more books, even offering to buy some from London for her. In *Eligible*, Darcy encourages Elizabeth with her job as a journalist. Because of that, Mr. Darcy is presented as a source of inspiration for every book boyfriend that comes after him. A very good example of that is a TikTok comparing him to Anthony Bridgerton (from *Bridgerton: The Viscount Who Loved Me* by Julia Quinn) with a description stating "same font"[79] that cumulates 387,300 likes and 1,661 comments, along them "Mr. Darcy is the blueprint of any romance novel man. He is the Adam of his own species" (liked 237 times, by @auroraditrapano).

To conclude, we can say that the concept of book boyfriend is very important when it comes to the expectations that readers have of male character in romance books today. The enduring appeal of Mr. Darcy can be attributed to the timeless qualities of his character and the masterful storytelling of Jane Austen. From the pages of *Pride and Prejudice* to numerous adaptations and modern retellings, Mr. Darcy's character has stood the test of time, and is beloved by readers and viewers. Furthermore, his widespread influence on the romance genre and the concept of a book boyfriend cannot be denied. He has set the standard for the attractive, enigmatic, and ultimately lovable hero that many subsequent male characters have sought to emulate in today's romance.

The importance and impact of social media, especially BookTok when it comes to romance is important and should not be underscored. BookTok can serve as a lens that analyzes and understands the fact the audience's understanding of Mr. Darcy is shaped by the cinematographic adaptations and the fanon representation. The platform has played a pivotal role in reshaping how Mr. Darcy is perceived, by promoting a book boyfriend based on a fanon representation that is very different from Austen's original character. Consequently, the contemporary image of Mr. Darcy can be characterized as fanon, born from these adaptations and retellings. These rewritings and cinematic versions provide valuable insights into what today's audience envisions for Darcy: a more humanized and eroticized character. This fanon representation has, in turn, established the benchmark for modern book boyfriends.

Understanding the reader's relationship to the genre of romance and their expectations is vital in order to continue researching it. Romance is a genre directed toward women, and it is interesting to see that the ideal male character is shaped by the female gaze, almost as a feminist response to patriarchal society. Romance is a genre that tends to be looked down upon as "silly love stories" but it can actually be considered a space where women can escape from patriarchy by finding "perfect" men supporting them and corresponding to their every standard and giving them the guarantee of a love story that has a happy ever after where they are respected, safe and treated well.

NOTES

1. Pamela Regis, *A Natural History of the Romance Novel* (Philadelphia, PA: University of Pennsylvania Press, 2007).
2. Sarah J. Maas, *A Court of Thorns and Roses* (New York, NY: Bloomsbury, 2018).
3. Stephenie Meyer, *Twilight—The Twilight Saga Book 1* (New York, NY: Little, Brown and Co., 2005).
4. E. L. James, *Fifty Shades of Grey* (New York, NY: Bloom Books, 2012).
5. Jane Austen, *Pride and Prejudice*, 1832, ed. Robert P. Irvine (Peterborough, Ontario, Canada: Broadview Press, 2020).
6. Regis, *Natural History of the Romance*.
7. Regis, "8. The Best Romance Novel Ever Written" chapter, in *A Natural History of the Romance Novel*, 75–84.
8. Katya Johanson et al., "What Is BookTok, and How Is It Influencing What Australian Teenagers Read?", *The Conversation*, May 9, 2022, https://theconversation.com/what-is-booktok-and-how-is-it-influencing-whataustralian-teenagers-read-182290.
9. Ronnie Gomez, "Breaking down BookTok: What Brands Can Learn from This Social-Literary Phenomenon," *Sprout Social*, July 26, 2022, https://sproutsocial.com/insights/BookTok/.
10. David Sanderson, "TikTok Rekindles Passion for Romance Novels," *The Times & The Sunday Times*, March 10, 2023, https://www.thetimes.co.uk/article/tiktok-romanic- fiction-booktok-publishing-0nhs0klkh.
11. Ibid.
12. See Appendix E, figure 1.
13. See Appendix E, table 1.
14. Matt Hills, *Fan Cultures*, 1st ed. (London, England: Routledge, 2002), 137.
15. Sarah K. Hanssen, "New Tools for the Immersive Narrative Experience," *International Journal of Emerging Technologies in Learning (iJET)* 14, no. 16 (August 29, 2019): 45.
16. Blogger Leslie, "The Best Book Boyfriends of 2022: Romance Heroes to Fall for This Year", *She Reads Romance Books*, January 18, 2023, https://www.shereadsromancebooks.com/book-boyfriends-2022/.
17. Hassan, "New Tools for the Immersive Narrative Experience," 45.

18. Blogger Lizz, "Obsession Runs Deep; or, What Is a Book Boyfriend?", *Lizz in Bookland*, February 8, 2016, http://www.lizzinbookland.com/2016/02/obsession-runs-deep-or-what-is-book.html.

19. Tricia Clasen, "Masculinity and Romantic Myth in Contemporary YA Romance," essay, in *Gender(Ed) Identities: Critical Rereadings of Gender in Children's and Young Adult Literature*, ed. Holly Hassel and Tricia Clasen (New York, NY: Routledge, 2017), 229.

20. Regis, *A Natural History of the Romance Novel*, 22.

21. See figure 2.

22. Janice A. Radway, "The Ideal Romance: The Promise of Patriarchy," chapter, in *Reading the Romance: Women, Patriarchy, and Popular Literature* (Chapel Hill, NC: The University of North Carolina Press, 2006), 128.

23. Ibid.

24. Regis, *A Natural History of the Romance Novel*, 113.

25. Dean Talbot, "Author Demographics Statistics," *Words Rated*, February 8, 2023, https://wordsrated.com/author-demographics-statistics/.

26. Patsy Stoneman, "Rochester and Heathcliff as Romantic Heroes," *Brontë Studies* 36, no. 1 (July 2011): 111.

27. Austen, *Pride and Prejudice*, 46.

28. Ibid.

29. Ibid.

30. Austen, *Pride and Prejudice*, 277.

31. Regis, "The Popular Romance Novel in the Twentieth Century," 113.

32. Jaden (@redformandumbazz), "The blueprint," TikTok post, November 12, 2020, https://vm.tiktok.com/ZGJEPMqvV/.

33. Nicole Perry, "Mr. Darcy: Literature's Romantic Hero or a Model for Unrealistic Expectations?", *The Sophian*, April 12, 2021, https://thesophian.com/mr-darcy-literatures-romantic-hero-or-a-model-for-unrealisticexpectations/.

34. Catherine Driscoll, "One True Pairing: The Romance of Pornography and the Pornography of Romance" in *Fan Fiction and Fan Communities in the Age of the Internet: New Essays* (Jefferson, NC: McFarland & Co., 2006), 88.

35. Cheryl L. Nixon, "Balancing the Courtship Hero: Masculine Emotional Display in Film Adaptations of Austen's Novels," in *Jane Austen in Hollywood*, ed. Sayre N. Greenfield and Linda Troost (Lexington, KY: Univ. Press of Kentucky, 2010), 33.

36. Lisa Hopkins, "Mr. Darcy's Body: Privileging the Female Gaze," in *Jane Austen in Hollywood*, ed. Sayre N. Greenfield and Linda Troost (Lexington, NY: Univ. Press of Kentucky, 2010), 112.

37. Silke Meyer, "'Spank Me Mr. Darcy': Pride and Prejudice in Contemporary Female (Hardcore) Erotica," in *Pride and Prejudice 2.0. Interpretations, Adaptations and Transformations of Jane Austen's Classic* (Göttingen, Germany: Vandenhoeck & Ruprecht, 2015), 261–73.

38. Hopkins, "Mr. Darcy's Body: Privileging the Female Gaze," 112.

39. A&E Television: "Behind the Scenes: Colin Firth as Mr. Darcy," July 20, 1997, http://www.aetv.com/scenes/pride/pride3b.html.

40. See Appendix E, figure 5.
41. See Appendix E, figure 3.
42. Josefine Smith and Kathleen W. Taylor Kollman, "Rank what you watch most often when you watch movies. Please rank the top three with 1 being the most common" question, in *Still Reading Romance survey* (Philadelphia, PA: Shippensburg University, 2022).
43. Meyer, "Spank Me Mr. Darcy," 266.
44. Radway, "The Ideal Romance," 150.
45. Deborah Kaplan, "Mass Marketing Jane Austen: Men, Women, and Courtship in Two Film Adaptations," in *Jane Austen in Hollywood*, ed. Sayre N. Greenfield and Linda Troost (Lexington: Univ. Press of Kentucky, 2010), 178.
46. Hannah Kerns, "Here's Why the 'Pride & Prejudice' Hand Flex Makes You Feel Things," *Elite Daily*, March 3, 2022, https://www.elitedaily.com/dating/pride-prejudice-hand-flex-tiktok.
47. *Pride & Prejudice*, directed by Joe Wright (Focus Features, 2005), 07:00.
48. Kerns, "Here's Why the 'Pride & Prejudice' Hand Flex,"
49. Sarah Emsley, "Why Has Mr. Darcy Been Attractive to Generations of Women?", *Literary Ladies Guide*, January 20, 2014, https://www.literaryladiesguide.com/literary- musings/why-is-mr-darcy-so-attractive/.
50. Imke Licherfeld, "Mr Darcy's Shirt—An Icon of Popular Culture," essay, in *Pride and Prejudice 2.0. Interpretations, Adaptations and Transformations of Jane Austen's Classic*, ed. Hanne Birk and Marion Gymnich (Göttingen, Germany: Vandenhoeck & Ruprecht, 2015), 194.
51. Gislind Rohwer-Happe, "The Mr. Darcy Complex—The Impact of a Literary Icon on Contemporary Chick Lit," in *Pride and Prejudice 2.0. Interpretations, Adaptations and Transformations of Jane Austen's Classic* (Göttingen, Germany: Vandenhoeck & Ruprecht, 2015), 207.
52. Rohwer-Happe, "The Mr. Darcy Complex," 208.
53. *Charlotte Brontë, Jane Eyre*, 1847, ed. Stevie Davis (London, England: Penguin Classics, 2006).
54. See Appendix E, table 2.
55. Regis, *A Natural History of the Romance Novel*, xi.
56. Regis, *A Natural History of the Romance Novel*, 3.
57. Janice Radway, "The Institutional Matrix," chapter in *Reading the Romance*, 19.
58. Dimitrije Curcic, "Romance Novel Sales Statistics," *Words Rated*, October 9, 2022, https://wordsrated.com/romance-novel-sales-statistics/.
59. Betsy Rosenblatt and Rebecca Tushnet, "Transformative Works: Young Women's Voices on Fandom and Fair Use," essay, in *eGirls, eCitizens: Putting Technology, Theory and Policy into Dialogue with Girls' and Young Women's Voices*, ed. Jane Bailey and Valerie Steeves (Ottawa, Canada: University of Ottawa Press, 2015), 387.
60. Curcic, "Romance Novel Sales Statistics."
61. Rohwer-Happe, "The Mr. Darcy complex," 209.
62. Staci Hart, *Pride & Papercuts: Inspired by Jane Austen's Pride and Prejudice* (New York, NY: Independently published, 2020).

63. Curtis Sittenfeld, *Eligible: A Modern Retelling of Pride and Prejudice* (New York, NY: Random House, Inc., 2016).
64. Lara S. Ormiston and Devleena Ghosh, *Unequal Affections: A Pride & Prejudice Retelling* (New York, NY: Skyhorse Publishing, 2017).
65. Linda Berdoll, *Mr. Darcy Takes a Wife* (Naperville, IL: Sourcebooks Landmark, 2020).
66. Hart, *Pride & Papercuts*, 10.
67. Austen, *Pride and Prejudice*, 49.
68. Sittenfeld, *Eligible*, 31.
69. See Appendix E, figure 4.
70. Hart, *Pride & Papercuts*, 189.
71. Berdoll, *Mr. Darcy Takes a Wife*, 45.
72. Radway, "The Ideal Romance," 147.
73. Clasen, "Masculinity and Romantic Myth in Contemporary YA Romance," 235.
74. Martine Voiret, "Books to Movies: Gender and Desire in Jane Austen's Adaptations," essay, in *Jane Austen and Co.: Remaking the Past in Contemporary Culture*, ed. Suzanne Rodin Pucci and James Thompson (Albany, NY: State University of New York Press, 2003), 229–46, 239.
75. See Appendix E, figure 3.
76. Clasen, "Masculinity and Romantic Myth in Contemporary YA Romance," 237.
77. Voiret, "Books to Movies: Gender and Desire in Jane Austen's Adaptations," 243.
78. See Appendix E, figure 7.
79. Manda Victoria (@manda_vm), "Same font," TikTok post, March 29, 2022, https://vm.tiktok.com/ZGEJEPPrTX/.

Chapter 15

Reading Romance and Erotic Literacy

Sara Partin and Josefine Smith

In the twenty-first century, sexuality and sexual intimacy are relevant in both personal and political contexts. Through the internet, sex—once considered a private act—is now laden with public meaning.[1] Public sexuality is pervasive: on social media, on television and film, in the news, as a form of work, and in fiction, which the public inherently uses to politicize and scrutinize, especially against women. Erotic romance is now a mainstream commodity, and readers are able to walk into a Walmart or Target and find authors like Ana Huang, Sara Cate, and Penelope Douglas in stock, or pick up the erotic graphic novel *Lore Olympus* off the shelf. Popular romance positions eroticism comfortably in the public sphere and normalizes intimate and romantic sexuality. This chapter will explore how romance fits within the larger context of public eroticism and how sexuality and feminine eroticism are constructed in popular romance fiction.

Sarah J. Maas's New Adult fantasy-romance series *A Court of Thorns and Roses* (*ACOTAR*) relies on sexual experience and encounters of the erotic: much of the series' plot progression and character development are placed around sexual encounters. Set in the fictional world of Prythian, *ACOTAR* tells the story of nineteen-year-old human Feyre in a world divided between human and fae.

When Feyre is taken to the fae lands after killing a faerie, both lands collide through the politics of magic, sex, and war. The romantic setting of the series, as well as its devoted online fanbase, are spaces to experiment with power dynamics and erotic couplings to imagine a more just, playful, and sexier future. This offers readers a platform to explore dynamics of female agency and feminized eroticism through the sexuality represented in the text. As the erotic intimacy of romantic texts like *ACOTAR* become popular and mainstream, those explicit situations could be a space for readers to develop their own sexual literacy that emphasizes their own sexual pleasure and consent.

Through reading Maas's complex depictions of sexuality, readers explore their own sexualities and question cultural norms, disrupting notions of shame and confusion to resituate sex positivity at the center of the female experience.

READING *ACOTAR*

Our reading of *A Court of Thorns and Roses*, both the book and the rest of the series, draws primarily from the original text. However, this exploration is in context of the larger collection focused on the cultural and personal experiences of reading romance. In Janice Radway's original research, bedhopping and explicit sex were highly ranked as elements that the Smithton readers felt should *never* be included in romance novels, and scenes with explicit sex were not considered an important ingredient of romance.[2] Indeed, Radway notes that sexuality in romance is still secondary to marriage, and female pleasure is at least not articulated as necessary to the erotic narratives.[3] In the contemporary iteration of the survey at the center of this volume, participants ranked "Lots of love scenes with explicit sexual description" in the top three most important ingredients, and explicit sex was only selected six times as something that should never be found in romance novels.[4] This indicates that the interest and value of erotic relationships has grown, which could suggest that the value of female pleasure in romance has shifted.

Radway notes American media tells women their "worth as individuals is closely tied to their sexual allure and physical beauty," yet they are also "educated by their families and churches to believe that their sexual being may be activated only by and for one other individual. The double message effectively produces a conflicted response to sexual need and desire."

Radway explains that often, women experience guilt for indulging in their desires, due to societal standards: "culture continues to value work over leisure and play," and that[5] "culture remains uneasy about the free expression of female sexuality."[6] Further, Easton and Hardy explain that heteronormativity teaches the female gender how they are "supposed to" enjoy sex.[7] While the series does engage in problematic sexual scenarios, there are erotic and sexual encounters that evolve beyond heteropatriarchal traditions. Often, as Radway notes, women "manipulate the culture of femininity" to "resist their situation . . . by enabling them to cope with the features of the situation that oppress them."[8] Women might use romance novels as an individual form of resistance as they address the consequences of their heteropatriarchal situations.

ACOTAR is notably a BookTok and cultural phenomenon, appearing on several bestseller and "best of" lists, its TikTok handle garnering over 8.9 billion views, and now being optioned for a TV adaptation.[9] Despite its popularity, scholarship directly exploring the cultural impact of *ACOTAR* is still relatively unexplored. Some scholars have explored themes of trauma and allegories represented in the text.[10] Like this chapter, some social science and humanities scholars have investigated themes of sexuality and the *ACOTAR* community. Little and Moruzi explore this work as a postfeminist text, considering the tensions between the sexual empowered heroine and the heteronormative and patriarchal realities all feminine texts must contend with.[11] Speese expands the conversation of *ACOTAR* as a postfeminist text that actually subverts hegemonic masculinity and rape myths by centering consent and feminine pleasure within *ACOTAR*'s erotic space.[12] Dudek, Grob, and Boyd seem to be in agreement with Speese regarding the potentially positive power of feminine erotic scripts creating a kind of sexual literacy.[13] This chapter weaves text and reader-response analysis together to show further evidence that ultimately erotic romance has the power to create sex-positive cultural understandings of female pleasure, and the mainstreaming of these narratives creates a sexual literacy that empowers female-identifying readers and normalizes female pleasure.

EROTICISM IN THE PUBLIC SPHERE

If looking at the specifically heterosexual erotic, contemporary erotic romance displaces the publicly accepted assumption that men have a monopoly on eroticism and sexual desire. In a generation of people who were raised by technology, phallocentric pornography is one way people develop their understanding of sexuality.[14] The question of eroticism and public spheres is fraught when applying feminist critiques. Amia Srinivasa posits pornography has become "an eroticization of gender inequality—from which there can be no true liberation without a revolution."[15] Erotic romance can redefine the narrative of the pornographic in fiction as something that further liberates female experience and challenges problematic depictions of sex. Phallocentric porn can be a "virtual training ground for male sexual aggression."[16] Audre Lorde notes that often, "[women] have been raised to fear the yes within [themselves], [their] deepest cravings."[17] Erotic fiction like Maas's series seeks to nullify this ideology and subvert conventions of phallocentric pornography. Female desire is often suppressed in the face of "patriarchal scripts" women have been subject to for centuries.[18] Not only have women been taught to be passive and unmotivated by sexual desire in the real world, but erotic fiction is regarded as taboo in its intense visibility. The explicit representations of sexual pleasures could be read as pornographic by some audiences, but Maas's goal is to redefine the terms of "porn." As erotic texts like pornography have centered on masculine pleasure and prioritized phallocentric pleasure, there is a potential for power in eroticization from a feminine perspective.

Critical understandings of romance distinguish erotic content from pornography in that the former promotes relationships. As Sylvia Day explains, erotic romance is a "story written about the development of a romantic relationship through sexual interaction."[19] Day, an author of erotic romance novels, explains the broader commentary on this genre: no matter what happens, the reader is assured that sex will drive the plot, and the couple will end up together. Further, erotic romance situates sex as paramount to the plot: "the [romantic] story would not make sense without the presence of sex."[20] Sexual desire and romantic love, as independent points, come together in the text. Erotic romance blends together the "generic structures of the romance novel and pornography. The former builds toward an emotional climax, while the latter is based on the repetition of sexual climaxes."[21] Women who read erotic romance can expect to find infinite pleasure through texts that offer sexual gratification through romance and titillation.

Recently, Jonathan Allen demonstrated that romance fiction can be studied through a similar lens as the popular understanding of pornography, with the major difference that it is directed toward a feminine audience and is concerned with feminine-focused fantasies of sexuality and the erotic in the context of sexual agency and desire.[22] As argued by Allen, the problem with the traditional perspective of studying erotic texts like pornography and popular romance is that it "pathologises the viewer of pornography. The problem is thus not 'pornography,' at least rhetorically, but rather the pathologizing impulses of critics, scholars, and commentators.... We can argue against the pathologization of viewers of pornography and readers of romance and still critique or celebrate the content and form of the text."[23] Erotic romance can redefine the narrative of the pornographic in fiction as something that further liberates female experience and challenges problematic depictions of sex.

Reconstructing our cultural perspective around female pleasure helps us reconstruct the naturalness of female sexual pleasure and better connect with our partners. Just as Audre Lorde posits that women have been raised to fear the "yes" in themselves, Susan Stiritz argues "when so many women in our culture experience sexual frustration and believe something is wrong with their genitals, we need to ask what part the misogynistic aggression we have briefly examined plays in their self-understanding and functioning."[24] Female sexuality can be reclaimed through explicitly intimate and erotic romance fiction to normalize female pleasure and subvert patriarchal traditions that represses feminine sexuality. Feminist Anne Zachary identifies a challenge with visual representations of the erotic: "whereas male sexuality is very visible, external, inserting, female sexuality is largely hidden, internal, inserted into."[25] Dudek, Grobbelaar, and Boyd see this as a strength of erotic romance because erotic romance articulates female pleasure on the page and erotic texts in general are a means to arousal for female consumers.[26] Instead of being concerned with how female characters should respond or being a tool in the male characters pleasure, erotic romance focuses on feminine pleasure. Interestingly, Dudek, Grobbelaar, and Boyd do have some concern that the female main character (FMC) often does not verbalize her pleasure and desire fully to her partner. However, if the main audience is a female readership, and the point is a fantasy of female pleasure, there is a level of relief that not only the FMC knows and wants pleasure, but that there is something intrinsic to the ideal partner that knows and understands her sexual desires. Readers see sex represented in the text, where they find depictions of female agency and sexual expressions that are sex-positive and give them a foundational level of sexual literacy to explore their own individual desires.

SEX POSITIVITY AND EROTIC ROMANCE

In Jane Ward's *The Tragedy of Heterosexuality*, "straight culture" is equated to sadness and boredom and is filled with trauma.[27] The question is thus: how do heterosexual women experience pleasure and consent in a positive form outside the boundaries of heteronormative structures? Today, negotiations of sex are especially relevant in personal as well as political contexts. Heteronormativity, as Lauren Berlant and Michael Warner claim in their landmark 1998 essay, is a constant project of saturation to remain dominant in public culture.[28] Not only is sex mediated in both the private and public spheres, but heteronormative sex is still privileged in society. Ward also understands heterosexuality to be a politics of exclusion, a "dysfunctional system" that queer bodies have since rejected to further liberate their sexual bodies.[29] A fantasy of romance is for the passion and love to be "all-consuming," and from a young age, women are taught that the most significant relationships they will have will be with a man.[30] Female-identifying readers, then, enter into the romance of *ACOTAR* with notions of patriarchy and heteronormativity that are reflected in culture and inherently prescribed to girls growing up.

Looking toward new methods of sexual expression may create new modes of sex positivity in culture. Berlant and Warner worked to deconstruct ideology surrounding heterosexuality by pointing out that "heteronormative conventions of intimacy block the building of nonnormative or explicit public sexual cultures," and heterosexual sex remains the "privileged example of sexual culture."[31] While heterosexual sex has been and still is the norm, and patriarchal cultural narratives offer little in the way of complete and candid sexual literacy, erotic and explicit romance offers readers a chance to experience sex in the safest space fashioned for their own bodies in mind. While this often requires a negotiation with the patriarchal frameworks often enmeshed within heterosexuality, it provides all the possibilities the romance genre offers to shift the narrative toward an inclusive, sex-positive space. *ACOTAR*'s predominantly female readership offers a model through which we might recontextualize how explicit material and identity work together to reclaim spaces that have once been dedicated to men. This allows us to look toward new methods of sexual expression that may create modes of sex-positivity in culture.

A Court of Thorns and Roses (*ACOTAR*) relies on sexual experience and encounters of the erotic: much of the series' plot progression is placed around heterosexual sexual encounters. Readers, then, find complex depictions of sexuality and eroticism in the text that allow them to negotiate sexual female agency and sexual expressions that are both sex-positive and sexually repressive. Moreover, this can be a tool to liberate their own sexualities and question cultural norms, disrupting notions of shame and confusion to resituate sex positivity at the center of the female experience. *ACOTAR*'s subversive potential does not solely lie in the reframing of the pornographic through the erotic; its explicit intimacy serves as a liberatory space where all forms of sex are welcomed and enjoyed. *ACOTAR*'s treatment of sexual relationships can be approached as a "challenge the more traditional representations of interpersonal relationships."[32][33] While readers have been changing their thoughts surrounding sexuality, society seems to still struggle with notions of liberation in sexual scenarios. Often, as Radway notes, women "manipulate the culture of femininity" to "resist their situation as women by enabling them to cope with the features of the situation that oppress them".[34] Female readers can use erotic romance as a space that challenges the boundaries of the romance novel to combine both making love and explicit sex to offer new models of relationships.

As *ACOTAR* is a romance, and its readership is predominantly female, we might use this series as a lens through which sex positivity is being interpreted in contemporary culture. The OED defines sex positivity as "promot[ing] a tolerant, progressive, or candid attitude towards sex and sexuality; pro-sex" (OED). As intimacy coach Jane Steckbeck notes, a "healthy erotic imagination can do wonders for a woman's libido and her experience of arousal."[35] Erotic imagination can be considered as any thoughts or mental images that stimulate sexual feelings. the strong attitudes women have toward their sexuality and their capabilities as women, encourage and inspire sex positivity and desire without shame in women of similar ages. In writing *ACOTAR*, Maas follows the same set of concerns as Srinivasan. Maas's intention in writing sex-positive relationships in *ACOTAR* was, as she notes in an interview, crucial to her own understanding of sex:

> I think it's important to have positive sexual relationships in books, especially where both parties are in love . . . not for the shock value. [I]t's OK not to just have

sex, but to enjoy it, and for young women [to see that]. I firmly believe that young women can be with as many men as they want, we can have as many boyfriends as we want, we can change our minds, there are no limits to what we can do.[36]

Women like Maas, Radway, and Srinivasan want a place of recognition where they can work through that which has previously been "unsaid" or "formerly unsayable" for women,[37] and readers find in *ACOTAR* a place of recognition for their desires. One survey participant said, "I use [romance] to learn more about people in a way that allows me to indulge in the fantasy of radical joy for everyone. . . . It's a way to find hope and connect with others who believe in the idea that love and joy is for everyone."[38] On reddit, *ACOTAR* fans suggest that romance and sexual fulfillment "[are] and should be for everyone" (u/lafornarinas), these examples suggest a desire and expectation for depictions of sexual expressions that are authentic fulfilling sexual experiences. Survey responses articulate the importance of romance to represent sexual freedoms that encourage them to be the "free, sexual and desired" women they want to be. Another response explains that romance fiction is a "safe haven for me in a sometimes-difficult world."[39] These narratives suggest that romance readers feel less shame for their sexuality—indeed, they expect a satisfying erotic life that values their pleasure as much as their partners'. Erotic romance as a genre sees this issue and validates its readers. Through recontextualization of sex in culture and attention to feminism of the 1970s and 1980s, we can recontextualize how sex is viewed in *ACOTAR*, and by extension, in contemporary culture. *Reading the Romance* and survey results helps us analyze how *ACOTAR* fans are understanding sexual expression in the series and our current culture. *ACOTAR* is a touchstone for sex in fantasy fiction; through readers' own understandings and application of the erotic and pornographic challenges power dynamics and erotic couplings to imagine ourselves into a more just, playful, and sexier future.

READING *ACOTAR* AS SEXUAL LITERACY

We wish to also consider the ways in which many of Maas's female characters are described and thus analyze sexual experience as it is utilized by characters to leverage power through erotic encounters. The "erotic" is that which we find "sexually desire[able] and arous[ing],"[40] so erotic fiction and romance is clearly desired by a female audience. The erotic becomes sexually stimulating to us, thereby heightening the complexity of human sexuality. "Erotic" romance as a genre is "softer" and "more acceptable" to a wider audience than perhaps what is considered "pornographic;"[41] given that certain works are not always as directly explicit, erotic romance is more palatable to certain audiences. In studying human sexuality, we must consider the "wider social, cultural, and psychological environments in which sexual desires are enacted."[42] *ACOTAR* uses erotic and explicit depictions of female sexuality and sexual encounters to negotiate power and agency in female characters. 19-year-old Feyre immediately establishes her sex positivity in the first novel, mentioning her "stolen" and "hungry" hours in a barn with a man she grew up with (*ACOTAR* 3). These experiences and Feyre's sexuality are unquestioned—she does what she wants with whomever she wants. Feyre never denies her sexual desires, thus allowing the erotic to "flow within [her] life with a kind of energy that heightens and sensitizes and strengthens all [her] experience."[43] Feyre uses the erotic as a guide in her life that consequently heightens her experience as a woman.

Feyre has two main love interests, and both explore complex facets of romantic and erotic relationships. Both Tamlin and Rhysand are problematic heroes in their own ways. Tamlin has never fully come to terms with his own trauma, which makes his character extremely toxic in the second book. Interestingly, Tamlin represents a more traditional male love interest bound by a patriarchal framework that does not allow for him to be emotionally vulnerable or egalitarian. Feyre's agency and sexual power are immediately complicated when she is forced to live with Tamlin, who is High Lord of the Spring. The entire premise of their relationship undermines Feyre's agency, as Tamlin forces her to live in indentured servitude until she dies.[44] Much of the explicit intimacy between Feyre and Tamlin explores the complex dynamics of consent, and one night Feyre encounters Tamlin after he performed a sexual ritual with a "maiden" to help keep his magic fruitful on the night of Calanmai. While Feyre has mixed emotions regarding her attraction to Tamlin's advances, the "fantastic setting" of the novel reframes this interaction as sexually arousing:[45] Feyre's body "goes loose and taut all at once," a direct result of Tamlin's words and actions (*ACOTAR* 196). As they grapple for power, Feyre is forced into submission which, according to Elizabeth Little and Kristine Moruzi, "naturalizes patriarchal dominance within an intimate relationship and presents it as desirable" that is necessary to a support their intimacy within a patriarchal model of a heterosexuality.[46] Feyre's erotic body has been diminished to an object of satisfaction rather than sharing a connection with Tamlin, and, as a result, she loses the power of erotic expression.

Feyre's actions of love to save Tamlin after he is kidnapped align strongly with what is expected of a submissive partner, acting under the patriarchal authority she is placed under (while also ending up the victim). While she chooses to save Tamlin after he has been kidnapped by an evil faerie general, Feyre's guilt about her role in his kidnapping is an important motivator.[47] With these scenes, Maas underscores the problems many women face in intimate relationships as they are taken advantage of and prevented from exercising their own agency.

Feyre may have once been a sexually independent woman, but here her agency is undermined through the physical and intimate partner violence she experiences with Tamlin. Notions of romance are further complicated as Feyre and Tamlin's relationship becomes more explicit and the pair engage in sexual acts. Feyre describes her sexual desire for Tamlin as something that develops from "longing" to "pounding," and their encounters become filled with increasing sexual tension.[48] Feyre also voices her desires to Tamlin, demanding he "[not] stop" as they have sex after a lengthy buildup.[49] Feyre consents with passion as a result of the bond she believes to have formed with Tamlin. However, because Feyre is originally brought to Tamlin's household as a captive, she has no opportunity to fully consent to any form of her relationship with him.

Little and Moruzi emphasize that often, romantic fiction justifies women's "submissiveness as romance."[50] Feyre's mixed feelings about Tamlin could be a result of "abuse without feeling;"[51] as Feyre is forced to leave Tamlin's land (so she is not captured and killed by other evil fae hunting her), she cannot bring herself to tell him she loves him as he has.[52]

This leads Feyre to her second relationship, with the morally gray, problematic fan favorite Rhysand. By introducing a new male presence, Maas complicates the romance genre and offers women a space to critique what is desirable in a relationship. An instant connection is formed between Rhysand and Feyre, who not only offers her help to save Tamlin, but also encourages her to find the strength to leave him when Tamlin's abuse grows in the second installment of the series, *A Court of Mist and Fury*.[53] While Tamlin represents the "hardness, indifference, and emotional cruelty" that Radway posits all women see but run from in their own relationships,[54] Rhysand has the potential to represent what women seek in erotic romance, and their own lives: "all popular romance originates in the failure of patriarchal culture to satisfy its female members."[55] Rhysand's presence offers women a glimpse of what those who enjoy romance desire outside of fiction, which is a vulnerable partnership between two individuals who love each other—and mind-blowing sex.

The generic conventions of erotic romance allow readers to see Feyre's encounters with her mate and husband, Rhysand, as a representation of egalitarian sex, though their relationship is still riddled with flaws. Though Tamlin is not presented as Feyre's "Happily Ever After" in the first novel,[56] Maas quickly shifts the narrative in Rhysand's favor in the second novel. After helping Feyre save Tamlin, Rhysand saves her from her wedding: "I heard you begging someone, anyone, to rescue you, to get you out. I heard you say no."[57] Feyre could not marry Tamlin—Tamlin's control became too much for her to handle as Tamlin locked her up in his mansion and she could not escape, leaving Rhysand to rescue her.[58] That dynamic, coupled with Tamlin's overbearing nature, pushes Feyre away for good. As a free citizen of Rhysand's court, Feyre now has the chance to experience love and desire in a healthy manner.

Feyre's sexual interactions with Rhysand evolve from brief touches to days-long "sex marathon[s]" (Orlando, White), which heightens Feyre's sexual agency as a complex feminine character. As Feyre and Rhysand get to know each other, friendship forms—their ability to be vulnerable with each other is what alters their relationship from friendship to love. Whereas Tamlin forbids Feyre from leaving his estate,[59] Rhysand constantly reminds Feyre she is free to enter and leave the Night Court as she pleases.[60] Feyre's body is no longer subject to Tamlin's violence, and instead can heal from the trauma of her death and abuse. Rhysand offers Feyre hope amid her own personal crisis. Reading in the twenty-first century is a communal act that dismisses broader issues of sexism and sexuality and embraces the women who read erotic romance in large numbers. Readers understand Feyre's journey as complex, rather than just good or bad. While Feyre has always been a sexual woman, she may now act freely without the constraints that prevented her from healing and engaging in true sex-positive pleasure.

As erotic fiction works to subvert boundaries placed on women, *ACOTAR* as a series seeks to empower women and celebrate their bodies. Rhysand encourages Feyre to empower herself, through her sexuality, past Tamlin's overbearing hold. Feyre is now a faerie, she is situated as an equal to Rhysand in power, but also in gender. Rhysand, as Srinivasan argues, offers Feyre a way to "emancipate" her politicized body following on the violence she experienced with Tamlin.[61] While in Rhysand's company, Feyre constantly recognizes the agony she felt with Tamlin. As their romance grows, so do their sexual interactions.

Feyre's relationship with Rhysand combines the erotic and the romantic to highlight modes of romanticized and emotionality-driven pleasure. After the pair admit their love for each other, Feyre notes that they are both "broken, and healing" but she is "honored" to be Rhysand's love and mate.[62] Feyre's acknowledgment of this bond between them is her consent to a future with Rhysand forever. The pair exchange their love for each other and have what has been deemed the infamous "sex marathon" wherein they have sex for three days straight.[63] Both Feyre and Rhysand note their multiple sexual climaxes, and Feyre knows they are "equals."[64] Between the moments of the sexual interactions, Feyre thinks about her future with Rhysand and how he has treated her during her stay with him, claiming "[their] souls had forged together," and they were "friends" first, then her "lover who had healed [her] broken and weary soul. [Her] mate who had waited for [her] against all hope, despite all odds."[65] Jodi McAlister notes that erotic romance is just as much about sex as it is about love[66]—Rhysand and Feyre obviously fall in love because they spend so much intimate time together, but their moments of physical and emotional healing are crucial to their developing a romantic relationship. Without their mutual vulnerability, they could not trust each other with love, as Feyre tells Rhysand: "I was never afraid of the consequences of being with you. Even if every assassin in the world hunts us . . . you are worth it."[67] Both characters and readers thus experience what Radway notes as "good" feelings of "emotional nurturance and erotic anticipation and excitation."[68] Both reassurance and declaration, Feyre has reclaimed her body from Tamlin's abuse and has made her own decision to have a future built in love and trust with Rhysand.

Without trust and honesty between the couple, the erotic relationship would not function to serve female readers in the ways they desire, nor would it be the ideal that Maas directs her fans toward. Feyre describes Rhysand as the ideal, "cliterate" man[69]—one who can make her orgasm over and over for days, but one who can also meet her needs emotionally and offer her the care she desires. As Srinivasan points out, sex has long been about male pleasure over female pleasure, so long as men get what they want.[70] Rhysand is a very skilled lover, and Feyre finds herself orgasming multiple times in one sexual encounter:

> The first lick of Rhysand's tongue set me on fire. I want you splayed out on the table like my own personal feast. He growled his approval at my moan, my taste, and unleashed himself on me entirely. A hand pinning my hips to the table, he worked me in great sweeping strokes. And when his tongue slid inside me, I reached up to grip the edge of the table, to grip the edge of the world that I was very near to falling off. He licked and kissed his way to the apex of my thighs, just as his fingers replaced where his mouth had been, pumping inside me as he sucked, his teeth scraping ever so slightly—I bowed off the table as my climax shattered through me, splintering my consciousness into a million pieces.[71]

Here, sex does not equal just penis and vagina: the female orgasm can be achieved through multiple modes of sexual pleasure. As Rhysand pushes Feyre to her climax not once, but twice orally, Maas offers the opportunity for women to orgasm outside of penetration. Sexual pleasure for women has long been ignored in patriarchal society because a vast majority of women cannot orgasm on phallic penetration alone.[72] Maas's exploration of multiple avenues toward the female orgasm subverts heteropatriarchal norms of penetrative sex by recentering the female orgasm at the core of the relationship. While women have been telling men what is going wrong in the bedroom for years, this novel offers a twenty-first-century model for what is right for women.

The explicit representations of sexual pleasures could be read as pornographic by some audiences, but Maas's erotic focus on Feyre's pleasure subverts patriarchal norms in other forms of explicit entertainment. Srinivasan explains that pornography has become a metonym for "problematic" sex because porn typically takes no account of women's pleasure.[73] Common porn tropes like sadomasochism, rape fantasies, and prostitution all cater to the male gaze. Aptly put, Srinivasan posits pornography has become "an eroticization of gender inequality—from which there can be no true liberation without a revolution."[74] Porn not only facilitates, but encourages, harmful perspectives for men in today's generation who are not learning adequate sex education in schools and are instead being raised by internet porn. Just as sex is everywhere, so too is pornography, and men are wrongly learning what they believe sex is through improper distributions of power that have become their own tropes.[75] Both Maas and Srinivasan redefine the narrative of the pornographic in fiction as something that further liberates female experience and challenges problematic depictions of sex.

Recontextualizing pornography to fit feminine desire is essential to foster spaces of support and mobilization. In a generation of people who were raised by technology, phallocentric pornography is the main educator for men, but women still encounter porn—just different porn. PornHub, one of the world's most popular porn sites, released their 2022 year in review, and women seem to be watching sex where they hold the power over men. Some of the most searched terms from women include "cowgirl," a position where the woman is on top, and "femdom," where the woman is in control of the man.[76] Women can try to revolutionize the internet, but it is moving too quickly for true traction to be gained here, especially in videos where "no" means "yes." Men who watch phallocentric porn are far more likely to support violence against women, which only means that porn has become a "virtual training ground for male sexual aggression."[77] People—specifically heterosexual men who watch porn—expect sex to be what they watch because they know nothing else, which is exactly why their female partners are not being sexually satisfied, and instead encounter sex that is forceful and aggressive. Today's generation has grown up around slut shaming, victim blaming, and rape culture, so there is still a double standard around women's sexual pleasure. Erotic fiction like Maas's series seeks to nullify this ideology and subvert conventions of phallocentric pornography.

In erotic fiction like *ACOTAR*, there is no space for a phallocentric lover. In the healthier relationships presented in the series, men and women are treated as equals and sex is not shamed. Feyre's female experience is centered to trouble heteropatriarchal assumptions surrounding sex, and, because erotic fiction is driven by sex, her experience models a different set of assumptions. John Stoltenberg's formula "pornography tells lies about women" but "tells the truth about men" rings true because internet porn blurs the distinction between fantasy and reality, and subsequently, power and authority.[78] In fiction like *ACOTAR*, women see the explicitly intimate as "optimistic" and "satisfying" due to erotic romance's subversive nature.[79] Here, the romance between Feyre and Rhys and is focused on the development of their relationship, which is just as crucial as their desires are to building a strong future together. Their relationship is focused on them being together, not just getting together, which is why the more explicit sex scenes are necessary: Feyre's sexual relationship with Rhysand is just as crucial to their relationship as their trust and honesty are. Jodi McAlister posits that erotic romance is, in fact, the safest space for women to encounter pornography. McAlister writes that erotic romance fuses together the generic structures of romance novels and pornography. The former builds toward an emotional climax, while the latter is based on the repetition of sexual climaxes. The erotic romance combines these apparently incompatible forms: in erotic romance, "pleasure is infinite and infinitely repeatable" in a 'safe' discursive space" for women.[80]

Pornography in erotic romance is the remedy for the problem Amia Srinivasan explains as women being taught from a young age to be docile, submissive, and sexually passive, and men expecting that to be the case thanks to porn. Indeed, Radway notes that women associate "typical" pornography with men's fantasies.[81] Erotic romances like *ACOTAR* offer women a space to see sex that is exciting, satisfying, and optimistic—sex that women want to have, with the kinds of partners they want to have it with. The pornographic, in these cases, are not used in excess to solely arouse, but to also show that sex is allowed to be enjoyed by women excessively. The romantic climax that is confessing one's love for another, when accompanied by the sexual climax, highlights the woman, who recognizes that pleasure is not only possible: it is a necessity.

Readers can see Feyre as the ultimate sex-positive character because she is not always the strong, stereotypical heroine that Judith Arnold claims fiction once reduced women to.[82] Feyre's complex womanhood aligns readers with her and represents women outside of the page. Toril Moi posits that women demand "representation of female role-models in literature" and "not only wants to see her own experiences mirrored in fiction, but strives to identify with strong, impressive female characters."[83] Here, the demand for impressive female characters is the demand for real women who not only show their flaws but embrace them.

Women can reclaim sexuality through erotic romance fiction to liberate themselves from heteropatriarchal traditions. *ACOTAR* explores variations of female sexual expression: after the trilogy surrounding Feyre ends, Nesta—Feyre's eldest sister—takes charge in the fifth installment to explore her own sexuality and personal healing, where sex acts as a "bonus" to identity.

Nesta is often described as "hot-tempered," "brutal," and even "death personified,"[84] which is true to her personality, but Nesta has also undergone a terrible fate after being kidnapped by Tamlin in a jealous rage and turned into a high fae against her will.[85] *A Court of Silver Flames* (*ACOSF*) explores Nesta's journey toward healing as well as a budding relationship with Cassian, Rhysand's brother, and fourth-in-command.

Whereas Feyre's sexuality functions as catharsis throughout her journey, thereby leading to audience-identification, Nesta's sexuality begins as a coping mechanism that does not offer healing qualities. After being "remade" fae—a vicious process of torture, death, and revival— Nesta turns to alcoholism and sex. After Feyre forces Nesta to heal, Nesta begins learning how to acknowledge her trauma. When she makes a deal with Cassian to have sex without feelings as he trains her in combat, the pair engage in a new, even more complex version of desire, as well as the "happily ever after" Nesta is reluctant to find for herself.[86] As Nesta recovers and begins processing her emotions, she becomes a healthier individual and falls in love with Cassian.

Nesta's sexuality as a result turns from coping to catharsis and helps her explore her identity as a woman.

Nesta's own sexuality is often described as "pornographic" by readers,[87] as it occurs often and in explicit detail. Nesta's installment offers the most sex in a single book Maas has yet to publish. As we argued earlier, though, sex in excess does not equate to obscenity—Nesta's pornographic sex is a "liberatory" act that heightens her journey toward healing and can in turn offer new methods of exploration to readers.[88] Nesta's sexual encounters with Cassian help us understand, as Jack Halberstam explains "sexualities and sexual self-understandings tend not to lend themselves to linear models of human identity."[89] Nesta's sexual journey is not linear in that it does not fit typical forms of pleasure and heroism—especially when compared to Feyre.

Nesta's own sexuality is far more radical than Feyre's because the pornographic is reframed to highlight "a version of woman that is messy, bloody, porous, violent, and self-loathing."[90] Nesta's body is a tool she uses to exercise choice and therefore associates herself more closely to female masochism and self-subjugation during sex. Nesta exercises control of her own body through a new form of pleasure, one that Halberstam argues can exist outside "a system that favors male masculinity."[91] Rather than finding pleasure through explicit intimacy, Nesta's sexuality exists outside of the patriarchy where her pleasure comes first, and she will go to any length to get it. Nesta embodies the "refusal to be or to become woman as she has been defined and imagined within Western philosophy."[92] Nesta's masochistic sexuality empowers her to find pleasure in moments that seem otherwise fraught.

Nesta's experiences with Cassian are extremely graphic; in one experience, after Nesta and Cassian return from a dangerous mission, the pair have sex as a bonding moment after they thought the other had died. Their agreement for "just sex" is abandoned whether they know it or not, as they both show their care for each other through sexual intimacy:

> Cassian pounded into her, a hand moving from her hip to her hair, tugging her head back, baring her throat. She gave herself over to it, to him, and the lack of control was heady, so pleasurable that she could barely stand it. He thrust harder, so deep with this angle that she might have been screaming again, might have been sobbing. His other hand drifted between her legs, his cock pounding into her, her hair gripped like reins in one hand, her pleasure in his other. She was utterly at his mercy, and he knew it—he was snarling with desire, slamming home so hard his balls slapped against her.[93]

After their rough sexual encounter, the pair both know that "nothing and no one would ever compare" to the feelings that arise from being intimate with each other.[94] As explained by Halberstam, Nesta's sexuality can be better described in terms of masochism. What appears violent in this case can be reframed as an act of care because sex is Nesta's ultimate act of self-mastery: Nesta's vulnerability in giving herself over to Cassian's sexual domination offers readers the understanding that Nesta cares for him. In an egalitarian sense, as Riane Eisler states, women's sexuality is associated with "feminine power" rather than powerlessness, and it exists outside of exploitative power structures of oppression.[95] As Nesta is incredibly sexual, she holds power in the bedroom, and she also works to reframe what sustaining care can look like between a man and a woman: sex between Cassian and Nesta is of great importance because it highlights "intimate choice."[96] Nesta's choice to enjoy sex for pleasure empowers "women [who] haven't been brought up to enjoy sex."[97] Nesta's journey toward healing allows her to be vulnerable and share trust with Cassian, and this moment highlights just how vulnerable she lets herself be with her lover. The bedroom is the one place Nesta allows herself to be dominated. The pornographic in this case is both a moment of coping and catharsis, of healing and pleasure, proving that sex can be simultaneously an added bonus and empowering to women. Nesta treats "as axiomatic [her] free sexual choices."[98] Nesta's complex sexual relationship with Cassian and the explicit sexual experiences they engage in also highlight the potential for varying sexual experiences outside of fiction. Sex, in addition to her healing experience, offers another option for readers to explore their own relationships with sex while simultaneously subverting ideology surrounding pornography. Sex, as a result, becomes the ultimate test of true emancipation through vulnerability: the more Nesta can be truly intimate with Cassian, the more she can truly accept genuine love, and in turn, can become a co-option of liberation through consent and intimacy.

ACOTAR READERS

In the survey detailed in the introduction of this book, 20% of people who listed their favorite romance novels mentioned *ACOTAR* by name, and over 21% listed Maas as a favorite author of theirs. Readers want to see varying sexual experiences as well: in ranking preference for explicit sex scenes, 9 readers ranked their number preference to read sex at 1, 33 readers ranked their preference at 2, and 77 readers ranked number 3. This represents a vast increase in the almost nonexistent preference in Radway's volume, where 9 readers ranked preferred explicit sex in the top 3.[99] Only 4 readers from the recent survey claimed explicit sex to be distasteful. Romance offers readers fuller sexual expression, where "bedhopping" and sexual education are not concerns for heroines.[100] This appears to indicate that women are embracing their bodies, trusting themselves, and creating spaces for themselves to celebrate their choice. Sex and love are not synonymous, but having sex can foreground a woman's love for herself. While the series is not wholly sex-positive, it is closer to being so than earlier romance novels would have been during the era of Radway's study. *ACOTAR* could be a space where readers, who, in a world of their own problems, might experience a world of candid sexual expression, ultimately understanding sexual pleasure and consent as devices that can thrive outside of the heteropatriarchal norm.

In examining culture, we can also see what has not changed in the last forty years: romances make women feel good, they offer them a man who can offer the same "attention, intuition, and understanding" they regularly afford men.[101] Romance novels remain the same; they build relationships through sex and communication, but reader interpretation has shifted. Women recognize these stories are fantasies, but that they do have real-world consequences: one reader notes romances "have shaped my opinion on how people should act in relationships, especially romantic ones. . . . I am more comfortable with saying what I want from a romantic and a sexual relationship because I have read so many novels about women who do the same thing."[102] Romance is still a genre that still favors cisgender, white, heterosexual relationships.

Many readers notice the lack of representation in romance and its potential to grow in that regard. LGBTQ+ romance is a growing field (as covered in several other chapters in this volume), yet the genre is still mostly heterosexual. While these romances at times reinforce "traditional female limitations,"[103] such as loving one's abuser or making personal sacrifices for love. They also offer counternarratives that encourage shifts in romantic thought.

Culture today seems to stress the importance of female autonomy and self-confidence; the reader's transformation is equally as important as the heroine's. Readers may indeed be engaging in romance fiction to challenge social orders and construct personal meanings.

These readers can both appreciate and challenge the touchstone of complex femininity in *ACOTAR*, through which they can counter narratives of heteropatriarchy and liberate heteropatriarchal spaces while still existing in them. Through examination of sex positivity in romance culture and attention to the second-, third-, and fourth-wave feminist movements of the last six decades, we can recontextualize how sex is viewed in *ACOTAR*, and by extension, in contemporary culture. Radway's *Reading the Romance* and both her and the present survey results help analyze how *ACOTAR* fans could understand sexual expression in the series and in current culture. *ACOTAR* is becoming a contemporary touchstone for sex in fantasy fiction; through readers' own understandings and application of the erotic and pornographic challenges power dynamics and erotic couplings that could imagine them into a more just, playful, and sexier future.

CONCLUSION

Sex and relationships play a large role in consumer culture today, especially as we move toward discourse surrounding new narratives of feminism. Indeed, Bernadette and David Barker-Plummer note that collective intelligence online "counter[s] normative and oppressive assumptions about women . . . and about feminism itself" romance is a dynamic and constantly evolving genre as it is shaped by its audience's desires.[104] Fan interaction only heightens meaning making, and the closer one is to the material, the more they might glean from it. The interwoven relationships between authors, readers, and wider romancelandia community creates a more decentralized (and perhaps more feminist) cultural environment for sex positive representations in popular romance to thrive, while the mainstreaming of romance enhances our erotic literacy. *ACOTAR*—and broadly, New Adult romance—wrestles with topics surrounding love, abuse, and trauma, claiming spaces of love and trust for women's bodies.

While not an uncommon theme in romance, Maas's romances emphasize multiple cultural shifts since Radway's volume: readers recognize that sex is a liberating act that can be messy (Radway 74) and does not have to be between two people inside of a marriage or with marriage as the end goal. There is hardly a concern for threat to conventional marriage; instead, there is concern for bodily autonomy, for orgasm equality, and for providing models to negotiate and deconstruct harmful relationships. Maas's series unabashedly claims the space for carefree and casual sex. It also claims a space for loving, intimate, and erotic sex. By exploring the spectrum of sex-positive intimacy, Maas develops the heroine's independence, intelligence, and trust in herself, and encourages readers to see the same in themselves.

NOTES

1. Lauren Berlant and Michael Warner's "Sex in Public" addresses how heterosexual sex, mediated in both the private and public spheres, permeates culture.
2. Janice A. Radway, *Reading the Romance: Women, Patriarchy, and Popular Literature*. 2nd ed. (University of North Carolina Press, 1991), 67, 75.
3. Radway, *Reading the Romance*, 16.
4. Josefine Smith and Kathleen Kollman, unpublished data from *Still Reading Romance survey*, June 9 2023.
5. Radway, *Reading the Romance*, 105–6.
6. Radway, *Reading the Romance*, 105.
7. Dossie Easton and Janet W. Hardy, *Radical Ecstasy: S/M Journeys in Transcendence* (Oakland, CA: Greenery Press, 2004), 250.
8. Radway, *Reading the Romance*, 12.
9. Constance Grady, "Why Half the People You Know Are Obsessed with This Book Series," *Vox*, February 27, 2024, https://www.vox.com/culture/24084037/sarah-j-maas-a-court- of-thorns-and-roses-acotar-romantasy.
10. Jeana Jorgensen, "The Thorns of Trauma: Torture, Aftermath, and Healing in Contemporary Fairy-Tale Literature." *Humanities* 10, no. 1 (March 1, 2021): 47. doi:10.3390/h10010047.; Kathleen Murphey, "Troubling Sex Trafficking Backstories to Heroines in Sarah Maas, Leigh Bardugo, and Christina Henry." *Pennsylvania Literary Journal* (2151–3066) 15, no. 3 (Fall 2023): 114–28. https://search.ebscohost.com/login.aspx?direct=true&AuthType=sso&db=asn&AN=174537948&site=eds-live&scope=site.
11. Elizabeth Little, and Kristine Moruzi. "Postfeminism and Sexuality in the Fiction of Sarah J. Maas." In *Sexuality in Literature for Children and Young Adults*, 81–95. Routledge, 2021.
12. Erin K. Johns Speese. "Came for the Smut, Stayed by Consent: Desire and Consent in Sarah J. Maas's Fictional Worlds." *Journal of Popular Romance Studies* 13 (August 1, 2024): 1–19. https://search.ebscohost.com/login.aspx?direct=true&AuthType=sso&db=edsdoj&AN=edsdo j.87eea1bd14524498a001e7922f9bdc7f&site=eds-live&scope=site.
13. Debra Dudek, Madalena Grobbelaar, and Elizabeth Reid Boyd, "Wondering about a Love Literacy: Unspoken Desire in Sarah J. Maas's A Court of Mist and Fury (2016)." *M/C Journal* 27, no. 4 (2024).
14. (PornHub).
15. Amia Srinivasan, *The Right to Sex: Feminism in the Twenty-First Century* (Macmillan, 2021), 35.

16. Srinivasan, *The Right to Sex*, 42.
17. Audre Lorde, "Uses of the Erotic." In *The Selected Works of Audre Lorde* (W.W. Norton & Company, 2020), 34.
18. Hannah McCann and Catherine M. Roach, "Sex and Sexuality." In *The Routledge Research Companion to Popular Romance Fiction*, edited by Jayashree Kamblé, Eric Murphy Selinger, and Hsu-Ming Teo (Routledge, 2020.), 421.
19. Day, qtd. in McAlister, "Erotic Romance," 214.
20. McAlister, "Erotic Romance," 214.
21. McAlister, "Erotic Romance," 217.
22. Jonathan Allan. *Men, Masculinities, and Popular Romance*. 1st ed. New York: Routledge, 2019, 7.
23. Allen, *Men, Masculinities, and Popular Romance*, 7.
24. Susan Stiritz "Cultural Cliteracy: Exposing the Contexts of Women's Not Coming." *Berkeley Journal of Gender, Law & Justice* 23, no. 2 (2008): 254.
25. Anne Zachary, *The Anatomy of the Clitoris: Reflections on the Theory of Female Sexuality* (Routledge, 2018), 91.
26. Dudek, Grobbelaar, and Boyd, "Wondering about a Love Literacy," *M/C Journal* 27 (4). https://doi.org/10.5204/mcj.3073.
27. Jane Ward, *The Tragedy of Heterosexuality* (NYU Press, 2022), 116.
28. Lauren Berlant and Michael Warner. "Sex in Public." *Critical inquiry* 24, no. 2 (1998): 547–566.
29. Ward, *The Tragedy of Heterosexuality*, 119.
30. Katherine Cruger, "Men Are Stronger; Women Endure: A Critical Analysis of the *Throne of Glass* and *The Mortal Instruments* YA Fantasy Series." *Journal of Media Critiques* 3, no. 10 (2017): 119.
31. Berlant and Warner, "Sex in Public," 553, 548.
32. Woledge, qtd. in Karen Hellekson and Kristina Busse, eds. *Fan Fiction and Fan Communities in the Age of the Internet: New Essays* (McFarland, 2006), 26.
33. Though Woledge is referring to slash fanfiction as the primary lens in her case study of erotic relationships, the concept of the intimatopic can be found throughout fan response and activism surrounding erotic fiction.
34. XXX
35. Jane Steckbeck, "Sparking Your Erotic Imagination," *Jane Steckbeck*, November 1, 2019. https://www.janesteckbeck.com/post/sparking-your-erotic-imagination. Accessed March 1, 2023.
36. Hilary White, "Badass Women and Ridiculously Sexy Romance? Yep, These Books Have It All," *PopSugar*, August 26, 2016, https://www.popsugar.com/love/sarah-j-maas- interview-41262845.
37. Srinivasan, *The Right to Sex*, xv.
38. Josefine Smith and Kathleen Kollman, unpublished data from *Still Reading Romance* survey, June 9 2023.
39. Smith and Kollman, unpublished data from *Still Reading Romance*.
40. DeWight R. Middleton, *Exotics and Erotics: Human Cultural and Sexual Diversity* (Waveland Press, 2002), 3.
41. Middleton, *Exotics and Erotics*, 117.

42. Middleton, *Exotics and Erotics*, 3.
43. Lorde, "Uses of the Erotic," 34.
44. Sarah J. Maas, *A Court of Thorns and Roses* (Bloomsbury, 2015), 37.
45. Elizabeth Little and Kristine Moruzi, in the Fiction of Sarah J. Maas." In *Sexuality in Literature for Children and Young Adults*, 81–95 (Routledge, 2021), 85.
46. Little and Moruzi, "Postfeminism and Sexuality in Maas," 85.
47. Maas, *ACOTAR*, 288.
48. Maas, *ACOTAR*, 156, 172.
49. Maas, *ACOTAR*, 246.
50. Little and Moruzi, 84.
51. Lorde, "Uses of the Erotic," 34.
52. Maas, *ACOTAR*, 251.
53. Maas, *A Court of Mist and Fury* (Bloomsbury, 2016), 65.
54. Radway, *Reading the Romance*, 151.
55. Radway, *Reading the Romance*, 151.
56. Catherine Roach, *Happily Ever After: The Romance Story in Popular Culture* (Indiana University Press, 2016), 165.
57. Maas, *ACOMAF*, 46.
58. Maas, *ACOMAF*, 125.
59. Maas, *ACOMAF*, 27.
60. Maas, *ACOMAF*, 48.
61. Srinivasan, *The Right to Sex*, 10.
62. Maas, *ACOMAF*, 435.
63. Christina Orlando "'Lots of Cursing and Sex': Authors Laurell K. Hamilton and Sarah J. Maas On Pleasure & Violence in Paranormal Romance." *Tor*, October 5, 2019. https://www.tor.com/2019/10/05/lots-of-cursing-and-sex-authors-laurell-k-hamilton-and-sarah-j- maas-on-pleasure-violence-in-paranormal-romance/. Accessed September 30, 2022; White, "Badass Women and Ridiculously Sexy Romance."
64. Maas, *ACOMAF*, 531.
65. Maas, *ACOMAF*, 533.
66. McAlister, "Erotic Romance," 213.
67. Maas, *ACOMAF*, 535.
68. Radway, *Reading the Romance*, 105.
69. Laurie Mintz, *Becoming Cliterate: Why Orgasm Equality Matters—and How to Get It* (HarperOne, 2017).
70. Srinivasan, *The Right to Sex*, 21.
71. Maas, *ACOMAF*, 531.
72. Anne Koedt, The Myth of the Vaginal Orgasm." In *Living with Contradictions*, 481–87 (Routledge, 2018), 481.
73. Srinivasan, *The Right to Sex*, 35.
74. Srinivasan, *The Right to Sex*.
75. Srinivasan, *The Right to Sex*, 36.
76. PornHub
77. Srinivasan, *The Right to Sex*, 42.

78. John Stoltenberg, *Refusing to be a Man: Essays on Sex and Justice* (Routledge, 2005), 106.
79. McAlister, "Erotic Romance," 213.
80. McAlister, "Erotic Romance," 23–33, 217.
81. Radway, *Reading the Romance*, 83.
82. Judith Arnold, "Women do." *Dangerous Men and Adventurous Women: Romance Writers on the Appeal of the Romance* (Routledge 1992), 135.
83. Toril Moi, *Sexual/Textual Politics: Feminist Literary Theory*. 2nd ed. (Routledge, 2002), 46.
84. Maas, *A Court of Silver Flames* (Bloomsbury, 2021), 586.
85. Maas, *ACOMAF*, 607.
86. Roach, *Happily Ever After*.
87. u/lafornarinas. Comment on "Sex scenes in romance books." *Reddit*, October 28, 2022, 4:18 p.m. https://www.reddit.com/r/RomanceBooks/comments/yfk4ty/sex_scenes_in_romance_books/.
88. Srinivasan, *The Right to Sex*, 33.
89. Halberstam, *Female Masculinity* (Duke University Press, 1998), 117.
90. Halberstam, *Female Masculinity*, 135.
91. Halberstam, *Female Masculinity*, 135.
92. Halberstam, *Female Masculinity*, 135.
93. *ACOSF*, 392.
94. *ACOSF*, 392.
95. Riane Eisler, *Sacred Pleasure: Sex, Myth, and the Politics of the Body* (HarperCollins, 1996), 339.
96. Eisler, *Sacred Pleasure*, 351.
97. Nancy Friday, *Women on Top: How Real Life Has Changed Women's Sexual Fantasies* (Pocket Books, 1991), 7.
98. Srinivasan, 84.
99. Radway, *Reading the Romance*, 74.
100. Radway, *Reading the Romance*, 105, 107.
101. Radway, *Reading the Romance*, 83.
102. See survey (Introduction Appendix B).
103. Radway, *Reading the Romance*, 214.
104. Bernadette Barker-Plummer and David Barker-Plummer. "Twitter as a Feminist Resource: #YESALLWOMEN, Digital Platforms, and Discursive Social Change." In *Social Movements and Media*, edited by Jennifer S. Earl and Deana A. Rohlinger. Emerald Publishing.

Conclusion

Through the preceding chapters, we hope that the variety of our contributors' interpretations of the data, preceding romance scholarship, romance texts, social media and organizations, and autoethnographic research can provide an updated picture of the state of romance readers, writers, and texts in the twenty-first century. Above all, our goal with this collection was to provide a new jumping-off point from which future scholars might be inspired to delve deeper into individual topics or reexamine our data much as we have reexamined Janice Radway's and updated her survey. Indeed, we recognize that even our survey already requires updating, and as new texts and genres emerge daily, a more comprehensive look at lesser-explored elements of romancelandia is already warranted, even as our project has just ended.

In the following sections, we wanted to provide additional unique resources. First, we conducted a virtual roundtable discussion with other members of the romance community, including authors, editors, and scholars, to get their perspectives on the state of romancelandia today. We also interviewed each other to provide additional context for how this book came about and where we see scholarly needs in both popular romance studies and popular fiction and pop culture studies more broadly. This collection also includes resources related to surveys, data, and other resources.

ROUNDTABLE

We interviewed several people who occupy the romance sphere in a variety of ways:

- Steve Ammidown is an archivist, collector, and historian of romance fiction. His expertise has been sought by venues such as *Texas Monthly*, *Men's*

Health, and *Library Journal*, among others. He co-hosts the podcast *Black Romance Has a History*.
- Traci Douglass is a *USA Today* Bestselling romance author who writes medical romance, small-town romance, paranormal romance, romantasy, M/M romance, and short stories. She has four successful medical romance series released by Harlequin.
- Rebecca Halsey is the author of the historical romance novel *Notes of Temptation*. She is currently the fiction editor and publisher of *Flash Fiction Online*, the professional ezine focusing on fiction of 500–1,000 words.
- Pepper McGraw is a *USA Today* Bestselling romance author who writes paranormal romance, with several series about monsters and shifters, faeries, and several cozy series about cats and witches. In her spare time, she advocates for animal rescue and cat TNR initiatives.
- Erin Young is an associate professor of literature and cultural studies at SUNY Empire State College. She was the managing editor of the peer-reviewed *Journal of Popular Romance Studies*. She has published several scholarly works in edited collections and journals like *Journal of American Culture* and *Extrapolation: A Journal of Science Fiction And Fantasy*. Her most recent work, "Race, Ethnicity, and Whiteness" can be found in *The Routledge Research Companion to Popular Romance Fiction*. Her research and teaching interests include popular romance fiction, Asian American fiction, and science fiction.

What follows is our interviews with each expert. These responses have in some cases been lightly edited for clarity.

What is your familiarity with Janice Radway's book *Reading the Romance*?

Ammidown
I first encountered *Reading the Romance* in the late 2000s while doing research on comics fandom for an anthropology class. For me at the time, it was just another fandom resource in an established canon of texts on the subject. It wasn't until I began to work with and study the history of the romance genre in 2016 that I came to understand how unique Radway's work was within romance scholarship.

Halsey
I'm not, but I *am* familiar with Regis's *A Natural History of the Romance Novel*.

Young
I was a graduate student working on a dissertation about popular romance in the mid-oughts when I first read *Reading the Romance*. It was one of the

seminal "first wave" texts I read to learn about the academic field of popular romance studies. I was a lifelong reader of romances before I became a romance scholar, so I really appreciated Radway's representation of the readership—and their relationship to the texts—as complex and smart. I was also keenly aware that the Smithton group of readers did not represent me or anyone with my lived experiences. (And by the time I encountered Radway's work, critiques of her study's limitations were already well-represented in the scholarship.) But I think Radway set the tone for the field's rigorous and respectful recognition of readers and their centrality to critical understandings of the romance genre. This is especially important in the digital age, when the boundaries between readers, authors, and scholars are much less distinct than they were when *Reading the Romance* was first published.

What do you think revisiting Radway's survey would reveal about differences in romance novel readers from the early 1980s to today?

Ammidown
I think an updated version of Radway's original survey would reveal that a broader cross-section of society are romance readers, for several reasons. The first is that the genre is so much larger now than when Radway did her original research. While many of the major publishers are the same as in the early '80s, the rise of self-publishing alongside the development of niche romances has meant that the number of books produced each month has skyrocketed, and almost any reader can find a book to their liking. Secondly, the changing acceptance of different gender identities and sexual orientations has created more space for both readers and writers. The stereotypes of Radway's Smithton readers—older, white, female, and heterosexual—are simply not representative of romance readers anymore. I think this shift will lead to a far more interesting and representative data set.

Young
I would hope BIPOC and LGBTQ+ romance novel readers would be better represented in an updated survey, and their responses would probably be much more heterogeneous. The demographic similarities among the Smithton readers meant, in part, that their reading processes involved negotiating US patriarchal and heteronormative structures from similar vantage points. Diverse readers have always interacted with romance novels in more dynamic ways than Radway's study alone revealed, and now they have access to more diverse texts (in terms of character representation, storytelling, genre, etc.). How queer readers in any era identify with protagonists—in both queer and non-queer romances—will likely not align with the identifications of hetero readers. This is, of course, also true for racialized and non-racialized readers.

How long have you been a romance novel writer, reader, and/or researcher/scholar? What got you into the genre in the first place?

Ammidown
I became interested in romance after taking a job at Bowling Green State University's Brown Popular Culture Library. Their romance novel related collections are enormous, and I was determined to learn more about the genre. The more I read within the genre and the more I studied, the more interested I became in how these seemingly ephemeral objects reflected (or in some cases did not reflect) the ever-changing society around them. I was hooked as both a reader and a researcher.

Douglass
I read my first romance novel when I was like twelve, I think. I wrote my first romance novel in 2011 and had my first romance published traditionally in 2013. I started writing romance because that's what I read. And when I couldn't find the story I was looking for, I decided to write it myself.

Halsey
I've been a romance reader since I was a teenager. Growing up in the Bible Belt, I was one of the only girls who had books with explicit content in it, and I would share all the best scenes with my friends. As a writer, I have always gravitated toward writing love stories. Even when I try to write in other genres, romance plots/subplots sneak into what I'm doing.

McGraw
Reader since I was eleven, so forty-two years. I've been writing since I was about that same age but publishing romance since 2015. From age eleven through my teens, I would steal my mom's romances. I was immediately hooked and eventually romance books became a line item in my personal budget. It remains my preferred genre today, though my subgenres have changed and developed over time.

Young
I started reading romance novels when I was about thirteen years old. I was a strong reader who transitioned to adult books early, and I read what was accessible in my parents' house: my dad's science fiction and my mom's romances. Today I teach courses on both! When I decided to study English in college, I relegated popular romances to the realm of "pleasure reading," the fun books I was allowed to read after studying "literature" all day. Fortunately, I had a good doctoral advisor who thought I had interesting things to say about romance novels, and I learned there was a field of academic study

devoted to the genre. Now it's been over thirty years that I've been reading and thinking about romance novels.

When you talk with romance readers today, what do they seem most enthusiastic about in terms of content? Least enthusiastic? Have you seen these elements change during your career?

Ammidown
I think a lot of readers I interact with are excited about the potential of romance. In recent years we have seen more books with BIPOC characters, diverse body sizes, non-neurotypical characters, and queer relationships. At the same time, readers are concerned that these changes seem more like trends than real shifts in the genre. Publishers seem happy to have just a few books by Black authors, or that contain fat characters, or autistic characters. While queer romances have exploded in popularity, the characters represented tend to still be sterotypically attractive, and there is a real concern about gay male romances being primarily written by women. Readers are also concerned with the packaging of romance. The disappearance of mass- market paperbacks in favor of trade paperbacks with cookie-cutter covers meant to look good on TikTok, or the ever-evolving recycling of subgenres as if they are new ideas- romcoms, romantasy, etc. I think long-time romance readers see these shifts as a threat to the stability of a genre that is so reliant on predictability.

Douglass
I think there is a romance out there for almost anything you might be looking for, which is great. Readers I talk to are most enthusiastic about the diversity present in the genre now vs. back in the 1980s and '90s. Least enthusiastic? That's hard to say, isn't it, because what one person might be sick of, another person loves. I do think people are generally over the "doormat" type protagonist who has no agency for themselves though. Yes, in the ten plus years I've been a published romance author, I've seen huge strides in diversity and representation within the genre. We still have a long way to go, but it's better than it was for sure.

Halsey
My friends love the romantasy books like Maas and Yarros. Everyone is into Emily Henry's witty dialogue. No one I know seems to be much interested in the rich, corporate bosses these days.

McGraw
Most enthusiastic: readers seem to want spicier content, and not just in the romance genre. There's a lot of genre-bending happening with the advent of

e-books and the expansion of who gets published. The result is a lot of other genres with romantic elements as integral parts of the books. Romance readers are voracious and will cross as many genres as are available if there's a promised HEA at the end. With the increase in who gets published and the online retailers, shelf space and a defined genre isn't as necessary as it once was. There has also been an increased acceptance of an HEA spreading out over multiple books, particularly with the new subgenres of reverse harem and academy romances. People have come to expect these HEAs to not be fully developed until the end of that series or sub-series. Least enthusiastic: cookie cutter characters and interchangeable heroes. Also, the demise of the bodice ripper. It's an interesting dichotomy because the concept of consent has been brought into the light in recent years, which has had a positive impact on the romance that's out there. Readers no longer want those forced seduction scenes where the concept of "no" means "yes," which was highly prevalent in romances of the '80s. At the same time, there has been a rise in bully romances and romances with an alphahole hero. In addition, the arrival of *Fifty Shades of Grey* over a decade ago resulted in a corresponding rise in BDSM romances becoming more mainstream. Of course, most of those romances today highlight the idea of consent, though many still skate that edge. Basically, I think romance has become edgier, but also more respectful of a woman's sexuality, her right to make her own choices and the role she plays in her own story.

Young
My main contact with other romance readers is through teaching romance novels; sometimes students are reading romances for the first time, but many students start the course as experienced romance readers. I find that there's a lot of enthusiasm for cross-genre texts with strong romance components. My students choose their own research projects, and it's not unusual for their proposals to focus on texts that bridge other genres (e.g., Sarah J. Maas's fantasy novels). There's a lot more genre overlap these days than when I started studying romances, so it makes sense that students' interests reflect this. It's also my experience that younger readers tend to be less tolerant of "alpha" heroes with traits that fall under the rubric of toxic masculinity.

This, too, makes sense considering the sociocultural changes that have taken place over the decades. I grew up on romance paperbacks from the '70s and '80s, which regularly contained domestic violence and sexual assault, many times perpetrated by the heroes themselves. These novels reflected the era of my childhood, during which marital rape was not yet considered a crime in every U.S. state. What readers will and will not tolerate in fictional characters reveals much about their time and place.

What is something about the romance genre that you don't think enough fan spaces, researchers, readers, or authors are talking about?

Ammidown
I think this is starting to change, but I've long believed that the history of the genre itself isn't well enough understood or widely enough studied. Genre fiction of all sorts, but especially romance, is shaped by decisions beyond the text on the page. Readers, editors and publishers are as important to understand as authors and texts when trying to track the evolution of the genre.

Douglass
Just the sheer number of books out there that cater to pretty much any taste. And the fact that we are a positivity-forward genre. In a world increasingly dark and violent, I think that's an amazing thing to offer people—hope, optimism, joy.

Halsey
Romantasy—at least that's how it feels.

McGraw
I'm not sure how much this is being discussed, but I'd really like to hear more about how it's *not* unrealistic for a woman to want sexual satisfaction in her relationships and it's *not* unreasonable to expect a man to spend his time learning what she needs and ensuring she receives it. I often hear complaints from men that basically insinuate, or even state outright, that romances cause women to have unrealistic expectations of their partners. What are women really expecting? A partner who listens, a partner who puts their satisfaction ahead of their own, a partner who is a true partner in all things. How is that unrealistic? I would also love to hear about the romances that highlight non-traditional matches. The couple that chooses not to get married. The couple that chooses not to have children. The three people who find love together. The bisexual couple, the gay couple, the lesbians finding their happily ever afters. More sapphic romances, more gay romances, more asexual romances. I do love that there are more of these romances available than ever before and that minority authors are being highlighted more. However, I do think we have more room for growth in this area: more spaces focused on exploring books written by minority authors, for romance readers to discover.

What is a fad in the romance genre that you have seen come and go, for better or worse?

Ammidown
Cover art is the most faddish aspect of the romance genre, and it's fascinating to see how things have changed (or not) over the decades. Deeply detailed

painted covers have come and gone, and photographed covers are becoming less common. But the thing I'm most happy to see fade away is the headless cover model. This began with illustrated headless women during the late 1990s during the "chick lit" era. The explosion in e-books led to a trend in the 2000s of photoshopped photographs of headless, shirtless men, which were eye-catching as tiny thumbnail images, but left something to be desired as visual representations of the text. However much people complain about the current trend of cartoonish illustrations, I'll always contend that the headless model era was worse.

Douglass
Oh gosh, there's so many, it's hard to keep up with. One that I'm personally not sad to see go (though I know there are tons of readers who love them) are the Omega books, where the guy gets pregnant. I mean, okay. I get where it might be nice to have the tables turned, but I'm just not into it. Of course, I'm not really into books where women get pregnant either, unless that's like a big goal of theirs, so . . .

Halsey
"New Adult" seems to have been a category for a hot minute that I don't really hear about anymore. It seemed like something the publishing industry wanted to put in place to bridge young adult to adult content. That turned out to be unnecessary. Interestingly, the young adult trope of writing in first person has become much more common in romance novels, a trend I think is a holdover from this moment when readers consuming young adult looked around for romance novels that captured the same feel as their favorite titles.

McGraw
Bodice rippers/forced seduction was around for quite some time. Was that a fad or simply something the romance genre grew out of? I'm not sure, but it's a positive that it's a thing of the past.

How do you think the research methods have evolved for popular romance research? How can mixed-methods approaches expand and complexify research in the field?

Ammidown
From the very beginning of romance research in the 1970s, we have seen research centered largely on textual analysis. One of the gifts of Radway's work was showing that including anthropological methods could create a more nuanced understanding of the genre. Unfortunately, much of the research over the following decades retreated into the texts. In the past few years, we've

seen an increase in mixed-methods research, which is a trend I hope continues because as I said earlier, the genre is so much more than the words on the page.

Douglass
I just think that romance is taken so much more seriously these days than it was and it makes my heart happy. People think writing a love story is easy, but the complexities of relationships and emotions are the basis of everything we do as humans. And getting those to work out in a way that makes the two protagonists happy and plausibly is hard.

How do you think cross-genre romance has evolved? How can cross-genre novels be a positive for the industry? Are there any downsides to how niche cross-genre writing in romance has become?

Ammidown
Cross-genre romance is nothing new and has been a feature of romance almost from the very beginning of the genre. Historical and contemporary romance have existed side by side for a century, with historical romance in particular exploring time periods both real and fantastical. Gothic romance brought horror into the genre in the 1970s, the same decade that brought us more romantic pirates and westerns. Science fiction and fantasy often featured romance as part of their genres, but elements of each began to creep into the romance genre in the 1980s. The current trends, whether it is true crime romantic suspense or "romantasy," are circular returns to books that have been around for years. While the new versions may frustrate longtime fans, a subgenre becoming trendy provides new on-ramps for readers to enter the genre and can provoke new interest in classic books and authors. To me, the trendiness of romance subgenres is almost always a net positive.

Douglass
Again, I think it goes back to the diversity issue and seeing that there is a unique reader base for just about anything, no matter how niche. As long as both parties are consenting, I'm all for it. Readers want to see themselves on the page. It's empowering and reassuring, letting them know they are not alone. There are no downsides. This table is plenty big for all of us.

Halsey
I think the OG cross-genre were the Western romances, back when "Westerns" were their own genre. Gritty urban fantasy romances predate the current fae-romance we see now. Cross-genre romances have always been there. The cross part has changed over time.

McGraw
Over the years, I've heard many hard-core sci-fi readers, mystery readers, fantasy readers, etc., complain that romance has "infiltrated" their genre. However, I always like to point out that romance is a part of life, and as such, that it's always been in those genres. Books I read in many other genres in the '70s, '80s, and '90s had people pairing up, having sex, and falling in love.

Having said that, I do think that romance writers have a unique gift for melding the elements of many different genres into rich, fully developed stories that are a true blend of those genres. Cross-genre romance makes for truly exceptional stories and the rise of the e-book and self-publishing has allowed more authors to explore their craft beyond the confines of one genre or subgenre.

Young
I'm not an industry expert, but I suspect the proliferation of cross-genre romance is largely profit-driven (i.e., about attracting as many different audiences (consumers) as possible). Of course, popular romance as we know it has always been produced under capitalism, so that part isn't new. I can think of a few "positives" from a teaching perspective. Every year I get students in my courses who become interested in romances through cross-genre texts, often located within the spectrum of speculative fiction. While still not common, there are more masculine students in my courses than I recall having in the earlier part of my career. Typically, these students are writers who understand—and take seriously—the prominence of romance conventions throughout the world of genre fiction. It could be said that cross-genre romances, at the very least, help push the popular romance from the margins of genre fiction to the center.

For a field that deals with popular culture, how do you see the relationship between the romance author, audience, and research? How do you see that all work together?

Ammidown
Romance authors and readers have always been interested in the perception of the genre by those outside of it. Feminist scholars of the 1970s and '80s, who took potshots at the genre in an attempt to build legitimacy for their own field of study, created tremendous animosity between those inside the genre and academia which lasted until the 1990s. Since the publication of the collection *Dangerous Men and Adventurous Women* in 1992, we've seen a shift in the other direction, with authors and readers taking a great interest in the work of academics regarding the genre. It's still a tenuous relationship, but I think the fact that more readers have become researchers has helped a lot, as has a shift towards outside researchers approaching the genre with more

respect than previous generations of scholars. Overall, I think that this shift is a positive one for both the genre and research, as more academic attention is good for the reputation of romance, and researchers can gain more access to readers than they might have had forty years ago.

Douglass
As an author, regardless of genre, I think it's important to understand your audience and what they want, to be successful. In romance especially, because you are dealing with relationships and emotions primarily, I believe that's extra important because people will know instinctively if you are not being true to the characters or the emotions. Also, researching setting, period, background, cultural references (especially if they are not your own) are incredibly important to tell truthful, relevant, resonant stories.

Halsey
Again, I don't do a lot of research, but I do think romance fans are more than happy to proclaim their loyalty and fandom. It's not a hidden secret anymore that romance exists and that fans read a heckin' ton of it. The fans pour feedback out into the world, whether the authors want it or not.

McGraw
In my opinion, as an author, it's all about understanding what my audience wants and delivering that in unique ways. For me, the best research is reading widely in the genre I write and living my life, interacting with people and studying the world around me.

How do you see the relationship between the romance genre and popular culture? How does popular romance reflect and influence cultural norms?

Ammidown
When it comes to popular culture, we've never seen the genre be more connected to the cultural zeitgeist than now. Romance plots now leak over from fan fiction and celebrity relationships with regularity. Sports romances, which didn't exist before the early '90s, have both reflected and driven cultural changes. A wave of auto racing romances has followed the increased popularity of Formula One racing, meanwhile the popularity of hockey romances has reportedly resulted in an increase in romance readers becoming hockey fans. Romantic suspense, which has risen and fallen in popularity in the past four decades, saw a resurgence in the late 2010s and early 2020s with the growth of true crime TV and podcasts, to the point where even Harlequin's Love Inspired Christian romance line has a suspense-oriented sub-line. At the same time as all of this, because the genre is not monolithic, romance has long straddled a

line between progressive and regressive when it comes to gender roles. For every genre-pushing book by Cat Sebastian, Katrina Jackson, or Olivia Dade there are twice as many books grounded in traditional heterosexual monogamy between two conventionally attractive people. You can more easily find a new traditionally published romance about a Nazi falling in love or a cowboy fighting "marauding" Native Americans than you can a romance with a fat male main character or a disabled main character of any gender. Publishers seek safety in the stories they know will sell and show little willingness to make changes to formulas they've found to be successful. And for better or worse, publishers seem to believe that regressive political ideologies and phony "both sides" stories sell better than those that move the genre forward. This isn't a new phenomenon—one need only look at the work of editor Vivian Stephens in the 1980s. As a Black woman, she saw value in bringing BIPOC voices to the table at both Dell/Candlelight and Harlequin. But as soon as she moved on from both publishers, any remaining non-white romances both publishers were considering were canceled and the very white norms resumed. Today, Harlequin insists that its "Inspirational" romances can come from any religion, but they are almost exclusively Christian, and almost exclusively white. Jewish and Muslim romances do exist, but do not receive the same publisher support. In what is probably a great metaphor for the broader culture, romance talks a very progressive game, but often embraces its most regressive elements. The independent authors who buck these trends provide a hope that the genre can move forward, but it will be slow going.

Douglass
Romance is a reflection of pop culture; how could it not be? Even if stories are set in the past or the future, we are still working out the issues of today within our pages. But I also think romance fiction offers readers a safe space to work out in their own heads and hearts who they feel about certain issues and the best way to address those in their own lives and situations. They influence each other, I suppose.

Halsey
Since 2010 at least, I think the push is for romance to show that there aren't any norms. I remember really being immersed in the romance writer conferences right after *Fifty Shades of Grey* did a cannonball into the marketplace, and suddenly it was ok to write about kink. Same thing with the slow proliferation of books with LGBTQ+ characters. My nonacademic guess is that this is both a reflection of and an influence on human behavior—a feedback loop. From an American perspective, I think the last twenty years have seen the romance genre become more ingrained in overall popular culture. Lifetime television used to be a joke, and now they've basically owned the joke and do what they

do best. There are always a couple news articles in which the author overexaggerates their shock that romance writers are serious about their craft, but for the most part I think that was news fifteen years ago. What was revealed with the collapse of RWA (to me at least) was that the romance writing community was historically insular, perhaps because they were looked down upon, perhaps because they were women. There was so much talk about how they'd finally found their people, the people that understand their need to write smutty scenes. I think that fear of not being accepted was what kept the old-timers from embracing new things and different people. They didn't realize that it isn't necessary anymore because there's no cultural imperative to hide what you're reading or writing these days. That isn't to say there aren't some communities that are trying to put the cat back in the bag. Some libraries out there have deshelved Maas for explicit content, but I think this is a deviation that has been overreported (as in, likely only affects a small number of libraries). I don't see de-shelving romance books as a trend that will have any lasting power. As I said, I grew up in the Bible Belt, and I'm willing to bet there will always be teenager like me ear-marking the sex scenes for their friends.

McGraw
I think the trends we see in popular culture pop up in our romance writing, and the trends in our romances pop up in popular culture. We write as products of the times and environments we're in and as such, everything around us influences what we create and put out into the world.

Romance and popular culture really can't be untangled because together, they weave a reflection of our world and the times we live in. Even when I write about shapeshifters and vampires and matchmaking cats, the essence of those stories reflects my own experiences and background, and the romances reflect my hope for humanity as a whole: that we will rise above all the ugliness and find our happily ever afters with the ones we love.

EDITORS' INTERVIEW

As part of our conclusion process, we interviewed each other over Zoom, basing our questions on those we asked of our roundtable but allowing the conversation to unfold organically as well. This has been lightly edited for length and clarity.

Discuss your role in the romance community.

Kollman
I have read romance and romance-adjacent books (Gothics, "soapy" epic women's fiction) since probably junior high or high school but took a detour

in college to consume much more horror and literary fiction. I came back to it when pursuing my MFA in writing popular fiction at Seton Hill University; even though my focus was on science fiction, fantasy, and horror, I took several romance modules and worked with a great many faculty and students who were enthusiastic romance readers and writers. One of my favorite genres outside of romance had slowly become urban fantasy (which was the genre of my first published novel), but when I discovered paranormal romance, I realized that was basically created for me, intersecting with all my genre interests. I read even more paranormal romance, wrote an award-winning paper on the changes in the genre regarding feminist perspectives, and presented it at a romance conference.

Later, I wrote a couple of contemporary romance novels under a pseudonym and might do more, although I will say romance is just one of many popular fiction genres I like. In working on this project, I've read even more widely formulated ideas for how I want to further include romance scholarship in my academic career, as well as how far I want to take my little author side hustle.

Smith

I started reading romance as an early teen and have been reading romance since. As an undergraduate student, I was interested in the relationship between popular culture stories and gender norms. This interest progressed in 2012 when I discovered New Adult fiction right at its inception, which inspired my research in popular romance and identity development, eventually becoming the topic of the thesis for my second master's in American studies.

I straddle the tricky line of both reader and scholar, both part of fan communities and curious about the cultural microcosm they represent. I've always been a voracious reader, but when I found romance, there's something about the relationship build that happens in romance that I don't think really happens in any other genre. By this I mean all relationships because it's such a feelings and emotion-centered, connection-centered genre in general. The friendships feel stronger and more intimate. The romantic relationships feel stronger and more intimate, even enemies and conflict feel more emotional or more feelings focused. I'm curious about how people relate to each other, and how people feel, and how emotions shape who they are and how they relate to others. I've always been a romance reader, always, and interested in coming-of-age fiction, like Young Adult Romance and gender construction in texts. I am very curious and like kind of the didactic themes that you find and why romance demonstrates quite a bit in terms of how to behave, how to be a successful gendered body and that kind of thing. I remember reading *Easy* by Tamara Webber, which is one of the early examples of popular New Adult fiction. I had never heard of it before. I had never heard of New Adult fiction before then, and I read it. This genre is not young adult. The first opening scene is like an attempted sexual assault right away, which doesn't happen in YA. So, there was a lot of trauma work for the main character. And part of that trauma work happened through her romantic relationship. So, there was all this stuff about consent. It was just very different. And so, I got really interested. And that's where I really started doing romance research. But now it's kind of evolving. I was reading it as an emerging adult, and so it very much spoke to my new adult era. But now I'm starting to become even more interested in the ways that romance constructs relationships and what intimacy looks like and what you can expect from your relationships and that kind of thing, but that's kind of the next project. But I'm definitely a reader and a researcher, and I am very active in the social media community. I give and get lots of book recs from there. I follow a lot of romance groups, too.

Kollman
I want to mention the overlap with horror. Just a little bit, because since I have not read as much romance and am not as enmeshed in the romance community as you. Romance is one genre that I really like, but I tend to read a little bit more diverse genres. But paranormal romance is such a good like overlap of several of my different genre interests. And I remember, one of the professors in my MFA program had talked about how he was mostly a horror writer, but he was pro-romance and talked about how horror and romance are both kind of castigated among even popular fiction and genre fiction, because they are genres that have to do with the body, whether it be for positive or negative outcomes. And there's such an overlap in terms of the reader affect that comes out when you read both of those genres.

Smith
A visceral response.

Kollman
Yes! So, I love paranormal romance. And I'm finishing reading a trilogy of vampire romance.

Smith
I'm actually reading a paranormal, because ever since you and I've been working on this book, I've been doing a little more paranormal romance.

Kollman
Cool! So yeah, I think that often people who think of reading as this wholly intellectual endeavor whether they read some genre like if they're okay with mystery, because it's a little more logos, and that horror and romance readers are all in for the pathos and a little bit of the ethos, because they do like you're mentioning identity and characters and that kind of thing. But it's the feeling we want. We want to feel.

Smith
It's the merging, it's the merging of the feeling and the ethos and the pathos. I like that.

How did you come to Radway's book initially?

Kollman
When I began my Ph.D. program, I took a social and cultural theory course my first semester, and Janice Radway's *Reading the Romance* was on the syllabus. I was so excited and found it fascinating from multiple standpoints. One of my last semesters of coursework, then, I took an entire class on romance fiction, in which we got to read a book of our own choosing every week. Even though when I first read it, *Reading the Romance* was already no longer reflecting then-current trends in romance fiction (this was in 2016), I could see its relevance for especially graduate students in any cultural studies program. *Reading the Romance* remains a very strong monograph that one can appreciate for its methodology, subject matter, and theoretical lens.

Smith
When I first started to research popular culture and romance fiction, the research of Radway, Modleski, Regis, and Light informed my theoretical perspective. I appreciated Radway's use of qualitative research and reader response to look at the process of romance reading, Modleski and Light's respect for both the genre and the agency of readers (instead of positioning them as victims), and Regis's historical and genre framework. I was intrigued by the mixed-methods and interdisciplinary framework that Radway used. Even though her work was published in the '80s, no one has really taken up the scope that she did. And that was the first time that I really saw a model, even if I don't always agree with some of her analysis. It's the first and only significant work that I've seen that has that level and model of curiosity about what the experience of reading is for women. That to me that in and of itself was always impactful. When I first read it, it was a very kind of emotional experience, because for some of the material, I reacted with a "Wow! I feel seen!" Some of it I didn't agree with at all, but it was

still very emotional. So that's kind of an interesting connection that I hadn't thought about.

Kollman
It is also interesting to me in researching how people came to it in places like the anniversary roundtable, that a lot of it was similar to where I encountered it in a theory class, whether you're doing a degree in literature or—like mine—American studies, or cultural studies.

Smith
She's common in American studies and cultural studies because she's an American studies person, that's where her discipline lives.

Kollman
Right. And so, it's very telling and cool that a work that is really examining women's reading habits is being given to students of all genders in intro theory class, almost universally. So, I'm really happy. But because of some of the ways that we can reflect on its need for updating, such as how do people today read their romances? That people who wouldn't continue with going into romance scholarship are kind of maybe only getting that early version of the data. And I think that's where our book can fill a gap there, that if people did want to see how it's changed and evolved. That was part of my interest in joining this project with you.

Smith
Yeah, I have a little bit of interest, because you're right when you say it's kind of a seminal text that we get in grad school with American studies, or something adjacent to that in interdisciplinary humanities. But when I've looked, I haven't seen any really great article doing a scoping review of this question. Just even looking at what has the romance genre developed into and what is the research about it? Because there's stuff from the 18th and 19th century. But popular romance fiction, the way that it has been pretty much, maybe, since the 1960s and '70s wasn't at all the same in terms of popularity, and the publishing industry around it. That's something that to me is surprising, because it's a pretty significant genre in terms of an industry perspective. And I haven't seen any serious examination of how all the different romance pockets relate to each other.

Kollman:
Yeah. I also don't know that I haven't looked for this, but I don't know that I've ever seen anyone do something that was similar to Radway study for a different popular fiction genre.

Smith
I don't think a lot of popular fiction research looks at reader response at the same level. The closest that I've seen, which is why New Adult fiction is so interesting, is in girlhood studies. There's some significant work there, and that's where I kind of lived before finding New Adult fiction.

Kollman
Okay. Well, there's another gap that perhaps could be filled. I would love to see more about cozy mystery readers or horror readers, or what have you.

How did you come to this project specifically?

Kollman
Covid caused several conferences I used to eagerly attend in person to move online, and that included the Popular Culture Associate (PCA) conference of 2022. I usually present in either a Gender Studies or some kind of visual media area, but that year I randomly submitted for the Disaster Studies area, presenting a paper on concert deaths that covered both the 2021 Astroworld Festival crowd crush as well as the Who concert in Cincinnati in 1979 that resulted in 11 deaths. While I really liked my work on that project, it wound up not feeling like a good fit for something I wanted to turn into a full-fledged paper for publication. So even though the panels I attended and moderated were still a good use of my time, I was a little adrift about my next scholarly project. That conference had some virtual networking boards set up, and I spotted Josefine's announcement that she was looking for collaborators on a romance project she had already begun. We conferred, hit it off, and it sounded like a great opportunity to gain new skills, get deeper into romance scholarship, and gain invaluable experience doing scholarly editing.

Smith
In 2019, I used Radway's survey in *Reading the Romance* to create my own. I wanted to explore how romance readers experienced romance and what that might indicate about constructions of gender and relationships. When I had a baby in 2020, and then the pandemic hit, I had all of this data and no capacity to explore it. I realize that it would be a much more interesting project to use the data in a collaborative project. I met Kathleen at PCA when she responded to my request for collaborators. To pick up the project, we did another round of survey distribution and doubled our data set. We developed the project into an edited collection and found an amazing interdisciplinary cohort of authors.

Kollman
Yeah. So, we met at PCA. We've never actually met in person.

Smith
No. One day we will.

Kollman
We will, we will. I think that one of the few upsides of virtual conferences during early pandemic days was that I think both of us might have been in a mood to be receptive to connect to potential collaborators. You sent out a connect, and it was just really nice.

Smith
It was a perfect convergence of both of our needs aligned at that moment. And then on top of that, we connected personally. I had all this data, and originally, I was thinking maybe I can do a book before I even had looked at creating the survey. And then I got pregnant and had a baby. And then Covid happened, and I was assuming the project was over because the world was burning. But then, when I came back to it because I still was passionate about the idea of trying to have some kind of mixed-methods text about romance readers' experience within the genre. And I really was interested in the tropes and things that people connected to, like the idea of what tropes do people like? How does that connect with like characters that they find really engaging? Because generally most pop fiction readers have their vibes that they like, especially if you read romance. You go through cycles, but usually you have subgenres you like or don't like. For example, I don't like love triangles. I avoid them often. I don't really love bully romances, but some people are really into them. I think that the tropes that people are into say a lot about what they care about and who they are. And so, I wanted to examine that, but I was feeling super overwhelmed. I couldn't do it alone. I needed a partner in this whose vision either inspired me or I could connect to their vision. I had sent out a couple of emails to people. And I hadn't really met anybody that I connected with. So, you know, I figured I'd do a long shot at PCA, which has a lot of cool people. I put something on the forum, and you reached out. You were so warm and professional, and I just really wanted to get to know you. When we talked, and within the first five minutes I decided I want to write something with this lady. I was excited that you seem to really be interested in the idea of having an edited collection, with a lot of disciplinary flexibility, and looking at one question from multiple perspectives and viewpoints. For me, that's where it really blossomed.

Kollman
And I think the thing I wanted to be able to bring to the table for you was some of these folks who write romance and are also scholars of it. A lot of our contributors had answered a call, and I was aware of their work already. I feel like that was exactly how, if I was going to update Radway, I would never have tried to do it on my own. I think that having this multiplicity of voices is absolutely the way to go. And I thought you, having already done a lot of the survey data gathering, did a lot of the heavy lifting already. We did another round of survey data gathering together later, but initially you were at a point in the project where it seemed like it was a good jumping in point. I had also, just prior to finishing my dissertation, taken a class from my grad school that was on romance fiction. Also, one conference that I was supposed to do that got canceled because of Covid was going to be a paper on lesbian romance novels. And because the conference was canceled, I never even wrote it. I decided that because it was so early in the process, I scrapped it, but I ended up using some of the research for part of a different project.

But I was able to bring a little bit of that into my chapter for this volume. So, it was just a great convergence. And, yeah, you were so professional and cool, and it just seemed like such a good partnership.

Smith
Yeah, I agree with you that I think one of the things that's so beautiful. And this kind of moves into one of the next questions. I think in terms of contributing. The field is kind of moving on from Radway, and I think one of the differences from when Radway published now is that romance is so much more a whole universe. It's not a one way, top-down structured industry anymore. You always kind of had book groups and stuff. But published authors didn't really participate in them back then. And then the whole readership was over here, and sometimes you get like readers that would write letters to an author or something or attend book signings and stuff like that. But it was all very much more static than it is now.

Kollman
Yes.

Smith
Between the changes in the publishing process and how people get noticed or gain a fan base, how they interact with their fan base, it's all changed now. I think one thing that this change in integration of fan and author is create a stronger community. And I am excited about some of our contributors who are looking at the social media component of that community. Writing

and being a romance author is not just being an author, usually. If you're a romance author today, you also are in the community significantly. The same is often true of romance researchers. I know Jodi McAlister is an author, for example. Several of our contributors are both readers and authors in addition to doing academic or independent scholarship. So, it's very much a multiple identity type of situation, what Catherine Roach calls an "acafan," and that I don't think was the case quite as much in the past. You would have someone like Lisa Kleypas, who got her undergrad degree at Wellesley in I think political science. And there are some historical romance writers who have an academic center. Or Jennifer Crusie, who's more contemporary but was also in academia, but I don't think it was as common. Now, there's a lot of Venn diagram overlap between romance readers, romance writers at romance research, and then the broader culture.

Kollman
Which I think is fantastic.

Smith
I was curious. We talked a little bit about some of the updating that needs to happen in terms of like the scope, and how we include different members of the romance community into research. But for Radway, specifically and thinking about some of the kind of feminist framework she uses in her initial research. What do you can you tell me a little bit more about what you think was a weakness of the text. In some cases, she couldn't have known at that point necessarily everything that wouldn't age well.

Kollman
Well, I think a couple of things. She's coming out of very much firmly enmeshed in second wave feminism, which we must position it in that context. The thing I most recently read was also her original article before her book.

Smith
Isn't it so interesting to read the original article?

Kollman
Yes. And I don't want to presume authorial intent, but one thing that perhaps was a struggle was the romance of the era, the late '70s.

Smith
Johanna Lindsey!

Kollman
Yeah. Books that we would probably today find certain elements to be not in line with twenty-first-century sensibilities. And so, the struggle becomes how these women are claiming space for themselves and their life. And they're taking back time from household duties, or the second shift, or their own work for themselves, in an era when there was no social media, or a lot of other opportunities to have feminine leisure time, and yet I think Radway also then found these books themselves to be so deeply problematic in terms of things that upheld the patriarchy, things that were reinforcing some very hegemonic and prescriptive gender roles, and that also contained dubious to outright nonconsensual activities, and you know I don't disagree with her. But she also wasn't necessarily predicting an era when these books would get a little bit more feminist, and the idea of some of the third and now arguably fourth wave feminist tropes that we would see in books today would also expand into an erotic space, and a very at times queer space that was not about any kind of patriarchy. There maybe wouldn't even be a hero in the book or no heroine, for example. Her sample was a little bit limited by the period, and by maybe not going into queer romance. Queer romance did exist in that era. It just was not in any sort of mainstream. And, the genre was very white then.

Smith
Full of classism.

Kollman
Super classist, yes. But she couldn't have predicted any of that necessarily, the changes we've seen in today's romance novels. So, I guess one of the things that I was curious to look at, and even our own survey did not get as diverse as it could have been in terms of diversity, and that's where that we need to open it up to the next set of researchers to be a little bit more focused on some of those areas. Also, in some ways her study felt incomplete maybe because of the friction between her own brand of feminism and academic feminism, like feminist theory versus what she was seeing in the texts themselves. She had very specific idea about these women that may not have been truly accurate. And I think what we also need to keep in mind is that some of the nonconsensual activity in those romance novels of the '70s is a product of trying to figure out how to let women be sexual without them being castigated for it. And that the nonconsensual trope is a compromise or a way around it.

Smith
This discussion relates my next projects. So probably part of this next stage of my work. I'm interested in how romance becomes both an escape and a

coping mechanism. It's safe to kind of play with as a fantasy. Like the idea of fated mates, which I know some people find very creepy, but the idea that you meet someone, and bio biology takes care of it for you. I don't have to worry about making sure that this guy is smart, nice, funny, respectful of my boundaries is going to have a partnership with me because both of us are at the mercy of our biology. So, we're going have to figure it out. Sometimes there's a relief in not having to fight so hard. I think that that's something that I wish Radway could have articulated. I don't know if she struggled with it as a person. But I think that that's something that for me felt like attention because she saw women enjoying these tropes. And I think it was a simpler thing to put them in this victim of this larger system role, as opposed to saying they might be holding two things, which is, that in real life they must deal with these things and in a fantasy space they maybe just accept those things. And somehow it still turns out well, because you get an orgasm, and someone who loves you forever. And it's not complicated; there's a relief in that simplified process when it's not real life.

Kollman
I think we could say that about a lot of fiction, or even things like true crime media.

Smith
One hundred percent.

Kollman
Knowing I wouldn't want to be in that situation. But it comes down to understanding that differentiation between fiction and reality.

Smith
For the longest time I would get really frustrated with Radway at the points where she implied these women are just victims of the patriarchy and they've been indoctrinated to think this is the best they can do. I think that that was the only way that she could understand their relationship with it, and I wish that there had been a better theoretical framework for the kind of complexity of both negotiating and subverting at the same time.

Kollman
Well, and that what like I kind of mentioned before, that was such a liminal period in terms of feminism. If you look at something like Susan Faludi's *Backlash*, which is one of my favorite books of feminist theory. Faludi covers the 1980s at the height of second-wave feminism. She was publishing that not long after Radway's book, and right after is when the mainstream

media started to get very patriarchal again, uncomfortable with second-wave feminism. And that's why in the '90s we then get a lot of girl power narratives.

How do we see this collection contributing to the field? How did it differ from our typical methodological approach?

Kollman
It seemed impossible for a single-author monograph to be able to walk in the footsteps of Radway's work. Taking this on as an edited collection with a shared data set, then, was a much better idea, because this way multiple voices can all contribute to the topic with a lot more diversity of thought. From a personal perspective, I so rarely deal with quantitative data that that was a good challenge, but by also opening up what we accepted for inclusion, we still got a great deal of textual analysis, which is usually more of what I do. I think ultimately having contributors do mixed methods greatly enhanced my own appreciation and understanding of the various ways to do this kind of research.

Smith
I have always gravitated towards interdisciplinary research, and I love to see so many perspectives about one topic. I hope this work is a step in growing the interdisciplinary and mixed-methods research in popular romance scholarship. I hope others will use the research, data, and developed survey to continue this work. There are still so many future directions to take this research—I am excited to see where it goes.

What are the strengths and weaknesses of Radway within the broader field of romance studies?

Kollman
Radway's original work opened up cultural studies to feminist theory and concerns that largely affected women. While not being the first such study of romance fiction, it is still one of the first *significant* studies, and one that did not rely solely on textual analysis of individual novels. In terms of weaknesses, however, those rest largely in the need of the information gathering to be more comprehensive, updated, and reflective of later trends in readership and content. I also think that not clearly being a member of the group which she was studying led Radway's conclusions to appear overly distant. This was likely a product of its time and the need for a researcher—especially a female one—to exhibit proper objectivity. However, in the years since *Reading the Romance*'s release, there have been trends toward

incorporating autoethnography and reflexivity within studies like Radway's, which we are delighted that several of our contributors have used in the present volume.

Smith
Radway was the first to publish robust romance reader focused research that implemented a mixed-methods framework with qualitative and ethnographic research. She was the first to ask readers about how romance reading functioned for them. The research is very much of the time—her participants were white straight middle-class women. There is so much opportunity to expand questions about the cultural process of reading romance with the diverse romance community. The other major issue with her research is her approach to the readers. Like many feminist analyses of popular culture, particularly third wave feminism, Radway often positioned participants purely as victims to a patriarchal system. Popular culture studies have evolved to understand the complicated system of subverting, negotiating and uphold patriarchal systems in genres like popular romance fiction.

Did anything surprise you about how different contributors interpreted or used the data?

Kollman
No; what's slightly ironic about the present study is that despite the clear need to gather updated data on reader practices, a lot of the results were very similar to Radway's in terms of how and why people consume romance novels. What I found most delightful was that even when there was overlap in how different contributors analyzed and discussed the data—or areas related to the data—there was enough uniqueness in everyone's approach that I think we succeeded in creating a book that is quite thorough while also reinforcing some common key findings.

Smith
I was pleasantly surprised to see a few contributors used some of their previous research to contextualize their chapter. I was also pleased to see a few contributors delve into the comments to do some qualitative research. Can you talk more about what you thought of the contributor interpretations of the data, or how they kind of used it?

Kollman
Yeah, I felt like they were in some ways finding some similar things about information comfort, in terms of why people read romance to begin with, but everybody's approach was kind of a little bit different. And I liked reading a

variety of some quantitative, some textual analysis, some blend, some bringing in their own area of particular focus. We've got some autoethnography from an author, for example. It was just such a nice blend of voices and confirming a lot of what we probably suspected updating the older material and quoting some of the interesting comments left in our data. I just thought it was a delightful mix. And I think it nicely brings things up to the present day.

Radway's career after *Reading the Romance* remained broadly focused on the intersection of book culture and feminist theory. Do you see your academic focus remaining with romance or are you more of a "Radwayist"?

Kollman
While Radway veering away from romance studies is something some researchers could point out as evidence of her not actually being a romance scholar, I like how diversified the rest of her academic writing has been thus far. I am the kind of scholar who chases personal interests in what I choose to write about rather than popular trends, which has led me to have articles published about fantasy fiction, music videos, vampires, and several TV series of vastly different genres. The common link between all my work, however, is looking at all these pop culture texts through the lens of intersectional feminist theory and focusing largely on issues related to gender and identity. I will always love romance fiction, will likely always read it, and may continue to write it or write about it, but I see myself moving to other subject areas as well. One of the common themes in a lot of the texts that I study, though, is the idea of "found families," and romance fiction is sort of the ultimate version of that, wherein a couple or family is literally established as the primary plot point of the work.

Smith
My research has always focused on popular romance and its cultural implications. I am constantly curious about how romance narratives construct individual identity, gender norms, and relational norms. As a romance reader myself, I feel like I am constantly negotiating my own values and constructions of reality, which I think is unavoidable with a genre or popular text that the audience loves and connects to. I hope to do a bit more research on New Adult fiction, the ways that romance influences social norms, romantic expectations, and how those cultural dynamics impact readers.

Kollman
We've discussed doing other projects together that are outside of that genre. And I would like to do more romance. But I'm a little bit like Radway, in

that I'm kind of using feminist theory to look at a lot of different type types of things, such as this idea of like found family or constructed family. And looking at how that works, when marginalized individuals coming together to create their own small community. A family that can be a romance that can be two people, or that can be something else.

Smith
I mean, that's literally the foundation from a psychological framework. That's literally the framework of a reverse harem romance.

Kollman
Yes, but also like even things that don't have a romantic relationship. Like a workplace sitcom, for example.

Smith
I think teen fiction, or adventure fiction typically has a found family component. Or fantasy fiction, where the main character's often an orphan, which means that they're required to do a found family situation.

Kollman
Your basic *Dungeons & Dragons* party is that.

Smith
Literally talk about the paratextual components of *D&D*, because you have the world, and then you have the game outside of the world, which is also a found family that get together, and then you have the cultural representations of the found family, like *Stranger Things*, where literally their group started because of *D&D*.

Kollman
So yeah, I do think of myself as a little bit more in line with what Radway's done with the rest of her academic career. But this is a realm that I really think is interesting. More broadly, popular fiction studies is just so cool, whether it's in literature or TV, or film.

Smith
I'm always going to gravitate towards romance, just because there's something about it that feeds my soul. But now that we've built this collaboration, I'm very excited about you pulling me into some of your projects so that I broaden into more pop culture research. Ultimately, what I like to do is look at the cultural meaning for people behind a cultural phenomenon. That's our biggest interest. That's our intersection, too.

Kollman

Yes, I think you know whatever type of pop culture text we're talking about, it's how people come to it, how they interpret it, how they use it. And also, I really am all about the representation within it, which is more important to me than worrying about how it was authored or constructed.

Smith

Yeah, I agree. I want to examine what kind of reality is being constructed in these narratives, as well as how audiences engage with them.

Bibliography

INTRODUCTION

Donahue, Deirdre. "NA Fiction is the Hot New Category in Books," *USA Today*, April 15, 2013, https://www.usatoday.com/story/life/books/2013/04/15/new-adult-genre-is-the-hottest-category-in-book-publishing/2022707/.

Fekete, Maleah. "Confluent Love and the Evolution of Ideal Intimacy: Romance Reading in 1980 and 2016." *Journal of Popular Romance Studies,* 2022, no. 11: 1–30.

Halverson, Deborah and Sylvia Day. *Writing NA Fiction.* Cincinnati: Writer's Digest Books, 2014.

Hubbard, Rita C. "Relationship Styles in Popular Romance Novels, 1950 to 1983." *Communication Quarterly* 33, no. 2 (1985): 113–25.

Kollman, Kathleen W. Taylor. "Contemporary Paranormal Romance: Theories and Development of the Genre's Feminism (Or Lack Thereof)." *Researching the Romance Conference, 2018, Bowling Green, Ohio*, ScholarWorks@BGSU, 2018.

Light, Alison. "'Returning to Manderley'—Romance Fiction, Female Sexuality and Class." *Feminist Review* 16, no. 1 (1984): 7–25.

Modleski, Tania. *Loving with a Vengeance: Mass-Produced Fantasies for Women.* New York: Methuen, 1984.

Naughton, Julie. "NA: A Book Category for Twentysomethings by Twentysomethings," *Publishers Weekly,* July 11, 2014, http://www.publishersweekly.com/pw/by-topic/industry-news/publisher-news/article/63285-new-adult-matures.html.

Radway, Janice A. *Reading the Romance: Women, Patriarchy, and Popular Literature.* Chapel Hill: University of North Carolina Press, 1991.

Radway, Janice A. "Women Read the Romance: The Interaction of Text and Context." *Feminist Studies* 9, no. 1 (1983).

Roach, Catherine M. *Happily Ever After: The Romance Story in Popular Culture.* Bloomington: Indiana University Press, 2016.

Selinger, Eric. "Reading the Romance: A Thirtieth Anniversary Roundtable, Editor's Introduction." *Journal of Popular Romance Studies*, vol. 4., no. 2 (2014): 1–2.
Selinger, Eric and Sarah SG Frantz. "Introduction." *New Approaches to Popular Romance Fiction: Critical Essays.* Frantz, Sarah SG, and Eric Murphy Selinger, eds. McFarland, 2014.
Sherwood, Kim. "Pride and Prejudice: Metafiction and the Value of Historical Romance in Georgette Heyer," in *Georgette Heyer, History and Historical Fiction*, edited by Samantha J. Rayner and Kim Wilkins. London: UCL Press, 2021, 75–87.
Walkerdine, Valerie. *Daddy's Girl: Young Girls and Popular Culture.* Cambridge, MA: Harvard University Press, 1998.

SECTION 1: VISITING ROMANCELANDIA: POPULAR ROMANCE FICTION AS A COMMUNITY

Chapter 1: Re-Reading Romance: Exploring Author, Reader, and Industry Perceptions of the Genre—Burgess and Kolodziej

Athwal, N., and L. C. Harris. "Examining How Brand Authenticity Is Established and Maintained: The Case of the Reverso." *Journal of Marketing Management* 34, no. 3–4 (2018): 347–69. https://doi.org/10.1080/0267257X.2018.1447008.
Burgess, Jacqueline, and Christian Jones. "Investigating Consumer Perceptions of Brand Inauthenticity in a Narrative Brand Ending." *Journal of Product & Brand Management* (2023). https://doi.org/10.1108/JPBM-03-2022-3897.
Carroll, Noël. "Narrative Closure." *Philosophical Studies* 135, no. 1 (2007): 1–15. https://doi.org/10.1007/s11098-007-9097-9.
Chappel-Traylor, Deborah. "To My Mentor, Jan Radway, With Love." *Journal of Popular Romance Studies* 4, no. 2 (2014): 1–4. https://www.jprstudies.org/2014/10/to-my-mentor-jan-radway-with-loveby-deborah-chappel-traylor/.
Curcic, Dimitrije. "Romance Novel Sales Statistics." Wordsrated. Accessed September 17, 2024. https://wordsrated.com/romance-novel-sales-statistics/.
Curcic, Dimitrije. "Fiction Book Sales Statistics." Wordsrated. Accessed September 17, 2024. https://wordsrated.com/fiction-books-sales/.
Fiske, John. "The Cultural Economy of Fandom." In *The Adoring Audience: Fan Culture*, edited by Lisa A. Lewis, 30–49. Abingdon, UK: Routledge, 1991.
Flood, Alison. "Romance Writers of America Aims for Happy End to Racism Row with New Prize." *The Guardian*, May 23, 2020. https://www.theguardian.com/books/2020/may/22/romance-writers-of-america-racism-row-new-prize-ritas-vivian.
Fritz, Kristine, Verena Schoenmueller, and Manfred Bruhn. "Authenticity in Branding – Exploring Antecedents and Consequences of Brand Authenticity." *European Journal of Marketing* 51, no. 2 (2017): 324–48. https://doi.org/10.1108/EJM-10-2014-0633.
Gleason, William A., and Erich Murphy Selinger. *Romance Fiction and American Culture: Love as the Practice of Freedom?* London: Routledge, 2016.

Goris, An. "A Natural History of the Romance Novel's Enduring Romance with Popular Romance Studies." *Journal of Popular Romance Studies* 3, no. 2 (2013): 1–4. https://www.jprstudies.org/2013/06/a-natural-history-of-the-romance-novels-enduring-romance-with-popular-romance-studies-by-an-goris/.

Jagodzinski, Mallory. "We've Come a Long Way, Baby: Reflecting Thirty Years After Reading the Romance." *Journal of Popular Romance Studies* 4, no. 2 (2014): 1–3. https://www.jprstudies.org/2014/10/weve-come-a-long-way-baby-reflecting-thirty-years-after-reading-the-romanceby-mallory-jagodzinski/.

Jenkins, Henry. *Textual Poachers: Television Fans and Participatory Culture, Updated Twentieth Anniversary Edition.* New York: Routledge, 2012.

Johnson, Allison R., Matthew Thomson, and Jennifer Jeffrey. "What Does Brand Authenticity Mean? Causes and Consequences of Consumer Scrutiny Toward a Brand Narrative." In *Brand Meaning Management* (Review of Marketing Research, Vol. 12), edited by Susan Fournier, 1–27. Emerald Group Publishing Limited, 2015. https://doi.org/10.1108/S1548-643520150000012001.

Kamblé, Jayashree, Eric Murphy Selinger, and Hsu-Ming Teo, eds. *The Routledge Research Companion to Popular Romance Fiction.* Routledge, 2021.

Klugman, Ema. "'They Are Like Printing Money': Sex, Rape, and Power in Romance Novels." *Unsuitable.* Accessed September 17, 2024. https://sites.duke.edu/unsuitable/rape-forgive/.

Kolodziej, Gaja. "Unforgettably in Love: Uses of the Amnesia Trope in Contemporary Romance." PhD diss., Massey University, 2021. Massey Research Online. http://hdl.handle.net/10179/16476.

Larson, Christine. "Open Networks, Open Books: Gender, Precarity and Solidarity in Digital Publishing." *Information, Communication and Society* 23, no. 13 (2020): 1892–1908. https://doi.org/10.1080/1369118X.2019.1621922.

Mittell, Jason. *Complex TV: The Poetics of Contemporary Television Storytelling.* New York University Press, 2015.

Moody, Stephanie. "From Reading the Romance to Grappling with Genre." *Journal of Popular Romance Studies* 4, no. 2 (2014): 1–3. https://www.jprstudies.org/2014/10/from-reading-the-romance-to-grappling-with-genreby-stephanie-moody/.

Moulard, Julia Guidry, Carolyn Popp Garrity, and Dan Hamilton Rice. "What Makes a Human Brand Authentic? Identifying the Antecedents of Celebrity Authenticity." *Psychology & Marketing* 32, no. 2 (2015): 173–86. https://doi.org/10.1002/mar.20771.

Prince, Gerald. *Dictionary of Narratology: Revised Edition.* Lincoln: University of Nebraska Press, 2003.

Putney, Mary Jo. "Welcome to the Dark Side." In *Dangerous Men and Adventurous Women: Romance Writers on the Appeal of Romance*, edited by Jayne Ann Krentz, 99–106. Philadelphia: University of Pennsylvania Press, 1992.

Radway, Janice A. *Reading the Romance: Women, Patriarchy, and Popular Literature.* Chapel Hill: University of North Carolina Press, 1991.

Regis, Pamela. *A Natural History of the Romance Novel.* Philadelphia: University of Pennsylvania Press, 2003.

Romance Writers of America. "About Romance Genre." Accessed September 17, 2024. https://www.rwa.org/Online/Romance_Genre/About_Romance_Genre.aspx.
Romance Writers of New Zealand. *The Beginner's Guide to Romance.* Accessed September 17, 2024. https://www.romancewriters.co.nz/about-us/beginners-guide-romance/.
Russell, Cristal Antonia, and Hope Jensen Schau. "When Narrative Brands End: The Impact of Narrative Closure and Consumption Sociality on Loss Accommodation." *Journal of Consumer Research* 40, no. 6 (2014): 1039–62. https://doi.org/10.1086/673959.
Saricks, Joyce G. *The Readers' Advisory Guide to Genre Fiction*, 2nd ed. Chicago: American Library Association, 2011.
Schell, Heather. "Love's Laborers Lost: Radway, Romance Writers, and Recuperating Our Past." *Journal of Popular Romance Studies* 4, no. 2 (2014): 1–5. https://jprstudies.org/wp-content/uploads/2014/09/LLL_Schell.pdf.
Selinger, Eric Murphy. "Rebooting the Romance: The Impact of *A Natural History of the Romance Novel*." *Journal of Popular Romance Studies* 3, no. 2 (2013): 1–5. https://www.jprstudies.org/2013/06/rebooting-the-romance-the-impact-of-a-natural-history-of-the-romance-novel-by-eric-murphy-selinger/.
Spencer, Lynn. "Adultery—The Great Romance Taboo." *All About Romance.* Accessed September 17, 2024. https://allaboutromance.com/adultery-the-great-romance-taboo/.
Walker, Kate. *Kate Walker's 12-Point Guide to Writing Romance.* Straightforward Publishing, 2018.
Williams, Rebecca. *Post-Object Fandom: Television, Identity and Self-Narrative.* New York: Bloomsbury Academic, 2015.

Chapter 2: From Private to Public: #Bookstagram as a Safe Space for Romance Readers—Rigato

Brouillette, Sarah. "Romance Work." *Theory & Event* 22, no. 2 (2019): 451–64.
Brower, Sue. "Fans as Tastemakers: Viewers for Quality Television." In *The Adoring Audience: Fan Culture and Popular Media*, edited by Lisa A. Lewis, 163–84. Routledge, 1992.
Brown, Trisha. "In with the DNF-ing, Out with Real World Settings: Results from the When In Romance Listener Survey." *BookRiot*, September 20, 2021. https://bookriot.com/pandemic-romance-reading/.
Bury, Rhiannon. *Cyberspaces of Their Own: Female Fandoms Online.* Peter Lang, 2005.
Curcic, Dimitrije. "Fiction Book Sales." Wordsrated, January 30, 2023. https://wordsrated.com/fiction-books-sales/.
Dezuanni, Michael, Sally Crichton, Sharon McLachlan, and Melissa Haugh. "Selfies and Shelfies on #bookstagram and #booktok – Social Media and the Mediation of Australian Teen Reading." *Learning, Media and Technology* 47, no. 3 (2022): 355–72.
Dixon, Jay. *Romance Fiction of Mills & Boon, 1909–1990s.* UCL Press, 1999.

Donald, Robyn. "Mean, Moody, and Magnificent: The Hero in Romance Literature." In *Dangerous Men and Adventurous Women: Romance Writers on the Appeal of the Romance*, edited by Jayne Ann Krentz, 81–84. University of Pennsylvania Press, 1992.

Krentz, Jayne Ann. "Trying to Tame the Romance: Critics and Correctness." In *Dangerous Men and Adventurous Women: Romance Writers on the Appeal of the Romance*, edited by Jayne Ann Krentz, 107–14. University of Pennsylvania Press, 1992.

Markert, John. "Publishing the Romance Novel." In *The Routledge Research Companion to Popular Romance Fiction*, edited by Jayashree Kamblé, 352–70. Routledge, 2020.

McGurl, Mark. *Everything and Less: The Novel in the Age of Amazon*. Verso, 2021.

Modleski, Tania. *Loving with a Vengeance: Mass-Produced Fantasies for Women*. Archon Books, 1982.

Nakamura, Lisa. "Afterword: Blaming, Shaming, and the Feminization of Social Media." In *Feminist Surveillance Studies*, edited by Rachel E. Bubrofsky and Shoshana Amielle Magnet, 221–28. Duke University Press, 2015.

Pressman, Jessica. *Bookishness: Loving Books in a Digital Age*. Columbia University Press, 2020.

Radway, Janice A. *Reading the Romance: Women, Patriarchy, and Popular Literature*. University of North Carolina Press, 1991.

Reddan, Bronwyn. "Social Reading Cultures on BookTube, Bookstagram, and BookTok." *Synergy* 20, no. 1 (2022).

Seidel, Kathleen Gilles. "Judge Me By the Joy I Bring." In *Dangerous Men and Adventurous Women: Romance Writers on the Appeal of the Romance*, edited by Jayne Ann Krentz, 159–80. University of Pennsylvania Press, 1992.

Schwartz, Deanna, and Meghan C. Sullivan. "Gen Z Is Driving Sales of Romance Books to the Top Bestseller Lists." NPR, August 29, 2022. https://www.npr.org/2022/08/29/1119886246/gen-z-is-driving-sales-of-romance-books-to-the-top-of-bestseller-lists#:~:text=Hourly%20News-,Gen%20Z%20is%20driving%20sales%20of%20romance%20books%20by%20Colleen,been%20aided%20by%20Gen%20Z.

Snitow, Ann B. "Mass Market Romance: Pornography for Women Is Different." In *Living with Contradictions: Controversies in Feminist Social Ethics*, edited by Alison M. Jaggar, 141–61. Routledge, 1994.

Struve, Laura. "Sisters of Sorts: Reading Romantic Fiction and the Bonds Among Female Readers." *Journal of Popular Culture* 44, no. 6 (2011): 1289–1306.

Thomas, Bronwen. *Literature and Social Media*. Routledge, 2020.

———. "The #bookstagram: Distributed Reading in the Social Media Age." *Language Sciences* 84 (2021): 1–10.

Wilkins, Kim, Lisa Fletcher, and Beth Driscoll. *Genre Worlds: Popular Fiction and Twenty-First-Century Book Culture*. University of Massachusetts Press, 2022.

Young, Erin S. "Race, Ethnicity, and Whiteness." In *The Routledge Research Companion to Popular Romance Fiction*, edited by Jayashree Kamblé, 511–28. Routledge, 2020.

Chapter 3: Romance Readers' Perceptions of New Adult Fiction—Smith

Arnett, J. J. "Emerging Adulthood: A Theory of Development from the Late Teens Through the Twenties." *American Psychologist* 55, no. 5 (2000): 469–80. http://dx.doi.org/10.1037/0003-066X.55.5.469.

Donahue, Deirdre. "NA Fiction is the Hot New Category in Books." *USA Today*, April 15, 2013. https://www.usatoday.com/story/life/books/2013/04/15/new-adult-genre-is-the-hottest-category-in-book-publishing/2022707/.

Halverson, Deborah, and Sylvia Day. *Writing NA Fiction*. Cincinnati, OH: Writer's Digest Books, 2014.

Lipsitz, George. "Listening to Learn and Learning to Listen." In *Locating American Studies: The Evolution of a Discipline*, edited by Lucy Maddox, 328–39. Baltimore: Johns Hopkins University Press, 1999.

McAlister, Jodi. *New Adult Fiction*. Cambridge: Cambridge University Press, 2021.

———. "Defining and Redefining Popular Genres: The Evolution of 'New Adult' Fiction." *Australian Literary Studies* 33, no. 4 (2018): 1–14.

———. "Messy Multiplicity: Strategies for Serialisation in New Adult Fiction." In *Prequels, Coquels and Sequels in Contemporary Anglophone Fiction*, 144–58. London: Routledge, 2018.

Naughton, Julie. "NA: A Book Category for Twentysomethings by Twentysomethings." *Publishers Weekly*, July 11, 2014. http://www.publishersweekly.com/pw/by-topic/industry-news/publisher-news/article/63285-new-adult-matures.html.

Pattee, Amy. "Between Youth and Adulthood: Young Adult and New Adult Literature." *Children's Literature Association Quarterly* 42, no. 2 (2017): 134–49.

Radway, Janice. *Reading the Romance: Women, Patriarchy, and Popular Literature*. Chapel Hill: University of North Carolina Press, 1991.

———. "Women Read the Romance: The Interaction of Text and Context." *Feminist Studies* 9 (1983): 54–55. http://www.jstor.org/stable/3177683.

Chapter 4: Which Women Want What? The Shifting Demographics and Perspectives of Romance Readers—Natalie Duvall and Matt Duvall

Auxier, Brooke, and Monica Anderson. "Social Media Use in 2021." *Pew Research Center* 1 (2021): 1–4.

Bly, Mary. "A Fine Romance." *The New York Times*, February 12, 2005.

Gee, James Paul. *Situated Language and Learning: A Critique of Traditional Schooling*. Psychology Press, 2004.

Heath, Shirley Brice. "What No Bedtime Story Means: Narrative Skills at Home and School." *Language in Society* 11, no. 1 (1982): 49–76.

Kaakinen, Markus, Anu Sirola, Iina Savolainen, and Atte Oksanen. "Shared Identity and Shared Information in Social Media: Development and Validation of the Identity Bubble Reinforcement Scale." *Media Psychology* 23, no. 1 (2020): 25–51.

Lois, Jennifer, and Joanna Gregson. "Sneers and Leers: Romance Writers and Gendered Sexual Stigma." *Gender & Society* 29, no. 4 (2015): 459–83.
Purcell-Gates, Victoria, Kristen H. Perry, and Adriana Briseño. "Analyzing Literacy Practice: Grounded Theory to Model." *Research in the Teaching of English* (2011): 439–58.
Purcell-Gates, Victoria, Erik Jacobson, Sophie Degener, and Victoria Purcell-Gates. *Print Literacy Development: Uniting Cognitive and Social Practice Theories*. Harvard University Press, 2009.
Radway, Janice A. *Reading the Romance: Women, Patriarchy, and Popular Literature*. University of North Carolina Press, 1991.
Radway, Janice A. "Women Read the Romance: The Interaction of Text and Context." *Feminist Studies* 9, no. 1 (1983): 53–78.
Raffaelli, Ryan. "Reinventing Retail: The Novel Resurgence of Independent Bookstores." Harvard Business School, 2020.
Teale, William H. "Parents Reading to Their Children: What We Know and Need to Know." *Language Arts* 58, no. 8 (1981): 902–12.
Teale, William H. "What Counts? Literacy Assessment in Urban Schools." *The Reading Teacher* 62, no. 4 (2008): 358–61.
United States. Bureau of the Census. *Money Income of Households, Families, and Persons in the United States*. US Department of Commerce, Bureau of the Census, 1987.

Chapter 5: Social Media, Critical Analysis, and Feminist Action: Popular YA's Role in Disseminating Theory Online—Caravaggio

Aubrey, Jennifer Stevens, Melissa Click, and Elizabeth Behm-Morawitz. "The Twilight of Youth: Understanding Feminism and Romance in Twilight Moms' Connection to the Young- Adult Vampire Series." *Psychology of Popular Media Culture* 7 (January 2018): 61–71.
Borgia, Danielle N. "Twilight: The Glamorization of Abuse, Codependency, and White Privilege." *The Journal of Popular Culture* 47 (March 2014): 153–73.
Chaudhuri, Shohini. *Feminist Film Theorists: Laura Mulvey, Kaja Silverman, Teresa de Laurentis, Barbara Creed*. New York: Routledge, 2006.
Chel. "Comment on Padilla, 'Replying to @Holly Boone802 CHAPTERS 30 and 31.'" August 28, 2023.
D'Amore, Laura Mattoon. *Vigilante Feminists and Agents of Destiny: Violence, Empowerment, and the Teenage Super/heroine*. London: Lexington Books, 2021.
Dietz, Tammy. "Wake Up, Bella! A Personal Essay on Twilight, Mormonism, Feminism, and Happiness." In *Bringing Light to Twilight: Perspectives on a Pop Culture Phenomenon*, edited by Giselle Liza Anatol, 99–112. New York: Palgrave Macmillan, 2011.
Fish, Stanley Eugene. *Is There a Text in This Class? The Authority of Interpretive Communities*. Cambridge: Harvard University Press, 1980.

Fish (@the.sequel.nobody.wanted). "Part 8: Someone Get Chris Hansen on This Case RIGHT NOW." TikTok. August 24, 2023. https://www.tiktok.com/@the.sequel.nobody.wanted/video/7270935511928163627.

Fish (@the.sequel.nobody.wanted). "Part 11: My Bad Thought Bella Was Actually Being Reasonable for a Second There." TikTok. August 25, 2023. https://www.tiktok.com/@the.sequel.nobody.wanted/video/7271384700428602670.

Fish (@the.sequel.nobody.wanted). "Reading This Was Certainly an Experience." TikTok. August 28, 2023. https://www.tiktok.com/@the.sequel.nobody.wanted/video/7272464386873232683.

hooks, bell. *Feminist Theory: From Margin to Center*. 2nd ed. London: Pluto Press, 2000 [1984].

Karla. "Comment on Padilla, 'Replying to @Holly Boone802 CHAPTERS 30 and 31.'" August 28, 2023.

Kliger-Vilenchik, Neta, et al. "Experiencing Fan Activism: Understanding the Power of Fan Activist Organizations Through Members' Narratives." *Transformative Works and Cultures* 10 (January 2011): 1–22.

Klo. "Comment on Padilla, 'Part 45: Replying to @moonbeenz THE RING.'" May 24, 2024. Kollman, Kathleen, and Smith, Josefine. *Still Reading Romance Survey Data*. 2023.

Kolodny, Annette. "Dancing Through the Minefield: Some Observations on the Theory, Practice, and Politics of Feminist Literary Criticism." *Feminist Studies* 6 (Spring 1980): 1–25.

Kori Lloyd 895. "Comment on Fish, 'Part 4: Edward's Personality Sure Is Something!'" August 22, 2024.

Kramar, Margaret. "The Wolf in the Woods: Representations of 'Little Red Riding Hood' in Twilight." In *Bringing Light to Twilight: Perspectives on a Pop Culture Phenomenon*, edited by Giselle Liza Anatol, 15–30. New York: Palgrave Macmillan, 2011.

Lorde, Audre. "'The Master's Tools Will Never Dismantle the Master's House.'" In *Feminist Postcolonial Theory: A Reader*, edited by Reina Lewis and Sara Mills, 25–28. New York: Routledge, 2003 [1984].

Maas, Sarah J. *A Court of Thorns and Roses*. London: Bloomsbury Publishing, 2015.

———. *A Court of Mist and Fury*. London: Bloomsbury Publishing, 2016.

———. *A Court of Wings and Ruin*. London: Bloomsbury Publishing, 2017.

———. *A Court of Silver Flames*. London: Bloomsbury Publishing, 2021.

Macdonald, D. L., and Scherf, Kathleen, eds. "Appendix A: The Revolutionary Moment." In *A Vindication of the Rights of Men; A Vindication of the Rights of Woman*, 345–92. Peterborough: Broadview Press, 2001.

McCullough, Steve. "Online Misogyny: The 'Manosphere.'" *Canadian Museum for Human Rights*. Accessed September 2023. https://humanrights.ca/story/online-misogyny-manosphere.

Meyer, Stephenie. *Twilight*. Boston: Little, Brown and Company, 2005.

———. *New Moon*. Boston: Little, Brown and Company, 2006.

———. *Eclipse*. Boston: Little, Brown and Company, 2007.

———. *Breaking Dawn*. Boston: Little, Brown and Company, 2008.

———. *The Twilight Saga: The Official Illustrated Guide*. Boston: Little, Brown and Company, 2011.
———. *Life and Death: Twilight Reimagined*. Boston: Little, Brown and Company, 2015.
———. *Midnight Sun*. Boston: Little, Brown and Company, 2020.
Mohanty, Chandra Talpade. "Under Western Eyes: Feminist Scholarship and Colonial Discourses." *Boundary 2* 12 (Spring–Autumn 1984): 333–58.
Mukherjea, Ananya. "Team Bella: Fans Navigating Desire, Security, and Feminism." In *Theorizing Twilight: Critical Essays on What's at Stake in a Post-Vampire World*, edited by Maggie Parke and Natalie Wilson, 70–86. Jefferson: McFarland & Company, Inc., 2011.
Mulvey, Laura. *Visual and Other Pleasures*. 2nd ed. New York: Palgrave Macmillan, 2009 [1989].
Myers, Abigail E. "Edward Cullen and Bella Swan: Byronic and Feminist Heroes… or Not." In *Twilight and Philosophy: Vampires, Vegetarians, and the Pursuit of Immortality*, edited by Rebecca Housel and J. Jeremy Wisnewski, 147–62. Hoboken: John Wiley & Sons, Inc., 2009.
Padilla, Connor (@connor_thebard). "Part 16: Replying to @tiffstokchronicles I PROMISE ILL READ FASTER." TikTok. May 9, 2023. https://www.tiktok.com/@connor_thebard/video/7231302760065453355.
Padilla, Connor (@connor_thebard). "Replying to @Holly Boone802 CHAPTERS 30 and 31." TikTok. August 28, 2023. https://www.tiktok.com/@connor_thebard/video/7272482480081390894.
Radway, A. Janet. *Reading the Romance: Women, Patriarchy, and Popular Literature*. Chapel Hill and London: The University of North Carolina Press, 1991.
Randolph, Bonnie Moore, and Ross-Valliere, Clydene. "Consciousness Raising Groups." *The American Journal of Nursing* 79 (May 1979): 922–24.
Sara Kirstine. "Comment on Fish, 'Part 7: The Cold Medicine Part Really Got Me.'" August 24, 2023.
Snooze. "Comment on Padilla, 'Part 2: Replying to @Abstract I Clearly Had a Lot to Say.'" May 2, 2024.
Urbanwitch101. "Comment on Fish, 'Part 11: My Bad Thought Bella Was Actually Being Reasonable for a Second There.'" August 26, 2024.
Violet. "Comment on Fish, 'Part 8: Someone Get Chris Hansen on This Case RIGHT NOW.'" August 24, 2024.

CONSULTED WORKS

Booth, Paul, ed. *A Companion to Media Fandom and Fan Studies*. Hoboken: John Wiley & Sons, Inc., 2018.
Click, Melissa A., and Scott, Suzanne, eds. *The Routledge Companion to Media Fandom*. New York: Routledge, 2018.

Clifford, John, ed. *The Experience of Reading: Louise Rosenblatt and Reader-Response Theory*. Portsmouth: Boynton/Cook Publishers, 1991.
Davis, Todd F., and Womack, Kenneth, eds. *Formalist Criticism and Reader-Response Theory*. New York: Palgrave Macmillan, 2002.
Hellekson, Karen, and Busse, Kristina, eds. *The Fan Fiction Studies Reader*. Iowa City: The University of Iowa, 2014.
Sullivan, John L., ed. *Media Audiences: Effects, Users, Institutions, and Power*. Los Angeles: SAGE Publications, Inc., 2020.
Veeser, Aram H., ed. *The Stanley Fish Reader*. Oxford: Blackwell Publishers, 1999.
Woods, Jack. "Reading Practices and the Formation of 'Interpretive Communities' in the Lodz Ghetto." *Holocaust Studies* 25 (May 2019): 467–91.

SECTION 2: A REAL MEET CUTE: ROMANCE GENRE AND SOCIAL PRACTICES

Chapter 6: Beyond the Bodice Ripper: Why Erotic Romance Is Feminist Literature—Stout

"About Passionate Ink." Passionate Ink - Some Like it Hot, December 21, 2021. https://passionateink.org/about-passionate-ink/.
Cron, Lisa. *Story genius: How to use brain science to go beyond outlining and write a riveting novel *before you waste three years writing 327 pages that go nowhere*. Berkeley: Ten Speed Press, 2016.
Gribble, J.L. "Escapism at its Finest," Review of *Between Sirs*, by Rachell Nichole. Amazon, May 18, 2020. https://www.amazon.com/gp/customer- reviews/RV FQZ80NKAP91/ref=cm_cr_dp_d_rvw_ttl?ie=UTF8&ASIN=B07ZK4F5GX
Kippert, Amanda. "Can He Rape Me If We're Married?" DomesticShelters.Org, domesticshelters.org, Accessed August 11, 2023, www.domesticshelters.org/articles/identifying-abuse/can-he-rape-me-if-we-re-married.
Lois, Jennifer, and Joanna Gregson. "Sneers And Leers: Romance Writers and Gendered Sexual Stigma." *Gender and Society* 29, no. 4 (2015): 459–83. Accessed June 14, 2023, http://www.jstor.org/stable/43669991.
McAlister, Jodi. "Erotic romance." *The Routledge Research Companion to Popular Romance Fiction* (2020), edited by Kamblé, J., Murphy Selinger, E., & Teo, H.-M. Routledge. https://doi.org/10.4324/9781315613468
Michelson, Anna. "Pushing the Boundaries: Erotic Romance and the Symbolic Boundary Nexus." *Poetics*, 94 (2022): 1–14, Accessed April 4, 2024, https://doi.org/10.1016/j.poetic.2022.101729.
Nichole, Rachell. *Love Affair in Times Square*. Philadelphia: Kindle Direct Publishing, 2019.
Radway, Janice. *Reading the Romance: Women, Patriarchy, and Popular Literature*. Chapel Hill: University of North Carolina Press, 1991: 17.
Regis, Pamela. *A Natural History of the Romance Novel*. University of Pennsylvania Press, 2013.

RZ. "Fiction." Review of Awakening Submission, by Rachell Nichole. Amazon, July 3, 2019, https://www.amazon.com/Awakening-Club-Dark-Side-Book-ebook/product-reviews/B07QDL1VBW/ref=cm_cr_unknown?ie=UTF8&reviewerTy pe=all_reviews&fil terbyStar=two_star&pageNumber=1

Simon, Jenni M.. *Consuming Agency and Desire in Romance : Stories of Love, Laughter, and Empowerment*. Lanham: Lexington Books/Fortress Academic, 2017. Accessed April 28, 2024. ProQuest Ebook Central.

Sue. "Ok." Review of Awakening Submission, by Rachell Nichole. Amazon, October 25, 2019, https://www.amazon.com/Awakening-Club-Dark-Side-Book-ebook/product- reviews/B07QDL1VBW/ref=cm_cr_arp_d_viewpnt_rgt?ie=UTF8&revie werType=all_re views&filterByStar=critical&pageNumber=1

Vivanco, Laura. 2012. "Feminism and Early Twenty-First Century Harlequin Mills & Boon Romances." *The Journal of Popular Culture* Vol. 45 No. 5: 1060–89. Accessed August 4, 2023, https://doi.org/10.1111/j.1540-5931.2012.00973.x.

Chapter 7: Reading Historical Romance / Reading Romance Historically—Sanders

Anderson, Rachel. *The Purple Heart Throbs: The Sub-Literature of Love*. London: Hodder & Stoughton, 1974.

Bowden, Martha F. *Descendants of Waverley: Romancing History in Contemporary Historical Fiction*. Lewisburg, PA: Bucknell University Press, 2016.

Byatt, A. S. "An Honourable Escape: Georgette Heyer." In *Passions of the Mind: Selected Writings*. 1969. New York: Turtle Bay Books/Random House, 1992.

Davies, Ben, Christina Lupton, and Johanne Gormsen Schmidt. *Reading Novels During the Covid-19 Pandemic*. Oxford: Oxford University Press, 2023.

Davisson, Amber, and Kyra Hunting. "From Private Pleasure to Erotic Spectacle: Adapting *Bridgerton* to Female Audience Desires." *Journal of Popular Television* 11, no. 1 (2023): 7–25.

Fahnestock-Thomas, Mary, ed. *Georgette Heyer: A Critical Retrospective*. Saraland, AL: Prinnyworld Press, 2001.

Ficke, Sarah H. "The Historical Romance." In *The Routledge Research Companion to Popular Romance Fiction*, edited by Jayashree Kamblé, Eric Murphy Selinger, and Hsu-Ming Teo, 118–40. *The Routledge Research Companion to Popular Romance Fiction*. London and New York: Routledge, 2021.

Fletcher, Lisa. *Historical Romance Fiction: Heterosexuality and Performativity*. Burlington: Ashgate, 2008.

Froide, Amy M. "The History Behind *Bridgerton*." *Journal of Popular Television* 11, no. 1 (2023): 55–60.

Gillis, Stacy. "The Cross-Dresser, the Thief, His Daughter and Her Lover: Queer Desire and Romance in Georgette Heyer's *These Old Shades*." *Women* 26, nos. 1–2 (2015): 57–74.

Gillis, Stacy. "Manners, Money, and Marriage: Austen, Heyer, and the Literary Genealogy of the Regency Romance." In *After Austen: Reinventions, Rewritings, Revisitings*, edited by Lisa Hopkins, 81–101. Houndmills: Palgrave Macmillan, 2018.

Gregson, Joanna and Jennifer Lois. "Social Science Reads Romance." In *The Routledge Research Companion to Popular Romance Fiction*, edited by Jayashree Kamblé, Eric Murphy Selinger, and Hsu-Ming Teo, 335–51. London and New York: Routledge, 2021.

Hodge, Jane Aiken. *The Private World of Georgette Heyer*. London: Bodley Head, 1984.

Hollows, Joanne. *Feminism, Femininity and Popular Culture*. Manchester: Manchester University Press, 2000.

Hopkins, Lisa. "Georgette Heyer: What Austen Left Out." In *After Austen: Reinventions, Rewritings, Revisitings*, edited by Lisa Hopkins, 61–79. Houndmills: Palgrave Macmillan, 2018.

Hughes, Helen. *The Historical Romance*. New York and London: Routledge, 1993.

Jensen, Klaus Bruhn. "Intermediality." In *The International Encyclopedia of Communication Theory and Philosophy*, edited by Klaus Bruhn Jensen and Robert T. Craig, 1–12. John Wiley & Sons, 2016.

Kamblé, Jayashree, Eric Murphy Selinger, and Hsu-Ming Teo, eds. *The Routledge Research Companion to Popular Romance Fiction*. London and New York: Routledge, 2021.

Kloester, Jennifer. *Georgette Heyer: Biography of a Bestseller*. London: William Heinemann/Random House, 2011.

McCann, Hannah, and Catherine M. Roach. "Sex and Sexuality." In *The Routledge Research Companion to Popular Romance Fiction*, edited by Jayashree Kamblé, Eric Murphy Selinger, and Hsu-Ming Teo, 411–27. London and New York: Routledge, 2021.

Paizis, George. *Love and the Novel: The Poetics and Politics of Romantic Fiction*. Basingstoke: Macmillan, 1998.

Prescott, Amanda-Rae. "After the Duke: Reflections on How *Bridgerton* Has Changed the Period Drama Conversation." *Journal of Popular Television* 11, no. 1 (2023): 61–73.

Radway, Janice A. *Reading the Romance: Women, Patriarchy, and Popular Literature*. Chapel Hill: University of North Carolina Press, 1984; rev. ed. 1991.

Radway, Jane A. "Romance and the Work of Fantasy: Struggles over Feminine Sexuality and Subjectivity at Century's End." In *Viewing, Reading, Listening: Audiences and Cultural Reception*, edited by Jon Cruz and Justin Lewis, 213–31. Boulder: Westview Press, 1994.

Radway, Janice A. "Women Read the Romance: The Interaction of Text and Context." *Feminist Studies* 9, no. 1 (1983): 53–78.

Rayner, Samantha J., and Kim Wilkins, eds. *Georgette Heyer, History and Historical Fiction*. London: UCL Press, 2021.

Regis, Pamela. *A Natural History of the Romance Novel*. Philadelphia: University of Pennsylvania Press, 2003.

Regis, Pamela. "Female Genre Fiction in the Twentieth Century." In *The Cambridge History of the American Novel*, edited by Leonard Cassuto et al., 847–60. Cambridge: Cambridge University Press, 2011.

Sherwood, Kim. "Pride and Prejudice: Metafiction and the Value of Historical Romance in Georgette Heyer." In *Georgette Heyer, History and Historical Fiction*, edited by Samantha J. Rayner and Kim Wilkins, 75–87. London: UCL Press, 2021.
Sipe, William Joseph. "Post-Racial Politics and the Mandate to Desire: Interracial Love as Liberation in *Bridgerton*." *Critical Studies in Media Communication* (2023): 1–14.
Stacey, Jackie, and Lynne Pearce. "The Heart of the Matter: Feminists Revisit Romance." In *Romance Revisited*, edited by Lynne Pearce and Jackie Stacey, 11–45. New York: New York University Press, 1995.
Vasudevan, Aruna, ed. *Twentieth-Century Romance and Historical Writers*. 3rd ed. With prefaces by Kay Mussell and Alison Light. London: St. James Press/Gale Research, 1994.
Westman, Karin E. "A Story of Her Weaving: The Self-Authoring Heroines of Georgette Heyer's Regency Romance." In *Doubled Plots: Romance and History*, edited by Susan Strehle and Mary Paniccia Carden, 165–84. Jackson: University Press of Mississippi, 2003.

Chapter 8: Romance Reading as a Social Activity- Michelson

Ahmed, Sara. *The Promise of Happiness*. Durham, NC: Duke University Press, 2010.
Berlant, Lauren. *Cruel Optimism*. Durham, NC: Duke University Press, 2011.
Brackett, Kim Pettigrew. "Facework Strategies among Romance Fiction Readers." *Social Science Journal* 37, no. 3 (July 2000): 347. https://doi.org/10.1016/S0362-3319(00)00073-2.
Bryson, Bethany. "What about the Univores? Musical Dislikes and Group-Based Identity Construction among Americans with Low Levels of Education." *Poetics* 25, no. 2 (November 1, 1997): 141–56. https://doi.org/10.1016/S0304-422X(97)00008-9.
Castell, D. "Up Close and Personal." *Romance Writers Report* 29, no. 4 (2009): 35–36.
Childress, C. Clayton, and Noah E. Friedkin. "Cultural Reception and Production: The Social Construction of Meaning in Book Clubs." *American Sociological Review* 77, no. 1 (2012): 45–68. https://doi.org/10.1177/0003122411428153.
Fletcher, Lisa, Beth Driscoll, and Kim Wilkins. "Genre Worlds and Popular Fiction: The Case of Twenty-First-Century Australian Romance." *The Journal of Popular Culture* 51, no. 4 (2018): 997–1015. https://doi.org/10.1111/jpcu.12706.
Frenier, Mariam Darce. *Good-bye Heathcliff: Changing Heroes, Heroines, Roles, and Values in Women's Category Romances*. New York: Greenwood Press, 1988.
Greenfeld-Benovitz, Miriam. "The Interactive Romance Community: The Case of 'Covers Gone Wild.'" In *New Approaches to Popular Romance Fiction: Critical Essays*, edited by Sarah S. G. Frantz and Eric Murphy Selinger, 195–205. McFarland & Company, Inc, 2012.
Krentz, Jayne Ann. "Why Romance?" *Romantic Times*, no. 72 (February–March 1990): 12–15.
Lois, Jennifer, and Joanna Gregson. "Sneers and Leers: Romance Writers and Gendered Sexual Stigma." *Gender & Society* 29, no. 4 (2015): 459–83. https://doi.org/10.1177/0891243215584603.

Long, Elizabeth. *Book Clubs: Women and the Uses of Reading in Everyday Life*. Chicago: University of Chicago Press, 2003.
López-Sintas, Jordi, and Tally Katz-Gerro. "From Exclusive to Inclusive Elitists and Further: Twenty Years of Omnivorousness and Cultural Diversity in Arts Participation in the USA." *Poetics* 33, no. 5 (October 1, 2005): 299–319. https://doi.org/10.1016/j.poetic.2005.10.004.
Markert, John. *Publishing Romance: The History of an Industry, 1940s to the Present*. McFarland and Company, 2016.
Michelson, Anna. "Redefining the Romance: Classification and Community in a Popular Fiction Genre." PhD diss., Northwestern University, 2022. https://doi.org/10.21985/n2-4tj1-6567.
Michelson, Anna. "The Politics of Happily-Ever-After: Romance Genre Fiction as Aesthetic Public Sphere." *American Journal of Cultural Sociology* 9, no. 2 (June 1, 2021): 177–210. https://doi.org/10.1057/s41290-020-00126-7.
Modleski, Tania. *Loving with a Vengeance: Mass-Produced Fantasies for Women*. 2nd ed. New York: Routledge, 1982.
Moody, Stephanie Lee. "Affecting Genre: Women's Participation with Popular Romance Fiction." PhD diss., University of Michigan, 2013. http://deepblue.lib.umich.edu/handle/2027.42/99818.
Peterson, Richard A., and Roger M. Kern. "Changing Highbrow Taste: From Snob to Omnivore." *American Sociological Review* 61, no. 5 (1996): 900–907. https://doi.org/10.2307/2096460.
Rabine, Leslie W. *Reading the Romantic Heroine: Text, History, Ideology*. Women and Culture Series. Ann Arbor: University of Michigan Press, 1985.
Radway, Janice A. *Reading the Romance: Women, Patriarchy, and Popular Literature*. Chapel Hill: University of North Carolina Press, 1984.
Roach, Catherine M. *Happily Ever After: The Romance Story in Popular Culture*. Bloomington: Indiana University Press, 2016.
Rubin, Gayle. "Thinking Sex: Notes for a Radical Theory for the Politics of Sexuality." In *The Lesbian and Gay Studies Reader*, edited by Henry Abelove, 3rd ed. Routledge, 1993.
"RWR News." *Romance Writers Report* 27, no. 12 (2007): 5.
Thumala Olave, María Angélica. "Reading Matters: Towards a Cultural Sociology of Reading." *American Journal of Cultural Sociology* 6, no. 3 (October 1, 2018): 417–54. https://doi.org/10.1057/s41290-017-0034-x.
Thurston, Carol. *The Romance Revolution: Erotic Novels for Women and the Quest for a New Sexual Identity*. Urbana: University of Illinois Press, 1987.

Chapter 9: Escaping the Negativity of "Escapism": Rethinking Romance Reader Notions of Why They Read—Barra

Adorno, Theodor W. "Culture Industry Reconsidered." *New German Critique* 6 (Autumn 1975): 12–19.
Ang, Ien. *Watching Dallas: Soap Opera and the Melodramatic Imagination*. New York: Routledge, 1985.

Bar-Haim, Gabriel. "Popular Culture and Ideological Discontents: A Theory." *International Journal of Politics, Culture, and Society* 3, no. 3 (Spring 1990): 279–96.

Barra, Andrea. *Beyond the Bodice Ripper: Innovation and Change in the Romance Novel Industry*. PhD diss., Rutgers, The State University of New Jersey-New Brunswick, 2014.

Bolus, Michael Peter. *Aesthetics and the Cinematic Narrative: An Introduction*. New York: Anthem Press, 2019.

Dyhouse, Carol. *Heartthrobs: A History of Women and Desire*. London: Oxford University Press, 2019.

Fowler, Bridget. *The Alienated Reader: Women and Romantic Literature in the Twentieth Century*. London: Harvester Wheatsheaf, 1991.

Fekete, Maleah. "Confluent Love and the Evolution of Ideal Intimacy: Romance Reading in 1980 and 2016." *Journal of Popular Romance Studies* 11 (May 2022): 1–30.

Gelder, Ken. *Popular Fiction: The Logic and Practices of a Literary Field*. New York: Routledge, 2004.

Guilluy, Alice. *'Guilty Pleasures': European Audiences and Contemporary Hollywood Romantic Comedy*. New York: Bloomsbury Academic, 2022.

Gunster, Shane. "Revisiting the Culture Industry Thesis: Mass Culture and the Commodity Form." *Cultural Critique* 45 (Spring 2000): 40–70.

Heilman, Robert B. "Escape and Escapism: Varieties of Literary Experience." *The Sewanee Review* 83, no. 3 (Summer 1975): 439–58.

Hirsch, Walter. "The Image of the Scientist in Science Fiction: A Content Analysis." *The American Journal of Sociology* 63, no. 5 (March 1958): 506–12.

Hirschman, Elizabeth C. "Predictors of Self-Projection, Fantasy Fulfillment, and Escapism." *The Journal of Social Psychology* 120 (June 1983): 63–76.

Katz, Elihu, and David Foulkes. "On the Use of the Mass Media as 'Escape': Clarification of a Concept." *The Public Opinion Quarterly* 26, no. 3 (Autumn 1962): 377–88.

Macpherson, Heidi Slettedahl. *Women's Movement: Escape as Transgression in North American Feminist Fiction*. Atlanta: Editions Rodophi B.V., 2000.

Owen, Mairead. "Reinventing Romance: Reading Popular Romantic Fiction." *Women's Studies International Forum* 20, no. 4 (July–August 1997): 537–46.

Rabkin, Eric S. *The Fantastic in Literature*. Princeton, NJ: Princeton University Press, 1976.

Radway, Janice. *Reading the Romance: Women, Patriarchy, and Popular Literature*. Chapel Hill, NC: University of North Carolina Press, 1984.

Roach, Catherine. *Happily Ever After: The Romance Story in Popular Culture*. Bloomington, IN: Indiana University Press, 2016.

Romance Writers of America. "About the Romance Genre." Last modified 2017. https://www.rwa.org/Online/Romance_Genre/About_Romance_Genre.aspx.

Rogers, Mary F. *Novels, Novelists, and Readers: Toward a Phenomenological Sociology of Literature*. Albany, NY: State University of New York Press, 1991.

Serazio, Michael. *The Power of Sports: Media and Spectacle in American Culture*. New York: NYU Press, 2019.

Span, Madeline. "Caring for the Self: A Case Study on Sociocultural Aspects of Reading Chick Lit." *Journal of Popular Romance Studies* 11 (June 2022): 1–18.
Stougaard-Nielsen, Jakob. "The Locked Room: On Reading Crime Fiction During the Covid-19 Pandemic." In *Lockdown Cultures: The Arts and Humanities in the Year of the Pandemic, 2020–21*, edited by Stella Bruzzi and Maurice Biriotti, 179–87. London: UCL Press, 2022.
Thumala Olave, María Angélica. "Reading Matters: Towards a Cultural Sociology of Reading." American Journal of Cultural Sociology 6, no. 3 (October 2018): 417–54.
Thurston, Carol. *Romance Revolution: Erotic Novels for Women and the Quest for a New Sexual Identity*. Chicago: University of Illinois Press, 1987.
Tuan, Yi-Fu. *Escapism*. Baltimore: The Johns Hopkins University Press, 1998.
Whissell, Cynthia. "The Formula Behind Women's Romantic Formula Fiction." *Arachne* 5, no. 1 (1998): 89–119.

Chapter 10: Love, Romance, Sex, and Happily Ever After: A Feminist Exploration of Women Romance Novel Readers—Kratzer

Alexander, Evie. *150 Romance Novel Tropes*. Evie Alexander, 2023. https://eviealexanderauthor.com/150-romance-novel-tropes/.
Ansley, L. "Townhouse Notes: Let's Talk About Romance Novels." *Perspectives on History* 59 (2021): 3.
Beckett, Laura. "Fifty Shades of White: The Long Fight Against Racism in Romance Novels." *The Guardian*, April 4, 2019. https://www.theguardian.com/books/2019/apr/04/fifty-shades-of-white-romance-novels-racism-ritas-rwa.
Birthisel, Jessica. "Erotic Romance Writing in a Post–*Fifty Shades of Grey* Landscape," in *Communication in Kink: Understanding the Influence of the Fifty Shades of Grey Phenomenon*, ed. J. M. W. Kratzer (Lanham, MD: Lexington Press, 2020), 53–76.
Burnett, H. E. "Shame Game: Romance Novels and Feminist Shame, A Mad Lib for Collective Feeling." *Women & Performance: A Journal of Feminist Theory* 23 (2013): 140–44. https://doi.org/10.1080/0740770X.2013.827374.
Burnett, H. E. "Reading Romance Novels: An Application of Parasocial Relationship Theory." North Dakota Journal of Speech & Theatre 13 (2000): 28–39.
Burnett, E., S. Handel, and J. Summers. "Even as Overall Book Sales Are Declining, Romance Novels Are on the Rise." Radio broadcast. NPR, June 2, 2023. https://www.npr.org/2023/06/02/1179850128/even-as-overall-book-sales-are-declining-romance-novels-are-on-the-rise.
Carson, C. "'People Are at Their Most Vulnerable When They're Naked Together': The Rise of Erotic Romance." *Salon*, January 4, 2014. https://www.salon.com/2014/01/04/people_are_at_their_most_vulnerable_when_theyre_naked_together_the_rise_of_erotic_romance/.
Cranny-Francis, Anne. *Feminist Fiction: Feminist Uses of Generic Fiction*. New York: St. Martin's Press, 1990.

Creswell, John W., and J. David Creswell. *Research Design: Qualitative, Quantitative, and Mixed Methods Approaches.* 6th ed. Thousand Oaks, CA: Sage, 2023.

Curcic, D. "Romance Novel Statistics." *Wordsrated*, October 9, 2022. https://wordsrated.com/romance-novel-sales-statistics/.

Dubino, Jeanne. "The Cinderella Complex: Romantic Fiction, Patriarchy, and Capitalism." *Journal of Popular Culture* 27 (1989): 103–18.

Fisher, M. L., and T. Meredith. "Evolutionary and Sociocultural Themes in Cover Art on Harlequin Romance Novels: A Temporal Analysis." *Evolutionary Behavioral Sciences* 16 (2022): 157–75. https://doi.org/10.1037/ebs0000258.

Ganguly, K. "Alien[ated] Readers: Harlequin Romances and the Politics of Popular Culture. *Communication* 12 (1991): 129–50.

Greer, Germaine. *The Female Eunuch.* New York: McGraw-Hill, 1970.

Holpuch, Amanda. "A Messy Relationship with Romance Novels." *The New York Times*, August 14, 2023. https://www.nytimes.com/2023/08/09/sports/hockey/hockey-romance-booktok-explainer.html.

James, E. L. *Fifty Shades of Grey.* New York: Vintage Books, 2012a.

James, E. L. *Fifty Shades Darker.* New York: Vintage Books, 2012b.

James, E. L. *Fifty Shades Freed.* New York: Vintage Books, 2012c.

James, E. L. *Grey: Fifty Shades of Grey as Told by Christian.* New York: Vintage Books, 2015.

James, E. L. *Darker: Fifty Shades Darker as Told by Christian.* New York: Vintage Books, 2017.

James, E. L. *Freed: Fifty Shades Freed as Told by Christian.* Naperville, IL: Bloom Books, 2021.

Jankowski, S. M. "Mommy Porn for the Suburban Wife." In *Communication in Kink: Understanding the Influence of the Fifty Shades of Grey Phenomenon*, edited by J. M. W. Kratzer, 97–113. Lanham, MD: Lexington Press, 2020.

Kolmes, K., and M. A. Hoffman. "Harlequin Resistance? Romance Novels as a Model for Resisting Objectification." *The Journal of Aesthetics and Art Criticism* 79 (2021): 30–41. https://doi.org/10.1093/jaac/kpaa004.

Kratzer, J. M. W., ed. *Communication in Kink: Understanding the Influence of the Fifty Shades of Grey Phenomenon.* Lanham, MD: Lexington Press, 2020a.

Kratzer, J. M. W. "Kinky People's Perceptions of the Fifty Shades of Grey Trilogy." In *Communication in Kink: Understanding the Influence of the Fifty Shades of Grey Phenomenon*, edited by J. M. W. Kratzer, 9–28. Lanham, MD: Lexington Press, 2020b.

Kratzer, J. M. W. "Kinky Access: Information Provided to Young Adult Kinksters by 'The Next Generation' Groups on Fetlife.com." In *Young Adult Sexuality in the Digital Age*, edited by R. Kalish, 194–209. Hershey, PA: IGI Global, 2020c. https://doi.org/10.4018/978-1-7998-3187-7.ch011.

Lawrey, J. A., A. McLuckie, B. J. Mulberry, E. K. Mullins, A. R. Shuler, and J. M. W. Kratzer. "Communication, Kink, and Sexual Education: What Young Women Learned from Fifty Shades of Grey." In *Communication in Kink: Understanding the Influence of the Fifty Shades of Grey Phenomenon*, edited by J. M. W. Kratzer, 77–96. Lanham, MD: Lexington Press, 2020.

Lindlof, Thomas R., and Brian C. Taylor. *Qualitative Communication Research Methods*. 4th ed. Thousand Oaks, CA: Sage, 2019.

Miles, Matthew B., and A. Michael Huberman. *Qualitative Data Analysis*. Thousand Oaks, CA: Sage, 1994.

Milliot, Jim. "Romance Books Were Hot in 2022." *Publishers Weekly*, January 13, 2023. https://www.publishersweekly.com/pw/by-topic/industry-news/bookselling/article/91298-romance-books-were-hot-in-2022.html.

Murphy, L. *The Ultimate Guide to the Romance Genre and Romance Tropes*. She Reads Romance Books, 2023. https://www.shereadsromancebooks.com/romance-genre-and-romance-tropes-guide/.

Nankervis, Madison. "Diversity in Romance Novels: Race, Sexuality, Neurodivergence, Disability, and Fat Representation." *Publishing Research Quarterly* 38 (2022): 349–63. https://doi.org/10.1007/s12109-022-09881-6.

Noland, Carey. "Self-Help in Kink: A Critical Look at Erotic How-To." In *Communication in Kink: Understanding the Influence of the Fifty Shades of Grey Phenomenon*, edited by J. M. W. Kratzer, 114–31. Lanham, MD: Lexington Press, 2020.

Rabine, Leslie W. *Reading the Romantic Heroine: Text, History, Ideology*. Ann Arbor: University of Michigan Press, 1985.

Radway, Janice A. *Reading the Romance: Women, Patriarchy, and Popular Literature*. Chapel Hill: The University of North Carolina Press, 1991.

Radway, Janice A. "Women Read the Romance: The Interaction of Text and Context." *Feminist Studies* 9, no. 1 (1983): 53–78.

Regis, Pamela. *A Natural History of the Romance Novel*. Philadelphia: University of Pennsylvania Press, 2007.

Roach, C. M. *Happily Ever After: The Romance Story in Popular Culture*. Bloomington: Indiana University Press, 2016.

"Sales of Romance Novels Are Rising in Britain." *The Economist*, March 6, 2023. https://www.economist.com/britain/2023/03/06/sales-of-romance-novels-are-rising-in-britain.

Smith, Dorothy E. *Institutional Ethnography: A Sociology for People*. Lanham, MD: AltaMira Press, 2005.

Smith, Dorothy E. *Writing the Social: Critique, Theory, and Investigations*. Toronto: University of Toronto Press, 1999.

Span, Megan. "Caring for the Self: A Case Study on Sociocultural Aspects of Reading Chick Lit." *Journal of Popular Romance Studies* 11 (2022).

Talbot, David. "Best-Selling Books of All Time." *Wordsrated*, October 11, 2023. https://wordsrated.com/best-selling-books-of-all-time/.

The Ripped Bodice. *The State of Racial Diversity in Romance Publishing Report*. The Ripped Bodice: A Romantic Bookstore, 2020. https://www.therippedbodicela.com/state-racial-diversity-romance-publishing-report.

Weisser, Susan Ostrov. "The Wonderful-Terrible Bitch Figure in Harlequin Novels." In *Feminist Nightmares: Women at Odds*, edited by Susan Ostrov Weisser and Jennifer Fleischner, New York: New York University Press, 1994.

SECTION 3: UNDER THE COVERS: TEXT ANALYSIS

Chapter 11: Coming of Age and Coming Out: The Intersection of New Adult and Queer Romance—Kollman

Amazon.com "Best Romance Books of 2023," https://www.amazon.com/best-romace-2023/b?ie=UTF8&node=17296235011.

Amazon.com "Amazon Best Sellers: Best Sellers in New Adult & College Romance," https://www.amazon.com/Best-Sellers-New-Adult-College-Romance/zgbs/digital-text/6487838011.

Baiocco, Roberto, et al. "Telling My Life: Narratives of Coming Out in LGB People between Certainty/Uncertainty and Revelation/Concealment." *Journal of Gay & Lesbian Mental Health* 27, no. 4 (October 2023): 458–82.

Barot, Len. "Queer Romance in Twentieth- and Twenty-First Century America" In *Romance Fiction and American Culture: Love as the Practice of Freedom?*, edited by William A. Gleason, and Eric Murphy Selinger, eds. Routledge, 2016): 389–404.

Betancourt, Manuel. "A New Novel Reinvents E.M. Forster's Classic Gay Love Story 'Maurice.'" *New York Times.* https://www.nytimes.com/2021/07/06/books/review/alec-william-di-canzio.html.

Black, Jessica E., and Jennifer L. Barnes. "Fiction and Morality: Investigating the Associations Between Reading Exposure, Empathy, Morality, and Moral Judgment." *Psychology of Popular Media* 10, no. 3 (2021): 149–64.

Ermac, Raffy. "Casey McQuiston." *Out.* https://www.out.com/out100/storytellers/casey-mcquiston.

Forster, E. M. *Maurice.* Avarang, 2023.

Forster, E. M. *A Room with a View.* Digireads, 2017. Routledge, 2016.

Guittar, Nicholas A. "'At First I Just Said "I Like Girls"': Coming Out with an Affinity, Not an Identity." *Journal of LGBT Youth* 11 (2014): 388–407.

Harris, Elizabeth A. "'I Just Want Something That's Gay and Happy': L.G.B.T.Q. Romance is Booming." *New York Times.* https://www.nytimes.com/2022/03/30/books/lgbtq-romance- novels.html.

Hoewe, Jennifer, and Lindsey A. Sherrill. "The Influence of Female Lead Characters in Political TV Shows: Links to Political Engagement." *Journal of Broadcasting & Electronic Media* 63, no. 1 (2019): 59–76.

Kollman, Kathleen W. Taylor. "'Getting Bi': Darryl Whitefeather as Bisexual Bellwether." In *Perspectives on Crazy Ex-Girlfriend: Quality Post-Network Television*, edited by Amanda Konkle and Charles Burnetts, Syracuse University Press, 2021.

Larson, Christine, and Ashley Carter. "Love is Love: Reverse Isomorphism and the Rise of LGBTQ+ Romance Publishing." *New Media & Society* (December 2023): preprint, 1–22.

Legate, Nicole, Richard M. Ryan, and Netta Weinstein. "Is Coming Out Always a 'Good Thing'? Exploring the Relations of Autonomy Support, Outness, and

Wellness for Lesbian, Gay, and Bisexual Individuals." *Social Psychological and Personality Science* 3, no. 2 (2012): 145–52.
Matelski, "I'm Not the Only Lesbian Who Wears a Skirt," and Len Barot, "Queer Romance in Twentieth- and Twenty-First Century America," In *Romance Fiction and American Culture: Love as the Practice of Freedom?*, edited by William A. Gleason, and Eric Murphy Selinger, eds. Routledge, 2016): 71–88.
McQuiston, Casey. *Red, White & Royal Blue*. St. Martin's Griffin, 2019.
Radway, Janice A. *Reading the Romance: Women, Patriarchy, and Popular Literature*. Chapel Hill: University of North Carolina Press, 1991.
Regis, Pamela. *A Natural History of the Romance Novel*. University of Pennsylvania Press, 2003.
———. "Ten Years After *A Natural History of the Romance Novel*: Thinking Back, Looking Forward." *Journal of Popular Romance Studies* 3, no. 2 (2013): 1–11.
Sedgwick, Eve Kosofsky. *Epistemology of the Closet*. University of California Press, 1990.
Sharma, Sakshi. "The Male Version of the Manic Pixie Dream Girl Has Arrived. But Is the Bar Too Low?" *Elle India* (blog), May 4, 2022. https://elle.in/male-manic-pixie-dream-girl-arrived/.

Chapter 12: Getting Love Out of the Margins: Race, Disability, and the Idea of a Happy After for Marginalized People—Linares

Allan, Jonathan A. "Gender and Sexuality." In *The Routledge Research Companion to Popular Romance Fiction*, edited by Jayashree Kamblé, Eric Murphy Selinger, and Hsu-Ming Teo, 428–53. New York: Routledge, 2021.
———. *Men, Masculinities, and Popular Romance*. London and New York: Routledge, 2020.
Baldoz, Rick. *The Third Asiatic Invasion: Empire and Migration in Filipino America, 1898–1946*. New York: New York University Press, 2011.
Baldys, Emily M. "Disabled Sexuality, Incorporated: The Compulsions of Popular Romance." *Journal of Literary & Cultural Disability Studies*, vol. 6, no. 2 (2012): 125–41.
Bargiela, Sarah, Robyn Steward, and William Mandy. "The Experiences of Late-Diagnosed Women with Autism Spectrum Conditions: An Investigation of the Female Autism Phenotype." *Journal of Autism and Developmental Disorders*, vol. 46, no. 10 (2016): 3281–94.
Bennett, Jenn. *Grave Phantoms*. New York: Berkley Sensation, 2015.
Chen, Eva Y. I. Chen. "Forms of Pleasure in the Reading of Popular Romance: Psychic and Cultural Dimensions" In *Empowerment versus Oppression: Twenty-First Century Views of Popular Romance Novels*, edited by Sally Goade, 30–41, Newcastle, United Kingdom: Cambridge Scholars Publishing, 2007.
Cheyne, Ria. "Disability Studies Reads the Romance." *Journal of Literary & Cultural Disability Studies*, vol. 7, no. 1 (2013): 37–52.

Conquergood, Dwight. "Performance Studies: Interventions and Radical Research." *TDR: Drama Review* 46, no. 2 (2002): 145–56.

Farrington, Brendan. "Florida sued for restricting Chinese citizens, other foreigners from buying property." The Associated Press. https://apnews.com/article/florida-chinese-citizens-property-law-4aeecc7a9470d03726658f1ef7b1d1f1. Accessed October 18, 2023.

Felicia. "Fans of Interracial Romance Discussion." *Goodreads*. https://www.goodreads.com/topic/show/18070597-lovers-of-black-women-asian-men-books. Accessed October 22, 2023.

Foster, Guy M. "What to do if Your Inner Tomboy is a Homo: Straight Women, Bisexuality, and Pleasure in M/M Gay Romance Fictions." *Journal of Bisexuality*, vol. 15, no. 4 (2015): 509–31.

Gill, Michael C. *Already Doing It: Intellectual Disability and Sexual Agency*. Minneapolis: University of Minnesota Press, 2015.

Hall, Alexis. "FAQ: About Me." *Alexis Hall*. quicunquevult.com/faq/faq-about-me/?Display_FAQ=12085. Accessed 30 Oct. 2023.

———.*Boyfriend Material*. Naperville, IL: Sourcebooks Casablanca, 2020.

———.*Husband Material*. Naperville, IL: Sourcebooks Casablanca, 2022.

Hsu, Madeline Y. "Race and the American Republic." In *Asian American History: A Very Short Introduction*, 25–51. Oxford, United Kingdom: Oxford University Press, 2017. https://doi.org/10.1093/actrade/9780190219765.003.0002

Jackson, Nicole M. "Freedom's Epilogue: Love as Freedom in Alyssa Cole's Historical Novellas." *Journal of Popular Romance Studies* 11, no. 1 (2022): 1–12.

Kamblé, Jayashree. "Female Enfranchisement and the Popular Romance: Employing an Indian Perspective" In *Empowerment versus Oppression: Twenty-First Century Views of Popular Romance Novels*, edited by Sally Goade, 148–71, Newcastle, United Kingdom: Cambridge Scholars Publishing, 2007.

———.*Making Meaning in Popular Romance Fiction: An Epistemology*. New York: Palgrave Macmillan, 2014.

Koch, Bea and Leah Koch. *The Ripped Bodice State of Racial Diversity in Romance 2021*. The Ripped Bodice, 2021. https://www.therippedbodicela.com/state-racial-diversity-romance-publishing-report

Kolawole, Emi. Black women face prejudice every day. I don't need it in online dating, too.: Asian men don't fare well on dating sites, either. WP Company LLC d/b/a The Washington Post, 2015. ProQuest, https://www.proquest.com/blogs-podcasts-websites/black-women-face-prejudice-every-day-i-dont-need/docview/1722816140/se-2.

Krishna, Nakul "Why is so much gay male romance fiction marketed at straight women?" Telegraph.co.uk, Apr 12, 2020. ProQuest, https://www.proquest.com/newspapers/why-is-so-much-gay-male-romance-fiction-marketed/docview/2388653121/se-2.

Liese, Chloe. *Always Only You*. Chloe Liese, 2020.

———.*Ever After Always*. Chloe Liese, 2021.

———.*Everything for You*. Chloe Liese, 2022.

———.*If Only You*. Chloe Liese, 2022.

———.*With You Forever*, 2021.

McCann, Hannah and Catherine M. Roach. "Sex and Sexuality." In *The Routledge Research Companion to Popular Romance Fiction*, edited by Jayashree Kamblé, Eric Murphy Selinger, and Hsu-Ming Teo, 411–27. New York: Routledge, 2021.

Mitchell, David T., and Sharon L. Snyder. "Narrative Prosthesis and the Materiality of Metaphor." In *Narrative Prosthesis: Disability and the Dependencies of Discourse*, 47–64. University of Michigan Press, 2000. http://www.jstor.org/stable/10.3998/mpub.11523.6.

Muñoz, José E. *Cruising Utopia: The Then and There of Queer Futurity*. New York: New York University Press, 2009.

Nankervis, M. "Diversity in Romance Novels: Race, Sexuality, Neurodivergence, Disability, and Fat Representation." *Pub Res Q* 38 (2022): 349–63. https://doi.org/10.1007/s12109-022-09881-6.

Papamarko, Sofi. Why black women and Asian men are at a disadvantage when it comes to online dating. ProQuest, Mar 21, 2017, https://www.proquest.com/blogs-podcasts-websites/why-black-women-asian-men-are-at-disadvantage/docview/1879536737/se-2.

Parreñas, Rhacel Salazar. "'White Trash' Meets the 'Little Brown Monkeys': The Taxi Dance Hall as a Site of Interracial and Gender Alliances between White Working Class Women and Filipino Immigrant Men in the 1920s and 30s." *Amerasia Journal* 24, no. 2 (1998): 115–34.

Piterman, Ashra. "Autistic Women and Masking: The Road to Closing the Gender-Based Gap in Autism Spectrum Disorder Diagnoses." ProQuest Dissertations Publishing, 2022.

Powers, Ráchael A., Kacy Bleeker, and Crystal Alcalde. "Anti-Asian Hate Crime in U.S. National News: A Content Analysis of Coverage and Narratives from 2010–2021." *Race and Justice* 13, no. 1 (2023): 32–54.

Radway, Janice A. *Reading the Romance: Women, Patriarchy, and Popular Literature*. Chapel Hill: University of North Carolina Press, 1991.

Rainey, Sarah Smith. *Love, Sex, and Disability: The Pleasures of Care*. Boulder: Lynne Rienner Publishers, 2011.

Rawitsch, Mark Howland, and Lane Ryo Hirabayashi. "Keep California White." In *The House on Lemon Street: Japanese Pioneers and the American Dream*. Denver: University Press of Colorado (2012): 129–46.

Schug, Joanna, et al. "Gendered Race in Mass Media: Invisibility of Asian Men and Black Women in Popular Magazines. *Psychology of Popular Media Culture* 6, no. 3 (2017): 222–36.

Schwab, Sandra. "'It Is Only with One's Heart That One Can See Clearly': The Loss of Sight in Teresa Medeiros's the Bride and the Beast and Yours Until Dawn." *Journal of Literary & Cultural Disability Studies* 6, no. 3 (2012): 275–89.

Selinger, Eric Murphy. "Rereading the Romance." *Contemporary Literature* 48, no. 2 (2007): 307–24.

Shah, Nayan. *Contagious Divides: Epidemics and Race in San Francisco's Chinatown*. 1st ed. Vol. 7. Berkeley: University of California Press, 2001. doi:10.2307/j.ctv1gwqmp3.

Shimizu, Celine Parreñas. *Straitjacket Sexualities Unbinding Asian American Manhoods in the Movies*. Stanford Stanford University Press, 2012.
Sohoni, Deenesh. "Unsuitable Suitors: Anti-Miscegenation Laws, Naturalization Laws, and the Construction of Asian Identities." *Law & Society Review* 41, no. 3 (2007): 587–618.
Thomas, Heather. "Before Brown v. Board of Education, There Was Tape V. Hurley: Headlines & Heroes." *The Library of Congress*, 5 May 2021, blogs.loc.gov/headlinesandheroes/2021/05/before-brown-v-education-there-was-tape-v- hurley/.
Wallenstein, Peter. *Tell the Court I Love My Wife: Race, Marriage, and Law—An American History*. New York: Palgrave Macmillan, 2002.
Wang, Katarina, Alice Guan, Janice Seto, Debora L. Oh, Kathie Lau, Christine Duffy, Esperanza Castillo, et al. "Asian American Women's Experiences of Discrimination and Health Behaviors during the COVID-19 Pandemic." *Journal of Immigrant and Minority Health* 26, no. 2 (2024): 421–25.
Whalen, Kacey. "A Consumption of Gay Men: Navigating the Shifting Boundaries of M/M Romantic Readership," master's thesis, DePaul University, 2017.
Whitlock, Alana, et al. "Recognition of Girls on the Autism Spectrum by Primary School Educators: An Experimental Study." *Autism Research*, vol. 13, no. 8 (2020): 1358–72.
Yam, Kimmy. "Anti-Asian hate crimes increased 339 percent nationwide last year, report says," January 31, 2022. https://www.nbcnews.com/news/asian-america/anti-asian-hate-crimes-increased-339-percent-nationwide-last-year-repo-rcna14282. Accessed October 22, 2023.
Yang, Chunyan. "Influences of Prepandemic Bullying Victimization and COVID-19 Peer Discrimination on Chinese American Adolescents' Mental Health during the COVID-19 Pandemic." *School Psychology* 39, no. 1 (2024): 20–30.
Young, Erin S. "Race, Ethnicity, and Whiteness." In *The Routledge Research Companion to Popular Romance Fiction*, edited by Jayashree Kamblé, Eric Murphy Selinger, and Hsu-Ming Teo, 511–28, Abingdon, Oxon; New York, NY: Routledge, 2021.
Yung, Judy. "Mary Tape, an Outspoken Woman: 'Is It a Disgrace to Be Born a Chinese?'" *Unbound Voices: A Documentary History of Chinese Women in San Francisco*, 1st ed. Oakland: University of California Press (1999): 171–76. JSTOR, https://doi.org/10.2307/jj.5973065.20.

Chapter 13: Retellings and Re-readings- Romance, Representation, and Reimaginations in *Self-Made Boys: A Great Gatsby Remix*—Babu

Anderson, Jill, et al. "Queer ecology: A roundtable discussion." *European Journal of Ecopsychology* 3, no. 1 (2012): 82–103.
Bittner, Robert, et al. "Queer and Trans-Themed Books for Young Readers: A Critical Review." *Discourse: Studies in the Cultural Politics of Education* 37, no. 6 (June 2, 2016): 948–64. https://doi.org/10.1080/01596306.2016.1195106.

Browne, Katelyn R. "Reimagining Queer Death in Young Adult Fiction," *Research on Diversity in Youth Literature* 2, no. 2, article 3. Available at: https://sophia.stkate.edu/rdyl/vol2/iss2/3.
Cole, Alayna. "Smashing the Heteropatriarchy: Representations of Queerness in Reimagined Fairy Tales." *Text* 22, no. 2 (October 29, 2018). https://doi.org/10.52086/001c.25181. Accessed July 9, 2021.
Kaufmann, Jodi. "Trans-Representation." *Qualitative Inquiry* 16, no. 2 (October 30, 2009): 104–15. https://doi.org/10.1177/1077800409350699.
McLemore, Anna-Marie. *Self-Made Boys: A Great Gatsby Remix*. Feiwel & Friends, September 6, 2022.
Sandilands, Catriona. "A Very Queer Nature: On Queer Ecologies, Gardens, and Flourishing Multispecies Practices." Sydney Environment Institute, January 1, 2018. www.academia.edu/49663781/A_Very_Queer_Nature_On_Queer_Ecologies_Gardens_and_Flourishing_Multispecies_Practices. Accessed April 22, 2023.

Chapter 14: Mr. Darcy as the Perfect Book Boyfriend— Schulmann-Darsy

A&E Television. "Behind the Scenes: Colin Firth as Mr. Darcy." Interview, July 20, 1997. http://www.aetv.com/scenes/pride/pride3b.html.
Austen, Jane. *Pride and Prejudice*. Edited by Robert P. Irvine. Peterborough, Ontario, Canada: Broadview Press, 2020.
Berdoll, Linda. *Mr. Darcy Takes a Wife*. Naperville, IL: Sourcebooks Landmark, 2020.
Blogger, Leslie. "The Best Book Boyfriends of 2022: Romance Heroes to Fall for This Year." *She Reads Romance Books*, January 18, 2023. https://www.shereadsromancebooks.com/book-boyfriends-2022/.
Blogger, Lizz. "Obsession Runs Deep; or, What Is a Book Boyfriend?" *Lizz in Bookland*, February 8, 2016. http://www.lizzinbookland.com/2016/02/obsession-runs-deep-or-what-is-book.html.
Clasen, Tricia. "Masculinity and Romantic Myth in Contemporary YA Romance." In *Gender(ed) Identities: Critical Rereadings of Gender in Children's and Young Adult Literature*, edited by Holly Hassel and Tricia Clasen, 228–41. New York, NY: Routledge, 2017.
Curcic, Dimitrije. "Romance Novel Sales Statistics." *WordsRated*, October 9, 2022. https://wordsrated.com/romance-novel-sales-statistics/.
Driscoll, Catherine. "One True Pairing: The Romance of Pornography and the Pornography of Romance." In *Fan Fiction and Fan Communities in the Age of the Internet: New Essays*, edited by Karen Hellekson and Kristina Busse, 79–96. Jefferson, NC: McFarland & Co., 2006.
Emsley, Sarah. "Why Has Mr. Darcy Been Attractive to Generations of Women?" *Literary Ladies Guide*, January 20, 2014. https://www.literaryladiesguide.com/literary-musings/why-is-mr-darcy-so-attractive/.
Gomez, Ronnie. "Breaking Down BookTok: What Brands Can Learn from This Social Literary Phenomenon." *Sprout Social*, July 26, 2022. https://sproutsocial.com/insights/BookTok/.

Hanssen, Sarah K. "New Tools for the Immersive Narrative Experience." *International Journal of Emerging Technologies in Learning (iJET)* 14, no. 16 (August 29, 2019): 40–54. https://doi.org/10.3991/ijet.v14i16.10591.

Hart, Staci. *Pride & Papercuts: Inspired by Jane Austen's Pride and Prejudice*. New York, NY: Independently published, 2020.

Hills, Matt. *Fan Cultures*. 1st ed. London, England: Routledge, 2002.

Hopkins, Lisa. "Mr. Darcy's Body: Privileging the Female Gaze." In *Jane Austen in Hollywood*, edited by Sayre N. Greenfield and Linda Troost, 111–21. Lexington: University Press of Kentucky, 2010.

Johanson, Katya, Amy Schoonens, Bronwyn Reddan, Leonie Rutherford, and Michael Dezuanni. "What Is BookTok, and How Is It Influencing What Australian Teenagers Read?" *The Conversation*, May 9, 2022. https://theconversation.com/what-is-booktok-and-how-is-it-influencing-what-australian-teenagers-read-182290.

Kaplan, Deborah. "Mass Marketing Jane Austen: Men, Women, and Courtship in Two Film Adaptations." In *Jane Austen in Hollywood*, edited by Sayre N. Greenfield and Linda Troost, 177–87. Lexington: University Press of Kentucky, 2010.

Kerns, Hannah. "Here's Why the 'Pride & Prejudice' Hand Flex Makes You Feel Things." *Elite Daily*, March 3, 2022. https://www.elitedaily.com/dating/pride-prejudice-hand-flex-tiktok.

Licherfeld, Imke. "Mr. Darcy's Shirt—An Icon of Popular Culture." In *Pride and Prejudice 2.0: Interpretations, Adaptations and Transformations of Jane Austen's Classic*, edited by Hanne Birk and Marion Gymnich, 189–203. Göttingen, Germany: Vandenhoeck & Ruprecht, 2015.

Maas, Sarah J. *A Court of Mist and Fury*. Bloomsbury, 2016.

———. *A Court of Silver Flames*. Bloomsbury, 2021.

———. *A Court of Thorns and Roses*. Bloomsbury, 2015.

Meyer, Silke. "'Spank Me Mr. Darcy': Pride and Prejudice in Contemporary Female (Hardcore) Erotica." In *Pride and Prejudice 2.0: Interpretations, Adaptations and Transformations of Jane Austen's Classic*, edited by Hanne Birk and Marion Gymnich, 261–73. Göttingen, Germany: Vandenhoeck & Ruprecht, 2015.

Nixon, Cheryl L. "Balancing the Courtship Hero: Masculine Emotional Display in Film Adaptations of Austen's Novels." In *Jane Austen in Hollywood*, edited by Sayre N. Greenfield and Linda Troost, 22–43. Lexington, KY: University Press of Kentucky, 2010.

Ormiston, Lara S., and Devleena Ghosh. *Unequal Affections: A Pride & Prejudice Retelling*. New York, NY: Skyhorse Publishing, 2017.

Perry, Nicole. "Mr. Darcy: Literature's Romantic Hero or a Model for Unrealistic Expectations?" *The Sophian*, April 12, 2021. https://thesophian.com/mr-darcy-literatures-romantic-hero-or-a-model-for-unrealistic-expectations/.

Radway, Janice. "The Ideal Romance: The Promise of Patriarchy." In *Reading the Romance: Women, Patriarchy, and Popular Literature*, 119–56. Chapel Hill, NC: University of North Carolina Press, 2006. Originally published in 1991.

———. "The Institutional Matrix: Publishing Romantic Fiction." In *Reading the Romance: Women, Patriarchy, and Popular Literature*, 19–45. Chapel Hill, NC: University of North Carolina Press, 2006. Originally published in 1991.

Regis, Pamela. *A Natural History of the Romance Novel.* Philadelphia, PA: University of Pennsylvania Press, 2007.

Rohwer-Happe, Gislind. "The Mr. Darcy Complex—The Impact of a Literary Icon on Contemporary Chick Lit." In *Pride and Prejudice 2.0: Interpretations, Adaptations and Transformations of Jane Austen's Classic,* edited by Hanne Birk and Marion Gymnich, 207–25. Göttingen, Germany: Vandenhoeck & Ruprecht, 2015.

Rosenblatt, Betsy, and Rebecca Tushnet. "Transformative Works: Young Women's Voices on Fandom and Fair Use." In *eGirls, eCitizens: Putting Technology, Theory and Policy into Dialogue with Girls' and Young Women's Voices,* edited by Jane Bailey and Valerie Steeves, 385–410. Ottawa, Canada: University of Ottawa Press, 2015.

Sanderson, David. "Tiktok Rekindles Passion for Romance Novels." *The Times & The Sunday Times,* March 10, 2023. https://www.thetimes.co.uk/article/tiktok-romantic-fiction-booktok-publishing-0nhs0klkh.

Sittenfeld, Curtis. *Eligible: A Modern Retelling of Pride and Prejudice.* New York, NY: Random House, Inc., 2017.

Smith, Josefine, and Kathleen W. Taylor Kollman. *Still Reading Romance Survey.* Philadelphia, PA: Shippensburg University, 2022.

Stoneman, Patsy. "Rochester and Heathcliff as Romantic Heroes." *Brontë Studies* 36, no. 1 (July 2011): 111–18. https://doi.org/10.1179/147489310x12868722453744.

Talbot, Dean. "Author Demographics Statistics." *Words Rated,* February 8, 2023. https://wordsrated.com/author-demographics-statistics/.

Voiret, Martine. "Books to Movies: Gender and Desire in Jane Austen's Adaptations." In *Jane Austen and Co.: Remaking the Past in Contemporary Culture,* edited by Suzanne Rodin Pucci and James Thompson, 229–46. Albany, NY: State University of New York Press, 2003.

Wright, Joe, director. *Pride & Prejudice.* Focus Features. 2005.

Chapter 15: Reading Romance and Erotic Literacy—Partin and Smith

Allan, Jonathan A. *Men, Masculinities, and Popular Romance.* 1st ed. New York: Routledge, 2019. https://doi.org/10.4324/9781351240024.

Arnold, Judith. "Women do." In *Dangerous Men and Adventurous Women: Romance Writers on the Appeal of the Romance,* edited by Jayne Ann Krentz, University of Pennsylvania Press, 1992, 133–39.

Barker-Plummer, Bernadette, and David Barker-Plummer. "Twitter as a Feminist Resource: #YESALLWOMEN, Digital Platforms, and Discursive Social Change." In *Social Movements and Media,* edited by Jennifer S. Earl and Deana A. Rohlinger. Emerald Publishing Limited, 2017. ProQuest Ebook Central. https://ebookcentral.proquest.com/lib/ksu/detail.action?docID=5018384.

Berlant, Lauren, and Michael Warner. "Sex in Public." *Critical Inquiry* 24, no. 2 (1998): 547–66. Cruger, Katherine. "Men Are Stronger; Women Endure: A Critical Analysis of the *Throne of Glass* and *The Mortal Instruments* YA Fantasy Series." *Journal of Media Critiques* 3, no. 10 (2017): 115–32. https://doi.org/10.17349/Jmc117208.

Duffett, Mark. *Understanding Fandom: An Introduction to the Study of Media Fan Culture*. Bloomsbury Publishing USA, 2013.
Easton, Dossie, and Janet W. Hardy. *Radical Ecstasy: S/M Journeys in Transcendence*. Oakland, Calif: Greenery Press, 2004.
Eisler, Riane. *Sacred Pleasure: Sex, Myth, and the Politics of the Body*. HarperCollins, 1996.
Friday, Nancy. *Women on Top: How Real Life Has Changed Women's Sexual Fantasies*. Pocket Books, 1991.
Grady, Constance. "Why Half the People You Know Are Obsessed With This Book Series." *Vox*, February 27, 2024. https://www.vox.com/culture/24084037/sarah-j-maas-a-court-of-thorns-and-roses-acotar-romantasy.
Halberstam, Jack. *Female Masculinity*. Duke University Press, 1998.
Halberstam, Jack. *The Queer Art of Failure*. Duke University Press, 2011.
Hellekson, Karen, and Kristina Busse, eds. *Fan Fiction and Fan Communities in the Age of the Internet: New Essays*. McFarland, 2006.
Koedt, Anne. "The Myth of the Vaginal Orgasm." In *Living with Contradictions*, 481–87. Routledge, 2018.
Little, Elizabeth, and Kristine Moruzi. "Postfeminism and Sexuality in the Fiction of Sarah J. Maas." In *Sexuality in Literature for Children and Young Adults*, 81–95. Routledge, 2021.
Lorde, Audre. "Uses of the Erotic." In *The Selected Works of Audre Lorde*. WW Norton & Company, 2020.
Maas, Sarah J. *A Court of Mist and Fury*. Bloomsbury, 2016.
———. *A Court of Silver Flames*. Bloomsbury, 2021.
———. *A Court of Thorns and Roses*. Bloomsbury, 2015.
McAlister, Jodi. "Erotic Romance." In *The Routledge Research Companion to Popular Romance Fiction*, edited by Jayashree Kamblé, Eric Murphy Selinger, and Hsu-Ming Teo, 212–28. Routledge, 2020.
McCann, Hannah, and Catherine M. Roach. "Sex and Sexuality." In *The Routledge Research Companion to Popular Romance Fiction*, edited by Jayashree Kamblé, Eric Murphy Selinger, and Hsu-Ming Teo, 416–32. Routledge, 2020.
Middleton, DeWight R. *Exotics and Erotics: Human Cultural and Sexual Diversity*. Waveland Press, 2002.
Mintz, Laurie B. *Becoming Cliterate: Why Orgasm Equality Matters—and How to Get It*. HarperOne, 2017.
Moi, Toril. *Sexual/Textual Politics: Feminist Literary Theory*. 2nd ed. Routledge, 2002.
Mulvey, Laura. "Visual Pleasure and Narrative Cinema." *Screen* 16, no. 3 (1975): 6–18.
Orlando, Christina. "'Lots Of Cursing And Sex': Authors Laurell K. Hamilton And Sarah J. Maas On Pleasure & Violence in Paranormal Romance." Tor, October 5, 2019. https://www.tor.com/2019/10/05/lots-of-cursing-and-sex-authors-laurell-k-hamilton-and-sarah-j-maas-on-pleasure-violence-in-paranormal-romance/. Accessed September 30, 2022.
Oxford English Dictionary (OED). "Pornography." n.d. In *OED.com*. Retrieved December 18, 2022, from https://www.oed.com/dictionary/pornography.

"Porn." Reddit (r/acotar). https://www.reddit.com/r/acotar/search/?q=porn&restrict_sr=1.

Radway, Janice A. *Reading the Romance: Women, Patriarchy, and Popular Literature*. 2nd ed. University of North Carolina Press, 1991.

Roach, Catherine M. *Happily Ever After: The Romance Story in Popular Culture*. Indiana University Press, 2016.

Srinivasan, Amia. *The Right to Sex: Feminism in the Twenty-First Century*. Macmillan, 2021.

Steckbeck, Jane. "Sparking Your Erotic Imagination." *Jane Steckbeck*, November 1, 2019. https://www.janesteckbeck.com/post/sparking-your-erotic-imagination. Accessed March 1, 2023.

Stiritz, Susan Ekberg. "Cultural Cliteracy: Exposing the Contexts of Women's Not Coming." Berkeley Journal of Gender, Law & Justice 23, no. 2 (2008): 243–66.

Stoltenberg, John. *Refusing to be a man: Essays on social justice*. Routledge, 2005.

"The 2022 Year in Review." *PornHub*, December 8, 2022. https://www.pornhub.com/insights/2022-year-in-review. Accessed March 10, 2023.

u/lafornarinas. Comment on "Sex scenes in romance books." *Reddit*, October 28, 2022, 4:18 p.m. https://www.reddit.com/r/RomanceBooks/comments/yfk4ty/sex_scenes_in_romance_boo ks/.

Ward, Jane. *The tragedy of heterosexuality*. Vol. 56. NYU Press, 2022.

White, Hilary. "Badass Women and Ridiculously Sexy Romance? Yep, These Books Have It All." *PopSugar*. August 26, 2016. https://www.popsugar.com/love/sarah-j-maas-interview-41262845.

Zachary, Anne. *The Anatomy of the Clitoris: Reflections on the Theory of Female Sexuality*. Routledge, 2018.

Appendix A
Demographic results

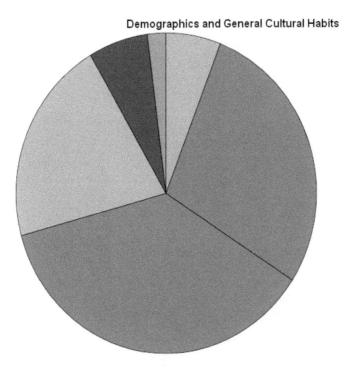

Figure A.1 Age

350 Appendix A

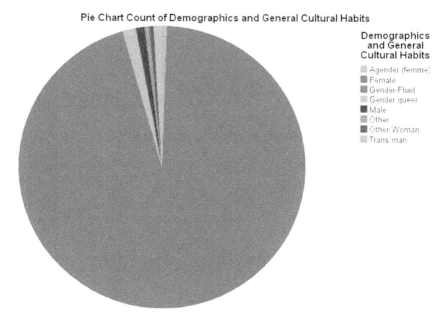

Figure A.2   Gender

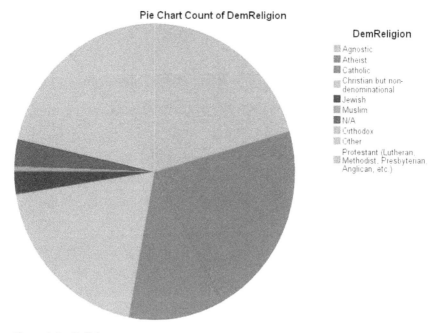

Figure A.3   Religion

Appendix A

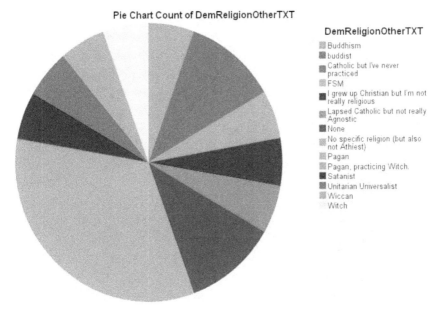

Figure A.4   Religion-other

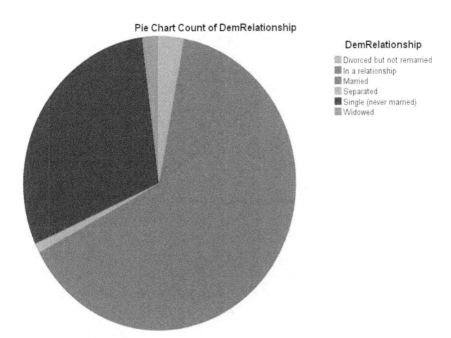

Figure A.5   Relationship Status

352 *Appendix A*

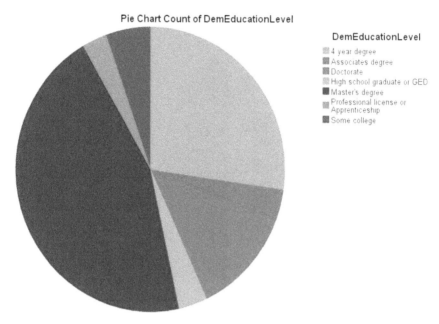

Figure A.6 Education

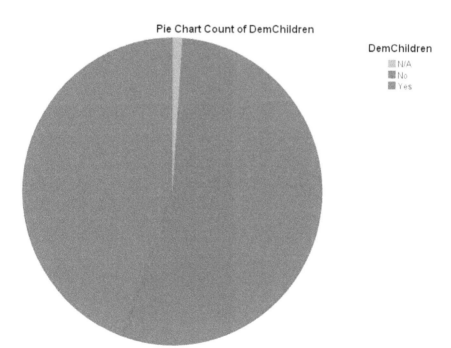

Figure A.7 Children

Appendix A

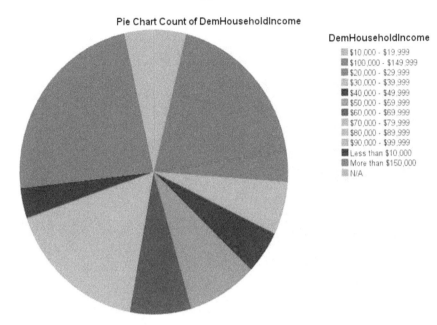

Figure A.8 Socioeconomic Status

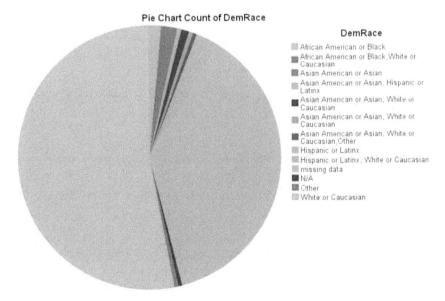

Figure A.9 Race

354 Appendix A

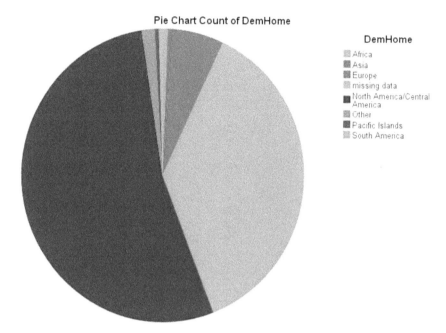

Figure A.10 Location

Appendix B

Survey

IRB

INTRODUCTION

This is an informed consent form to outline what it means to participate in a research project being carried out by the primary researchers, Josefine Smith and Kathleen Kollman. In this study, we explore how romance readers think and feel about romance novels and how those stories affect the reader's life. The following questions will ask you about your personal attitudes and opinions about the romance books you read.

BENEFITS TO TAKING PART IN THE STUDY

Our ideas of what it means to be a woman are shaped by cultural definitions and images of women. With this study, I hope to understand how the romance novels you read affects you and how you think about being a woman in the 21st century. By investigating those relationships, women can be both more aware of the cultural definition of womanhood we are faced with and recognize how cultural definitions of womanhood have changed.

CONFIDENTIALITY

Results will be safeguarded based on the collection method. We will take the following steps to keep participants information confidential, and to protect it from unauthorized disclosure, tampering, or damage:

1. Only the primary researcher, Josefine Smith, will have access to the raw data and records through a password-protected account on Qualtrics.

Hard copies of notes from surveys and demographic information will be kept in a filing cabinet in a locked office. Electronic files will be stored on a network and password-protected by a security login. Laptop computers used to access or store data files will have an automatic log-out feature after five minutes of inactivity

2. Web-based participation will not collect IP addresses to safeguard participants' anonymity and confidentiality. The data will be described in comparison to other data points or through statistical interpretations if published or shared with others. The data will be aggregated into one data collection and demographic information will be linked to survey data using a coded system. At no point during the study will personally identifying information (names, birth dates, or addresses) be collected. As the data collected will not be sensitive or include identifying information, and it will not be encrypted.

RISKS

There are no direct risks associated with this study. There may be risks that cannot be predicted. There are some questions on the survey that mention rape and other traumatic events, and may bring up thoughts or memories that that could cause distress. Individuals experiencing distress from participation in this study are encouraged to contact the following organizations for support:

RAINN (Rape, Abuse & Incest National Network)

- Rainn.org: The nation's largest anti-sexual violence organization.
- National Sexual Assault Hotline (800) 656-HOPE (4673): The National Sexual Assault Hotline is a safe, confidential service staffed by local sexual assault service providers. For more information, see their about page: https://www.rainn.org/about-national-sexual-assault-telephone-hotline.
- Online Hotline (https://hotline.rainn.org): RAINN has taken extensive measures to ensure that your Online Hotline interaction is safe and confidential. You'll never be asked for personally identifying details, like your name, age, or location. To ensure your safety, RAINN has partnered with the country's top technology and online security companies to build a hotline that is as safe and secure as current technology allows.

SAMHSA'S (Substance Abuse and Mental Health Services Administration)

- National Helpline/Treatment Referral Routing Service (1-800-662-HELP (4357) or TTY 1-800-487-4889): A confidential, free, 24-hour-a-day,

365-day-a-year, information service, in English and Spanish, for individuals facing mental and/or substance use disorders.

RIGHTS AS A RESEARCH PARTICIPANT

Participation in this study is voluntary. You have the right to stop participation, or leave the study, at any time. Participants may choose not to answer any particular question(s) that they do not feel comfortable answering for surveys or focus groups. Deciding not to participate or choosing to leave the study will not result in any penalty or loss of benefits to which you are entitled. If you wish to withdraw from the study, let the primary investigator (Josefine Smith) know and your responses will be removed from the pool.

CONTACT FOR QUESTIONS OR PROBLEMS

Contact Josefine Smith (717-477-1634, jmsmith@ship.edu) if you have questions about the study. Contact Shippensburg University's IRB committee, Committee on Research with Human Subjects (irb@ship.edu), or IRB/Human Subjects Chairperson Dr. Todd Whitman via email (tkwhit@ship.edu) or phone (717.477.1654) with any problems, unexpected physical or psychological discomforts, or think that something unusual or unexpected is happening.

I acknowledge that I am at least 18 years old, and that I understand my rights as a research participant as outlined in the consent form. I acknowledge that my participation is voluntary.

Upon signing, the subject or the legally authorized representative can retain a copy of this form the subject's research record.

○ I agree
○ I disagree

READING HABITS

At what age did you first begin reading for pleasure?

○ 5–10 years
○ 11–20 years
○ 21–30 years
○ 31 or above

Which of the following was your most favorite kind of book as a teenager?

○ Biography
○ Historical fiction other than romance
○ Westerns
○ Historical romances
○ Contemporary romances
○ Mysteries
○ Science fiction
○ Comic books
○ Fantasy
○ None. I didn't read for pleasure.
○ ☐ Other

At what age did you first begin reading romances regularly?

○ Under 10
○ 10–14 years
○ 15–19 years
○ 20–24 years
○ 25–29 years
○ 30–39 years
○ 40 or older

How many romances do you read each month?

○ 1–4
○ 5–9
○ 10–14
○ 15–19
○ 20–24
○ 25 or more

About how many books other than romances do you read each month?

○ None
○ 1–4
○ 5–9
○ 10–14
○ 15–19
○ 20–24
○ 25 or more

How often do you discuss romances with others?

○ Never
○ Rarely
○ Sometimes
○ Often
○ Always

Who do you discuss romances with most often?

○ My mother
○ My daughter
○ My sister
○ My friend(s)
○ Social media community
○ [   ] Other

Where do you get most of the romances you read?

○ In-store purchase
○ Online merchant (Amazon, Barnes & Noble, Google Books)
○ Author website/Author Direct
○ Library
○ Fan fiction Website
○ Borrow from a friend or relative
○ [   ] Other

Which of the following kinds of romances do you read? Here you may check as many as you like.

☐ Contemporary mystery romances
☐ Historical romance
☐ Contemporary romances
☐ New Adult romance
☐ Erotica
☐ Family sagas
☐ Supernatural romance
☐ Queer/LGBTQ romance
☐ Spy/thriller
☐ [   ] Other

Which of the following best describes what usually makes you decide to read a romance or not?

○ I like the cover.
○ I have already read something by the author and liked it.
○ I like the title.
○ The book description (publisher's blurb or back of the book) sounds interesting.
○ Someone else recommended it to me.
○ [   ] Other

ROMANCE FICTION

What are the three most important ingredients in a romance? Please rank the top three with 1 being the most important quality.

☐ A happy ending
☐ Well-developed emotional intimacy between the heroine and hero
☐ A long conflict between the hero and heroine
☐ Punishment of the villain
☐ A slowly but consistently developing love between hero and heroine
☐ A setting in a particular historical period (Romances should be Regencies, Edwardians, about the Civil War, etc.)
☐ Lots of love scenes with explicit sexual description
☐ Lots of love scenes with little or no explicit sexual description
☐ Some detail about the heroine and hero after they have finally gotten together (ex: epilogue)
☐ A specific kind of hero and heroine (Romance heroes/heroine should have certain characteristics all the time). Please describe. [   ]
☐ Other [   ]

Which of the following do you feel should never be included in a romance? Please rank the top three with 1 being the most distasteful quality.

☐ Rape
☐ Explicit sex
☐ Sad ending
☐ Physical torture of the heroine or the hero

Appendix B

- [ ] An ordinary heroine
- [ ] Bed-hopping
- [ ] Adultery
- [ ] A cruel hero
- [ ] A weak hero
- [ ] A cruel heroine
- [ ] A weak heroine
- [ ] A hero who is stronger than the heroine
- [ ] A heroine who is stronger than the hero

What qualities or characteristics do you like to see in a heroine? Please rank the top three with 1 being the most desirable quality.

- [ ] Intelligence
- [ ] Independence
- [ ] Beauty
- [ ] A sense of humor
- [ ] Assertiveness
- [ ] Femininity
- [ ] Aggressiveness
- [ ] Sexual inexperience
- [ ] Other _____

What qualities or characteristics do you like to see in a hero? Please rank the top three with 1 being the most desirable quality.

- [ ] Intelligence
- [ ] Tenderness
- [ ] Protectiveness
- [ ] Strength
- [ ] Bravery
- [ ] A sense of humor
- [ ] Independence
- [ ] Attractiveness
- [ ] Other _____

How closely do you think the characters in romances resemble the people you meet in real life?

○ A great deal
○ A lot
○ A moderate amount
○ A little
○ Not at all

How closely do you think the events in romances resemble events that occur in real life?

○ A great deal
○ A lot
○ A moderate amount
○ A little
○ Not at all

Does the romantic heroine's reactions and feelings toward people and events resemble your own?

○ A great deal
○ A lot
○ A moderate amount
○ A little
○ Not at all
○ Not Applicable

How closely do you feel that the romantic hero's emotional responses to the heroine resemble your partner's emotional response?

○ A great deal
○ A lot
○ A moderate amount
○ A little
○ Not at all
○ Not Applicable

Which of the following best describes your attitude to the way the stories are told?

○ I like stories to be told by the heroine, in first person. (For example, "I couldn't believe my eyes, there was the most arrogant man I had ever seen.")
○ I dislike stories that are told by the heroine, in first person, but I will read them sometimes. My favorites give the point of view of both the heroine and hero.
○ I prefer to read romance novels that give the point of view of both the heroine and hero.
○ I have no preference whether the story is told by the heroine or by a narrator who gives the point of view of both the heroine and the hero.

Which of the following reasons best describe why you read romances? Please rank the top three with 1 being the most important reason.

☐ To escape my daily problems.
☐ To experience faraway places, different times, or experiences different then my own.
☐ For simple relaxation.
☐ Because I wish I had a romance like the heroine's.
☐ Because reading is just for me. It is my time.
☐ Because I like to read about the strong, interesting heroines.
☐ Because romantic stories are never sad or depressing.
☐ Other (please describe) ⬚

NEW ADULT FICTION

Are you familiar with the romance subgenre New Adult?

○ Yes
○ No

Describe the difference between New Adult Romance and other romance fiction.

About how many New Adult romances do you read each month?

○ None
○ 1–2
○ 3–4
○ 5–6
○ 7 or more
○ Click to write Choice 6

Which of the following best describes what usually makes you decide to read a New Adult romance or not?

○ I like the cover.
○ I have already read something by the author and liked it.
○ I like the title.
○ The book description (publisher's blurb or back of the book) sounds interesting.
○ Someone recommended it to me.
○ [   ] Other

Which of the following coming of age storylines in New Adult romances do you read? Check as many as you like.

☐ Senior year of high school/ going to college
☐ Like a moderate amount
☐ Graduating college First professional job
☐ [   ] Other

Which of the following tropes are your favorite in New Adult romance?

○ Sports Romance
○ Unlikely romance (nerd-popular, wrong side of the tracks, etc.)
○ Student-teacher
○ Workplace romance
○ [   ] Other

Please rank the importance of the following ingredients in a New Adult romances.

    Settings/events that support the heroine's coming of age (new school, new job, graduating college, moving)
    The heroine goes through a coming of age process
    A long conflict between the hero and heroine
    Punishment of the villain
    Lots of scenes of explicit sexual description
    First mature romantic relationship for the heroine
    Some detail about the heroine and hero after they have finally gotten together
    Strong supporting characters
    Challenging relationships with authority (parents, teachers, boss, etc.)
    Other ▢

Which of the following do you feel should never be included in a New Adult romance? Please rank the top three with 1 being the most distasteful element.

- ▢ Rape
- ▢ Explicit sex
- ▢ Sad ending
- ▢ Physical torture of the heroine or the hero
- ▢ An ordinary heroine
- ▢ Bed-hopping
- ▢ Adultery
- ▢ A cruel hero
- ▢ A cruel heroine
- ▢ A weak hero
- ▢ A weak heroine
- ▢ A hero who is stronger than the heroine
- ▢ A heroine who is stronger than the hero

What qualities or characteristics do you like to see in a New Adult heroine? Please rank the top three with 1 being the most desirable quality.

- ▢ A sense of humor
- ▢ Assertive
- ▢ Beauty
- ▢ Bravery

☐ Feminist
☐ Independence
☐ Innocence
☐ Intelligence
☐ Kindness
☐ Strength
☐ Other [   ]

How important are the following qualities or characteristics for a New Adult hero? Please rank the top three with 1 being the most desirable quality.

☐ A sense of humor
☐ Attractiveness
☐ Bravery
☐ Intelligence
☐ Kindness
☐ Protectiveness
☐ Strength
☐ Socially conscious (woke)
☐ Other [   ]

How closely do you think the characters in New Adult romances resemble people you meet in real life?

○ A great deal
○ A lot
○ A moderate amount
○ A little
○ Not at all

How closely do you think the events in New Adult romances resemble events that occur in real life?

○ A great deal
○ A lot
○ A moderate amount
○ A little
○ Not at all

How closely do you think the New Adult heroine's reactions and feelings towards people and events resemble women in their 20s?

◯ They are almost identical to women in their 20s that I know.
◯ They are a great deal like women in their 20s that I know.
◯ They are somewhat like women in their 20s that I know.
◯ They are rarely like women in their 20s that I know.
◯ They are not like women in their 20s that I know.

How closely do you feel that the New Adult hero's emotional responses to the heroine resemble the way men in their 20s behave?

◯ They are almost identical to men in their 20s that I know.
◯ They are a great deal like men in their 20s that I know.
◯ They are somewhat like men in their 20s that I know.
◯ They are rarely like men in their 20s that I know.
◯ They are a not like men in their 20s that I know.

What are your three favorite New Adult romances?

What are your three favorite New Adult authors?

DEMOGRAPHICS

What is your gender?

◯ Male
◯ Female
◯ Trans man
◯ Trans woman
◯ Gender queer
◯ [   ] Other

What is your age?

○ 18–23
○ 24–34
○ 35–44
○ 45–54
○ 55–64
○ 65 or over

3. With which race/ethnicity do you identify? (Select all that apply)

☐ African American or Black
☐ American Indian or Alaska Native
☐ Asian American or Asian
☐ Hispanic or Latinx
☐ Middle Eastern or North African
☐ Pacific Islander
☐ g. White or Caucasian
☐ ⬚ Other

4. Where is your home located?"

○ North America/Central America
○ South America
○ Europe
○ Africa
○ Asia
○ Australia
○ Caribbean Islands
○ Pacific Islands
○ ⬚ Other

What is your current relationship status?

○ Single (never married)
○ In a relationship
○ Married
○ Widowed
○ Separated
○ Divorced but not remarried

Do you have any children?

○ Yes (Please specify age and gender)
○ [   ] No

What is your employment status?

○ Employed full-time (either for employer or self-employed)
○ Employed part time
○ Unemployed looking for work
○ Unemployed not looking for work
○ Retired
○ Student
○ Disabled
○ Stay-at-home parent

What is your occupation or job title?

[   ]

If in a relationship, what is your partner's occupation?

[   ]

What is your total household income? (That is, not just yours if there are others contributing to the family income)

○ Less than $10,000
○ $10,000–$19,999
○ $20,000–$29,999
○ $30,000–$39,999
○ $40,000–$49,999
○ $50,000–$59,999
○ $60,000–$69,999
○ $70,000–$79,999
○ $80,000–$89,999
○ $90,000–$99,999
○ $100,000–$149,999
○ More than $150,000

How many years of education have you completed?

○ Some high school
○ High school graduate or GED
○ Associate's degree
○ Professional license or Apprenticeship
○ Some college
○ 4 year degree
○ Master's degree
○ Doctorate

If married, how many years of education has your spouse completed?

○ Some high school
○ High school graduate or GED
○ Associate's degree
○ Professional license or Apprenticeship
○ Some college
○ 4 year degree
○ Master's degree
○ Doctorate

What is your religious preference?

○ Atheist
○ Agnostic
○ Catholic
○ Christian but nondenominational
○ Hindu
○ Jewish
○ Mormon
○ Muslim
○ Orthodox
○ Protestant (Lutheran, Methodist, Presbyterian, Anglican, etc.)
○ [   ] Other

Rank what you read most often when you read magazines. Please rank the top three with 1 being the most common.

☐ I don't read magazines
☐ Lifestyle (*Cosmopolitan, Rolling Stone, Vanity Fair*)
☐ Parenting magazine
☐ Auto

Appendix B

- [ ] News & Politics (*Time, New Yorker, Newsweek*)
- [ ] Entertainment & TV
- [ ] Home & Garden
- [ ] Travel
- [ ] Science & Nature
- [ ] Cooking
- [ ] Other _____

About how many hours per week do you watch television for entertainment?

- ○ 3 hours or less
- ○ 4–7 hours
- ○ 8–14 hours
- ○ 15–20 hours
- ○ 21 hours or more

Rank what you watch most often when you watch television? Please rank the top three with 1 being the most common.

- [ ] Historical dramas
- [ ] Situation comedies (*The Office, Blackish, Friends*, etc.)
- [ ] Supernatural dramas
- [ ] Teen dramas
- [ ] News
- [ ] Variety or specials
- [ ] Police procedural
- [ ] True crime
- [ ] Game shows
- [ ] Sports
- [ ] Other _____

Rank what you watch most often when you watch movies. Please rank the top three with 1 being the most common.

- [ ] Period films
- [ ] Action/Adventure
- [ ] Paranormal
- [ ] Teen or children's films
- [ ] Documentaries
- [ ] Pornography or erotica
- [ ] Romantic comedy
- [ ] Comedy

☐ Horror
☐ Drama
☐ Science fiction
☐ Other

ROMANCE AND COMING OF AGE

What is one important thing for me to know about how reading romance novels shapes your feelings, opinions and identity?

Powered by Qualtrics

Appendix C

Tables for Chapter 8

Table C.1 Age Began Reading Romance

	Count	Percent
Under 10	3	1.0%
10–14 years	68	22.6%
15–19 years	85	28.2%
20–24 years	41	13.6%
25–29 years	42	14.0%
30–39 years	39	13.0%
40 or older	21	7.0%
N/A	2	0.7%
Total	**301**	**100%**

Table C.2 How often you discuss romance novels with others?

	Count	Percent
Never	13	4.3%
Rarely	59	19.6%
Sometimes	124	41.2%
Often	88	29.2%
Always	15	5.0%
N/A	2	0.7%
Total	**301**	**100%**

Table C.3 Who do you discuss romances with most often?

	Count	Percent
My mother	5	1.7%
My daughter	0	0.0%
My sister	17	5.6%
My friend(s)	109	36.2%
Social media community	133	44.2%
Other	21	7.0%
N/A	3	1.0%
Blank—Never discuss	13	4.3%
Total	**301**	**100%**

Table C.4 Where do you get most of the romances you read?

	Count	Percent
In-store purchase	12	4.0%
Online merchant (Amazon, Barnes & Noble, Google Books)	183	60.8%
Author website/Author Direct	0	0.0%
Library	91	30.2%
Fan fiction Website	5	1.7%
Borrow from a friend or relative	2	0.7%
Other	6	2.0%
N/A	2	0.7%
Total	**301**	**100%**

Table C.5 What usually makes you decide to read a romance or not?

	Count	Percent
I like the cover.	3	1.0%
I have already read something by the author and liked it	80	26.6%
I like the title	1	0.3%
The book description (publisher's blurb or back of the book) sounds interesting	158	52.5%
Someone else recommended it to me	49	16.3%
Other	8	2.7%
N/A	2	0.7%
Total	**301**	**100%**

Table C.6 How many books other than romances do you read each month?

	Count	Percent
None	53	17.6%
1–4	193	64.1%
5–9	43	14.3%
10–14	8	2.7%
15–19	2	0.7%
20–24	0	0.0%
25 or more	1	0.3%
N/A	1	0.3%
Total	**301**	**100%**

Appendix D

Participant Reading List for Chapter 10

This list is a compilation of recommendations from participants (and a few of my own). Enjoy!

STAND ALONE NOVELS

A Deadly Education by Naomi Novik
Archer's Voice by Mia Sheridan
Balance by Lucia Franco
Beach Read by Emily Henry
Begins with Us by Colleen Hoover
Black Sun by Rebecca Roanhorse
Book Lovers by Emily Henry
By A Thread by Lucy Score
Caraval by Stephanie Garber
Dirty Curve by Megan Brandy
Find Me by Ashley R. Rostek
Howl's Moving Castle by Dianna Lynne Jones
Kings of Quarantine by Twisted Sisters
Kiss Quotient by Ana Hong
Legend Born by Tracy Deonn
Lessons in Chemistry by Bonnie Garmus
Lost and Chosen by Ivy Asher
Made in Malice by Albany Walker
Maggie Moves On by Lucy Score
Meet You in the Middle by Devon Daniels
One Last Stop by Casey McQuiston

People We Meet on Vacation by Emily Henry
Red, White, and Royal Blue by Casey McQuiston
Remarkably Bright Creatures by Shelby Van Pelt
Reminders of Him by Colleen Hoover
Rock Bottom Girl by Lucy Score
Say You Swear by Megan Brandy
Seeing Sound by Albany Walker
Something Borrowed by Emily Giffin
Something Wilder by Christina Lauren
Still Beating by Jennifer Hartman
The Dating Playback by Farrah Rochon
The Hating Game by Sally Thorne
The Idea of You by Robinne Lee
The Love Hypothesis by Ali Hazelwood
The Priory of the Orange Tree by Samantha Shannon
The Spanish Love Deception by Elena Armas
The Things We Leave Unfinished by Rebecca Yarros
The True Love Experiment by Christina Lauren
Three Kings by Freydis Moon
Too Late by Colleen Hoover
Verity by Colleen Hoover
Zodiac Academy by Caroline Peckham

NOVEL SERIES

A Court of Thorns and Roses (ACOTAR) series by Sarah J. Maas
A Ruin of Roses by KF Breene
Beautiful series by Christina Lauren
Back to the Burbs by Tracy Wolff and Avery Flynn
Bennett Boys Ranch by Lauren Landish
Bridgerton by Julia Quinn
Black Light series by Livia Grant
City of Gods and Monsters by Kayla Edwards
Clover Leaf Farm series by Melanie Harlow
Club Shadowlands by Cherise Sinclair
Collector series by Stacie Marie Brown
Crossfire series by Sylvia Day
Dark Hunter series by Sherrilyn Kenyon
Demigods of San Francisco by KF Breene
Dreamland Billionaire by Lauren Asher
Earthsinger Chronicles by Elle Penelope

Evalyn Maynard Trilogy by Caydence Snow
Fantasy Lover series by Shrrilyn Kenyon
Fifth Season by N. K. Jemisin
Fourth Wing series by Rebecca Yarros
Girl Meet Duke series by Tessa Dare
Graceling by Kristin Cashore
House of Earth and Blood/Crescent City series by Sarah J. Maas
Ice Planet Barbarians by Ruby Dixon
Infinity Chronicles by Albany Walker
Kingdom of the Wicked Series by Kerri Maniscalco
Mead Mishaps series by Kimberly Lemmings
Mortal Instrument series by Cassandra Clare
Night Huntress by Jeaniene Frost
Outlander by Diana Gabaldon
Plated Prisoner/Gild Series by Raven Kennedy
Road to Hell series by Brenda K. Davies
Ruthless Rwals series by Kate Bateman
Savage Lands by Stacie Marie Brown
Sooki Stackhouse/The Southern Vampire Mysteries series by Charlane Harris
Soulmate Equation by Christina Lauren
Spindle Cover series by Tessa Dare
The Bliss Wars by L. Penelope
The Brentwood Boys series by Meghan Quinn
The Bromance Book Club by Elena Armas
The Monstrous series by Lily Mayne
The Song of Achilles trilogy by Madeline Miller
The Twelve Kingdoms series by Jeffe Kennedy
The Vancouver Agitators series by Meghan Quinn
True North Small Town Romance series by Sarina Bowen
Twisted by Ana Hong
Ultimate series by Lori Foster
Villain series by Katie Roberts
Wild series by K.A. Tucker
Winternight trilogy by Kathryn Arden
Wolf Queen by Sam Hall

ROMANCE NOVEL AUTHORS

Abby Jimanez
Alexandra Belfore
Alexis Hall

Ali Hazelwood
Alona Andrews
Amanda Quick
Aurora Rose Reynolds
Avery Flynn
Beverly Jenkins
Carrie Ann Ryan
Darian Alexis
Denise Williams
Elizabeth Hunter
Elle Kennedy
Elsie Silver
Emily Henry
Grace Dravin
Jane Ann Krentz
Jane Castle
Julia Quinn
K.F. Breen
K-J Charles
Kathleen Brooks
Kristen Ashley
L.J. Shen
Les Hernandez
Megan Miranda
Meghan Quinn
Mia Sheridan
Noel Adams
Nora Roberts
Olivia Waite
Sarah J. Maas
Serena Bowen
Simone St. James
Stephanie Garber
Tessa Baily
V.E. Schwab

FACEBOOK GROUPS

Ashley Spivey book club
Big Book Energy with author Kierra Lewis (also does a zoom call with group members)

Bitchy Bookworms
Book Addicts
Cliterati
FB Peloton Book Club
Kindle Girlies Group
L.J. Shen
SJM Recovery and Support and Spoiler Group

TIKTOK

Big Book Energy with Kierra Lewis
Chelsea Reads
Daniel Alexander (handle: DaleCSander)
Elite Reading
Ladybug Books
Spicy booktok

INSTAGRAM

Dominique Wesson (fan art Sarah J. Maas and others)
Magic Naanavi (fan art)

YOUTUBE

Lily Reads with Kenya

PODCASTS

Fated Mates
Learning the Tropes
SFF Yeah
TBR
When in Romance

OTHER

The Steamy Box by Melissa Salvador – sends romance novels with sex toys

Appendix E

Tables and Figures for Chapter 14

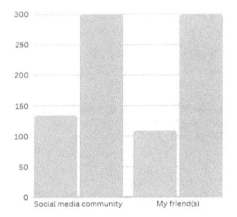

Total number of answers (may vary depending on how far they completed the survey).

Total of participants who chose this option.

Figure E.1   Whom do you most frequently discuss romances with? Survey results from *Still Reading Romance Survey,* by Josefine Smith and Kathleen W. Taylor Kollman

Appendix E

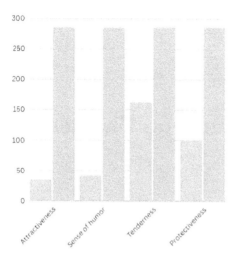

Figure E.2 **What qualities or characteristics do you like to see in a hero?** Please rank the top three with 1 being the most desirable quality. Survey results from *Still Reading Romance Survey,* by Josefine Smith and Kathleen W. Taylor Kollman

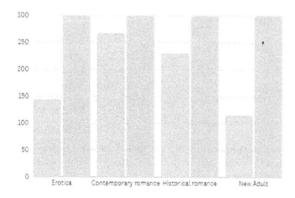

Figure E.3 **Which of the following kinds of romances do you read?** Here you may check as many as you like. Survey results from *Still Reading Romance Survey,* by Josefine Smith and Kathleen W. Taylor Kollman

Appendix E 385

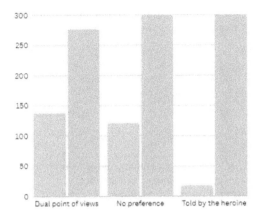

▢ Total number of answers (may vary depending on how far they completed the survey).

▢ Total of participants who chose this option.

Figure E.4 Which of the following best describes your attitude to the way the stories are told? Survey results from *Still Reading Romance Survey*, by Josefine Smith and Kathleen W. Taylor Kollman

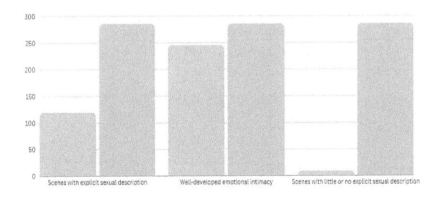

▢ Total number of answers (may vary depending on how far they completed the survey).

▢ Total of participants who chose this option.

Figure E.5 What are the three most important ingredients in a romance? Please rank the top three with 1 being the most important quality. Survey results from *Still Reading Romance Survey*, by Josefine Smith and Kathleen W. Taylor Kollman

Appendix E

Table E.1 Answer in the option "Other-Text" to the question: "Which of the following coming of age storylines in New Adult romances do you read? Check as many as you like."

| Footnote n.12 | Participant CE198 | "I don't seek out New Adult romances or any of their storylines, I only read one if its recommended, usually by someone on social media |

Survey results from *Still Reading Romance Survey*, by Josefine Smith and Kathleen W. Taylor Kollman

Table E.2 Answer to the question: "What is one important thing for me to know about how reading romance novels shapes your feelings, opinions, and identity?"

Endnote n.47	Participant CE186	"I started reading more mature and explicit romance novels when I was starting our high school and I feel like it really altered my perception of men and sex growing up. . . . I want 'the man who was written by a woman' type guy. I've come to understand that the perfect romance that I read about in books isn't really a thing, but I guess I still kinda hold out hope just in case."
Endnote n.51	Participant CE83	"I am not ashamed that romance isn't 'real literature.' I don't think that I am any less intelligent because I only read romance."
Endnote n. 70	Participant CE160	"The Romance genre has taught me a lot . . . including what it looks like to have a partner that respects you as an equal (and that equality in a romantic relationship is okay to expect and should be expected). They've opened my mind and my worldview, which I'm so grateful for. They are empowering and important."

Survey results from *Still Reading Romance Survey*, by Josefine Smith and Kathleen W. Taylor Kollman

Appendix F

Contributor Book Recommendations

Please enjoy this list of recommendations from our contributors!

CHAPTER 1

Katherine Center
Mariana Zapata
Nan Fischer
Mary Balogh
Amalie Howards
Fern Michaels
Ashley Winstead
Ashley Poston
Helen Hoang
Jude Deveraux
Sofi Laporte
Joanna Barker
Robyn Carr
Liz Tomforde
Elizabeth Lowell
Laura Moher
Sally Britton
Emma Hart
Susan Lee

CHAPTER 7

Jane Austen, *Northanger Abbey*
Emily Brontë, *Wuthering Heights*
Elinor Glyn, *Three Weeks*
Alison Goodman, *The Benevolent Society of Ill-Mannered Ladies*
Georgette Heyer, *Sylvester, or The Wicked Uncle*
E. M. Hull, *The Sheik*
Sophie Irwin, *A Lady's Guide to Fortune-Hunting*
Sarah MacLean, *Nine Rules to Break When Romancing a Rake*

CHAPTER 10

The Vancouver Agitators series by Meghan Quinn

- Tropes include: forced proximity, best friend's sister, fake dating, friend's to lovers, roommates to lovers

Ice Planet Barbarians series by Ruby Dixon

- Paranormal with several tropes
- Trigger warning for brief SA in the first few books

Archer's Voice by Mia Sheridan

- Emotional, slow burn

More than Words by Mia Sheridan

- Friends to lovers, second chance

By a Thread by Lucy Score

- Workplace romance, grumpy boss

Back to the Burbs by Tracy Wolff and Avery Flynn

- Neighbors to lovers

Love Lines series by Cara Bastone

- Close proximity, friends to lovers

The Highland Fling by Meghan Quinn

- Grumpy sunshine, forced proximity

Bennett Boys Ranch series and *Tannen Boys Ranch* series by Lauren Landish

- Cowboy romance, friends to lovers, grumpy sunshine, forced proximity, second chance

CHAPTER 12

Young Adult
I'll Be the One by Lyla Lee (also APIDA and LGBTQIA+)
There's Something About Sweetie by Sandyha Menon (also APIDA)

LGBTQIA+
Pansies by Alexis Hall
For Real by Alexis Hall
A Lady for a Duke by Alexis Hall
Red White and Royal Blue by Casey McQuiston (also Latino/x)

Asian Pacific Islander Desi American (APIDA)/Neurodiversity/Disability
The Bride Test by Helen Hoang
The Heart Principle by Helen Hoang

Manga
My Love Mix-Up by Wataru Hinekure, Aruko (also Young Adult and LGBTQIA+)
Cherry Magic by Yu Toyota (also LGBTQIA+)
Sweat and Soap by Kintetsu Yamada
Perfect World by Rie Aruga (also Disability)

Science/Grad School
The Love Hypothesis by Ali Hazelwood

African American
Forbidden by Beverly Jenkins

Wild Card
Anne of Green Gables (and all the books with Anne as heroine) by L. M. Montgomery
Lone Pilgrim by Laurie Colwin
The Moving Finger by Agatha Christie

CHAPTER 13

The Hating Game by Sally Thorne

- Genre/Trope: Enemies-to-lovers, Office Romance
- Description: A fun, witty read with tension and banter between two coworkers who start as rivals but find themselves in unexpected territory.

Red, White & Royal Blue by Casey McQuiston

- Genre/Trope: LGBTQ+, Enemies-to-lovers, Political Romance
- Description: A romance between the First Son of the U.S. and the Prince of England. This book is charming, heartwarming, and hilarious.

Beach Read by Emily Henry

- Genre/Trope: Contemporary Romance, Opposites Attract
- Description: Two writers with very different styles challenge each other to write in the other's genre over one summer, leading to both professional growth and a slow-burn romance.

The Kiss Quotient by Helen Hoang

- Genre/Trope: Contemporary Romance, Autism Representation
- Description: A fresh take on the "fake relationship" trope, featuring a neurodiverse protagonist and a romance that's sweet and steamy.

The Flatshare by Beth O'Leary

- Genre/Trope: Contemporary Romance, Forced Proximity
- Description: Two people share an apartment but never meet—one works days and the other nights. A quirky and heartwarming romance develops as they communicate through Post-it notes.

Index

aca-fan, 2, 4, 130
acquiring romance novels, 90, 130, 134–135
Adorno, Theodor: Culture industry and escapism, 145–147
Ahmed, Sara: Criticism of happiness in romance, 130
Alexander, Evie, 167
Alien Land Law, 214
Allan, Jonathan A., 211–212, 216, 218, 224, 226
Altman, Mary, 224
Always Only You (Liese), 191, 210–211, 219–223, 225; disabled heroine forms an equitable partnership, 210–211, 219; focus on the development of relationship, 221; marginalized characters, 191; story of a disabled heroine, 210
American Studies Association, 2
Ammidown, Steve, 293
Anne, Jayne, 33, 139
Ansley, Laura, 170
anti-miscegenation laws, 211, 217–218
Aubrey, Jennifer Stevens, 72
Austen, Jane, 89, 111, 114, 192, 196, 254, 258, 260–261, 266
Autism Spectrum Disorder (ASD), 219
Ayres, Ruby, 90

Babu, Christina M., 192, 196
Backlash (Faludi), 206, 224, 315
Baiocco, Roberto, 202
Baldoz, Rick, 217
Bamboo and Lace (Wick), 213
Bar-Haim, Gabriel, 146
Barker-Plummer, Bernadette, 287
Barker-Plummer, David, 287
Barnes, Jennifer L., 60, 134, 202
Barra, Andrea, 90–91
BDSM erotic romance, 97
Bennett, Elizabeth, 260
Bennett, Jenn, 191
The Bergman Brothers And Sisters Series (Liese), 219–223
Berlant, Lauren, 130, 275
"beta" traits, 61, 65
Between Sirs (Nichole), 104–105
Bhabha, Homi, 212
BIPOC, 295, 297, 304; diversity of representation, 112, 124, 297; feminists, 100; narratives in historical romances, 90
Birthisel, Jessica, 91, 165
Bittner, Robert, 239–241
Black, Jessica E., 202
black moment, 199–200, 203
Blackwood, Oliver, 225
bluestocking, 37

Blushing Books, 96
bodice ripper historical romances, 33, 37, 89, 93, 104, 298, 300
Bolus, Michael Peter, 145
book boyfriend: common characteristics of, 260; definition, 252–253; Hill's theory of hyperdiegesis, 251; Mr. Darcy as. *See* Mr. Darcy as a book boyfriend; notion of a male archetype, 253–254; popularity of Mr. Darcy as, 254; romantic or heroic acts, 253
Book clubs, 2, 9, 31, 34, 75, 120, 129, 138, 169, 173, 184
bookfluencers, 33–34, 36–39, 41
bookish communities online, 34
Book Riot's pandemic, 34
#Bookstagram, 12, 31, 34; change in the fandom and the genre, 34; criticism of romance fiction, 33; historical and contemporary romances, 33; sense of community, 32–34; on social media, "close-knit" a community, 32
@bookswithemilyfox, 35
BookTok, 14, 34, 72–77, 79, 81, 111, 132, 138, 169, 186, 192, 249–257, 260, 262, 266, 272; Austen Project, 262–263; book boyfriend. *See* book boyfriend; description, 250–251; impact, 249; influence on romance reading habits. *See* romance reading; modern retellings of *Pride And Prejudice*, 261–264; sentimental hero, 250; theoretical framework, 250
#BookTok or *#Bookstagram*, 34
Bowling Green State University Latino Issues Conference 2021, 213
Boyfriend Material (Hall), 206, 223–228
Bride and the Beast and *Yours Until Dawn* (Medeiros), 211
Bridgerton, 111–112, 114, 123, 266
Brontë, Charlotte, 89, 111–112, 114, 126
Brontë sisters, 89
Brower, Sue, 41
Buchanan, Tom, 237–238, 240, 242–245
Burgess, Jacqueline, 11
Bury, Rhiannon, 31

Canadian Museum for Human Rights, 76
Can't Escape Love (Cole), 219
Caravaggio, Jessica, 13
Carson, Chloe, 167, 169
Carter, Ashley, 201, 204–205
Cate, Sara, 271
Charlotte Temple (Rowson), 112
Chen, Eva Y. I., 227
Clasen, Tricia, 72, 252, 265
Cole, Alyssa, 124, 212–213, 219
coming of age: intersection with queer romance, 195. *See also* New Adult (NA) fiction or romance; queer
A Consumption of Gay Men: Navigating the Shifting Boundaries of M/M Romantic Readership, (Whalen), 211
coping mechanism, 284, 315
A Court of Mist and Fury (*ACOMAF*), 79–80
A Court of Silver Flames (*ACOSF*) (Maas), 80, 284
A Court of Thorns and Roses (*ACOTAR*) (Maas), 72, 76, 79–80, 82, 192, 271–273, 275–278, 280, 282–283, 286–287; complex femininity in readers, 287; cultural impact of, 272–273; erotic content and pornography, difference, 274; female readership, 276; feminine-focused fantasies of sexuality, 274; Feyre, characteristics of, 278–279; generic conventions of erotic romance, 279–280; heteronormativity, 272; heteropatriarchal norms, 272, 281; LGBTQ+ romance, 286; Nesta's sexuality, 284–285; OED, 276; pornography in erotic romance, 283; reading, 272–273, 277–286; recontextualizing pornography, 282; sex marathon, 280; sex positive cultural understandings of female pleasure, 273; sexual experience, 276; as sexual literacy, 277–286; treatment of sexual relationships, 276; understandings of female pleasure, 273, 281

Index

COVID-19, 34, 120, 192, 214, 310–312
Cranny-Francis, Anne, 168
Creswell, J. David, 174
Creswell, John W., 174
Cron, Lisa, 107
cross-genre romance, 301–302
cross-genre texts, 298, 302
cultural omnivores, or consumers, 90, 136
culture, escape in, 145–147; anxiety and social dislocation, 146; culture industry, 145; definitions of escape, 146; escapism and engagement in reading habits, 146; link between ideology and popular culture, 146; mass culture, 146; sociology of reading, 147; use of fiction, 147; views of escape, 145
Curtis, Richard, 226

Dade, Olivia, 304
Dancing Through the Minefield: Some Observations on the Theory, Method, and Politics in Feminist Literary Criticism (Kolodny), 82
Dangerous Men and Adventurous Women: Romance Writers on the Appeal of Romance, 40, 302
Dark Desires (Feehan), 94
Davies, Andrew, 123
de Gouges, Olympe, 75
Deleuze, 239
Dell, Ethel M., 90, 124
demographics and studies, 367–372; age, 349; age began reading romance, 373; attitude, 385; benefits of participation (IRB), 355; books per month, 375; children, 352; confidentiality, 355–356; contact for questions or problems, 357; decide to read a romance or not, 374; discussing romance novels, 373–374, 383; education, 352; gender, 350; getting the romances to read, 374; impact of reading romance novels, 386; ingredients in a romance, 385; kinds of romances, 384; list of recommendations, 377–381, 387–391; location, 354; new adult fiction, 363–367; new adult romances, 386; qualities or characteristics in a hero, 384; race, 353; RAINN (Rape, Abuse & Incest National Network), 356; reading habits, 357–360; relationship status, 351; religion, 350–351; rights as a research participant, 357; risks, 356–357; romance and coming of age, 372; romance fiction, 360–363; SAMHSA'S (Substance Abuse and Mental Health Services Administration), 356–357; socio-economic status, 353; subject's research record, 357–360. *See also* survey data of *still reading romance*

Dev, Sonali, 213
de Wilde, Autumn, 123
disability, 219–223. *See also* marginalized couples/groups
diversity in romance: increase in LGBTQ+ and BIPOC representation, 112, 209. *See also* LGBT/LGBTQ+/LGBTQIA+
Dixon, Jay, 33, 40
Dixon, Ruby, 35, 169
Donald, Robyn, 40
Douglas, Penelope, 271
Douglass, Traci, 294
Driscoll, Beth: genre worlds 129
DuBois, W.E.B., 219
Duvall, Matt, 13
Duvall, Natalie, 13

E-books, 96–97, 137
editors' interview, 305–320
Ellora's Cave, 96
Emily Hamilton (Vickery), 205
Emma (de Wilde), 123
erotic literacy: complex femininity in readers, 287; eroticism in the public sphere, 273–275; heterosexual sex, 275; LGBTQ+ romance, 286; methods of sexual expression,

275; romance novels and sexual education, 271; straight culture, 275. *See also* erotic romance

erotic romance: act of feminist rebellion, 95; adult content, 94; autoethnography, 94–95; BDSM romance, 99, 103; bodice rippers, 104; consent, 104–105; culture of slut-shaming romance authors, 99; Domestic Discipline, 103; emancipatory narratives, 102; explicit love scenes, 103; feminism, 100; happy ending expectation, 105–106; legitimized, 96–97; male dominant-female submissive books, 105; "marriage equals an HEA" concept, 106; mechanism of social control, 97; mock approval, 98; open-door discussions of sex, 98; outsiders, 98; patriarchy, commentary and exploration of, 104; qualities, 93; queer characters and relationships, 105; rape and sexual assault, 104; resistance within the romance community, 96; Risk-Aware Consensual Kink (RACK), 104; romance-only book signings, 97; self-pleasure, 102; sex, 95–97; sex- positive characters, 101; and sex positivity, 275–277; slut-shaming, 98–100; socially acceptable, 102; soft porn or porn for women, 98; spicy or high-heat romance, 96; 1950's-style relationship, 103; sweet savage romance, 104; writing as an act of rebellion, 94

escape/escapism: culture. *See* culture, escape in; desire for a relationship like the characters, 160; emotional escapism, 156; emotional expectation, 155; guarantee of the couple ending up together, 156; identification, 159; identify with main character, 144; notion of guilt, 157; as primary reason for reading, 144; in Radway's study, 144–145; real life depression, 158; redefinition in romance reading, 143; for romance readers, 152, 156–161; romantic media. *See* romantic media, escape in; stereotypes about romance readers, 160

Ever After Always (Liese), 221
An Extraordinary Union (Cole), 124

Facebook, 1, 5, 61, 114, 169, 173, 183
Faludi, Susan, 315
fan communities, 306; online discussions and BookTok engagement, 72. *See also* BookTok; online romance bookish communities
fanon representation, 255–258, 266
fantasy romance, 76, 176, 192, 271, 301
Feehan, Christine, 94
Fekete, Maleah, 3, 4, 158
female gaze, 79, 181, 254, 256, 259–260, 267, 282
feminism/feminist, 4–5, 40, 93, 95, 97, 99–100, 103–104, 107, 163, 277, 287, 313–316, 391; academics/themes/theories/theorists, 3, 13, 72, 76, 79–80, 83, 86, 130, 314–319, 390, 390; anti-feminist stereotype, 40; beliefs, 80; consciousness-raising, 72, 76, 80, 84, 390; criticism, 72, 79; emancipatory action, 80; erotic romance as feminist literature. *See* erotic literacy; feminine adolescence and young adulthood, 12, 45, 390; feminine coming-of-age., 47; feminine power, 285; feminized eroticism, 271. *See also A Court of Thorns and Roses (ACOTAR)* (Maas); focused fantasies of sexuality, 274; fourth-wave, 4, 100, 287, 314; hierarchy of interpretation, 82; historical romances. *See* historical romance; ideal being portrayed in writing, 64; interpretations of

romance novels, 197; movements, 14, 224; narratives, 102; pornography to fit feminine desire, 282; queer, BIPOC and polyamorous characters as, 100; rebellion, 93, 95, 98, 100; relationship with romance reading, 2, 40, 100; scholars, 33–34, 82, 302; second wave, 287, 313, 315; self-proclaimed, 148; social media reader communities, 81–83; standpoint, 171; theory. *See* feminist theory; third-wave, 4, 287, 317

feminist theory: affective nature of romance texts, 83; calls for men to read novels written by women, 82; hierarchy of interpretation, 82–83; romance reading as pleasurable, 82; sisterhood, 82; and social media reader communities, 81–83; variously focused criticisms, 83

Feminist Theory: From Margin to Center (bell hooks), 75

Ficke, Sarah H., 112

Fifty Shades of Grey (James, E.L.): impact on romance readership, 91, 95, 97, 165–167, 169–170, 251, 298, 304, 391

Fish, Stanley, 72, 77

Fletcher, Lisa, 129

FMC (Female Main Character), 175, 178, 275

formula of genre fiction, 158

Four Weddings and a Funeral (Curtis), 226–227

Fowler, Bridget, 148, 158

Gelder, Ken, 146

"genre worlds" approach, 129

gender representation: inclusion of nonbinary and trans characters, 235. *See also The Self-Made Boys: A Great Gatsby Remix* (McLemore)

genre evolution, historical and contemporary trends. *See #Bookstagram;* historical romance

Gen Z, 34, 100, 125

Gill, Michael, 221

Gingerbread Photography (Nichole), 105

Glyn, Elinor, 124

"good" romance book, 68

Grave Phantoms (Bennett), 191, 210–211, 213–215, 218, 225; casual and legalized racism as barriers, 211; discrimination, 214; discrimination and laws curtailing Asian American rights, 214; interracial relationship, 210; obstacles created by white supremacy for Asian Americans, 218; relationship after marriage, 209; stereotypical tropes, 211

Greenfeld-Benovitz, Miriam, 129

Greer, Germaine: criticism of romance novels, 168

Gregson, Joanna, 98–99

Guattari, 239

guilty pleasure, 75, 117, 144, 261

Halberstam, Jack, 284

Hall, Alexis, 124, 206, 210, 224

Halsey, Rebecca, 294

Happily Ever After: The Romance Story in Popular Culture (Roach), 4

Happily Ever After (HEA), 19, 105–106, 113, 116–119, 127, 130, 138, 155, 169, 175, 177, 298; desire to read books with happy endings, 177; expectation of happy ending, 105–106; New Adult fiction priority, 55; pleasurable experience and happy feeling, 91, 155. *See also* romance reading

Happy for Now (HFN), 19, 105, 113, 117, 155

Harlequin, 33, 67, 100, 136–137, 224, 258, 294, 303–304

harlequinization, 258

Heath, Laura, 41

Herrera, Adriana, 124

Heyer, Georgette, 90, 111, 114, 122

Hirschman, Elizabeth, 146
His Road Home (Richland), 219
historical romance: community, 120; definitions of romance, 113; developing empathy, 121–122; discourses, 116–122; evolution and audience preferences, 111; form of self-care, 119; future reader-response studies, 123–124; genres and subgenres of romance, 115; for happy ending, 118; historicizing romance, 112–114; historiography of romance scholarship, 113–114; hopeful experience and happiness, 118; methodology, 114–116; notion of compensatory function, 122–123; notion of escapism. *See* escape/escapism; positive aspects of sexuality, 119; practice of reading for pleasure, 117; queer (m/m) romance, 118–119; Regency romance, 111, 114, 123–126; satisfying ending, 119; sense of comfort, 120; significance of "descriptive detail," 121; Smithton readers, 120; understanding of the past, 121
Hoang, Helen, 219
Hoffman, M.A., 170
An Honourable Escape: Georgette Heyer (Byatt), 122
hooks, bell, 75
Huang, Ana, 167, 271
Hull, E. M., 124
Hunting, Helena, 102
Husband Material (Hall), 223–228

Ice Planet Barbarians (Dixon), 35, 169
identical, factory-produced commodities, 17
inspirational romances, 304
Instagram, 6, 9, 12, 31, 34–36, 38, 40, 76
International Association for the Study of Popular Romance Digital Forum 2020, 213

interpretive communities, 72, 76–77, 80, 82; and BookTok. *See* BookTok; chat by posting live comments, 77; communal reading, 77; interpretations, 80; interpretive communities, concept of, 77–78; vertical patriarchal power structure, 81
intersectionality: romance and feminist discourse, 13, 76, 209, 212

Jane Eyre (Brontë), 114, 124
Jankowski, S.M., 168
Journal of Popular Romance Studies, 111, 205

Kamblé, Jayashree, 211
Katrina Jackson, 304
Kauffmann, Jodi, 237
The K Club Dark Side (Nichole), 99
Kirstine, Sara, 79
Kleypas, Lisa, 313
Kollman, Kathleen W. Taylor, 1, 6, 20, 34, 72, 115, 191, 305–306, 355
Kolmes, K., 170
Kolodny, Annette, 72, 82–83
Kolodziej, Gaja, 11
Kratzer, Jessica, 91
Krentz, Jayne Ann, 33, 40
Kushner, 242

Larson, Christine, 201, 204
Lawrey, J.A., 169
lesbian, gay, and bisexual (LGB), 202
LGBT/LGBTQ+/LGBTQIA+, 38, 90, 96, 97, 112, 124, 130, 137, 167, 187, 191, 195, 224, 226, 228, 286, 295, 304; historical and modern representation, 195, 211, 235. *See also* BIPOC
Liese, Chloe, 191, 210–211, 219–224
literacy as a social practice: beta traits, 65; good romance book, 68; healthy sexual relationships, 64; intelligence and sense of humor, 64; literacy

events, 62–66; model of, 62–63; reasons for reading romance, 66–68; relaxation and self-fulfillment, 65. *See also* erotic literacy; romance
Literature/Film Association Conference 2016, 213
Little, Elizabeth, 278
Lloyd, Lydia, 37
Lois, Jennifer, 98–99
Loose Id, 96
Lorde, Audre, 81, 273–274
Lord of Scoundrels (Chase), 96
Lore Olympus, 271
Love and the Novel: The Poetics and Politics of Romantic Fiction (Paizis), 113
love stories, 20, 25, 100, 130, 144, 167, 267, 296; narrative structure and reader expectations, 167

Maas, Sarah J., 13, 72, 192, 271, 298
male/female gaze, 13, 76
male gaze, 79, 181, 186, 257, 282
male/male (M/M), 65, 206, 211
marginalized couples/groups, 68, 130, 205, 209, 225; *Always Only You* (Liese), 210–211, 219–223; antimiscegenation, 210; Asian American masculinity, 211; attacks on APIDAs, 214; *The Bergman Brothers And Sisters Series* (Liese), 219–223; *Boyfriend Material* (Hall), 223–228; Cole, Alyssa (Black romance writer), 212; disability, 219–223; discrimination, 214, 217; double consciousness, 219; *Grave Phantoms* (Bennet), 213–218; *Husband Material* (Hall), 210, 223–228; hybridity, 212; interracial relationships, 210–211; male/male (M/M) tropes, 211; marriage laws, 217; minority reader and scholar, 212–213; negative stereotypes about homosexuality, 225–226; race, 213–218; race, disability, and sexuality, 209; sexuality, 223–228

"marriage equals an HEA" concept, 106
mass-market: paperbacks, 136; publishing, 222
"The Master's Tools Will Never Dismantle the Master's House" (Lorde), 81
Matelski, Elizabeth, 196
Maurice (Forster, E.M.), 191, 197–201, 203, 206
McAlister, Jodi, 46, 55, 281, 283, 313
McCullough, Steve, 76
McEwan, Stacey, 41
McGraw, Pepper, 294
McLaren's Bride (Dier), 213
McLemore, Anna-Marie, 192, 236
media representation: social media's role in romance discussions, 72. *See also* social media
#MeToo movement, 192
Meyer, Stephenie, 13, 72, 76, 256–257
Michelson, Anna, 90, 129
Midwest Popular Culture Conference 2020, 213
Mills & Boon, 33, 100
Mitchell, David T., 223
modern romance novel, 89, 102–103, 105, 107, 258
Modleski, Tania, 3, 33
Mohanty, Chandra Talpade, 82
monogamy, 102, 168, 173, 304
Moody, Stephanie, 130
Moruzi, Kristine, 273, 278–279
Mr. Darcy as a book boyfriend: analysis of the representation of, 256; character presentation, 265; cinematographic adaptations, 266; erotic representations, 257; erotization of, 256–260; evolution of the romantic hero, 249; fanon representation, 255–258, 266; female erotica, 257; hand flex in *Pride & Prejudice*, 258; harlequinization, 258; Mr. Darcy Complex, 259; patriarchal parenting arrangements, 265; popularity, 254; spicy scenes,

257; wet shirt scene, 259. *See also Pride and Prejudice* (Austen)
Mulvey, Laura, 72, 80–81
Muñoz, José Esteban, 227
Myers, Abigail E., 180

narratives: brands, 16; common devices, 17, 167; counternarratives, 286–287; emancipatory, 102; erotic, 272–274; fan-created, 261; of feminism, 287, 315; fictional, 257; heteronormative, 95; patriarchal, 107, 275
A Natural History of the Romance Novel (Regis), 113, 196–197, 200, 205, 250, 253, 294
negative stigma surrounding romance novels, 91
New Adult (NA) fiction or romance, 1, 6, 12–13, 46–56, 196, 203, 306–307, 310, 319; adult characters with developing agency, 47; characteristics ranking, 51; coming-of age as NA characteristic, 51; concept of coming-of-age, 47, 55; descriptive statistical techniques, 48; difference between Young Adult (YA) and romance fiction, 46; discussion, 54–55; emergence, 45; expectations for heroes and heroines, 55; familiarity with new adult fiction, 49; favorite new adult storylines, 50; first mature relationship ranking, 51; future research, 55–56; genre, 50; hero characteristics ranking, 52; heroine characteristics ranking, 53; hero's and heroine's emotions and men in their 20's, 53–54; identity exploration, 46; methodology, 47–48; new adult fiction characters and real life, 54; new adult questions, 49; number of fiction per month, 49; ranking of setting as NA fiction characteristic, 50; readers, 4; reflections, 53; representation and norms, 56; results, 48; setting, 54–55; stories and real life, 53

Nixon, Cheryl, 256
Noland, Carey, 170

O'Donnell, Luc, 225
OG cross-genre, 301
Olave, Thumala, 139, 147, 151
online merchants, 134
online romance bookish communities: birth control in historical romances, 37; bluestocking heroines, 37; case studies, 36; coded language within the romance genre, 40; collaborative posts, 38–39; curate books, 37–38; discussions among romance fandoms, 41; humour and "inside jokes," 39; Instagram, 35; LGBTQ+ books, 36; narrowed-down recommendations lists, 37; qualitative research on selected bookish accounts, 35; romance bookfluencers, 36; stigmas associated with romance, 36; tongue-in-cheek content, 39; toxicity in romance, 39
Orczy, Baroness, 112
#OwnVoicesStory, 222

Padilla, Connor, 79–81
Paizis, George, 113, 125
Pamela (Richardson), 112
paranormal romance novel, 3, 38, 94–95, 167, 294, 306–307
Partin, Sara, 192
patriarchal scripts, 273
patriarchy, 3, 33, 59, 75, 80, 94–95, 97, 102, 104–105, 107, 139, 168, 224, 235, 267, 275, 284, 287, 314, 315
Pattee, Amy, 46
phallic worship, 38
phallocentric pornography, 273, 282
pinkwashing, 204
pleasure reading, 111, 296
pop culture, 146, 293, 304, 319–320
Popular Culture Association (PCA), 1, 205, 213, 310

Index 401

popular romance studies: overview of recent scholarship, 111. *See also* historical romance
pornography, 168, 180, 186, 257, 273–274, 282–283, 285
Pride and Prejudice (Austen), 114, 192, 250, 255–263, 265–266; *Eligible*, 262; modern retellings, 261–264; *Mr. Darcy Takes a Wife*, 262, 264; *Pride and Papercuts*, 262–263; *Unequal Affections*, 262–264
problems with romance genre: bondage where the heroine, 168; mommy porn, 168–169; objectification, 168; romance novels and porn, difference, 169
project, development of: contents, 8; demographic results, 7–8; ethnographic and reader response perspective, 3; interviews and surveys, 5; limitations, 6–7; methodological concerns, 5; nationality focused question, 6; non-Judeo-Christian traditions to the question, 6; racial identity question, 6; research about reading romance, 1–2; romancelandia, 2; subtypes of romance novels, 5; survey, methodology and demographics, 6; updating the survey, 5
prostitution, 282
publishing industry, 96, 124, 129, 136–137, 222–223, 300, 309; changes in romance novel sales and distribution, 111; and e-book technology, 96, 137; institutional matrix, 136; rise in self-publishing, 124
Purcell-Gates, Victoria, 62–63
Puritan heritage, 146

queer, 7, 65, 73, 76, 95, 97, 100, 105, 112–113, 115, 118, 133, 138–139, 152, 173, 191–192, 195–197, 201, 203–205, 210–212, 224–228, 235–246, 275, 295, 297, 314; coming-of-age, 203; Forster's contributions, 197–200; LGBTQA+ and new adult romance scholarship, 196–200; methodology, 192; m/m romance, 118–119; and NA romance, intersection, 192; Radway's survey and data, 204–205; *red, white & royal blue* (McQuistin), 200–203; Regis, contributions, 196–197; *Room with a View* (Forster), 198–199; same-sex pairing, 204; trans and nonbinary characters in romance, 235. *See also* LGBT/LGBTQ+/LGBTQIA+

race and romance: and disability, 219; and geographic location, 7; intersectionalities of class and gender, 235, 237, 246; laws, 215; mixed-race progeny, 218; privilege of gender, 216; race/ethnicity, 115, 368; the representation of BIPOC characters, 209–210. *See also* marginalized couples/groups; racism
Race, Ethnicity, and Whiteness (Young), 210, 294
racism, 102, 210–211, 216, 240
Radway, Janice, 1–2, 6, 17, 32–33, 47, 59, 71, 113, 123, 129, 143, 195, 197, 200, 204, 235, 250, 253, 272, 293–294, 308; mixed methods in cultural studies research, 3; questionnaire, 2
Rai, Alisha, 219
RAINN (Rape, Abuse & Incest National Network), 356
rape fantasies, 282
readathons, 31
Reading Historical Romance/Reading Romance Historically (Sanders), 89
Reading the Romance: Women, Patriarchy, and Popular Literature (Radway), 32, 71, 82, 113, 235, 250
reasons for reading romance: demographic categories, 153–154; developing empathy and experience, 111; identification with the heroine, 152; me time, 150; notion of guilt, 157; pleasure, joy and escape. *See* escape/escapism; positive feelings

and self-care, 157; by preference order, 150; relaxation, 151; relaxing hobby, 149; safe space for self-care and community, 111; stereotypical romance reader, 152; survey demographics, 150. *See also* demographies and studies; romance reading
Red, White & Royal Blue (McQuiston), 191, 200–204, 206
Reddan, Bronwyn, 34
Reddit, 5, 76, 277
Regency romance, 111, 114, 123–126
Regis, Pamela, 17, 19, 112–113, 168, 170, 191, 196–200, 205–206, 249–250, 253, 255, 261, 294, 308
representation: gender and diversity shifts in romance, 33, 55, 112, 123, 139, 241, 297. *See also* gender representation; race and romance
Researching the Romance Conference 2018, 209, 212–213
Rich, Adrienne, 242
Richardson, Samuel, 112
Richland, Anna, 219
Ridley, Erica, 124
Rigato, Ayegül, 12
The Rights of Woman (de Gouges), 75
Risk-Aware Consensual Kink (RACK), 104
Roach, Catherine, 4, 11, 130, 155, 166, 226
Roe vs. Wade, 192
Rohwer-Happe, Gislind, 259, 261
Roldan v. Los Angeles County, 217
romance and feminist discourse. *See* intersectionality; feminism/feminist
romance: coded language, romance genre, 40; demographics and perspectives of readers, 65–68; elements, never be included, 64; Facebook, 1, 5, 61, 114, 169, 173, 183; fantasy. *See* fantasy romance; fiction categories, 168; form of escape, 33; genres and subgenres of, 115; healthy sexual relationships, 64; heroes, characteristics of, 66; heroines, characteristics of, 65; historical. *See* historical romance; ingredients of, 63; intelligence and sense of humor, 64; literacy events, 62–66; model of literacy as social practice, 62–63; porn for women or mommy porn, 38; pre-Amazon romance readers, 60; reading. *See* romance reading; reasons for reading romance, 66–68; relationships through emotional bonds, 60–61; relaxation and self-fulfillment, 65; romance-friendly connections, 61; romance novels as "phallic worship," 38; sex in romance, 38; "smut" in romance books, 38; social practice. *See* literacy as a social practice; sweet savage, 104; trashy or guilty pleasure, 261. *See also* problems with romance genre
romance bookstagram/bookstagrammers, 31, 36–37, 39–41
romance formula, Regis's, 156, 158, 249–250
romancelandia, 2, 5, 35, 38, 94–96, 209, 287, 293
Romance Readers Survey, 12
romance reading: acquiring romance novels, 134–135; age began reading romance, 131; blend of reality and fantasy, 89; community and social connection, 130; concept of cultural omnivores, 90; cultural consumption patterns, 136; discussing with others, 132–134; Dot's recommendations, 135; early 1980s to today, differences in readers, 295; e-books and the internet, 137; entertainment consumption patterns, 135–136; "happily-ever-after," 91, 130; independently published romance, 140; institutional matrix of

romance, 131, 136–140; justifiable or "educational" pastime, 90; methods, 131; mommy porn, 91; normalization of romance novels, 138; notion of escapism, 90; pathways to romance reading, 130–132; plot template of eight points, 198; from a reader's perspective, 101; realization about asexual/aromantic identity, 138; results and discussion, 131; shape the views, 139; social context, 136–140; social media community. *See* social media; word-of-mouth reviews, 135
Romance Writers of America (RWA), 18, 94–95, 106, 113, 137
romantic media, escape in: escapist fantasies, 148; idealism and realism, 149; sense of reality and flight from reality, 148; sympathetic treatments of escape, 148
Rosenblatt, Betsy, 261
The Routledge Research Companion to Popular Romance Fiction note, 17, 113
Rowson, Susanna, 112

sadomasochism, 282
Sanditon (Davies), 114, 123
sapphic romances, 206, 299
#sapphicsemptember, 31
Schulman-Darsy, Louise, 192
Scott, Sir Walter, 112
Sebastian, Cat, 304
Sedgwick, Eve Kosofsky, 196
Seidel, Kathleen Gilles, 33
The Self-Made Boys: A Great Gatsby Remix (McLemore), 236; binary identities, 237–242; coming of age and LGBTQA+, 236; European affair, American version of, 244; impact of reimagined characters, 239–242; intersection of queer theory and political ecology, 238; Mexican-American heritage, 236; queer ecologies, 245–246; queer lives and American dream, 242–246; racial identity, 238; racial mindset, 240; reimagining queer death in young adult fiction, 241; representations of sexuality problems, 239; reproductive futurism, 245; sex-gender misalignment, 238; sex-reassignment surgery, 237; unequal distribution of wealth, 245; West Egg and East Egg, 244
sex-positivity, 38–39, 101, 272, 275–278, 283, 287–288, 391; treatment in modern romance, 93, 271. *See also* modern romance novel
sexual empowerment, 95
sexual intimacy, 221, 271, 285
sexuality, 38–39, 60, 75, 95, 97–99, 101–102, 104, 112, 119–121, 139, 152, 159, 168–169, 177–178, 180, 196, 198, 201, 211, 216, 221, 223–225, 238–239, 241, 245, 257, 271–278, 280, 283–285, 298
shame: associated with sexual expression, 71; BDSM romance, 99; culture of "slut-shaming" romance authors, 99; feminism, 100; key mechanism of social control, 97; mock approval, 98; open-door discussions of sex, 98; outsiders, 98; romance-only book signings, 97; of romance reading, 75, 80, 83, 97–98; sex-positivity. *See* sex-positivity; shamed aspect, 32; slut-shaming, 98–100; surrounding romance and sex, 99, 103; women embracing sexual agency, 102
Simon, Jenni M., 100, 102
Smart Bitches and Trashy Books (SBTB), 41, 129
Smith, Josefine, 1, 6, 12, 21, 72, 95, 114, 124, 192, 196, 306–307, 355, 357
Smithton women, 32, 73–74, 82–83, 91, 123, 134, 138–139, 144, 150, 151, 224
Snitow, Ann B., 33, 38

Snyder, Sharon L., 223
social media, 1, 6, 11, 14, 21, 31–32, 34–35, 61, 67–68, 72–74, 76, 81–83, 111, 132–134, 138, 168, 175, 181–184, 186, 192, 204, 250–252, 254, 256, 263, 266, 271, 293, 307, 312, 314; *#Bookstagram*. *See #Bookstagram*; BookTok and romance readership. *See* BookTok; communication and friends, 183–184; feminist theory. *See* feminist theory; focus on aesthetics, 34; impact on romance fiction communities., 12; romance groups, 1; romance reading as social activity. *See* romance reading. *See also* BookTok
social organization, 171–172, 174, 186
Span, Megan, 157, 170, 187
spicy scenes, 257
sports romances, 303, 364
Srinivasan, Amia, 276–277, 280–283
standpoint theory, 91, 167, 170–172, 174, 185; activities and social relations, 171; cultural norms for women, 172; lived experiences, 171; relations of ruling, 172; research questions, 172; text and social organization, 172
Stephens, Vivian, 304
stereotypes, romance readers, 31–34, 160
Stiritz, Susan, 274
Stoltenberg, John, 282
Stout, Joann, 89
Struve, Laura, 32
survey data of *still reading romance:* concerns about women being separated, 74; feminist theories and concepts, 76; shame of romance reading. *See* shame; Smithton women. *See* Smithton women; social media reader communities, 73; stresses and expectations of patriarchal systems, 75; structure of a survey, 73
sweet savage romance, 104
Swipe Right (Rai), 219

Tate, Andrew, 14, 76
Thomas, Bronwen, 34–35
Threads, 6
Thurston, Carol, 148
TikTok, 6, 14, 34–35, 76–81, 132, 162, 168–169, 183, 186, 192, 250–252, 255, 259, 266, 272, 297; influence of BookTok on romance reading, 72, 249
Toril Moi, 283
@ toriloves_heas. Tori, 36, 38
Toronto van attack, 2018, 76
toxic masculinity, 13, 76, 216, 298
The Tragedy of Heterosexuality (Ward), 275
#transrightsreadathon or #sapphicsemptember, 31, 38
tropes in romance, 5–6, 12, 33, 37, 50, 60, 89, 156, 167, 169, 195, 197, 204, 211–212, 224, 227, 252, 282, 311, 314–315; common narrative devices, 17, 167; counternarratives, 286–287; emancipatory narratives, 102; erotic narratives, 272–274; fan-created narratives, 261; fictional narratives, 257; heteronormative narratives, 95; in historical romances centering BIPOC and LGBTQ+, 90, 124; narrative brands, 16; narratives of feminism, 287, 315–316; patriarchal cultural narratives, 275; patriarchal narrative, 107; pornographic, 282
A Tropical Rebel Gets the Duke (Las Léonas series), 124
Tushnet, Rebecca, 261
Twilight Saga (Meyer), 72, 76, 78
Twitter/X, 5, 35, 114

Under Western Eyes: Feminist Scholarship and Colonial Discourse (Mohanty), 82

Vickery, Sukey, 205
Visual and Other Pleasures (Mulvey), 81

Vivanco, Laura, 100
Voiret, Martine, 265

Ward, Jane, 275
Warner, Michael, 275
Watching Dallas (Ang), 148
Wayne Pop 2020 Virtual Conference, 213
Whalen, Kacey, 211–212, 223
white supremacy, 218
white women as a woman of color (WOC), 209
Wick, Lori, 213
The Wild Rose Press, 96
Wilkins, Kim, 129
With You Forever (Liese), 221
women, reading romance novels: agency, 170; benefits of the romance genre, 169; bringing sexy back, 179–180; communication, social media and friends, 183–185; cultural expectations, 182; current trends, 167–168; data analysis, 174; data collection, 173–174; discussion, 185–187; educational benefits, 169–170; escape, 176; female agency, 181–183; happily ever after, 177; ladies' choice, 175, 178–179, 186; literature review, 167; methods, 173–174; participants, 173; problems. *See* problems with romance genre; read porn like a lady, 180–181; reflexivity, 175; relationship, 185–187; self-reflection, 177–178; social benefits, 169; social relations of daily organization, 187; subgenres and tropes, 167–168; symbols and standards for living, 185; themes, 175; validation strategies, 174–175; women's standpoint theory. *See* standpoint theory

X, 5

Yi-Fu Tuan, 145
Young, Erin S., 210, 294
Young Adult (YA) fiction or romance, 13–14, 46, 76

Zachary, Anne, 274

About the Editors' Statements

Kathleen W. Taylor Kollman holds a PhD in American Culture Studies from Bowling Green State University. She is currently on the faculty of Miami University in Ohio, where she teaches courses in media and communication, women's studies, and American studies. Previously, Kollman taught at Wright State University and The Ohio State University. She received an M.F.A. in Writing Popular Fiction from Seton Hill University in 2015. In addition to her scholarly work, she writes speculative fiction and has had multiple novels and short stories appear in print. Her articles and reviews have been published in edited collections on the TV shows *Crazy Ex-Girlfriend* and *Severance*, the history of fantasy novels, and in the journals *Rock Music Studies*, *The Journal of Dracula Studies*, *The Journal of American Culture*, and *The Popular Culture Studies Journal*. Kollman is currently working on a monograph on fictional representations of female U.S. presidents for Lexington Books.

Josefine Smith is a librarian and associate professor at Shippensburg University. She completed an M.L.I.S. in Academic Librarianship from the University of Pittsburgh and an M.A. in American Studies from Penn State, Harrisburg. As an academic librarian her research portfolio encompasses librarianship topics like information literacy and information consumption and student identity and cultural studies studies related to gendered identity development and popular texts. Smith is currently finalizing publications on gender representations in *Masters of the Universe: Revelation* and the cultural implications of New Adult fiction as a genre, and pursuing a third master's in counseling. She is constantly curious about the relationship between popular culture and personal and relational identities.

About the Contributors

Christina M. Babu is an instructional designer at IBM with a background in English and Cultural Studies. She holds a Master's degree in English and Cultural Studies and has diverse experience in academia and industry, including roles as a college professor and instructional designer. Christina's professional journey is marked by her passion for creating engaging learning experiences and her expertise in curriculum design. Her interests span across cultural studies, pop culture, gender studies, and queer ecologies, aligning with her future aspirations of pursuing a PhD in these fields. Christina is also enthusiastic about exploring the intersections of culture, technology, and education. She is currently based in India and is open to global opportunities that allow her to merge her interests in research, education, and instructional design.

Andrea C. Barra received her MA and PhD in Sociology from Rutgers University. Her dissertation (2014) focused on innovation and change in the romance novel industry using a mixed-methods approach interviewing readers and authors, analyzing romance's influence on electronic publishing, and categorizing novel themes. She is currently the Director of Assessment in the Office of the Provost at Emory University in Atlanta, GA. She has over a dozen years of experience in student learning outcomes, accreditation, and institutional effectiveness at various universities. Andrea is also an adjunct professor of Sociology, teaching various subjects including research methods, race, culture, media, and religion.

Dr. Jacqueline Burgess is an award-winning researcher and educator based at the University of the Sunshine Coast, Queensland, Australia as a Lecturer in International Business and the Program Coordinator. Her research investigates the marketing and business aspects of the creative industries, has been published in multiple international journals, presented at various academic conferences, and covered by local and international news outlets. Jacqueline also collaborates with creative practitioners, associations, and industry groups and regularly facilitates marketing workshops for the creative industries.

Jessica Caravaggio is a PhD Candidate at Queen's University working under the supervision of Dr. Jane Tolmie (feminist theory, queer theory, speculative fiction) and Dr. Glenn Willmott (popular culture studies, new media, speculative fiction). Her dissertation project investigates trends in popular young adult (YA) literature such as representations of femininity, sexuality, and reproduction to make connections between these trends and popular feminist theory. Her work also comments on the feminist consciousness-raising potential of popular YA texts within social media reader communities. Jessica's areas of interest include feminist theory and literature, young adult literature, genre studies, and reader-response theory. In 2025, she is teaching the undergraduate course, "Literature and the Fantastic: Women and Girls of YA Fantasy Fiction" at Queen's University.

Matthew Duvall is a learning scientist. His dissertation research focused on using Goodreads, a social media application built around readers and books, to engage high school students in English language arts. With partner Natalie Duvall, Duvall created the student motivational software Relate to Motivate (R2M), has presented at various conferences on both teaching and writing, and co-compiled the Amazon bestselling charity anthology, *Hazard Yet Forward*.

Natalie Duvall is the director of the Professional Institute for Educators and MEd programs at the University of the Arts and a full-time high school English teacher. In addition to her work in education, she is a published fiction writer and instructor. With partner Matthew Duvall, Duvall created the student motivational software Relate to Motivate (R2M), has presented at various conferences on both teaching and writing, and co-compiled the Amazon bestselling charity anthology, *Hazard Yet Forward*.

Dr. Gaja Kołodziej is a Polish novelist and a creative writing teacher residing in New Zealand. She wrote Young Adult fiction, New Adult fiction, women's fiction and romances available in paperback, e-book, and audiobook, as well as a series of creative writing textbooks. She has a master's degree in psychology and a doctoral degree in creative writing, and is a member of

Polish Writers' Association, European Association of Creative Writing Programmes, and Romance Writers of New Zealand.

Jessica M. W. Kratzer (Ph.D., University of Missouri) is an associate professor of communication studies at Northern Kentucky University. Her research focuses on interpersonal and sexual communication, gender, sexual communities, and sexuality in media. Dr. Kratzer's research includes publications on senior citizen sexual communication, online kink communities, hookup culture, and sexuality in television shows, movies and books. Dr. Kratzer has edited two collections, *Communication in Kink: Understanding the Influence of the "Fifty Shades of Grey" Phenomenon* and *The Cruel and Reparative Possibilities of Failure*.

Trinidad Linares (MA in Popular Culture) is the Library Associate for MLBSSA at Bowling Green State University. She has given presentations about romance and marginalized identities at the Literature/Film Association Conference (Rowan University); Telling & Retelling Stories: (Re)imaginingPopular Culture (Wayne State University); Researching the Romance (BGSU); International Association for the Study of Popular Romance's Digital Forum; and American Culture Association/Popular Culture AssociationConferences. *Bitch*, *Meridians*, and *The Projector* have published her writings. Her chapter "Alternate, Not Arrested Development: Bryan Fuller's Female Protagonists" is in *Buffy to Batgirl: Essays on Female Power, Evolving Femininity and Gender Roles in Science Fiction and Fantasy*.

Anna Michelson is an assistant professor of sociology in the Behavioral Sciences Department at McPherson College. She received her PhD from Northwestern University. Her dissertation focused on the social process of classification and meaning-making in the romance community, 1981–2021. Other research projects have explored social patterns of music taste, the Local Color literary movement, and the popularization of erotic romance novels. Her work has been published in *Sociological Forum*, *Music and Arts in Action*, *Poetics*, and the *American Journal of Cultural Sociology*.

Sara Partin is a master's student at Kansas State University studying English and Cultural Studies. Sara is especially interested in depictions of female sexuality as they intersect with popular culture, social media, and fandom. She is also interested in sex-positive feminism and gender studies. In her free time, Sara enjoys reality television and spending time with her family.

Ayşegül Rigato is a fourth-year PhD student in the Institute for Comparative Studies in Literature, Art, and Culture at Carleton University. After completing her undergraduate degree in American Literature and Culture at Hacettepe University, she immigrated to Canada for her master's in American studies at Western University. Her master's research focused on women's literature in the 20th century and the depictions of women's bodily autonomy and reproductive rights. Her doctoral research examines the contemporary romance readership and the #BookTok phenomenon. As a romance fan, she aims to understand what draws readers to the genre and why it is still stigmatized despite being one of the most popular genres.

Louise Schulmann-Darsy is a graduate student from Auburn University (AL). She is currently getting her master's degree in English literature with a minor in gender studies. Originally from France, she has been studying in the United States for the past two years. Her academic interests are twenty-first-century popular romance, chick lit, modern mythology retellings, and cultural studies. She plans to pursue a PhD to become a university professor, a desire that was confirmed by being a teaching assistant.

Lise Shapiro Sanders is Professor of English Literature and Cultural Studies at Hampshire College in Amherst, Massachusetts. Her books include *Consuming Fantasies: Labor, Leisure, and the London Shopgirl, 1880–1920*; *Bodies and Lives in Victorian England: Science, Sexuality, and the Affliction of Being Female*, coauthored with Pamela K. Stone; *Embodied Utopias: Gender, Social Change, and the Modern Metropolis*, co-edited with Amy Bingaman and Rebecca Zorach; *Temples of Luxury*, a primary source collection coedited with Susanne Schmid; and a critical edition of Millicent Garrett Fawcett's 1875 novel *Janet Doncaster*. Her articles have appeared in several edited collections and in journals including *Early Popular Visual Culture*, *English Language Notes, The Journal of Modern Periodical Studies, Modern Fiction Studies*, and *Women's History Review*. She has coedited special issues of *Feminist Theory, The Journal of Modern Periodical Studies*, the *International Journal of Fashion Studies*, and *Women: A Cultural Review*, and she serves on the *Feminist Theory* Editorial Collective. She is currently at work on a book on working women and the modern romance in interwar Britain entitled *Reading for Pleasure*.

Jo Stout is an educator, romance author, and all-around lover of learning. She has been analyzing the romance genre for more than two decades and earned an MFA in writing popular fiction from Seton Hill University. The author of more than twenty romance novels, Jo has worked with several publishers and also published independently, with her work spanning the genres of nonfiction, short fiction, poetry, and novels. As an instructor at Southern New Hampshire University, Jo works with MFA students to help them craft novels in multiple genres, and with her work at Thomas Jefferson University, she works with new writers to help them embrace their writing styles and learn the rhetorical moves necessary to succeed in the professional world. Jo lives outside of Philly with her family, a mountain of books, and a raging caffeine addiction.

www.ingramcontent.com/pod-product-compliance
Lightning Source LLC
LaVergne TN
LVHW021602060925
820435LV00004B/53